SUMMER JOBS BRITAIN 2007

SUMMER JOBS BRITAIN 2007

Including Vacation Traineeships

EDITORS

David Woodworth
Guy Hobbs

Assisted by Amy Tyndall

Distributed in the USA by
The Globe Pequot Press, Guilford, Connecticut

**Published annually by
Vacation Work, 9 Park End Street, Oxford
www.vacationwork.co.uk**

Thirty-eighth edition

SUMMER JOBS IN BRITAIN 2007
By David Woodworth and Guy Hobbs

ISBN 13: 978-1-85458-366-6 (hardback)
ISBN 10: 1-85458-366-2 (hardback)

ISBN 13: 978-1-85458-365-9 (softback)
ISBN 10: 1-85458-365-4 (softback)

ISSN 0143 3490

Statement for the purposes of
The Employment Agencies Act 1973:
The price of Summer Jobs in Britain
is £16.95 (hardback) or £10.99 (softback) and is for the book and
the information contained therein; it is not refundable.

Cover design by mccdesign ltd

Maps by Andrea Pullen

Typeset by Brendan Cole

Printed and bound in Italy by Legoprint SpA, Trento

Preface

Whatever your plan for the summer, whether it be boosting your bank balance, enhancing your CV, or helping others over the summer vacation, **Summer Jobs in Britain** is full of opportunities for the avid job hunter. The book is bursting with ideas for a fulfilling summer, from paid jobs to voluntary work as well as internships and work experience – we hope that you will find what you are looking for within these pages.

The summer has always been a period when employers in Britain look for large numbers of additional staff. Even when the recession of the early nineties was at its worst people still, for example, ate fruit and vegetables and went on holiday, so agriculture and tourism continued to provide a reliable source of short-term work. Summer Jobs in Britain is designed to help you in your search for a job, whether you wish to work near home or further afield. Alongside the many vacancies in tourism and agriculture the book features a growing Vacation Traineeships and Internships section, as well as other more varied work ranging from joining archaeological digs to providing sports tuition.

In this book we have collected details of job vacancies supplied to us by employers in England, Scotland, Wales and Northern Ireland. The jobs have been arranged in regional chapters under the following headings: Business & Industry, Children, Holiday Centres & Amusements, Hotels & Catering, Language Schools, Medical, Outdoor and Sport, Voluntary Work and Vacation Traineeships & Internships, the latter providing on-the-job work experience for students in business and industry.

Many employers in the book express a willingness to take on overseas applicants. While nationals of EU and EEA countries, young nationals of Commonwealth countries and American students can seek work in the UK without too much difficulty, it can be hard for most other foreign citizens. Nevertheless, there are a number of special schemes recognised by the Home Office which give non-EU nationals the opportunity to work for a limited period in this country. Detailed information is given about all such programmes in the introduction.

The companies and individuals listed in Summer Jobs in Britain are for job-seekers to apply to directly; the publishers cannot undertake to contact individual employers or to offer assistance in arranging specific jobs.

The Directory is an annual publication and is VALID FOR 2007 ONLY. A thoroughly revised edition for 2008 will be published in November 2007.

David Woodworth
Guy Hobbs
Oxford, October 2006

Contents

Working this Summer

Overview

After a steady fall in unemployment from its highest point as long ago as 1993, the UK job market seems to have slowed again. The number of unemployed people rose by 108,000 to 1.54 million between January and March 2006, pushing the jobless rate to its highest in 3 years at 5.1%. The situation may not have been helped by the estimated 600,000 migrant workers (rather than the initial estimate of 15,000) who have flocked to the UK from Eastern European nations which joined the EU in 2004. This influx of workers seems to have filled gaps in the UK labour market in the administration, business and management and hospitality and catering sectors. The competition for jobs may be tough therefore, but the temporary market still seems buoyant. Figures published by the Royal Bank of Scotland suggest that in London at least, temporary hiring increased at its strongest rate in 19 months in June 2006, reflecting rising workloads. Another plus for temporary job workers is the trend in shedding full-time employees for part-time staff. Registering with a temping agency, whatever your preferred field of work, appears to be a very prudent and lucrative move for the summer jobseeker and can lead to a permanent role in the same organisation.

Summer employment is a must for most university students. Bursaries worth more than £300 million, from 118 universities, are being offered to 400,000 British students from 2006 to ensure that the less well-off are not discouraged from going to university. However, according to recent reports, a student on a three-year course, who takes out a maximum student loan and defers the £3,000 tuition fees introduced in 2006 each year, will owe £22,000 at the end of the degree. In the light of this it has become vital for young people to keep their finances very firmly under control. Dwindling investment in graduate trainees means that students are increasingly leaving university not only in a mire of debt, but also with no immediate prospect of paying it off. However, these increased pressures are producing a new generation of budget-conscious students in the UK; a survey by the National Union of Students suggests that over 90% of students take on work to pay their way through their increasingly expensive higher education. This book is designed to be a guide to the large variety of work that can be found in Britain during the summer months of 2007 in order to help keep the banks off your back, gain some CV points and enjoy your summer.

CATEGORIES OF WORK

To make this book easier to use we have divided the jobs listed into the following categories.

Business and Industry

This category includes working as Drivers, Temps, Office Workers, Labourers and Cashiers, among others.

Temping. Britain has the largest temporary workforce in Europe – the Recruitment and Employment Confederation estimates the number of UK citizens on temporary contracts as 1.2 million. The Royal Bank of Scotland reported that while demand for permanent staff is slumping fast, the demand for temps continues to rise, with over 40% of employment agencies reporting growth in the first quarter of 2006. Work as a 'temp' involves providing short-term cover for staff away on holiday, sick leave, and so on, and is usually arranged by an agency. Jobs are available in virtually all corners of business and industry, though the majority are clerical/office-based and favour those with secretarial or computer skills, or experience of an office environment.

Temping work is attractive as it is available at any time of the year (though much more in popular holiday periods), can offer flexible hours, and can be found at short notice. Length of placements is immensely variable and so you can often decide which weeks you would like to work, as opposed to committing to a full summer of work. Now would appear to be the best time to consider taking temporary work, in comparison with the last few years. Using temporary staff is increasingly popular with employers, especially small companies who need to pick up and discard skilled staff easily to cope with peaks and troughs in business. Current economic uncertainty can also be seen as a bonus for temps – companies are more likely to bolster themselves against recession by avoiding commitment to new permanent staff. The temporary market has received another boost since the increase of standard maternity leave from 18 to 26 weeks, along with the introduction of paternity leave at the same time.

The average temping pay in London is £11 per hour before tax, but some office-based jobs pay hourly rates well into the teens. You should however, be prepared for anything as low as £5.35 depending on skill level and location. 2006 did see temping pay rise to a new high. Those with relevant skills, such as a high level of competency in popular software packages, can command a lucrative wage for their knowledge. Temping can also be valuable to those looking for a more vocational experience as well as cash over the summer. You could secure a placement in a sector where internship schemes are rare, such as marketing or media, giving you vital insight as well as an edge over other candidates if you eventually apply for permanent jobs in that sector. Even if ultimately you target a different sector, having demonstrated and practised transferable skills as a temp will help secure employment. One should be aware, however, that with the increase in popularity of taking on temporary staff, that employers seem to require ever more of their temps: agencies report that large numbers of prospective employers now call temporary staff to interview. While this may seem like a daunting step, it certainly suggests that the days of temporary employees doing little more than filing, photocopying and coffee-making are over.

In addition to the agencies listed in this book, most towns have several agencies specialising in temporary work. If you are looking for more than financial reward, it pays to be choosy, as different agencies specialise in different areas – for example, Judy Fisher Associates (☎020-7437 2277) carries only media placements. To find agencies in your area, look under *Employment Agencies* in the *Yellow Pages* or try the employment agencies' association at www.rec.uk.com.

Shop Work. Recent developments in retail mean that there is sizeable demand for extra staff in the summer. The explosion of out-of-town retail parks with huge stores, and the super or 'extra' store, demonstrated in Walmart's ASDA take-over and stores such as B&Q Warehouse, has created large numbers of casual vacancies. The trend for late-night and 24-hour shopping has prompted similar vacancies in supermarkets. Those willing to work antisocial hours are in demand, and working the night shift generally ensures a significantly bigger pay packet. Most jobs are part-time, but if a full-time summer job becomes available, already working there makes you more likely to be chosen as a replacement.

If you are applying for a full-time job, then be aware that more upmarket stores like Marks and Spencer will favour applicants with an interest in eventually working there permanently. Marks and Spencer run a placement scheme, Marks and Start, aimed at those areas of society that find it difficult to gain employment. These groups include both sixth-form and university students, with significant benefits to be gained from their Student Support Scheme. For further information, go to the Careers pages at www. marksandspencer.com. Other stores with less emphasis on continuous customer service are less picky. Seasonal demand is also raised by tourism and permanent staff going on holiday.

Sales. The idea of employment as a sales person conjures up outdated images of traipsing from house to house trying to sell dusters or encyclopaedias. While this type of work still exists, telesales (which involves selling a product over the telephone) is a more popular method nowadays, usually operating from large purpose built call centres. As internet shopping becomes more popular and retail space becomes more expensive, the number of centres is expected to grow. Call centre staff tend to be young, and staff turnover high, as there is sometimes a burn-out problem when staff may be continuously monitored to assess their performance. In view of the long term future of the industry, though, effort is now being made to enhance the working environment. Pay is often fairly good – Recruitment UK estimates £6-£8+ per hour. Hours can be flexible as many firms open well into the evening to cater for customers who are at work all day. The only thing that those wishing to gain employment in a call centre should bear in mind is the current trend among large companies of transferring entire call centres to places such as India, where running costs are much cheaper.

A good telephone manner may be all you need to get a sales job with a holiday tour operator, though the ability to speak a European language will give you the edge over monoglots; work with holiday companies needs to be arranged early, in the spring. Some companies may offer pay solely on a commission basis; it is wise to check whether you will be dealing with customers looking to buy, as with holiday companies, or making unsolicited 'cold calls', for which you may need to be a bit more thick-skinned and may earn less commission. Make sure you know the exact conditions before you sign a contract.

Cleaning. Office and industrial cleaning is another area that offers temporary vacancies. Most cleaning companies prefer to employ staff for long periods, but they will occasionally take people on temporarily for jobs such as cleaning newly-built or refurbished office blocks, or for the annual deep-clean of those factories which still shut down for a couple of weeks each summer. Local councils are sometimes a good source of such jobs, as they tend to implement big clean-ups of local schools and facilities once term finishes.

Factory Work. Spending the summer on a production line may not sound the most thrilling way of spending one's summer, but the potential for work in this field is good. The factories most likely to require extra staff are those preparing for the Christmas rush, as they begin to increase production in August, or those that deal with the packaging and processing of seasonal food. Huge quantities of fruit and vegetables are harvested between late spring and early autumn and must be preserved by canning or freezing. The main vacancies in this business are for line workers, packers and delivery drivers.

Be prepared for early mornings, shift work and high levels of boredom. Pay is not outstanding, but starts at around £5.35; shift work can be much more lucrative.

Children

This category includes opportunities as *Leaders, Playworkers, Instructors* and even *Managers*.

In response to the desperation of parents trying to occupy their children in the long summer holidays, recent years have seen a boom in American-style holiday centres, camps and playschemes for the younger generation. These have become increasingly important as more parents go out to work and private child-care costs rocket. Activities offered range from horse riding and archery to learning how to perform circus tricks, and in order to maintain a broad appeal, new courses offered recently include recording a pop CD, film-making and constructing a personal website.

Playschemes and centres vary in size and content; some are run by big operating chains, like PGL, who attend to more than 140,000 children a year, and some others by local councils. Work for the latter may be on a voluntary basis as budgets are tight. The long-term potential for work in this area is high. The main season is from around the start of April until mid-September, but longer-term work is available as PGL operate centres from February until October. Ages of many of those attending these centres range from 7-17, so anyone looking to be a secondary school teacher could gain valuable experience, as well as primary teachers-to-be.

For these jobs, applicants often will not require formal qualifications. UK legislation, however, means that most employers will require successful applicants intending to work with children to undergo a Criminal Records Bureau check - be aware that it may be expected even if not mentioned in the job advert. Some centres no longer offer sports such as rifle-shooting or climbing, which require a higher level of competence, in response to parental fears, and those that do will require solid qualifications from teaching staff. Preference is likely to be given to those with experience of working with children. Trainee primary school teachers are particularly well suited.

Jobs on holiday camps can vary from teaching sports to organising discos. Since much of the work is similar to that in camps geared towards children and/or adults, more details are given below under *Holiday Centres*.

Holiday Centres and Amusements

Tourism. Although the annual summer congestion around Britain's airports testifies to the fact that most families now prefer to holiday abroad rather than here, the British tourist industry remains huge. The trend for short breaks and long weekends away within the UK is currently very strong, backed by industry pushes to promote such getaways. As a nation we have also shown a large leap in visits to the UK's tourist attractions, with large sites, such as Alton Towers, in Staffordshire, and the London Eye, where 20 million people have so far enjoyed its views across the capital. Farms, gardens and countryside attractions appear to have recovered from the crippling effects of the 2001 foot and mouth outbreak, and free entry to museums and art galleries has had a huge impact on visitor numbers, particularly in London where strict security measures have been put in place since the terrorist attacks on the city in July 2005 and terror threats in August 2006. Attractions such as the Eden Project in Cornwall and the Imperial War Museum in Manchester, are boosting regional tourism, while events like the Commonwealth Games encouraged international interest in Britain, as will the Olympic Games to be held in London in 2012. As a result, there has been an unprecedented growth in tourism, with 29.95 million international visitors in 2005 spending £14.3 billion in the UK – an 8% increase on the previous year. Coupled with the information

that Britons alone spend over £33 billion each year on day trips, it is perhaps easy to see why there are more than 2.1 million people in employment related to UK tourism.

In spite of the events that have threatened and dramatically upset the tourist industry in the past few years: the foot and mouth outbreak of 2001, September 11th and the subsequent global fear of terrorism, with the SARS virus and the war in Iraq, indications seem to be that tourism in the UK is finally recovering. While the numbers of tourists from America are still down, reports show that the major impact on the tourism industry has been generated by those from Western Europe and from long-haul destinations outside of the US, with the number of passengers up by 6.7% from last year. The tourist authorities are currently reporting success in increasing American travel to the UK through advertising and magazine campaigns.

Television and films are a major force in marketing different regions as predominately more tourists want to retrace the steps of film stars and see for themselves the setting of their favourite film. The British film industry's international successes, including the *Harry Potter* series and *Bridget Jones' Diary*, have increased tourist interest in London and the UK as a whole. Most recently *The Da Vinci* Code has seen international visitors flock to London, Lincoln and Edinburgh. Glen Nevis in Scotland annually attracted over a million *Braveheart* fans, while Whitby, the setting for TV's *Heartbeat* series, continues to attract hordes of nostalgic viewers.

Holiday Centres. One of the greatest recent trends in UK tourism has been the growth of holiday camps, activity centres and theme parks. These centres are some of the largest seasonal employers in the country. Not only do they take on thousands of staff between them - the largest can take on hundreds each - but they also offer a diverse range of jobs, both unskilled and skilled. Many chains of holiday centres, such as Butlins, have been refurbished and updated, distancing themselves from the 'Hi-De-Hi' image, and may require receptionists, lifeguards, car park attendants, entertainers, shop assistants and so on. Chains of upmarket leisure resorts like CenterParcs and Oasis capitalise on the demand for short fitness-enhancing breaks, and so are likely to want specialised sports instructors as well as offering unskilled employment. As a result of the number and type of posts offered, they are often popular and competitive - the opportunity to spend a summer working with many other young people in a holiday environment can prove quite attractive. It is essential to apply as soon as possible because many of the big employers start recruitment early in the year. Although extra people are hired later in the season, to cover bank holidays and busy weeks, these are frequently contacted from a reserve list compiled from the surplus of earlier applications.

If you fail to find employment with one of the centres listed in the book, try a speculative, personal approach. Visit Britain (☎020-8846 9000; www.visitbritain.com) can provide information on the major theme and leisure parks throughout England. Visit Scotland (☎0131-332 2433; www.visitscotland.com); Visit Wales (☎0870-830 0306; www.visitwales.com); and Visit Northern Ireland (☎078-6873 4813; www. visitnorthernireland.com) provide the same information for Scotland, Wales and Northern Ireland. They are a service primarily providing information about accommodation and attractions in their respective areas; they are not a recruitment service in themselves. The book *Explorer Britain* (AA Publishing, £12.99) also provides a comprehensive directory of attractions that you might contact.

Hotels and Catering

Hotels and catering establishments offer a range of jobs including work as *Waiting, Bar and Chamber Staff, Receptionists, Chefs and Kitchen Assistants.*

Many of the temporary hotel and restaurant jobs during the summer season are to be found in the country's main tourist resorts and beauty spots. Big hotel chains may provide the best opportunities for those based in or near cities, as they employ large numbers of staff and have a relatively fast turnover, meaning short-term vacancies can be available at any time of the year. In order to combat the dip in hotel occupancy rates during the last couple of years due to increased security threats, hotels all over the country, and especially those in London, are constantly offering rock bottom prices and special deals to entice guests both from the UK and abroad.

The appearance of hotels at many large motorway service stations around the country provides another source of potential work. The disadvantage is that major chains are less likely to provide accommodation and are more likely to want, and be able to get, experienced and trained staff for certain duties.

Working in a large and impersonal hotel in a city is likely to be more regimented and formal than spending the summer in an independent, family-run guest house on the coast, and so perhaps less friendly and enjoyable (unless you end up working for a Basil Fawlty). If you choose a remote area with a lower cost of living and/or fewer opportunities to spend, such as the Scottish Highlands or the Black Mountains, you will find it easier to save the money you earn. Many hotels start advertising for summer staff before Easter, and generally applicants who can work for the entire season are preferred.

Hotel work can be hard and tiring, and you are usually expected to work shifts, sometimes at unsociable hours. Hotel and restaurant kitchens are particularly hot and frantic, with chefs notorious for their short tempers. On good days, however, hotel work is lively, varied and can be exciting. Before taking up a job offer, though, always ask for precise details about your duties. Many job titles do not provide a clear definition of the work and may vary in meaning between different establishments: 'kitchen porter', for example, may translate as 'general dogsbody' in one place, and refer to a specific role in another. Small hotels tend to employ general assistants for a range of duties as diverse as cleaning toilets to working on reception.

Fast food restaurants generally have a high turnover of staff at any time of the year; the main chains, including McDonalds and Pizza Hut, employ large numbers of people throughout the country. Motorway service stations and roadside restaurants like Little Chef also need extra workers in the summer.

Unless you are applying to be a chef, you will seldom require qualifications to work in a hotel or restaurant; while experience is often preferred, it is by no means always essential. A neat appearance and resilient nature may be enough; increasingly language skills can be an advantage.

Wages. Standard pay in bars and restaurants tends to be at the national minimum rate, but higher for silver service and in London, and usually lower for fast food restaurants. Hotels usually offer a similar rate, but often offer added perks like use of their leisure facilities. Often, tips can be a substantial bonus to waiting and bar staff. However, centrally pooled and divided tips may be included in the national minimum wage, and a recent European Court of Human Rights ruling set a precedent for including cheque and credit card tips as part of waiters' minimum wage.

Youth Hostels. The YHA employs Seasonal Assistant Wardens to help run its 227 Youth Hostels in England and Wales. Work is available for varying periods between February and October. Contact details for further information about working in a Youth Hostel can be found in the entry in the Nationwide chapter.

Language Schools

The staff needs of language schools are principally for *EFL Teachers* and *Social Organisers*.

Teaching English as a foreign language (TEFL), also known as TESOL (Teaching English to Speakers of Other Languages), is perhaps no longer the major growth industry it was a decade ago, but it still offers a large number of summer jobs that often pay better than average. Starting from around June, people of all nationalities and ages, though usually teenagers and students, come to Britain to learn or improve their English and absorb some British culture. The schools that cater for them proliferate along the south coast and in major university/tourist cities like Oxford, Cambridge, Edinburgh and London.

Most British language schools require their teachers to have a TEFL or TESOL qualification, though some will take on graduates with an English or languages degree, or PGCE students; a few employ undergraduates in those disciplines. Recognised language schools will require a formal qualification. There are a vast number of TEFL/ TESOL courses and qualifications on offer, varying widely in length, location and cost. Check the advertisements for those that seem most respected before committing to a course. It is important to choose a course which offers teaching practice as this will give you the skills and confidence you need to teach effectively. One of the most widely recognised and required certificates is the Cambridge CELTA (Certificate in English Language Teaching to Adults). CELTA courses can be taken at 250 approved centres in the UK and overseas. They can be taken full-time over four or five weeks, or part-time over a longer period. For more information and to find a centre, contact

University of Cambridge (ESOL Examinations, 1 Hills Road, Cambridge CB1 2EU; ☎01223-553997; e-mail ESOLhelpdesk@CambridgeESOL.org). Contact the centres directly for details of course costs as these vary (£750 to £1,200 is an average guide).

The other major certificate, carrying equal recognition to the CELTA, the Cert TESOL, is awarded by Trinity College London (Trinity College London, 89 Albert Embankment, London SE1 7TP; ☎020-7820 6100; fax 020-7820 6161; e-mail tesol@trinitycollege.co.uk; www.trinitycollege.co.uk), which stipulates a minimum of 130 hours of scheduled course input over a four- to five-week period (or part-time over a longer period – anything up to nine months). Both the Trinity CertTESOL and the Cambridge CELTA are accepted by the British Council as initial TESOL training qualifications in its accredited English teaching organisations in the UK and its own teaching centres abroad. Many of the courses advertised cost between £800 and £1,000, some of which include exam and accommodation costs. For a full guide to TEFL courses, see *The EL Gazette Guide to English Language Teaching around the World* (price £13.95 plus £2 postage, distributed by Book Systems Plus (BSP House, Station Road, Linton, Cambridgeshire CB1 6NW; ☎01223-894870; fax 01223-894871) which includes tables comparing costs, duration, dates and locations.

The majority of residential language schools often take on staff to work as social supervisors and organisers, both at the school outside of teaching time and on day trips. The bigger ones may also require sports and activity instructors. These positions frequently require no qualifications other than interest and an ability to work with young people.

Medical

This category consists largely of opportunities for *Nurses and Care and Support Workers*.

Britain's care industry is currently suffering both from a shortage of health professionals and the pressure of an ageing population. Much of the work available is with the elderly, though some is available with the sick and disabled (applicants in these areas should be aware that UK legislation may require Criminal Records Bureau checks on those intending to work with vulnerable adults).

Overall, then, there should be little difficulty in finding work in this field. Often agencies do not even require experienced applicants as on-the-job training is given. Generally, though, applicants must be over 18 and having your own transport can be an advantage. In addition to the vacancies in this book, specialist nursing agencies can be found in the Yellow Pages or at www.rec.uk.com.

Outdoor

The majority of vacancies in this category are for *Fruit Pickers, Farm Staff and Marquee Erectors*.

Agriculture. While increased mechanisation has reduced the number of pickers required at harvest time, agriculture remains the second largest source of seasonal work after tourism. Soft fruit is still hand-picked, and since some other crops do not necessarily ripen at the same time machines can not always be used. Crops such as hops, strawberries and apples are very labour intensive, demanding lots of hard-working labour for a short time. Furthermore, fruit sold in supermarkets must comply with increasingly precise European legislation on size and shape, and so extra staff are needed to help with selection. However, the rise in numbers of pick-your-own farms has affected the number of picking jobs in some places.

Food processing factories cannot pick their own, and so pickers and packers will always be required. In recent years tons of fruit has gone unpicked because of a shortage of seasonal workers to pick them. The solution to this problem has been a vast increase in foreign agricultural labour. Farmers are taking on an assortment of foreigners from Kosovans to Brazilians, where local people are unwilling to do manual farm work. Due to the enlargement of the EU in May 2004, the traditional Seasonal Agricultural Workers Scheme (SAWS), which had been increasing annually to meet farmers' needs, has actually been reduced. Since those who benefited most from this scheme were those who lived in the new EU member states (and thus were able to work in the UK anyway), it was by no means a drastic change. Even under the new points-based system of entry (see *Work Permits and Special Schemes*), under which most of the special schemes for entry have been assimilated, SAWS will remain in use until 2010.

The best areas for summer fruit and vegetable picking work in the summer are from the Vale of Evesham over to the River Wye (in the Midlands), Kent, Lincolnshire, East Anglia (especially the Fens) and north of the Tay in Scotland (especially Perthshire). Harvest types and times vary between regions, so raspberries may ripen two weeks later in Scotland than in the south of England. Strawberries and gooseberries are among the first fruits to ripen in southern Britain, usually in June. Processing and packing work is generally available in the Vale of Evesham after the main harvest season. Work involving harvesting outdoor salad crops is also available in the Hampshire and West Sussex area.

Kent and Herefordshire are the centres of hop picking, and the harvest is in September. A high degree of mechanisation is now used, but people are still needed to drive tractors, strip hop flowers from vines and so on. Women can be automatically allocated the indoor work, so make it clear if you are looking for an outdoor job.

The apple harvest runs from August until mid-October and offers traditionally more lucrative work. The industry is currently threatened by an increasing number of cheap foreign imports, but recent moves attempting to commit supermarkets to certain quotas of home produce may shore it up. Climate changes mean that it is now possible for British apple growers to produce crops of Braeburn, allowing greater competition with continental growers.

The fledgling English wine industry has been growing in reputation over recent years and there are some 350 vineyards throughout England and Wales, producing around two million bottles a year. Warmer winters and summers, probably due to global warming, are allowing UK wine producers to expand into new varieties such as the Chardonnay and Pinot Noir grapes. These vineyards, located mainly throughout the southern half of England, may require workers, though the grape harvest is unpredictable as the sugar content depends on the often elusive sun. The grape harvesting season is fairly late, usually beginning in September and finishing mid-November, although it depends largely on a number of factors such as the region, the weather and the variety of grape. For more information, or for a copy of *The Vineyards of England and Wales*, priced £5.50, contact English Wine Producers (PO Box 5729, Market Harborough LE16 8WX; ☎01536-772264; fax 01536-772263; e-mail info@ englishwineproducers.com; www.englishwineproducers.com).

Over the last two decades the number of areas of farmland devoted to cherry growing has shrunk from over 4,000 acres to under 800. However, a variety of dwarf tree developed by the supermarket chain Tesco may begin to rejuvenate the industry, not least because workers will not have to climb ladders to reach the fruit, as previously.

While fruit picking is generally short-term, it is possible to string several jobs together by following ripening crops around the country, or by choosing a farm with several crops that will ripen in sequence. On the spot applications are often productive, with no interview required, and it is sometimes possible to secure employment at very short notice (note that most farmers prefer the first approach to be via telephone). Jobs available may be increased by later or better harvests, by the farmer underestimating the number of pickers required, or by workers with other commitments leaving before the harvest is over. Conversely, even if you have secured a position, bad weather may mean no work on a particular day, and thus lost income.

Picking fruit can be exhausting and backbreaking – it is wise to watch more experienced workers to pick up any good techniques – although some farms have tried to make things easier for pickers, for example by growing strawberries on tables so they can be picked comfortably from a standing position. Due to the economy and temporary nature of much accommodation offered by farmers, a comfortable night's sleep may not always follow a tiring day's work. Some provide comfortable bunkhouses and meals, but others require you to bring your own tent and cater for yourself. Some provide communal cooking facilities, but these can sometimes be in a poor state of cleanliness as upkeep is no-one's direct responsibility. The Food and Farming Information Service also advises workers to take out insurance to cover personal belongings, and to visit farms in advance if possible.

Fruitfuljobs.com is a web-based agency which helps people find jobs with accommodation on UK farms; although the main season runs from March to October work is available throughout the year in the agricultural and horticultural industries - from organic farming to operating a forklift truck. You can also call ☎0870-0727 0050, or e-mail info@fruitfuljobs.com, for more information. Another useful website that details agricultural jobs in both the UK and overseas is www.pickingjobs.com.

Farmers can recruit students from any part of the EU. Some farms take part in the Seasonal Agricultural Workers scheme, as mentioned previously, enabling them to recruit student pickers from outside the EU. This is done through organisations such as Concordia (YSV) Ltd. (Heversham House, 2nd Floor, 20-22 Boundary Road, Hove, East Sussex BN3 4ET; ☎01273-422293; fax 01273-422443; e-mail info@concordia-iye.org.uk; www.concordia-iye.org.uk). These organisations only accept overseas applicants for fruit and vegetable harvesting and all participants pay a service charge. In return Concordia and the other scheme operators exercise control over participating farms and expect certain standards. The farms take from one up to as many as several hundred workers at one time, of many different nationalities, often largely from southern and eastern Europe. Further information about the Seasonal Agricultural Workers scheme is given under *Work Permits and Special Schemes*.

In addition to harvesting work, there are also opportunities for other types of farm work: as a general assistant on a family farm or as a groom, for example. Both this type of work and picking jobs are listed in the Outdoor sections of the regional chapters in the book. Some organic farms take on volunteers: for details of one scheme see the entry for WWOOF in the Voluntary Work section in the *Nationwide* chapter.

Wages. Pay varies according to the fruit and the difficulty involved in the picking process. Many farmers pay piecework rates, which means that you are paid according to the quantity you pick. This method can be very satisfactory when a harvest is at its peak but when fruit is scarce earning more than the minimum can be much more difficult. However, even if you are paid on a piecework basis the amount you earn for each hour worked must average the rates set out in the Agricultural Wages Order. You should obtain a copy of the current order from the Agricultural Wages Board before you start work. If you have any queries about the rate you are being paid, the Agricultural Wages Helpline staff should be able to advise you. Be prepared to cope with frustration when three days of rain means no picking and therefore no wages.

The Agricultural Wages Board (Ergon House, Horseferry Road, London SW1P 2AL; ☎020-7238 6523) sets minimum weekly and hourly rates for agricultural workers in England and Wales. As of 1 October 2006, a new grading structure was applied to people working in the industry. The minimum rate for standard workers (different rates apply in Scotland and Northern Ireland) is £5.74 an hour. For basic trainee workers, the minimum rate for workers aged 19 and over is £5.35 an hour. The minimum rate for an Initial Grade worker under 16 is £2.68 per hour. The six-tier grading structure is as follows:

- Grade 1 – Initial Grade £5.35
- Grade 2 – Standard Worker £5.74
- Grade 3 – Lead Worker £6.31
- Grade 4 – Craft Grade £6.77
- Grade 5 – Supervisory Grade £7.18
- Grade 6 – Management Grade £7.75

Many farmers calculate wages by a combination of piecework and hourly rates of pay. Remember that the farmer is legally obliged to pay you at least the appropriate minimum rate for your age for the hours worked. Ask exactly how much you will be paid before accepting a job: some people have been paid as little as 12p for picking a pound of strawberries. The Department for Environment, Food and Rural Affairs (DEFRA) has a helpline for both employers and employees who want to know more about the Agricultural Wages Order: Agricultural Wages Helpline, DEFRA, Freepost NAT 12176, London SW1P 2BR; ☎0845-000 0134; www.defra.gov.uk.

Gangmasters. Gangmasters can be involved in the recruitment of seasonal summer staff on farms. While most gangmasters treat their workers fairly, a significant minority are connected to the criminal underworld and could exploit their workers in some way. Exploitation can take different forms and might involve underpayment of wages, unsafe working conditions, use of illegal workers, and illegal deductions from pay for transport and accommodation. Some are also involved in the forgery of passports and documents and some help to arrange false benefits claims. Fears of a developing 'shadow economy' have led the government to crack down on those employing illegal workers. The matter was brought further into the public eye when over 20 Chinese cockle pickers drowned in Morecambe Bay in February 2004. In July 2004, men related to the incident were charged with their manslaughter, along with several charges relating to the trafficking of illegal immigrants into the country to be used as cheap labour. There are incidents of people in similar situations being paid £3 for cutting down 1,000 daffodil heads, and of up to thirty workers living in one suburban house, or in accommodation with partitions forming rooms and no water, while being charged extortionately for the experience.

Consequently, the Gangmasters Licensing Authority (GLA) was set up in 2005 with the aim of curbing the exploitation of workers and ensuring a level playing field for all businesses. The GLA has information for workers available on its website www.gla.gov.uk. If a worker feels that their rights have not been met they can phone the GLA Helpline on ☎0845-602 5020 or phone Crimestoppers on ☎0800-555 111 at any time. Alternatively, you can ask for a copy of the leaflet *Working on a Farm or Packhouse; Your Rights Explained* from DEFRA Publications, quoting product code PB8744 (Admail 6000, London SW1A 2XX; ☎020-8957 5242; fax 020-8957 5012; www.defra.gov.uk).

Useful Addresses. Many farmers have entries in this book, but you may find a local farm which is too small to need to advertise nationally. Economic pressures have forced farmers to diversify, and an increasing number of farms are being opened to the public, sometimes generating extra jobs for guides, cleaners and so on. Temporary jobs are sometimes advertised in *Farmers Weekly*, though prospective employers are likely to require some experience.

Organic farms often rely on voluntary assistance too. EU volunteers should send a s.a.e. to WWOOF (World Wide Opportunities on Organic Farms), PO Box 2675, Lewes, Sussex BN7 1RB (www.wwoof.org.uk) for details of membership and the opportunities available on organic farms in the UK and worldwide throughout the year. In return for their help, workers receive free meals, accommodation, the opportunity to learn and transport to and from the local station.

Removals and Marquee Work. While manual jobs with removal firms are available at any time of year, the summer is a real boom time for marquee erectors. During the sunny season there is a never-ending round of agricultural shows, festivals, wedding receptions and so on. And while a village fair may require just one marquee, a music festival will require a whole range of tents plus large amounts of furniture and equipment. All this has to be loaded and unloaded from lorries, as well as driven to and from a depot; for this and other driving work possession of an HGV driving licence would be a useful advantage. Overtime is often available, so marquee work can be lucrative. The disadvantage for women is that most employers specify a minimum height for loading work and only take on men.

Sport

The range of jobs under this category includes, among others, *Instructors, Coaches, Boat Crew, Stable Staff, and Walk Leaders.*

Sports holiday centres often specialise in sea, river or mountain activities and as such are often found in remote and beautiful places such as Scotland and the Lake District. They almost always need to recruit live-in workers. While there are opportunities for unskilled staff, most vacancies are for sports instructors, teachers and camp managers. Applicants will normally require governing-body qualifications and a reasonable amount of experience; growing concern about insufficient supervision and instruction at activity centres in the past has resulted in new tougher controls.

Recent sporting events and successes have increased interest in certain areas of sport, and if you have qualifications in these areas then your chances of finding work could be increased. *Watersports*, for example, are increasingly popular as advances in wetsuit and equipment technology mean participants no longer have to freeze in British coastal waters and lakes, and that beginners can experience relative success very quickly. Teaching centres along the south and west coasts particularly are keen to recruit windsurfing, sailing and canoeing instructors in ever-increasing numbers. Several lake centres also advertise in this book. Similarly, recent English success on the cricket pitch has had a positive impact on the uptake of the game at lower levels, prompting the need for more coaching schemes, often run by local authorities.

Anyone with life-saving qualifications could consider working as a lifeguard at a leisure centre. Several local authorities advertise such vacancies in this book.

Riding: Riding schools and trekking centres (which are particularly common in Wales) may take on experienced riders. Since a lot of the work is dealing with groups, the ability to get on well with people is also important.

There might be a riding school or holiday centre in your area where you could ask about the possibility of a temporary job. The British Horse Society (☎0870-120 2244; fax 01926-707800; e-mail enquiry@bhs.org.uk; www.bhs.org.uk) publishes a list of more than 900 approved establishments, available on the above website and also in the publication, *The BHS Directory of where to Ride, Train and Keep Your Horse, Including the Register of Instructors*, price £14.99 for non-members or £13.50 for members, available by mail order from the BHS Bookshop, Stoneleigh Deer Park, Kenilworth, Warwickshire CV8 2XZ.

The Association of British Riding Schools (Queen's Chambers, 38-40 Queen Street, Penzance, Cornwall TR18 4BH; ☎01736-369440; fax 01736-351390; e-mail office@abrs-info.org; www.abrs-info.org) provides a free directory of its members on their website. You should also contact them for information about trekking holidays and centres. Employment can also be found with racing stables, which sometimes require stable staff.

If you are looking for employment as a sports coach, it is advisable to check the listings for children's camps as they often also require qualified instructors.

Voluntary Work

The category of voluntary work encompasses a large range of activities including *Archaeology, Children, Conservation and the Environment, Heritage, Physically/ Mentally Disabled, Social and Community Schemes and Workcamps.*

Many organisations throughout the UK need volunteers to help with a host of different types of work, from caring for people with disabilities or the elderly to taking part in conservation and archaeological projects.

Voluntary experience can provide the dual benefit of giving you an insight into a particular area of work as well as boosting your CV. Statistics from Student Volunteering UK suggests that employers look favourably on candidates with voluntary work on their CVs: 73% state they would employ a candidate with volunteering experience over one without and 94% believing volunteering indicates skill acquisition and development. Another 94% of employees who had volunteered to learn new skills had benefited either by getting their first job, improving their salary or being promoted.

Some organisations represent sectors, such as arts and charity administration, that are particularly difficult to get into as a graduate – experience with them could give you an edge over other candidates in the future. Most of the voluntary organisations in this book do not require specific skills; willingness and enthusiasm are the most important attributes.

Working among people with special needs is both physically and emotionally demanding, however, many volunteers find the challenge to be both a rewarding and maturing experience. Most organisations provide free board and lodging, sometimes a small amount of pocket money and help with travel expenses. Many social or community projects need volunteers all year round, but there is always a demand in the summer for extra staff to help with outings and holidays.

Conservation and archaeological projects are increasingly popular. However, they do tend to be short-term and often require a contribution from the volunteer. The level of contribution depends on what it is for; some placements simply need a donation to cover board, lodging and travel, while others are arranged by agencies that will require a fee.

Museums, stately homes and gardens frequently operate on a very tight budget and may be pleased to receive offers of voluntary help; some may even pay a small wage. They will often offer accommodation and flexible working hours, in order to allow you to see some of the local area. *Hudson's Historic Houses and Gardens* (price £12.95, published by Norman Hudson & Co.) is crammed full of addresses. *The National Trust Handbook*, which lists all the UK properties open to the public, is free with membership or available from all good bookshops for £5.00. The Trust also produces a variety of free leaflets about properties in certain areas.

Festivals and events are a good source of temporary voluntary work, though very short-term. Cheltenham Festival of Literature and the Hay Festival of Literature are among the larger advertisers here – you can apply personally to smaller local events, particularly in university or historical towns. You might be paid travel and other expenses and will usually get free entrance to all the events of the festival.

If you are interested in becoming involved in local issues in your area, contact Millennium Volunteers through the Department for Education and Skills (Room E4c, Moorfoot, Sheffield S1 4PQ; e-mail millennium.volunteers@dfes.gsi.gov.uk; www.mvonline.gov.uk). Millennium Volunteers is a UK-wide, government-funded initiative providing 130 volunteering opportunities for young people aged between 16 and 24. Volunteers contribute to a range of voluntary organisations from their local Citizens Advice Bureau, to joining a conservation project organised by BTCV (see entry), to projects such as sports coaching and music and dance. A national online database of voluntary work is available at www.do-it.org.uk. Those completing 200 hours of voluntary activity in a year receive an award of excellence signed by the Secretary of State. Most UK universities also have thriving Community Action groups offering a range of volunteering opportunities in the local area.

Sources of Information. *The International Directory of Voluntary Work* (£12.95, published by Vacation Work, 9 Park End Street, Oxford OX1 1HH) has been fully revised and includes information on both short- and long-term opportunities. The National Council for Voluntary Organisations (Regent's Wharf, 8 All Saints Street, London N1 9RL (☎0800-279 8798; fax 020-7713 6300; www.ncvo-vol.org.uk) publishes the *Voluntary Agencies Directory*, price £35 plus £5.50 postage and packing for non-members, which lists more than 2,000 organisations countrywide.

Volunteering England (☎0845-305 6979; e-mail volunteering@ volunteeringengland.org; www.volunteering.org.uk) produces information sheets on finding out about volunteering opportunities. The website details voluntary organisations, ideas about the types of volunteering available and where to find your nearest Volunteer Centre for local volunteering opportunities.

Information on voluntary work in Wales can be obtained from Wales Council for Voluntary Action (Baltic House, Mount Stuart Square, Cardiff Bay CF10 5FH; ☎0870-607 1666; fax 029-2043 1701; e-mail help@wcva.org.uk; www.wcva.org. uk). They also have offices in Colwyn Bay (☎01492-539800); Newtown (☎01686-611053); Pontypridd (☎01443-491110); Carmarthen (☎01267-229322); and Lampeter (☎01570-424150).

Vacation Traineeships & Internships

This heading covers placements and schemes which aim to provide young people with an opportunity to gain on-the-job training during their holidays. They are variously referred to by firms as 'work placements', 'internships', 'vacation schemes', 'training schemes' as well as a myriad of other names. 'Internship' is originally an American term formerly used only by US-based or international firms, but rapidly gaining currency in the UK. They are generally short-term placements for students lasting from two weeks to the whole summer holiday.

Traineeships and internships may not appeal to those wanting a summer job just to have fun or to earn enough money for a holiday or to repay an overdraft. Some employers offer fantastic remuneration, with some City internships paying up to £650 a week. Others see the reward as the experience itself and just pay expenses. In the long run, a work placement can prove to have been the most valuable investment of your vacations.

The content and style of traineeships and internships varies from one firm to another. Some, especially large banks, accountants and consultancies, will put you into a position of real responsibility so you can learn the ropes of the business from its centre. Others operate more of a 'work-shadow' scheme where you are expected to follow and observe a member of staff, and perhaps help them with their work. Companies in areas like computer programming will only recruit applicants who already have particular skills, and therefore focus on helping you to apply those skills in a business environment, rather than teaching you new skills.

Advertised traineeships and internships tend to be most numerous in areas of Science, Technology and Engineering, since these industries have seen a serious decrease in numbers of students coming into them. In other areas, like finance and law, competition is likely to be strong. Traineeships and internships in oversubscribed areas tend to be the unpaid ones; media and marketing among others. If you are looking for a traineeship in a large blue-chip organisation it is wise to consult their website for details, since they often don't feel it necessary to advertise or to recruit beyond major universities.

The Advantages of Vacation Training & Internships. Since the introduction of tuition fees and abolition of grants, the financial rewards of doing a traineeship/internship have become increasingly alluring: many schemes pay impressive salaries. Even so, for many the value of the experience gained far outweighs that of the salary. Traineeships/ internships can give you a valuable insight into potential careers, especially as you are likely to be given a meaningful role rather than simple menial tasks. It is an incredible advantage, when looking for permanent jobs, to have had a taste of various industries without having had to make a commitment to any, and perhaps more importantly to have it listed on your CV. This is particularly true in the current economic climate. Graduate vacancies recently shrunk to an all-time low and while firms continue to create jobs, they are reluctant to invest in graduate trainees. The competition for jobs that do exist currently stands at 42 applications for every vacancy. With such fierce competition, it is increasingly vital for students to seek work placements as an initial step into the job market. Employers are more far likely to value a candidate who spent a summer gaining experience and skills, and probably cultivating a more mature approach to work, than one who worked sporadically at a local pub.

In addition, when it comes round to interview time for graduate jobs, you will have already been able to practice and will be better prepared as a result. Having done a traineeship/internship will also provide a good source of interview conversation. Employers frequently say that they are looking for work experience, practical business skills, personality and initiative, and if you are able to demonstrate these on your CV a minimum degree requirement for the job may be waived.

Many companies also treat their schemes as extended assessment periods: while you are getting an insight into them, they can assess your suitability for a permanent position. Some interns leave with a permanent job offer in the bag and even sponsorship for their final year. Even if the company does not make you a job offer, a good reference from them can help you find work elsewhere. Experience in sectors where placements are rare, like media or the arts, can enable you to build up a bank of contacts that would help enormously in future job hunts.

Experience and Qualifications. Most employers specify a preferred field of study relevant to the job. Unsurprisingly, arts undergraduates are not generally targeted by engineering or computing firms. The internship schemes of larger companies are geared towards university students, with many specifying further that they must be in their penultimate year of study. Some, particularly unpaid and work shadow schemes, will offer work to pre-university students. Others may operate special or informal schemes for those trying to get experience during a gap year or after A Levels – here a personal approach or use of personal contacts often pays.

More generally, employers are looking for self-motivated students with a positive attitude, with the ability to work well in a team and an aptitude to analyse and solve problems quickly and effectively. If you give the impression that you really want just a holiday job, you are unlikely to be considered for a post.

Further guidance and advice on work placements and internships can be obtained from the National Council for Work Experience (www.work-experience.org).

Au Pair, Home Help and Paying Guest Agencies

Among the types of job to be found in this category are positions for *Au Pairs, Mother's Helps, Playscheme Leaders and Paying Guests.*

Playschemes. Most local authorities organise playschemes for children during the summer holidays, as a cheaper alternative to private childcare. Throughout the country dozens of playleaders and assistants are needed to run activities for children of all ages. Cash limits mean that some councils ask specifically for volunteers. Councils will usually advertise in local newspapers a few months before the end of the school term, or you can contact their education or leisure departments to find out what they will be offering.

Domestic Work. Anyone preferring closer contact with children should consider working in a family as a mother's help or (for applicants from overseas) as an Au Pair. This work usually requires some experience and involves light housework and looking after children. Mother's helps and au pairs work to assist the mother, not replace her as a nanny might, and therefore qualifications are not usually necessary.

There are many agencies in the UK which specialise in placing home helps. Details of these and other au pair opportunities are listed in the Au Pair, Home Help and Paying Guest chapter towards the end of the book. If you prefer to find work independently, job advertisements appear in *The Lady* magazine and occasionally in *Horse and Hound*, both available from newsagents.

Further Sources of Information and Employment

Jobcentre Plus. The Department of Work and Pensions runs the Jobcentre Plus Network where a full range of temporary vacancies can be found by searching on touch-screen terminals known as Jobpoints. In London, the Hotel & Catering Jobcentre Plus, on Denmark Street, runs a Temporary Desk for those seeking work in the catering and hospitality sectors. At other Jobcentre Plus offices, such as Fountain Street in Manchester, you can ask to join a Temporary Jobs Register covering a range of employment sectors. Jobcentre Plus advertises all of its vacancies at www. directgov.gov.uk/employment and on its own website, www.jobcentreplus.gov.uk.

To find the address of your nearest Jobcentre Plus either look in the telephone directory under 'Jobcentre Plus' or search on the website mentioned above.

Jobseeker Direct (☎0845-606 0234) is a phone service designed to help you find a full or part-time job. Telephone advisors have access to jobs nationwide and can help match your particular skills and requirements to vacant positions. Anyone without a job can use the service whether or not they are claiming Jobseeker's Allowance. In addition, the self-service Jobpoint terminals located in every Jobcentre Plus give access to a database of over 400,000 vacancies and are available for use by anyone looking for work.

The Jobcentre Plus (www.jobcentreplus.gov.uk) also advertises nationwide vacancies, particularly those in more specialised fields on its website: it has access to all the jobs currently available to Jobseeker Direct.

Big companies such as Butlins like to recruit early and advertise vacancies through their local Jobcentre Plus in the spring. In the summer, many jobs are available on the spot too. The organisers of big local events and farmers, for example, sometimes use Jobcentre Plus to recruit staff.

Increasingly, local Jobcentre Plus offices request that people searching for jobs call Jobseeker Direct on ☎0845-606 0234 rather than the office itself, since Jobseeker Direct and its companion website (www.jobcentreplus.gov.uk) provide a comprehensive nationwide service.

Employment Agencies. While the number of agencies dealing with temporary work in London can be positively daunting, outside the capital the range is much narrower. It is worth registering with as many agencies as possible in order to enhance your chances of finding work. The jobs offered are frequently office based, though increasingly agencies specialise in different industry sectors. Brook Street Bureau and Reed, which have branches all over the UK, both tend to concentrate on clerical work. Manpower, also with offices nationwide, has information on labouring and warehouse jobs. You can find their local agencies under 'Employment Agencies' in the Yellow Pages.

Under the Employment Agencies Act it is illegal for an agency to charge a fee for finding someone a job: agencies make their money by charging the employers.

The Internet. The internet can be an invaluable aid to the jobseeker. Details of new vacancies are posted on www.vacationwork.co.uk, which also has links to other relevant sites. Other extremely useful websites include www.seasonworkers.com and www.anyworkanywhere.com, whilst the websites of most local newspapers have weekly updated employment pages.

National Institutes. One way of finding out more about Vacation Training opportunities within a specific field is to contact the relevant national professional body or institute. Institutes do not themselves offer traineeships, but may be able to offer general advice and/or give names and addresses of companies within their field. Here are a few – others can be found under *ASSOCIATIONS-TRADE* at www.yell.com.

Hotel & Catering International Management Association: Trinity Court, 34 West Street, Sutton, Surrey SM1 1SH (☎020-8661 4900; fax 020-8661 4901; www.hcima. org.uk).

Institute of Chartered Accountants in England and Wales: Gloucester House, 399 Silbury Boulevard, Central Milton Keynes MK9 2HL (☎01908-248040; e-mail careers@icaew.co.uk; www.icaew.co.uk/careers).

Institute of Chartered Accountants of Scotland: Head Office, CA House, 21 Haymarket Yards, Edinburgh EH12 5BH (☎0131-347 0100; fax 0131-347 0105; www.icas.org.uk).

Chartered Institute of Public Relations: 32 St James' Square, London SW1Y 4JR (☎020-7766 3333; fax 020-7766 3344; e-mail info@cipr.co.uk; www.ipr.org.uk).

International Federation of the Periodical Press: Queen's House, 55-56 Lincoln's Inn Fields, London WC2A 3LJ (☎020-7404 4169; fax 020-7404 4170; e-mail info@

fipp.com; www.fipp.com).

Royal Institute of British Architects: 66 Portland Place, London W1B 1AD (☎020-7580 5533; fax 020-7255 1541; e-mail info@inst.riba.org; www.riba.org).

Royal Town Planning Institute: 41 Botolph Lane, London EC3R 8DL (☎020-7929 9494; fax 020-7929 9490; www.rtpi.org.uk). This organisation runs a Vacation Employment Register which is designed to put prospective employers in touch with planning students on RTPI accredited courses who are looking for work over the summer vacation.

TAX AND NATIONAL INSURANCE

Income Tax. Single people are entitled to a personal tax allowance, which means that you do not pay income tax until your yearly earnings exceed £5,035 (2006/7 figure). Few people are likely to earn this much over the vacation. You may earn between £5,035 and £7,185 at a tax rate of 10%. If you earn any more than this you will have to pay tax at 22%.

To avoid paying tax you need to fill out the right form; if your employer uses the PAYE system, new employees will usually be taxed under an 'emergency code' until the Tax Office receives this form from your employer. Students working in their holidays should fill in form P38(S), and school/other students or individuals starting to work for the first time should fill in a P46. A P38 allows employers to pay students without the deduction of tax. However, if you are not planning to be a student after 5 April of the next year, or if your total income (excluding student loans, scholarships and educational grants) in the tax year exceeds £5,035, you should not fill in a P38. Students who work during term time as well as during holidays are also not eligible to fill out a P38. If you pay any tax before you are put on the correct tax code, then you can claim a rebate during the year if your estimated yearly earnings do not exceed the personal allowance. If you have not been put on the right tax code by the time you leave your job, send a repayment claims form (P50) to the Tax Office together with your P45, which you will get when you finish work. If you are being paid by cash or cheque, not PAYE, then worrying about codes and rebates should not be necessary, although strictly speaking any income should be reported to your local tax office. Further information and figures for 2007/8, when available, can be found at www.hmrc.gov.uk/students.

National Insurance. National Insurance contributions are compulsory for employees over 16 years of age if they earn over a certain limit. The rate you pay is calculated according to your wages. Currently, anyone who earns less than £98 a week pays nothing and then 11% of earnings above that figure.

If you require information in addition to that given above, contact your local HM Revenue & Customs, the new department responsible for the former Inland Revenue and HM Customs and Excise offices, or visit www.hmrc.gov.uk or else your local Citizens Advice Bureau.

The National Minimum Wage

The UK has a national minimum wage, which on 1 October 2006 was raised to £5.35 per hour for those aged 22 and over and £4.45 per hour for those aged 18-21. Most workers in the UK, including home workers, agency workers, commission workers, part-time workers, casual workers and pieceworkers, are entitled to the national minimum wage. The minimum wage has been extended to cover 16 (who have ceased to be of compulsory school age) and 17 years olds, at a rate of £3.30 per hour. There are a small number of other cases in which the minimum wage does not apply, for example, for people living with and working for a family business or if a worker is aged under 26 and in the first year of an apprenticeship; in addition if an employer provides accommodation he can also deduct up to £29.05 per week (£4.15 per day) of a worker's pay for the cost of providing it. So, a low wage that appears to be breaking the law may in fact be legal.

This is a general overview. Those wanting more detailed information, leaflets or to register a complaint should call the National Minimum Wage (NMW) Helpline on ☎0845-600 0678, write to NMW Enquiries, BP7102, Benton Park View, Newcastle-upon-Tyne NE98 1ZZ, or visit www.dti.gov.uk/employment/pay.

Creating Your Own Job

You might not want to spend time sending off speculative letters or phoning around potential employers chasing a job vacancy that might not exist or may already have been filled. The alternative is to make a job for yourself, by creating a service that people in your area might be willing to pay for. Shell Livewire is a free support service, founded and supported by Shell UK, open to all 16-30 year-olds considering starting, or already running, a small business. It gives young people access to free business start up information and support tailored to their needs. This is provided online at www. shell-livewire.org, via training events, and through a *Start A Business Toolkit* CD-Rom. The toolkit contains essential information on planning, starting, and running a business, including an enterprise route map; ideas generation and personal assessment tools; video role models; and a resource bank to help plan the business. The website also provides online networking with other aspiring entrepreneurs, and links to local business advice and gives details of its Shell Springboard funding programme and Entrepeneur of the Year Awards. Young entrepreneurs can also put questions to online mentors who can draw on their own experiences of launching and running their own businesses. Further information is available from Shell Livewire (Design Works Unit 15, William Street, Felling, Gateshead, Tyne and Wear NE10 0JP; ☎0845-757 3252; fax 0191-423 6201; e-mail shell-livewire@one.org).

Window cleaning, car-washing, housework and babysitting are a few of the most obvious odd-jobs you could offer to do, and there are many more. Before becoming self-employed you should ask yourself some questions:

1. What do people want? Do a little market research among neighbours and friends, read local papers and look at adverts placed in local shops. Try to identify particular needs in the area.

2. What can I offer? It is surprising how easily existing skills or hobbies can be turned into financially rewarding enterprise. Some suggestions:

- *Academic qualifications:* private tuition, translation.
- *Carpentry:* simple woodwork, mending gates, making/putting up shelves.
- *Cooking:* lunch and dinner party catering or sandwich-making.
- *Cycling:* bicycle repairs (highly recommended), courier work (suitable for those with a mountain bike who live in a big city).
- *Gardening:* grass-cutting, weeding or pruning.
- *Knitting:* making jumpers, cardigans on commission.
- *Music:* busking, playing in pubs, DJ-ing or giving music lessons.
- *Sewing:* dressmaking, repairs and alterations, cushion-making.
- *Word-processing:* CV-typing, report and essay typing.
- *Walking:* dog exercising, tourist guiding or shopping for the elderly.

3. Who wants me? After you have identified a job you can do and for which you think there is local demand, you need to publicise your services. The best way to start is with advertisements in local shop windows and supermarket notice boards, which are either very cheap or free. It is worth thinking about your market as you do this – if you are offering music lessons it is probably more worthwhile to advertise in a music shop than a grocer's store. If you can afford it, you could place an ad in the local newspaper. It is also useful to deliver a handbill to your target area.
4. Is it worth it? Before getting too carried away imagining yourself as the next

Richard Branson, stop and ask yourself how much money you are hoping to make and whether you will be able to do so using your particular idea. Work may well be sporadic, unpredictable and even only occasional. If you need a regular income, think very carefully.

The principal feature of successfully creating a job for yourself is your reputation. If you impress someone with your hard work, promptness and efficiency, they will tell others.

Tips on Applying for a Job

1. Most employers like to make their staff arrangements in good time, so apply early and according to the dates mentioned in the job details.

2. Before applying for a position, ensure that you fulfil all the requirements, such as age and qualifications. Employers usually have definite reasons for setting requirements and will stick to them, so you are wasting both your time and theirs if you apply for a job for which you are clearly not suitable.

Period of work: employers generally prefer to take on one person for the whole season. If you are able to work for longer than the minimum period quoted, you are more likely to get the job.

Accommodation: it is particularly important to note whether or not lodging is provided, especially for those who are coming from abroad. In areas which attract many tourists over the summer, temporary rented accommodation can be either difficult to find or prohibitively expensive. Some employers can recommend lodgings in the area or be of more positive help, but often they are reluctant to recruit those without pre-arranged accommodation.

3. Prepare an application. This will normally be in the form of a covering letter and a *curriculum vitae* (CV). The point of the application is to show (i) that you want the job, (ii) that you want to work for that organisation, and that (iii) you have had the appropriate experiences and demonstrated the relevant skills and qualities so that the employer wants you.

In order to achieve these three objectives you must first consider why the specific job interests you and secondly what are the key qualities and skills needed - typically these may include social/interpersonal skills, organisational abilities, leadership, verbal and written communication skills, numeracy, intelligence, diligence, conscientiousness, thoroughness, work processing, and so on. Once these factors have been worked out, it is time to write a CV and covering letter to show that you are the best person for the job.

Curriculum Vitae: This should be typed on one or two full A4 sides in note form and include the following details, ordered in titled groups of information:
(a) Personal details (name, address, telephone number, nationality, age, marital status);
(b) Educational qualifications and current place and subject of study if you are a student, otherwise your present occupation;
(c) Relevant experience, which may include work experience, organising social events, captaining a football team or activity in school or university societies;
(d) Skills such as computing, word processing, other languages, driving licence;
(e) Interests and Hobbies;
(f) Referees - preferably one from work/place of education and one personal.

Covering Letter: this should be fairly short (one side of A4) and tidy, preferably typed. This is your chance to explain why the job must be given to you in terms of points (i), (ii) and (iii) above, using the information on the CV to support your argument. Use positive, enthusiastic language and include the following information, possibly in separate paragraphs:
(a) Which exact position you have chosen and why it appeals to you (and also make

it clear which geographical region you have chosen if there are several to choose from);
(b) Why you have chosen that particular organisation - here it is worth being extremely complimentary towards them – making it clear you have researched their business where possible;
(c) Why they should employ you - and use your CV to prove that your claims are true.

4. Address the letter to the person specified in the entry, whether this gives an actual name or merely the title, e.g. Personnel Manager, Student Training Officer.

5. Always enclose a stamped addressed envelope (s.a.e.) or, if you are applying from abroad, an International Reply Coupon (IRC). IRCs are available from any post office and cost £0.95. It can be both expensive and inconvenient for employers to reply to a large number of applicants, especially once the positions have been filled. Some employers simply will not respond to applications without a s.a.e. or IRC.

6. When an interview is necessary, and this applies in particular to firms offering vacation traineeships, you should be able to show a basic knowledge of, and interest in, the activities of the company in question, as well as demonstrate that you are seriously considering a career in that particular field. In other words, you must demonstrate premeditated enthusiasm for the employment sector, the work and the organisation. It is also essential to realise that how you say it is as important as what you say - be positive, friendly and enthusiastic.

7. If you receive a job offer, check all the relevant information: the job details given in this book are supplied by the employer, but it is wise to confirm them before accepting the position. Things to check include wages, board and lodging, hours and the conditions of work. Some staff have ended up working unpaid overtime, others have been sacked without warning, so clarify **all** terms and conditions in advance.

Ask your employer to put the relevant details in writing (though for these to become legally binding, both parties must sign a contract).

8. If you are offered more than one job, decide quickly which you prefer and inform all employers of your decision as soon as possible, especially for jobs where vacancies advertised were limited.

9. Some young people regard their summer job as a holiday, but this is seldom the attitude taken by the employer. If the job details indicate that a hotel needs an assistant to serve three meals a day six days a week, or a hop farmer needs pickers to work seven days a week in all weathers, then you should be well aware that there will be far more work than holiday.

10. Finally, ask for a reference when you leave your job, since this should enhance your chances of finding work in the future. In some fields, such as retail and childcare, the ability to produce a reference is considered important.

Work Permits and Special Schemes

In a sense the title of this chapter is inaccurate in that work permits as such are no longer issued; the term is used as most readers will understand what is meant by a work permit. Before writing letters to prospective employers, overseas applicants should clarify the terms under which they may visit and work in Britain. Anyone arriving at UK Immigration without the necessary visa, letter of invitation or other required documentation could be sent back home on the next available flight. An outline of the regulations is given below. For further information, contact the nearest British Consulate or High Commission. Foreign readers should be aware that although the number of applications from asylum-seekers fell by 21% in 2005, with the levels remaining roughly the same in the first quarter of 2006, immigration controls are tight and those attempting to work in the UK without the appropriate documentation will not be treated lightly. On the other hand, increasing fears of an asylum crisis have led to a number of new measures intended not just to crack down on illegal workers, but also to increase the opportunities for foreigners to work legally in this country where the labour is required.

The primary route for entry into the UK for the purpose of employment was previously the work permit system. Work permits were issued only where a genuine vacancy existed and where particular qualifications or skills were required that were in short supply from the resident and EEA labour force. In 2005, the government announced its intention to implement a Five Year Strategy for Immigration and Asylum. This represented a major overhaul of the work permit arrangements, as well as rules on immigration and asylum. Consequently, a new points-based system, designed to enable the UK to control immigration more effectively was introduced in March 2006 to replace the 80 different entry routes by which a non-EEA national could come to the UK to work.

Visa Requirements

All those who are **not** British or EEA nationals will need a visa or entry clearance for all stays in the UK over six months

Since November 2003, nationals of 10 "phase one" countries require entry clearance for stays of over 6 months. These countries are Australia, Canada, Hong Kong SAR, Japan, Malaysia, New Zealand, Singapore, South Africa, South Korea, and the USA. From November 2006, nationals of a further 55 "phase two" countries also require the same entry clearance. These include much of South America, the Caribbean island states and some African nations. For the full list of "phase two" countries and for the latest information on visa requirements, it is advisable to check the UK visa website at www.ukvisas.gov.uk.

Entry under the Points-Based System for Migration

Wherever relevant, entries in this book specify if the company or organisation in question welcomes applications from overseas. Unfortunately, this does not mean that all foreigners can work for them legally in this country. It is an offence under the Asylum and Immigration Act of 1996 to take employment in breach of conditions of stay: a person found to be working illegally may be fined and may also be liable to deportation. An employer employing overseas nationals whom he or she knows to be working in breach of their landing conditions may also be liable to prosecution and a fine of up to £5,000.

EEA Citizens. Nationals of the European Economic Area are free to enter the United Kingdom to seek employment without a work permit. At present this applies to citizens of EU countries, EEA member states of Norway, Iceland and Liechtenstein, and the European Free Trade Agreement (EFTA) member state of Switzerland. However EEA nationals still require a permit for the Channel Islands and the Isle of Man. The EU itself expanded in May 2004, increasing the number of countries by ten. These new countries are: Estonia, Latvia, Lithuania, Poland, Czech Republic, Slovakia, Hungary, Slovenia, Malta and Cyprus. However, nationals from eight of these states – Czech Republic, Estonia, Hungary, Latvia, Lithuania, Poland, Slovakia, and Slovenia – who find a job in the UK are required to register with the Home Office under the new Worker Registration Scheme as soon as they find work. This currently carries an initial charge of £70 (fees are reviewed regularly). This scheme was set up so that the government could monitor the impact of EU accession on the UK labour market and restrict access to benefits. Nationals from Malta and Cyprus have free movement rights and are not required to obtain a workers registration certificate. January 2007 will see the expected entry to the EU of Bulgaria and Romania. At the time of going to press, it is still unclear as to whether nationals from these countries will enjoy the same unlimited access to jobs in Britain as other member states.

EEA nationals intending to stay longer than six months may apply for a residence permit, although there is no obligation on them to do so.

Non-EEA Citizens. Until the Points-Based Entry system (PBS) was introduced, the general position under the Immigration Rules was that overseas nationals (other than EEA nationals) coming to work in Britain should have work permits before setting out. Permits were normally issued only for specific jobs requiring a high level of skill and experience for which resident or EEA labour was not available. In other words, a UK employer could not receive a work permit for a non-EEA citizen unless it was a job for which there was no EEA National available.

The new points-based system of migration to the UK is still in the early stages of implementation. It is designed to control migration more effectively, tackle abuse and identify the most talented workers by consolidating entry clearance and work permit applications into one single-step application. The plan is to ensure that only those who benefit Britain can come here to work. These criteria are only for those workers from outside the EEA who wish to work or train in the UK. The system is based on 5 tiers:

- ○ Tier 1: Highly skilled workers, e.g. scientists or entrepreneurs;
- ○ Tier 2: Skilled workers with a job to offer, e.g. nurses, teachers or engineers;
- ○ Tier 3: Low skilled workers filling specific temporary labour shortages, e.g. construction workers for a particular building project;
- ○ Tier 4: Students;
- ○ Tier 5: Youth mobility workers and temporary workers, e.g. working holiday makers.

For each tier, applicants will need sufficient points to gain entry clearance to the UK. Points can be scored for skills or attributes which predict a worker's success in the labour market. For Tiers 3-5, under which most summer employment falls, points will be awarded depending on whether the applicant has: a valid certificate of sponsorship from an approved sponsor; adequate funds to live in the UK; proven compliance with previous immigration conditions and in some cases English language ability. A web-based self-assessment programme, which allows applicants to understand whether they meet the UK's criteria for entry can be found on the Home Office website. The system is being introduced tier by tier, so whilst the new scheme automatically abolishes some of the previous work permit arrangements (see below), such as the Sectors Based Scheme, others will remain in place for the foreseeable future.

Further details about the PBS are available at www.workingintheuk.gov.uk and the Home Office Immigration and Nationality Directorate (www.ind.homeoffice.gov. uk). Queries should be directed to Work Permits (UK)'s Customer Contacts Centre on ☎0114-207 4074.

Citizens of Commonwealth Countries: Nationals of Commonwealth countries (including Australia, New Zealand, Canada and South Africa) between the ages of 17 and 30 are permitted to visit the UK under Tier 5 of the new system (previously known as the 'Working Holiday Maker' scheme). This allows them to take up casual employment which will be incidental to their holiday, but not to engage in business or to pursue a career. The period which can be spent in the UK is two years and of that time, 52 weeks may be spent working full-time or part-time at no more than 20 hours per week.

Commonwealth citizens with at least one British-born grandparent may wish to apply for 'UK Ancestry employment entry clearance' from the British High Commission: this altogether eliminates the need for a work permit. Married couples must apply for separate entry clearance before travelling.

Canadian students, graduates and young people should contact the Student Work Abroad Programme (SWAP), which provides support to those wishing to work in Britain. It is administered by the Canadian Universities Travel Service, which has over 40 offices in Canada. For details see www.swap.ca.

Australians and New Zealanders should contact International Exchange Programmes (IEP), a non-profit organisation specialising in sending young Australians and New Zealanders on working holidays overseas. For more details visit www.iep. org.au or www.iep.co.nz.

Students from the USA. US students seeking temporary work in the UK will fall under Tier 5 of the new system (previously known as the 'Work in Britain Program'). This allows full-time US college students and recent graduates over the age of 18 to look for work in Britain, finding jobs through BUNAC listings or through personal contacts. Jobs may be pre-arranged, though most participants wait until arrival in Britain to job hunt. US students on study abroad programmes through an American University overseas are also eligible for the programme. When students apply to BUNAC they will receive a 'Blue Card'. The Blue Card must be presented to immigration on arrival in the UK. It is valid for six months and cannot be extended, although it is possible to obtain a second Blue Card in another calendar year if they again fulfil the eligibility requirements. The Blue Card costs $290 from BUNAC, PO Box 430, Southbury, CT 06488 (☎1-800 GO BUNAC; e-mail wib@bunacusa.org; www.bunac.org).

Seasonal Agricultural Work Scheme (SAWS).: This is one of the few schemes that remains in place after the PBS has come into effect. The government plans to maintain the scheme until 2010, from when it will fall under Tiers 3 and 4. Farm camps under this scheme are authorised by the Home Office and are the main hope for non-EEA and non-Commonwealth nationals wishing to work in this country. Special 'Work Cards' are issued to a certain number of non-EEA nationals each year. Places fill up very quickly and it is necessary to apply in November to have any chance of obtaining a card for the following year.

The recruitment for these farms is handled by nine agencies, known as SAWS operators, including Concordia (for address see *Agriculture* above). Between them they recruit pickers for over 160 farms throughout the year. Prospective participants should be aged 18 or over and full-time students in their own country. An invitation to work is only valid if the work card is issued by an official operator and *not* by individual farmers. The SAW scheme has undergone some large changes since 1 January 2004. Whereas in previous years the scheme only ran from May until November, it now runs all year long, taking in a much wider breadth of work for those involved, from daffodil picking to working with livestock. The numbers have been reduced, in the light of the addition of new EU states who can no longer participate in the scheme and would use the Workers' Registration Scheme route. The upper age limit of 25 has been removed. The only requirement is that the applicant is a full-time student, currently studying in higher education residing in a country outside of the EEA and not in their last year of studies. You can take part in the scheme for a minimum of five weeks and a maximum of six months at a time. Applicants should note that a reasonable charge may be made for the accommodation and other services provided. Applicants can participate in the scheme for longer than six months, as long as they return to their home country for a minimum of three months before applying again.

Voluntary Work. Overseas nationals seeking voluntary work in the UK will fall under Tier 5 of the new system. Overseas nationals may be admitted for up to 12 months for the purpose of voluntary work providing their sponsor is a charity or non-charitable philanthropic organisation and the applicant is receiving no remuneration other than pocket money, board and accommodation. The work which they do must be closely related to the aims of the charity i.e. working with people, and they must not be engaged in purely clerical, administrative or maintenance work. Volunteers are expected to leave the United Kingdom at the end of their visit.

Vacation Traineeships & Internships. Again, these will fall under Tier 5 of the new system. Permission can be given for overseas nationals with pre-arranged work placements to obtain permits for professional training or managerial level work experience for a limited period of 12 months.

While many companies in this book are happy to employ overseas students as trainees since most of them run their schemes in order to try out potential employees, they may not be keen to take on anyone who cannot return to them after their studies.

Non EEA Students Studying in the UK. These students fall under Tier 4 of the new system. Overseas students studying in Britain who wish to take up vacation work no longer have to obtain permission to do so. This is on the basis that they do not pursue a career by filling a full-time vacancy or work for more than 20 hours per week during term time, except where the placement is a necessary part of their studies, with the agreement of the educational institution.

Au Pairs. Overseas Au Pairs now fall under Tier 5 of the new system (previously known as the Au Pair Placement scheme). For details of regulations affecting au pairs see the chapter *Au Pair, Home Help and Paying Guests* at the end of the book.

Japanese Students: Japanese nationals fall under Tier 5 of the new system (previously known as the *Youth Exchange Scheme*). This allows Japanese students aged between

18 and 25 to come to the UK for an extended holiday for up to 12 months with the intention of taking work as part of your holiday. There is a quota of 100 participants each year.

Further Information

Once in the UK, general information about immigration matters can be obtained from the Home Office Immigration and Nationality Directorate, Lunar House, 40 Wellesley Road, Croydon CR9 2BY (☎0870-606 7766; www.ind.homeoffice.gov. uk): be prepared to wait in line for your call to be answered, it will be eventually. Guidance leaflets are also available from the Correspondence Unit, UK Visas, Foreign and Commonwealth Office, King Charles Street, London SW1A 2AH (☎020-7008 8438), or can be downloaded from www.ukvisas.gov.uk/forms. Further information and guidance can be found at www.ukvisas.gov.uk/guidance. Work Permits (UK), Home Office, PO Box 3468, Sheffield S3 8WA (☎0114-207 4074; fax 0114-207 4000; www.workingintheuk.gov.uk) can advise employers on the rules of the entry scheme.

ABBREVIATIONS

approx.	approximately	max.	maximum
a.s.a.p.	as soon as possible	min.	minimum
B & L	board and lodging	p.a.	per annum
CV	curriculum vitae	s.a.e.	stamped addressed envelope
IRC	International Reply Coupon	w.p.m.	words per minute
NMW	National Minimum Wage		

Glossary of Qualifications

The following list of qualifications (often the name of the institute or association which issues them) are listed in alphabetical order.

ACA/ACCA – (Chartered) Association of Certified Accountants
BASI – British Association of Ski Institutes
BCU – British Canoe Union
BHSIC – British Horse Society Instructor's Certificate
BTEC – Business and Technology Education Certificate
CELTA – Certificate in English Language Teaching to Adults
CIMA – Chartered Institute of Management Accountants
City and Guilds 706/1, 706/2 – catering qualifications
DELTA – Diploma in English Language Teaching to Adults
GCSE – General Certificate of Secondary Education
GNAS – Grand National Archery Society
HGV – Heavy Goods Vehicle driving licence
HND – Higher National Diploma
LGV – Light Goods Vehicle driving licence
LTA – Lawn Tennis Association
MLTB – Mountaineering Leadership Training Board
NAMCW – National Association for Maternal and Child Welfare
NGB – National Governing Body
NNEB – National Nursery Examination Board
OND – Ordinary National Diploma
PCV – Passenger Carrying Vehicle
PLG – Pool Life Guard
RGN – Registered General Nurse
RLS (S) – Royal Life Saving (Society)
RSA – Royal Society of Arts (Examinations Board)
RYA – Royal Yachting Association
SEN – Senior Enrolled Nurse
TEFL/EFL – (Teaching) English as a Foreign Language
TESOL – Teaching English to Speakers of Other Languages

Summer Jobs Nationwide

Organisations which have branches in various parts of Britain

Business and Industry

ANGEL HUMAN RESOURCES plc: Angel House, 4 Union Street, London Bridge, London SE1 1SZ (☎020-7940 2000; fax 020-7940 2018; e-mail hq@angelhr.org; www.angelhr.org). Angel was founded in 1965 and adheres strictly to the codes of practice laid down by its professional bodies. It specialises in recruiting in the commercial, hospitality, industrial, and healthcare markets. Open 7am-6pm Monday to Friday with branch offices throughout the UK.

Chefs, Cooks, Waiting and General Catering and Kitchen Assistants; work may be offered in catering environments, throughout the year. Work may also be offered to experienced **Office Staff, Warehouse and Factory Staff** and experienced or qualified **Social Workers.** Pay may vary between £5.35 and £16.00 per hour dependent on experience and qualifications.

Applicants from abroad should note that placements can only be made after arrival in the UK; Angel cannot enter into correspondence prior to arrival in the UK. Work can usually be offered within a few days. Angel cannot assist with accommodation.

Apply to the office in person or by phone on arrival in London.

BETTERWARE: Head Office, Stanley House, Park Lane, Castle Vale, Birmingham B35 6LJ (☎0845-121 1010; fax 0845-129 4653; www.betterware.co.uk).

Distributors to deliver and collect Betterware's Household Products brochure. Expected earnings £40 to £200 per week, dependent on hours available. To work full or part-time, at least 8 hours per week. Vacancies exist in all parts of the UK at all times of the year. Full-time career opportunities in sales management also exist for the right candidates.

For more details or to make an *application* please call Betterware Recruitment on 0845-125 5000 (local rate).

BLUE ARROW LIMITED: 800 The Boulevard, Capability Green, Luton, Bedford LU1 3BA (☎0800-085 5777; fax 01582-749084; e-mail enquiries@bluearrow.co.uk; www.bluearrow.co.uk).

Temporary/Permanent Staff (500,000 per year) to work in offices, catering, industry and construction around the UK. Benefits include competitive pay rates, paid holiday, variety of work, hours to suit. Relevant previous experience may or may not be required. Minimum age 16.

Those interested should *visit* the website or contact one of Blue Arrow's 150 branches around the country.

HORIZON HPL: Signet House, 49-51 Farringdon Road, London EC1M 3JB (e-mail horizonhpl.london@btinternet.com). A training centre established in 1991 which organises paid work placements in hotels, shops and companies in the UK and in France for EU citizens, including English and French tuition and preparation to sit British and French examinations.

Company Staff. Placements are available all year round (in a variety of fields) from 3 months to 1 year. They receive a trainee wage and accommodation if working in a hotel. Applicants from 17-50 years. An interview is necessary.

Applicants should contact the agency 2 months in advance of intended work date.

MAJESTIC WINE WAREHOUSES: Majestic House, Otterspool Way, Watford WD25 8WW (☎01923-298200; fax 01923-819105; e-mail careers@majestic.co.uk; www.majestic.co.uk). Majestic is the UK's foremost by-the-case retailer of wines, beers and spirits. There are over 100 stores throughout England, Scotland and Wales and expansion plans for another 8 to 10 stores a year.
Temporary Drivers to help with delivery driving, merchandising and dealing with customers. Wages vary according to location. Vacancies available in most holiday periods, particularly at Christmas and during the summer. Applicants should enjoy working with the public, must have held a driving licence for at least a year, and must be 20 or over. The job is physically demanding. No accommodation is provided.
Application forms can be obtained by phoning 01923-298210 or by writing to the Recruitment Manager at the above address.

PROMOTIONAL SUPPORT LTD: 100 Sydney Place, Bath BA2 6NE (☎01225-443434; e-mail info@promotionalsupport.co.uk; www.promotionalsupport.co.uk). Organises roadshows, exhibitions and events and supplies promotional staff for clients such as Walkers, Robinsons, Pepsi, Loreal, Bounty and other blue chip clients.
Temporary Promotional Contracts available. Wages from £50-£80 per day. To work 8-10 hours a day. Minimum period of work 1 day at any time of year. No accommodation available.
Applicants should have bubbly, outgoing, attractive personalities. Overseas applicants considered. Interview preferred, but not necessary.
Applications at any time to Promotional Support at the above address, by e-mail (info@promotionalsupport.co.uk), or post a CV and photograph with s.a.e.

Children

ACTIVE TRAINING & EDUCATION: Kildare, Manby Road, Malvern, Worcestershire WR14 3BD (☎08454-561205; fax 01684-562716; e-mail info@ate.org.uk; www.ate.org.uk). An educational trust which runs residential holidays in various rented premises, including boarding schools, field study centres and conference centres, in various parts of the UK.
Caterers (3-4). £300 per week.
General Assistants (10-20). £100 if under 18, or £140 if over 18. B & L provided.
Matrons (3-4). £200 per week. B & L provided.
To work on residential children's holidays. Period of work from July to August.
Applications to Helen Fairest, Deputy Director, at the above address.

ARDMORE LANGUAGE SCHOOLS: Hall Place, Berkshire College, Burchetts Green, Maidenhead, Berkshire SL6 6QR (☎01628-826699; fax 01628-829977; e-mail info@theardmoregroup.com; www.ardmore-language-schools.com). Ardmore offers summer junior vacation courses in English to overseas students at residential and homestay centres located throughout Britain.
Centre Directors, Academic Programme Mangers, Recreational Programme Managers, Centre Administrators, Sports Leaders and Lifeguards needed for residential colleges and homestay centres around the UK. Wages by arrangement. Those aged 19 or over preferred. Period of work 3-8 weeks during July and August.
For further details *visit* the above website and if interested in working for Ardmore during the summer download an application form.

BARRACUDAS SUMMER ACTIVITY CAMPS: Bridge House, Bridge Street, St.Ives, Cambridgeshire PE27 5EH (☎01480-497533; fax 01480-492715; e-mail

jobs@barracudas.co.uk; www.barracudas.co.uk). Barracudas runs summer day camps for 5-14 year olds.
Camp Managers (20), Assistant Camp Managers (20), Senior Group Leaders (15). Wages on application. Experience in teaching and management required.
Group Co-ordinators (150). Wages from £175 per week. Experience with children/ sports necessary.
Group Assistants (150). Wages from £175 per week. A wish to work with children and to ensure their safety necessary.
Football Coaches (50). Wages from £175 per week. Experience in football coaching and excellent knowledge of the game needed.
Arts and Crafts Instructors (50). Wages from £175 per week. Experience in arts and crafts needed.
Dance and Drama Instructors (50). Wages from £175 per week. Drama and dance experience necessary.
Lifeguards (50). Wages from £190 per week. Should be NPLQ/NARS qualified.
All staff to work 40 hours per week. Minimum period of work of 2 weeks. Staff required from mid-July to end of August. Minimum age 18. Foreign applicants with fluent English are welcome; B & L is limited for qualified teachers, managers and lifeguards. Training is available for all staff: some courses lead to nationally recognised qualifications.
Applications should be made from November onwards to Rachel Fabb at the above address or on the website. Interview with references required; police check and security checks made.

CCUSA: First Floor North, Devon House, 171-177 Great Portland Street, London W1W 5PQ (☎020-7637 0779; fax 020-7637 0779; e-mail info@ccusa.co.uk; www. ccusa.com). With over 20 year's experience and 150,000 participants from around the world, CCUSA offers renowned work and travel programmes.
Camp Counsellors (500) required to work at one of CCUSA's summer camps across the UK. Wages dependent on position within the camp, B & L is provided. Applicants must be available for a 9-week period of commitment. Minimum age 19 or over by 1 July 2007. All staff must have previous camp experience or experience of working with children aged 11 to 17. Foreign applicants are welcome provided they speak English to the standard of a native speaker.
Application forms and more information can be found online at the above website.

EAC ACTIVITY CAMPS: First Floor, 59 George Street, Edinburgh EH2 2LQ (☎0131-477 7570; fax 0131-477 7571; e-mail sdonnelly@eac4english.com; www. activitycamps.com). Multi-activity day and residential camps in Edinburgh, Glasgow, Canterbury, York, Ramsgate and Ashford. For children aged 5-16.
Camp Directors (6). Accommodation available at most sites; must be over 21.
Assistant Camp Directors (6). Must be over 21.
Qualified Instructors required for archery, swimming, football and tennis. Relevant qualifications essential for lifeguard and archery positions: RLSS Life Saving/NPLQ/ Bronze Medallion. For archery: GNAS. Additional recognized coaching qualifications are a distinct advantage.
Group Captains (40). Group Monitors (80). Activity Leaders (40). Must be at least 18.
Salaries dependant on position and experience. Accommodation and food provided on most sites. Must have all round sporting ability and be enthusiastic. Sporting qualifications and coaching awards preferred. All staff to work 42 hours per week,

between June and August, with various contracts available. The work is hard but good fun and very rewarding. Overseas applicants welcome but they must have a police check from their own country before starting work. All applicants must be available for interview. An enhanced CRB check is required for all successful applicants.

Applications from February to Susan Donnelly, HR and Recruitment Manager.

KIDS FOR LIFE: Innovation House, 14 Farnborough Street, Farnborough, Hampshire GU14 8AG (☎0845-450 8411; fax 01252-516577; e-mail talent@kidsforlife.co.uk; www.kidsforlife.co.uk). Kids for Life has been providing parents with safe, registered childcare for children aged 4 to 16 with exciting, innovative activities every school holiday for over 10 years. They run 2 types of camp: KFL Camps (range of activities) and KFL Sports. They run 44 camps across the UK.

Activity Instructors (300). Competitive rates of pay. Instructors are required to work long hours, this is not a 9 to 5 job. Staff required all summer from July to September. Accommodation available at some camps. Applicants must be 17 or over. Relevant coaching qualifications or experience is preferred, but extensive training is provided. First-aid qualification is also favoured. Instructors should be imaginative, enthusiastic, caring and responsible.

Application forms should be downloaded from the above website and returned to either talent@kidsforlife.co.uk, or to the above address.

THE KINGSWOOD GROUP: Group Operations, Kingswood House, Alkmaar Way, Norwich, Norfolk NR6 6BF (☎01603-309350; fax 01603-404904; e-mail jobs@kingswood.co.uk; www.kingswood.co.uk). Kingswood operates year round educational activity centres for kids, including Camp Beaumont Summer Camps, which have been running for 23 years at various locations across the UK.

Group Leaders (60-80) are responsible for round-the-clock welfare of a group of children at our Camp Beaumont Summer Camps, including overnight dormitory supervision. Also to instruct and initiate games and non-specialist activities, and to monitor the welfare needs of individual children in their group. National minimum wage applies according to age. Camps run for 8 weeks from the start of July to the end of August. Accommodation provided at a cost of £24.50 per week and food at a cost of £39.95 per week. Comprehensive training is provided. Applicants must be aged between 19 and 25 and have some previous experience working with children and/or a well developed interest in sports, music, drama, art and crafts or any recreational pursuits. Foreign applicants with fluent English welcome.

Kingswood also recruits throughout the year for **Activity Instructors** to supervise various high and low adventure activities such as caving, go-karting, rock-climbing and archery. No experience is necessary, though a friendly and outgoing personality and a love for working with children is a must. Activity Instructors are employed on an initial 12-month Training and Development Package with food, accommodation, nationally recognised qualifications and a training allowance provided throughout the year.

Applications should be sent to the HR department at the above address in the spring. Telephone interviews and an assessment weekend required.

PGL TRAVEL LTD: Alton Court, Penyard Lane, Ross-on-Wye, Herefordshire HR9 5GL (☎0870-401 4411; e-mail recruitment@pgl.co.uk; www.pgl.co.uk/recruitment). PGL recruit around 2,000 staff each year to assist with the running of their children's activity centres throughout the UK, including Devon, the Isle of Wight, Lincolnshire, the south coast, Surrey, Shropshire, Perthshire and Wales. Europe's largest provider of adventure holidays for children has offered outstanding training and work opportunities to seasonal staff for almost 50 years. PGL jobs provide a break from the 9-5 routine. If you are enthusiastic, energetic and looking for real experience and responsibility in a stimulating environment, PGL could have the job for you.

Activity Instructors in canoeing, sailing, windsurfing, fencing, archery, motorsports, pony trekking and more. Qualifications not essential for all positions as full training will be provided. Minimum age 18.

Group Leaders also needed to take responsibility for groups of children, helping them to get the most out of their holiday. Previous experience of working with children is an advantage. Minmum age 18.

Support Staff to assist the catering, domestic and maintenance teams.

From £70-£100 per week plus free B & L. Positions available from February to November, for the full season, as little as eight weeks, or any period in between, although there are very few summer-only vacancies.

Applications can be made online, downloaded from the website, or call for an information pack.

SUPER CAMPS LTD: Park House, Milton Park, Abingdon, Oxon OX14 4RS (☎01235 832222; fax 01235 831991; email employment@supercamps.co.uk). Runs multi-activity Half-Term, Christmas, Easter and Summer day camps for children aged 4-13 in schools in South and Central England. Super Camps is committed to providing safe and fun-packed activities (including art/craft and sports) for all children attending its camps.

Site Leaders (50). From £400 per week. Qualified teachers with camp experience.

Second In Charge (50). £275 per week. Qualified/trainee teachers or individuals with substantial children's camp experience.

Swimming Pool Lifeguards (40). £250 per week. Must have experience and hold a recognised and up-to-date life saving/coaching qualification (NPLQ/NARS).
Activity Instructors (400). From £210 per week. To teach a range of activities to children aged 4-13 years. First aid and relevant childcare qualifications/camp experience an advantage. Training is provided, therefore enthusiastic individuals with an interest in sports or arts and crafts and a genuine interest in working with children are welcome to apply.

Staff needed for half-terms, Christmas, Easter, July and August. Good experience for those wishing to go into a teaching, childcare or recreation/leisure profession.

Applications all year round to Personnel at the above address.

Holiday Centres and Amusements

BOURNE LEISURE LIMITED: 1 Park Lane, Hemel Hempstead, Hertfordshire HP2 4YL. Owns and operates 35 holiday parks in resorts throughout England, Scotland and Wales under the brand names of Haven and British Holidays.
Bar Team Members, Catering Team Members, Cooks, Shop Assistants, Cleaning Team Members and Lifeguards. Competitive salary and full training given. Some accommodation is available dependent on the park. Applicants must possess an outgoing personality, smart appearance and be willing to work flexible hours. Vacancies exist between the months of March and October for team members who are available to work for a minimum of 8 weeks.

For more information on work at any Bourne Leisure's parks please go online at www.bournejobs.co.uk or contact Human Resources on 01442-203952.

BUTLINS SKEGNESS: Roman Bank, Skegness, Lincolnshire PE25 1NJ (☎01754-762311).
BUTLINS MINEHEAD: Minehead, Somerset TA24 5SH (☎01643-703331).
BUTLINS BOGNOR REGIS: Bognor Regis, West Sussex PO21 1JJ (☎01243-820202; www.butlinsonline.co.uk).
Team required for on-going positions at all 3 resorts in the following departments: Guest Catering, Accommodation, Sports and Leisure, Security, Retail Catering, Technical Services, Guest Services, Bars, Shops and Supermarkets, Nursery, Entertainments, Funfair, Administration, Lifeguards, Environment, Gardens. Competitive rates of pay and benefits. Training available. Accommodation on resort may be available.

Applications to above address marked for the attention of Human Resources. More information available at www.butlinsonline.co.uk or www.bournejobs.co.uk. Interview required.

MOTORSPORT VISION LTD: Fawkham, Longfield, Kent DA3 8NG (☎01474-872331; fax 01474-879259; www.motorsportvision.co.uk). Operates several major British motor sport leisure venues. Seasonal staff are always needed to work venues around England, but especially at Brands Hatch, Cadwell Park, Oulton Park and Snetterton.
Marshals required to marshal track activities. Includes some weekend work. Must be flexible and able to work as part of a team.
Bar Assistants required to work behind a busy bar. Variable hours to include evening work and weekends. Experience in cash handling and stock rotation an advantage. Must be flexible and able to work long hours.
Catering Assistants required for duties including some cooking, serving, cash handling, general hygiene and maintenance. Variable hours to include evening work and weekends. Cash handling and food production experience essential.

General Assistants required for variable hours to include evening work and weekends. To assist the Catering Department and help ensure that all services are provided to the highest standard.

Cleaning Operatives required to ensure that all areas are maintained in a clear, tidy safe and hygienic manner.

Wages available on application. Staff are required from March to November, to work as and when required on a fixed term contract. Overseas applicants must have a valid work permit.

Applications to the Human Resources Administrator, from March, at the above address.

PONTINS LTD: Sagar House, Eccleston, Chorley PR7 5PH (☎01257-452452; fax 01257-452270). Pontins is one of the UK's leading holiday companies, entertaining over 600,000 guests every year at 8 coastal locations, and employing over 2,000 people throughout the UK. The centres are located in Blackpool, Lancashire; Burnham on Sea, Somerset; Rye, Sussex; Hemsby, Norfolk; Lowestoft, Suffolk; Clwyd, North Wales; Southport, Merseyside; and Brixham, South Devon.

Fast Food Assistants to serve food and drinks, operate the tills and perform general cleaning duties in a number of fast food outlets.

Restaurant Staff to serve meals and clean dining areas in a variety of self and waiter service restaurants, which seat up to 2,000 people.

Catering Staff including qualified and experienced chefs, cooks and kitchen assistants. Duties include catering for large numbers, preparing and cooking fast food, taking orders, collecting money and general cleaning of the catering areas.

Bar Staff to serve drinks, operate the tills and clean in busy bars.

Shop Staff to be responsible for sales, operating the tills and the merchandising of stock.

Reservations Staff to book in guests and allocate apartments.

Security to patrol the centre and implement and report on health and safety measures.

Lifeguards to supervise the heated indoor pools and the safety of guests.

Leisure Staff to supervise and operate all leisure amenities.

Accommodation Staff to help prepare the accommodation for the arrival of guests, including the making up of beds and cleaning of kitchens and bathrooms.

Maintenance Staff. Positions are available for qualified electricians, plumbers and joiners as well as those who have experience in general maintenance.

Cleaners/Gardeners for internal and external cleaning and maintenance of gardens.

Wages at national minimum and above, to work 40 hours over 6 days per week. Staff are taken on on both seasonal and permanent contracts, but positions are available all year round. Minimum period of work 6 months. Limited accommodation is available. Food is subsidised. Applicants must be at least 18 years of age for all positions. Qualifications and experience are not always necessary, except in specialist areas, as induction training is provided.

Open days are held at all of the eight coastal locations at various times throughout the year and are advertised in local newspapers and job centres. Road shows are also held across the country at Easter.

To apply call the Recruitment Line (☎01257-452452) or e-mail jointheteam@ pontins.com from February onwards for summer positions.

ROYAL COLLECTION ENTERPRISES LTD: Buckingham Palace, London SW1A 1AA (☎020-7930 4832; fax 020-7360 7122; e-mail recruitment@royal.gsx. gov.uk). Royal Collection Enterprises is responsible for the opening of the Official

Residences of The Queen, including Buckingham Palace, Windsor Castle, the Palace of Holyroodhouse and the official London Residence of HRH The Prince of Wales at Clarence House. Front-line staff play a vital role in ensuring that visitors have an enjoyable and memorable experience.

Wardens & Retail Assistants (200) for the summer opening of the State Rooms at Buckingham Palace. Wages £6.15 per hour. To work 35-40 hours per week. Period of work mid-July to end of September.

Ticket Sales and Information Assistants (20) to work at Buckingham Palace (with some work at Windsor Castle) from mid-June to end of August or September. Wages £6.15 per hour. To work 35-40 hours per week. Must possess excellent communication skills, a good telephone manner and a working knowledge of Microsoft Office packages.

Guiding Wardens to provide guided tours of Clarence House and to carry out ticket and security checks from July to mid-October. Applicants must have clear, confident communication skills and the ability to engage the attention of an audience. Previous experience of tour guiding and language skills would be an advantage. Wages £7.00 per hour.

Wardens and Visitor Service Assistants to work at Windsor Castle from May/June to the end of September/October. Wages £6.16 per hour.

Visitor Service Assistants (15) to work at The Palace of Holyroodhouse, carrying out a range of duties including warden, retail, ticketing and café work. Positions available from July to end of September. Wages £5.86 per hour.

All positions require regular weekend work. We offer excellent training, free lunches and uniform, a friendly team atmosphere and a stimulating, unique working environment. For all positions applicants must be between 18 and 65 years old and some customer/visitor care experience would be beneficial. Individuals should be enthusiastic, reliable, smart in appearance and service orientated. Employment is subject to satisfactory references and full security clearance. Foreign applicants with fluent English and a valid work permit/visa welcome. No accommodation available.

For further information and to download an application form and job description, *visit* the recruitment pages at www.royal.gov.uk. Provisional closing date for applications is 28 February 2007.

Hotels and Catering

ANGLO CONTINENTAL PLACEMENTS AGENCY: 9 Wish Road, Hove, East Sussex BN3 4LL (☎01273-776660, fax 01273-776634; e-mail sharon@anglocontinentalplacements.com; www.anglocontinentalplacements.com). A friendly agency established in 1988 who operate throughout the UK. The office is open from 8.30am to 5.30pm Monday-Friday. Hotel and Catering Staff placed all over the UK.

Chefs, Waiting Staff, Receptionists, Commis Chefs, Chefs de Parties, Porters, etc. required. Positions available in all aspects of the hotel industry.

Live-in positions available. Staff wanted from New Zealand, Australia and South Africa and the EU. Previous work experience not essential. Minimum period of work 6 months.

Applications including CV and references to Sharon Wolfe at the above address.

CEI LONDON AND CEI DUBLIN: 164-168 Westminster Bridge Road, London SE1 7RW (☎020-7960 2600; fax 020-7960 2601; e-mail info@cei-frenchcentre.com; www.cei-frenchcentre.com); 5-7 O'Connell Street, Dublin 1 (☎00-353 1 887 0100; fax 00-353 1 872 8773; e-mail Dublin@cei-frenchcentre.com).

The CEI specialises in youth tourism and programmes in the hotel and catering sectors,

English classes and accommodation in London. Candidates must be 18 or over and from an EU country. Programme prices vary.

Applications should be made at least 8 weeks before arrival in the UK, to the Employment Consultant at the above address.

CHEF CENTRE LTD: 1 Kingly Street, London W1B 5PA (☎020-7439 0771; fax 020-7287 3576; e-mail info@chefcentre.com; www.chefcentre.com). A recruitment agency established 30 years ago with a long-standing client base and contacts. **Temporary/Seasonal Chef Work.** Wages negotiable, often living-in; to work as required. Accommodation is frequently available as part of the package. Staff required from March to December. Must have a City and Guilds 706.II or equivalent NVQ and food hygiene certificate. Overseas applicants with relevant experience, qualifications and documentation are welcome.

Applications at least one month before intended work date to Alison, Suzi, Emily or Mike at the above address.

CHOICE HOTELS EUROPE: 112 Station Road, Edgware, Middlesex HA8 7BJ (☎020-8233 2001; fax 020-8233 2080; e-mail fbernardon@choicehotelseurope. com). Owns, manages and franchises over 500 hotels in 13 European countries. Guidance can be offered with finding jobs in Europe, but posts are primarily for the UK and Ireland.

Receptionists, Chefs, Waiting and Bar Staff. Salary in accordance with minimum wages regulation. Minimum period of work of 6 months; 1 year in Front Office. 39 hour week spread over 5 days. Applicants are considered all year round and in all parts of the UK.

Applicants must be over 18, customer orientated, smart and pleasant. Priority given to those with hotel qualifications and/or experience of the business. Good working knowledge of English essential (must be fluent for Receptionist positions, preferably with hotel experience or qualifications).

Applications in writing to Françoise Bernardon, Group Human Resources Officer, at the above address.

DEE COOPER: Culloch Schoolhouse, Comrie, Perthshire PH6 2JG (☎01764-670001/679765; fax 01764-679728; e-mail dee@livein-jobs.demon.co.uk; www. livein-jobs.co.uk; www.londonpubjobs.co.uk). Agent working with more than 1,000 hotels in England, Scotland and Wales. Free service. **Live-in Hotel Staff.** Wages and hours variable, all positions live-in. Foreign applicants with permission to work in the UK welcome.

For a list of relevant available jobs, *contact* Dee Cooper using the above details.

DE VERE HOTELS & LEISURE: 2100 Daresbury Park, Warrington WA4 4BP (☎01928-712111; fax 01928-756341; www.deveregroupplc.co.uk). De Vere Group Plc is a highly focused company concentrating on two growth markets – hotels and health and fitness. The company has two distinctive hotel brands; De Vere Hotels and Village Leisure Hotels.

Waiting Staff, Room Attendants, Porters, Bar Staff, Commis Chefs and Casual Banqueting Staff. Must be over 18 and available to work for a minimum of 4 weeks between May and October. Accommodation may be available, although it is not guaranteed. Overseas applicants who speak fluent English and are eligible to work in the UK may apply.

Applications should be forwarded directly to the Human Resources Manager at the desired location. Addresses of individual hotels can be obtained from our website www.deveregroupplc.co.uk.

GRAFHAM WATER CENTRE: Perry, Huntingdon, Cambridgeshire PE18 0BX (☎0845-634 6022; fax 01480-813850; e-mail info@grafham-water-centre.co.uk; www.grafham-water-centre.co.uk). Provides activity and special interest holidays with centres in Cambridgeshire and Derbyshire.

Catering Assistants (10). Wages £214 per week plus food. To work 37 hours per week from May to July; minimum period of work 2 months. Work also available for 10 months. Accommodation provided at a charge. Food hygiene certificate preferred. Overseas applicants welcome.

Applications from January to Mr Ian Downing, Head of Centre, at the above address.

HATTON HOTELS GROUP: Hatton Court, Upton Hill, Upton St Leonards, Gloucester GL4 8DE (☎01452-617412; fax 01452-612945; e-mail lianne@hatton-hotels.co.uk; www.hatton-hotels.co.uk). A privately-owned collection of character hotels in Gloucestershire, Somerset and Jersey.

Bar Staff, Restaurant Staff, Housekeeping Staff. Good rates of pay plus B & L and tips. 5 day working week on rota. Excellent training and incentives provided.

Applications should be sent to Personnel at the above address.

HORIZON HPL: Signet House, 49-51 Farringdon Road, London EC1M 3JB (e-mail horizonhpl.london@btinternet.com). A training centre established in 1991 which organises paid work placements in hotels and companies in the UK and France for EU citizens, including English and French tuition and preparation to sit British and French examinations.

Hotel Work. Placements are available all year round (in a variety of fields) from 3 months to 8 months. They receive a trainee wage and free accommodation. Applicants from 17-50 years. An interview is necessary.

Applicants should contact the agency 2 months in advance of intended work date.

MICHAEL WISHER AND ASSOCIATES: Head Office, Griffin House, Nottingham Trent University, Clifton Campus, Nottingham NG11 8NS (☎0115-984 6000; fax 0115-984 6001; e-mail enquiries@michaelwisher.co.uk; www.michaelwisher.co.uk). Specialises in providing temporary hospitality staff to major corporate and sporting events across the UK, with offices in the Midlands, Manchester and Nottingham.

Bar Staff, Waiting Staff, Catering Assistants and Kitchen Porters. Wages from £5.05 to £6.50 per hour. Hours of work are variable depending on the event and venue. The work is flexible so staff can choose hours to suit. Work is available throughout the year, however the summer months are the busiest period with many sporting events taking place over this time. Transport is always provided, free of charge, to and from the venues. No experience necessary. Applicants should be 18 and over. Overseas applicants with fluent English, relevant work permits and documentation are welcome to apply.

Application forms should be downloaded from the above website and returned to the relevant office. Telephone interview required.

MILL HOUSE INNS LTD: Barclay House, Falcon Close, Quedgeley, Gloucester GL2 4LY (☎01452-887222; fax 01452-887333; e-mail info@millhouseinns.co.uk; www.millhouseinns.co.uk). Owns a current estate of 60 managed houses all over the UK. Most are located in wonderful countryside settings with a focus on casual family dining.

Bar Staff, Waiting/Table Service Staff, Kitchen Porters, Chefs, Receptionists/

Administration Staff. Wages depend on site location. Flexible working hours. Accommodation available, but not always at places of work, at a cost deducted from pay. Full training is provided. Minimum period of work 8 weeks between March and October. Overseas applicants are considered, but must be proficient in written and spoken English and have necessary work authorisation. Applicants should have a neat appearance and a pleasant personality.

Applications from March to Personnel at the above address; they will provide further information on positions available at individual establishments.

WA SHEARINGS HOTELS: Miry Lane, Wigan, Lancashire WN3 4AG (www. WAshearings.com). WA Shearings Hotels is one of the UK's largest hotel groups, with more than 40 hotels in the UK. Most hotels operate 48 weeks of the year with a season which extends from February to December, including Christmas and the New Year. **Housekeeping, Restaurant and Kitchen Staff.** Wages typically £5.05 per hour, live out. To work 39 hours per week. Minimum period of work 3 months. Experience in hotel work valuable but not essential. Live-in accommodation is available. Foreign applicants need to have English of at least an intermediate standard.

Applications to Tricia Grewar, Personnel and Training Office, Argyll Business Centre, 204 Argyll Street, Dunoon PA23 7HA, or visit the website.

TOWNGATE PERSONNEL LTD: 3 Alum Chine Road, Westbourne, Bournemouth, Dorset BH4 8DT (☎01202-752955; fax 01202-752954; e-mail enquiries@towngate-personnel.co.uk; www.towngate-personnel.co.uk). A recruitment agency specialising in the hospitality industry. Also recruits permanent management staff and experienced operational staff for seasonal positions (March-October).
Short-term live-in assignments in hotels throughout England.
Silver Service Waiting Staff (50). £200-£300 per week.
Chefs: All Grades (50). £220-£500 per week. To work in various hotels throughout the UK mainland, the Channel Islands and the Isle of Man. To work a 5 to 6 day week. Previous experience essential.
Hotel Receptionists (20) for hotels on the Channel Islands. £200-£300 per week. To work 5 to 6 day week. Hotel reception experience a must.
All staff required for a minimum of 6 months between April and September. Accommodation included at a cost of approx. £40 per week.

Applications from March to James Tucker, Operations Manager, at the above address.

YHA: Personnel and Training Department (Recruitment Hostel Staff), PO Box 6030, Matlock, Derbyshire DE4 3XA (☎01629-592570; e-mail jobs@yha.org.uk; www. yha.org.uk). The YHA, a registered charity, is the largest budget accommodation provider in Britain with 220 youth hostels in diverse locations throughout England and Wales.
General Assistants needed to help run the YHA's youth hostels throughout England and Wales. Work is available for varying periods (minimum 3 months), between January and October each year. Preferred minimum age 18 years. Assistants undertake a variety of tasks including catering, cleaning, reception and general maintenance. Experience in one or more of the above areas is desirable, but customer service experience and enthusiasm are essential. Non-EU nationals require a valid work permit. All posts are subject to an interview, usually at the hostel where the vacancy exists.

For an *application* form call the YHA National Recruitment line on ☎01629-592570 between September and June. Alternatively, visit the YHA website at www. yha.org.uk.

Language Schools

ANGLO EUROPEAN STUDY TOURS LTD.: 8 Celbridge Mews, London W2 6EU (☎020-7229 4435; fax 020-7792 8717; e-mail anglo@aest.co.uk; www.aest. co.uk). Runs summer courses for 10 to 18 year olds all over the UK, offering general English plus sports, entertainments and excursions.

EFL Teachers. Wages £190 to £220 per week. To work 22 hours a week, Monday to Friday, at centres all over the UK. Staff required June to August. Applicants must have a TEFL qualification (RSA or Trinity) and a degree. Mainly non-residential posts available.

Applications to Suzy Taylor, Director of Studies, at the above address.

ARDMORE LANGUAGE SCHOOLS: Hall Place, Berkshire College, Burchetts Green, Maidenhead, Berkshire SL6 6QR (☎01628-826699; fax 01628-829977; e-mail info@theardmoregroup.com; www.ardmore-language-schools.com). Ardmore offers summer junior vacation courses in English to overseas students at residential and homestay centres located throughout Britain.

EFL Teachers needed for residential colleges and homestay centres around the UK. Wages by arrangement. Those aged 19 or over preferred. Period of work from 3 to 8 weeks during July and August.

For *further details* visit the above website and if interested in working for Ardmore during the summer download an application form.

EF INTERNATIONAL LANGUAGE SCHOOLS: 74 Roupell Street, London, SE1 8SS (☎020-7401 8399; fax 020-7401 3717; e-mail steve.allen@ef.com@ef.com; www.ef.com).

EFL Teachers required for July and August to work full-time. Wages vary according to location and experience. Candidates should have at least a first degree and CELTA.

Applications with CVs should be sent to the Director of Studies at the above address.

EF LANGUAGE TRAVEL: 114A Cromwell Road, London. SW7 4ES (☎020-7341 8612; fax 020-7341 8501; e-mail ltrecruitment@ef.com; www.ef.com). Language courses with free time programmes for international students in locations throughout the UK.

Group Leaders and Teachers (1000 nationwide). Both residential and non-residential staff required. Full board and accommodation available for residential appointments only. Salary varies depending on region and experience. Minimum age 19 years. Teaching or leadership experience preferred but not essential. Applicants must have a standard of English as high as that of a native speaker.

Activity Organisers (30 nationwide) to plan an activity programme for all students in one particular town or residential centre. Salary varies depending on region and experience. Minimum age 20 years. Previous organisational experience essential.

All staff to work flexible hours, 6 days a week. Minimum period of work 3 weeks between late May and late August. All applicants must be available for interview.

Apply on-line or by e-mail at the above addresses. Alternatively contact Fraser Davis at fraser.davis@ef.com or at the above postal address for an application form or further information.

EMBASSY CES: Lorna House, 103 Lorna Road, Hove, East Sussex BN3 3EL (☎01273-322353; fax 01273-322381; e-mail vacjobsuk@embassyces.com; www.

embassyces.com/jobs). Organises summer schools for international students, combining English lessons and an activity/excursion programme at schools and universities around the UK.

Activity Leaders (250) to organise a variety of daytime, evening and weekend activities. Experience of working with children or in the leisure or tourism industry is desirable but full training will be given. All applicants must speak fluent English, have enthusiasm and initiative and be hardworking.

EFL Teachers (350). Applicants must be 18+ and have RSA CELTA or Trinity cert. TESOL. Previous experience is desirable.

Wages dependent on experience. 6 days work per week. Positions are available from June to September. Full board accommodation is available at residential centres.

Apply from January onwards either online (click on www.embassyces.com/jobs and follow the summer jobs links) or contact the Recruitment Department for an application pack. Interview necessary, usually by telephone.

THE ENGLISH COUNTRY SCHOOL: 18 Riverside, Winchcombe, Cheltenham, Gloucestershire GL54 5JP (tel/fax 01242-604067; www.countryschools.co.uk). British Council accredited English language summer schools in Southern England and the Lake District, for children and teenagers providing 'fun, friendship and learning in a healthy, natural environment'.

EFL Teachers (8) to teach English and assist with sports and crafts. Wages from £300 per week live-in, with time off. Must have EFL qualifications, and/or PGCE/B.Ed.

Sports Organisers (2). Wages from £300 per week live-in, with time off. Must have relevant sports coaching qualifications.

Minimum period of work 3 weeks between mid July and mid August.

Applications from April to the Director. Interview necessary.

INTERNATIONAL QUEST CENTRES: 33 Queens Terrace, Southampton SO14 3BQ (☎023-8033 8858; fax 023-8033 8848; e-mail education@internationalquest. net; www.internationalquest.net).

Teachers and Activity Leaders (400) to work in up to 30 vacation study centres in England, Wales, Scotland and Ireland. 2 to 6 week contracts available late June to mid-August. Most of the positions for activity leaders are residential, whereas most of the positions for teachers are not. Teachers must be native English speakers; TEFL qualifications or previous experience an advantage but pre-season briefing and in-house materials provide much useful guidance and support for all staff.

Apply on-line at www.internationalquest.net, via e-mail or by post to the above address.

ISIS EDUCATIONAL PROGRAMMES: 259 Greenwich High Road, Greenwich, London SE10 8NB (☎020-8293 1444; fax 0208-293 1199; e-mail recruitment@ isisgroup.co.uk; www.isisgroup.co.uk). ISIS runs Language/Activity Centres in summer at 15 locations around the UK including London, Oxford, Cambridge, Winchester, York and Edinburgh.

EFL Teachers (150) to teach mainly teenagers on courses from 18 June to 27 August. Wages £200 to £250 per week. To work 3 hours teaching mornings and 3 hours of repeat lessons in the afternoon (i.e. 30+ hours a week but lesson preparation for only 15 hours). Teaching qualification needed.

Activity Leaders (100+). Wages start from £165 per week. To lead 13 sessions (mornings and afternoons) per week. Period of work 18 June to 27 August. Hours are guaranteed. No special qualifications necessary. Appointments are personality based.

The above wages include full board and lodging, but non-residential arrangements also possible with higher wages.
Applications to the H.R. Manager, at the above address.

STAFFORD HOUSE STUDY HOLIDAYS: 19 New Dover Road, Canterbury, Kent CT1 3AH (☎01227-811506; fax 01227-787740; e-mail recruitment@staffordhouse. com; www.ceg-uk.com/staffordhouse_studyholidays). British Council accredited language school that has been running EFL summer schools for several years.
Management Staff, EFL Teachers, Activity Leaders required to work at centres throughout the UK. Good rates of pay and excellent working conditions.
For *further information* please e-mail the above address.

TWIN GROUP: 67-71 Lewisham High Street, London SC13 5JX (☎020-8297 1132; fax 020-8297 0984; www.twinuk.com).
EFL Teachers. Wages from £210 to £275 per week. Involves both teaching and running activities, with groups of up to 15 students. Must hold at least Cert. TEFL qualifications.
Activity Organisers, Administration Officers and Welfare Officers. Wages of £250 per week.
Work is available in July and August in schools mainly in the south of England and London. Some centres require applicants to be residential and some do not.
Applications to the above address as soon as possible.

UNIVERSAL LANGUAGE SERVICES SUMMER SCHOOLS: 43-45 Cambridge Gardens, Hastings, East Sussex TN34 1EN (☎01424-438025; fax 01424-438050). Various summer schools for foreign students throughout the UK and in Malta.
EFL Teachers. Wages on application. All applicants must have CELTA or TESOL qualifications.
Activity Organisers. Wages approximately £5.35 per hour.
Positions available in June, July and August. Minimum period of work 1 week. Minimum age 18.
Applications should be sent to the above address.

WELS GROUP OF INTERNATIONAL HOUSE SCHOOLS: International House Summer in England, Ash Hill Road, Torquay TQ1 3HZ (☎01803-210943; fax 01803-291501; e-mail richard@ih-westengland.co.uk; www.ihwelsgroup.com). English language programmes at four centres in Buckinghamshire, Oxford, Salisbury and Sussex; also three year-round schools running summer English programmes for juniors in Bath, Salisbury and Torquay. Part of a group with over 120 affiliated schools in 40 countries.
EFL Teachers (40-50). Salary £250-£350 per week. Minimum period of work three weeks. Staff required 1 July to 29 August. Must have a university degree and a minimum of a Cambridge CELTA or Trinity Cert. TESOL. Accommodation provided free of charge at residential centres.
Contact Richard Gubbin at the above address from February 2007.

Medical

ACTIVE ASSISTANCE: 5a Brewery Lane, Sevenoaks, Kent TN13 1DF (☎01732-779353; fax 01732-779134; e-mail enquiries@activeassistance.com; www. activeassistance.com/careers/careers.htm). Active Assistance provides live-in Personal Care Assistants (Pas) to physically disabled clients in their own homes.
Personal Care Assistants are required for live-in positions nationwide, working with physically disabled adults. Wages start at £54 per day including free food and

accommodation. Free training also provided. Must be 21 or over and have a valid driving licence and work permit. Suitably qualified foreign applicants with good spoken English are welcome.

Applications are accepted at any time by completing the online form at the above website.

ALL CARE SOUTH WALES: 228 Holton Road, Barry, Vale of Glamorgan CF63 4HS (☎01446-701020; fax 01446-722788; www.all-care.org).
Home Care Workers (6) needed between July-September to work various hours and days. Wages start at £5.75 per hour. Applicants must be over 21.
Applications to Emma James at the above address.

CHRISTIES CARE LTD: The Old Post Office, High Street, Saxmundham, Suffolk IP17 1AB (☎01728-605000; fax 01728-603601; e-mail recruit@christiescare.com; www. christiescare.com). Founded in 1987, the company provides live-in care to dependent adults in their own homes nationwide.
Carers for live in positions with clients in their own homes. Clients are all dependent adults with many different needs who require varying degrees of care such as incontinence management, hoist work for paraplegics, experience of dealing with dementia and the bedridden. All need help with cooking, shopping and housekeeping. Salary up to £450 per week. Staff required all year round; minimum period of work 7 full days. Applicants with experience preferred but training provided. Minimum age of 18. Must be able to work legally in the UK.
Applications to the Recruitment Department at the above address.

CONSULTUS: 17 London Road, Tonbridge, Kent TN10 3AB (☎01732-355231; fax 01732-360693; e-mail office@ConsultusCare.com; www.ConsultusCare.com). Founded in 1962 by the present Managing Director, Consultus is one of the major providers of live-in care in Britain. Their aim is to help the elderly remain happily and safely in their own homes for as long as possible. Work available across the UK.
Live-in Carers needed nationwide to perform domestic duties and some personal care for elderly private clients. NMC-registered nurses also welcome. Duties may include cooking, cleaning, housekeeping, driving, shopping and a varying degree of personal care of the client. Wages from £55-£70 per day, with own room in client's house, to work on two-week live-in assignments. Positions are available all year. Applicants over 21 preferred. Some experience of care of the elderly/disabled preferred. Overseas applicants with relevant permits and clear English welcome.
Applications should be made at any time to the above address. Interview in either UK or South Africa.

CURA DOMI-CARE AT HOME: Guardian House, Borough Road, Godalming, Surrey GU7 2AE (☎01483-420055; fax 01483-420053; e-mail curadomi@aol.com; www.curadomi.co.uk).
Carers required to care for elderly and disabled people in their own homes. Wages vary according to the position being offered but are typically £353 to £447 a week for live in work, plus accommodation and travel expenses, or from £6.60 to £9.30 per hour for daily work, as relevant. Period of work by arrangement. Positions are either residential for live in work (south of England) or non-residential (local to Guildford, Surrey for daily work). Applicants are given an interview and 3-day training session. Qualified moving and handling courses available free to all carers plus 24-hour office support. Overseas applicants with fluent English and the necessary documents to work in the UK welcome.
Applications to the above address.

NURSES DIRECT: 26 Harmer St, Gravesend, Kent DA12 2AX (☎0800-376 6154; fax 0870-011 8613; www.nursesdirect.co.uk). With offices serving over 100 locations across the UK, Nurses Direct employ trained nurses and experienced carers to work for various organisations.
Trained Nurses (50), Care Assistants (75), Learning Disability Support Workers (35). Wages are competitive. To work weekdays or weekends. No minimum period of work. Positions are available all year. Minimum age 18. Required qualifications depend on the position sought but experience is essential. Foreign applicants are welcome if they are authorised to work in the UK and have a good standard of English. CRB checks will be necessary.
To apply, find details of your nearest branch on the above website.

Outdoor

EVENTS STAFF LTD: 25 York Road, Northampton NN1 5QA (☎01604-627775; fax 01604-627004). A recruitment company that supplies staff to events such as the British Grand Prix, large scale outdoor events and shows, and various horse racing fixtures across the country.
Stewards, Programme Sellers, Ticket Sellers, Car Park Attendants, Waiting and Bar Staff (1000+ at peak of summer) to work at various events; wages and details of work by arrangement.
Applications welcome any time. Applicants must be over 16, and willing to work long hours outside. Call the above number for an information pack.

FIELD AND LAWN (MARQUEES) LTD: Southlands, Leeds Road, Thorpe Willoughby, North Yorkshire YO8 9PZ (☎01757-210444; fax 01757-210104; e-mail robbie.gibb-kirk@fieldandlawn.com; www.fieldandlawn.com). A young and enthusiastic company which takes a pride in its product and employees. Work hard, play hard atmosphere.
Marquee Erectors required to work long hours erecting marquees throughout England and Wales. Wages starting at £5.35 per hour. The work is very strenuous so fitness is essential. Overseas applicants, particularly from New Zealand, South Africa and Australia, welcome. Positions are available from May to November.
Applications from 1 April through to end of September to the Operations Manager at the above address or telephone number or e-mail robbie.gibb-kirk@fieldandlawn. com.

LEAPFROG INTERNATIONAL LTD: Riding Court Farm, Datchet, Berkshire SL3 9JU (☎01753-580880; fax 01753-580881; e-mail enq@leapfrog-int.co.uk; www.leapfrog-int.co.uk).
Events Crew (up to 100), needed to help set up and run outdoor activities such as team-building challenges, family fun days and 'It's a knockout' tournaments. Wages are a set figure per event; hours of work vary from day to day. Period of work between May and September. Events take place all around the UK. Travel to events is organised by Leapfrog International from their headquarters in Datchet. Aged 18-40, applicants should be enthusiastic and outgoing and should enjoy working with people. A clean driving licence is an advantage; previous experience not essential as training will be given.
Please call The Event Management Team on 01753-589300 for an application form.

MOBENN HIRE SERVICES: Mobenn House, Naunton Parade, Cheltenham, Gloucestershire GL51 7NP (☎01242-584515; fax 01242-222705; e-mail enquiries@ mobenn.co.uk; www.mobenn.co.uk).
Marquee Erectors for work all over the country. Wages £40-£50 per day; same daily rate paid for long and short days. No accommodation available. Period of work by arrangement. Applicants need a clean driving licence; the work is quite strenuous so it is necessary to be fit and active. This company is for those who like outdoor work. Hard days, good days and a great team spirit can all be found.
Applications to R. Allen, Administrator, at the above address.

Special Schemes for US Citizens

BUNAC's *Work in Britain* program offers full-time students and recent graduates the chance to spend up to six months in the UK.

- Special Blue Card work permit
- On-the-spot support from our London and Edinburgh offices
- Job and accommodation listings online
- New friends, new skills and new experiences

1-800-GO-BUNAC
info@bunacusa.org
www.bunac.org

BUNAC USA, PO BOX 430, Southbury, CT 06488, USA

BUNAC USA: PO BOX 430, Southbury, CT 06488, USA (☎(203) 264 0901; e-mail info@bunacusa.org; www.bunac.org).
Work in Britain was established by BUNAC 40 years ago as part of a reciprocal student work exchange programme between the UK and the USA. Participants apply for the unique BUNAC Blue Card allowing them to work in the UK in any type of job for up to six months at any time of year. *Work in Britain* is a government-approved programme allowing thousands of students every year to legally work and live in Britain.
    To be eligible for the programme you must be a full-time degree level student at an American university, either in the US or as part of a US university approved study abroad programme. So no matter where in the world you are currently studying, eligible US passport holders who are over 18 can apply to *Work in Britain.* Graduates can apply within a semester of graduating in the US. The cost of the programme is

$290 in 2006/7.
  Participants receive a programme handbook before they leave the US, which is full of information including job listings, Income Tax, National Insurance, accommodation, travel and much more. BUNAC has well established resource centres in London and Edinburgh to make finding work as easy and as stress-free as possible. Participants do a wide variety of jobs from working in a law firm to serving in a pub. Students can also take part in BUNAC's social programme ranging from Halloween Ghost walks to horse riding in Wales.
  For further information see www.bunac.org or contact BUNAC USA, PO BOX 430, Southbury, CT 06488. Tel: (203) 264 0901.

Sport

GRAFHAM WATER CENTRE: Perry, Huntingdon, Cambridgeshire PE18 0BX (☎0845-634 6022; fax 01480-813850; e-mail info@grafham-water-centre.co.uk; www.grafham-water-centre.co.uk). Runs special interest and activity holidays and courses with centres in Cambridgeshire and Derbyshire.
Activity Instructors (20) wanted for canoeing, windsurfing, sailing, archery, climbing and mountain biking. Wages £214 per week plus food. To work 37 hours per week from February to October; minimum period of work 2 months. Positions also available for 10 months. Accommodation available at a charge. Must have N.G.B. qualifications. Overseas applicants welcome.
  Applications from January to Mr Ian Downing at the above address. Interview required.

HF HOLIDAYS LIMITED: Leader Recruitment Manager, Redhills, Penrith, Cumbria CA11 0DT (☎01768-214528 quoting SJA7; www.walkleaders.co.uk). The UK's leading walking holiday company (founded 1913) is a non-profit seeking organisation which owns 17 country house hotels based in some of the most scenic parts of Britain.
Walk Leaders required to lead walks catering for all levels of walker. Full board and accommodation, travel expenses and training opportunities will be provided. Applicants may choose where, how often and when they want to lead week-long walking holidays (from 2-30 weeks per year). Applicants should be experienced walkers with leadership potential, fully competent in the use of map and compass, considerate and tactful. Residential assessment courses are held during the winter and spring (difficult for applicants living abroad) so application by February is essential.
  For *applications* or an information pack contact the above address or visit www. walkleaders.co.uk.

PGL TRAVEL LTD: Alton Court, Penyard Lane, Ross-on-Wye, Herefordshire HR9 5GL (☎0870-401 4411; e-mail recruitment@pgl.co.uk; www.pgl.co.uk/recruitment). PGL recruits around 2,000 staff each year to assist with the running of their children's activity centres throughout the UK, including Devon, the Isle of Wight, Lincolnshire, the south coast, Surrey, Shropshire, Perthshire and Wales. Europe's largest provider of adventure holidays for children has offered outstanding training and work opportunities to seasonal staff for almost 50 years. PGL jobs provide a break from the 9-5 routine. If you are enthusiastic, energetic and looking for real experience and responsibility in a stimulating environment, PGL could have the job for you.
Activity Instructors in canoeing, sailing, windsurfing, fencing, archery, motorsports, pony trekking, and more. Qualifications not essential for all positions as full training will be provided. Minimum age 18.

Group Leaders also needed to take responsibility for groups of children, helping them to get the most out of their holiday. Previous experience of working with children is an advantage. Minimum age 18.

Support Staff to assist the catering, domestic and maintenance teams.

From £70-£100 per week plus free B&L. Positions available from February to November, for the full season, as little as eight weeks, or any period in between, although there are very few summer-only vacancies.

Applications can be made online, downloaded from the website, or call for an information pack.

Websites

ANYWORK ANYWHERE: www.anyworkanywhere.com. This organisation provides a free source of information to people looking for work throughout the UK and worldwide via their website.

Tour Guides, Overland Drivers, Ski /Board Instructors & Guides, Chalet Chefs & Hosts, All levels of Hotel & Pub Staff, Nannies, Barge & Yacht Crew, Care Workers, Teachers, Nurses, Holiday & Theme Park, Campsite and Summer Resort Staff are among the jobs listed as well as a wide and changing variety of many others. Interested candidates can simply contact their chosen advertiser and apply direct, with no registration, no fee or hassle. The site also provides a broad range of other resources for work and travel worldwide.

For further information *consult* www.anyworkanywhere.com.

FRUITFULJOBS: (e-mail info@fruitfuljobs.com; www.fruitfuljobs.com). Fruitful Ltd can offer both seasonal work for backpackers and permanent positions for those looking to develop a career in the UK (anything from farm managers to logistics assistants). The seasonal work Fruitful can offer on UK/European farms and within the produce industry includes working as field, packhouse and camp supervisors, quality controllers, drivers, pickers, packers, production operatives and tractor drivers. Jobs can be from a few weeks to 12 months. Peak employment is from March until October, but work is available throughout the year.

The majority of seasonal jobs have cheap accommodation available; they are out of the city and in the countryside, giving the opportunity to earn some money. The workforces are multi-national which is great for the social side of things and also means that the growers have plenty of experience employing overseas travellers.

Please *see* www.fruitfuljobs.com or call/sms +44 77-4008 6555.

WWW.VOOVS.COM: 26 Vine Close, Welwyn Garden City, Hertfordshire AL8 7PS (☎01707-396511; e-mail info@voovs.com). A seasonal recruitment website offering the following positions.
Summer Jobs: Beach resort/camping/activity/lakes and mountains/barges/flotilla jobs from April to October. Vacancies for instructors, nannies, couriers, chefs, bar and hotel staff. Wages start at £50 per week, with accommodation and transport provided. To usually work a 6-day week.
Cruise Ships & Yachts: Cruise ship/yachting jobs available around the year. Varied contracts. Wages from £500 a month.
Ski Resort And Winter Jobs: Ski resort jobs including work in chalets, hotels, bars & ski and snowboard hire retail shops, ski technicians, ski instructors, as reps, ski guides, nannies, resort admin, accounts, sales, resort and area managers. Wages start at £50 per week; ski pass, transport to resort and accommodation/food provided. To work a 6-day week.
Gap Year: Gap year job ideas for around the globe. Voluntary to TEFL, ski and snowboard instructor courses and useful information and links on gap year activities. Hospitality and Leisure: other jobs on offer include hotel, restaurant and bar work, theme park jobs, TEFL and fruit picking.
For most positions applicants must be aged over 18. Positions available in UK and Ireland, across Europe and around the globe.
For further details see www.voovs.com.

Voluntary Work

Archaeology

COUNCIL FOR BRITISH ARCHAEOLOGY: St Mary's House, 66 Bootham, York YO30 7BZ (☎01904-671417; fax 01904-671384; e-mail info@britarch.ac.uk; www.britarch.ac.uk).
Archaeology for All: The CBA is an educational charity working throughout the UK to involve people in archaeology and to promote the appreciation and care of the historic environment for the benefit of present and future generations.
Details of **Excavations** and other fieldwork projects are given on the Council's website and in the Council's publication *British Archaeology*. The magazine is published six times a year. An annual subscription costs £25 (£19 for the first year); however, it also forms part of an individual membership package which is available for £32 per year and brings extra benefits.
Having studied the magazine you should make *applications* to the Director of the projects which interest you.

Children

ACTIVE TRAINING & EDUCATION: Kildare, Manby Road, Malvern, Worcestershire WR14 3BD (☎08464-561205; fax 01684-562716; e-mail info@ate.org.uk; www.ate.org.uk).
An educational trust which runs residential holidays in various rented premises, including boarding schools, field study centres and conference centres, in various parts of the UK.
Volunteer Monitors (20-30) to work on 7-day residential children's holidays; work is demanding but very rewarding, working with a group of children 24/7 with a half

day off per week. Duties include every aspect of the children's day, offering continual supervision and support. £50 pocket money, free board and lodging and travel to the camp are provided. Minimum age 17; attendance of a one-week training course in July is essential. Period of work July-August.

Applications to Helen Fairest, Deputy Director, at the above address.

SCRIPTURE UNION: 207-209 Queensway, Bletchley, Milton Keynes, Buckinghamshire MK2 2EB (☎01908-856177; fax 01908-856012; e-mail holidays@ scriptureunion.org.uk; www.scriptureunion.org.uk).

An International non-denominational Christian movement that has been running residential holidays for children and young people throughout England and Wales for more than 100 years.

Volunteers to help as team members on Scripture Union residential 7 to 10 day holidays around the UK for young people aged from 8-18. Volunteers are expected to be on site 24 hours a day to help organise activities during the holiday as part of a team; training is given before the beginning of the holiday.

Volunteers pay for their own accommodation and meals, but a Volunteer Grant Fund may assist with some of the costs. Minimum period of work one week. Applicants must be committed Christians in sympathy with the aims of Scripture Union and aged 18 or over; there are particular needs for people with qualifications in catering, first aid, life-saving, sports, mountaineering and working with disabled people.

Applications should be sent to the Holidays Administrator at the above address.

Conservation and the Environment

BTCV: Sedum House, Mallard Way, Potteric Carr, Doncaster DN4 8DB (☎01302-388883; e-mail information@btcv.org.uk; www.btcv.org).

BTCV is the UK's leading practical conservation charity. Every year it involves more than 130,000 volunteers in projects to protect and enhance our environment.

BTCV offers a programme of **Conservation Working Holidays** each year in the UK and overseas. These last from just a couple of days to a few weeks, and include wetland management, dry stone walling and habitat management in various places throughout the UK and abroad such as Cornwall, Derbyshire, Iceland and South Africa.

No experience is required, just plenty of enthusiasm and energy. Prices start at £60 for a weekend and £90 for a week to cover food, accommodation and training in conservation skills (£350 plus for international holidays). Volunteers typically work from 9am-5pm with evenings free and a day off during the week. Accommodation ranges from village halls to youth hostels and field centres.

For further information *contact* the above address or visit the BTCV website.

EARTHWATCH: 267 Banbury Road, Oxford OX2 7HT (☎01865-318831; fax 01865-311383; e-mail info@earthwatch.org.uk; www.earthwatch.org).

An international environmental charity that engages people worldwide in scientific field research and education to promote the understanding and action necessary for a sustainable environment.

Earthwatch recruits **Paying Volunteers** to help research scientists on environmental projects worldwide. Around 4,000 volunteers take part each year, on projects lasting from three to eighteen days. They currently offer around 140 projects in 50 countries, including 9 in the UK. You could work as part of a team helping to conduct a study of Britain's basking sharks, tracking dinosaurs on the Yorkshire coast, or monitoring mammals in Oxfordshire's ancient Wytham Woods.

No special skills are required since any necessary training is given in the field.

All English speaking volunteers over 16 are welcome. Volunteers pay a share of the project costs, which start from £150. Prices include food and accommodation, but travel is extra.

For *further details* and availability contact Earthwatch at the address above.

THE NATIONAL TRUST: Heelis, Kemble Drive, Swindon SN2 2NA (☎0870-6095383; e-mail volunteers@nationaltrust.org.uk; www.nationaltrust.org.uk/volunteers).
Leading conservation and environmental charity.
The National Trust has a range of **Volunteering Opportunities** if you are looking to fill a gap year, change career or gain work experience. Roles range from assisting with house stewarding and interpretation to events and conservation. All located at beautiful Trust sites. Training is provided and accommodation may be available; some placements are available through the New Deal scheme; out-of-pocket expenses covered.

For an *information pack* call 0870-609 5383, e-mail, or visit the website.

ROYAL SOCIETY FOR THE PROTECTION OF BIRDS: The Lodge, Sandy, Bedfordshire SG19 2DL (☎01767-680551; fax 01767-692365; e-mail volunteers@rspb.org.uk; www.rspb.org.uk/volunteering).
Nationally, the RSPB has more than 13,000 volunteers.
Local Volunteer Opportunities available on more than 150 reserves throughout the UK, via 13 regional and country offices and with over 250 youth and local groups. Applicants need not be bird experts. Volunteers of any age required. For further information about volunteering in general, contact the Volunteers Co-ordinator at the above address and ask for the *Volunteering Information* brochure, or visit the above website for a current list of volunteering opportunities.
Residential Volunteers are taken on 39 reserves throughout the UK. Accommodation is provided. Tasks/activities available include: management of reserves, work with visitors, research, survey & monitoring, species protection. Specialist skills are not always required. Volunteers must be over 16 (18 in some cases) and must stay a minimum of 1 week. They must also have a genuine interest in and enthusiasm for conservation issues. Volunteers from overseas are welcome; a permit is not ordinarily necessary as this is unpaid work, but please check with your local British Embassy or High Commission before travelling. Overseas applicants must be over 18 and speak good conversational English.

Further information can be found in the RSPB's free publication on residential volunteering, *Do Something Different*, available from the above address.

Applications should be made to the Residential Volunteering Development Officer, at the above address.

WWOOF UK (World Wide Opportunities on Organic Farms): PO Box 2675, Lewes, Sussex BN7 1RB (tel/fax 01273-476286; e-mail hello@wwoof.org.uk; www.wwoof.org.uk and www.wwoof.org).
An opportunity to help organic growers get into the countryside (UK and worldwide) and meet like-minded people to learn and share in an atmosphere of mutual trust.
Volunteers are needed to spend time helping on organic farms, gardens and smallholdings around the UK: organic farming avoids the use of artificial fertilisers and pest killers, and can be labour intensive. Simple accommodation and food are provided. Short and long stays available. Applicants must have a genuine interest in furthering the organic movement. Applications welcomed from students/individuals of any nationality all year round. EU applicants do not need work permits, Australians,

New Zealanders and Canadians need vacation work permits, all others must have right of entry. Work permits are not issued for WWOOF work.

For further information and *applications* send a s.a.e. to the above address or go to their website.

Festivals and Special Events

OXFAM STEWARDS: Brunswick Court, Brunswick Square, Bristol BS2 8PE (☎0117-916 6479; fax 0117-916 6476; e-mail stewards@oxfam.org.uk; www.oxfam. org.uk/stewards).

Oxfam has been providing volunteer stewards for music festivals since 1993 and now offer stewarding places at 10 festivals. This service forms part of the Oxfam Events team.

Festival Stewards (up to 3,500). Stewarding is about providing a safe environment for everyone at a festival. It usually involves talking to people and answering general enquiries. On occasions, you may be called upon to deal with serious incidents or emergencies. It is vital for the safety and security of a festival that the emergency services have competent stewards that can be relied upon to assist in the effective management of a major incident.

Stewards are required to work a minimum of 3 shifts per festival; shifts last 8 hours. The festivals run from June to September. Applicants are asked to pay £120 at the beginning of the summer, which is returned once all stewarding duties are completed. In return, stewards receive free entrance to the festival, a meal ticket for every shift worked, and a separate camping area with toilets and showers.

Applications should be made from late February. Please visit the website for an application form.

Heritage

WATERWAY RECOVERY GROUP: PO Box 114, Rickmansworth, Hertfordshire WD3 1ZY (☎01923-711114; fax 01923-897000; e-mail enquiries@wrg.org.uk; www.wrg.org.uk).

The National co-ordinating body for voluntary labour on the inland waterways of Great Britain.

Volunteers needed to restore Britain's derelict canals: work may involve restoring industrial archaeology, demolishing old brickwork, driving a dumper truck, clearing mud and vegetation and helping at a National Waterways festival. To work either on weekends or weeklong canal camps. Work is available year round; minimum period of work 1 day. No experience or qualifications are necessary but volunteers should be between the ages of 18 and 70.

Accommodation and food provided for £42 per week/£6 per day. Overseas applicants welcome, but must be over 21.

Apply to The Enquiries Officer at the above address.

Physically/Mentally Disabled

THE CAMPHILL VILLAGE TRUST: Delrow House, Hilfield Lane, Aldenham, Watford, Herts WD25 8DJ (☎01923-856006; www.camphill.org.uk).

The Association of Camphill Communities runs working communities for mentally handicapped adults and children throughout Britain. They are based on anthroposophy, as founded by Rudolf Steiner.

Voluntary Helpers are required for the household, workshop or on the land. Free B &

L and a small personal allowance are provided. There are a limited number of summer jobs available, otherwise the minimum period of work is 12 months. Minimum age is 20. Overseas applicants welcome.

Apply in writing to Delrow House for a list of the addresses of Camphill Village Trust centres.

LEONARD CHESHIRE: c/o GAP Activity Projects, GAP House, 44 Queen's Road, Reading RG1 4BB (☎0118-959 4914; fax 0118-957 6634; e-mail volunteer@gap. org.uk; www.gap.org.uk).
Leonard Cheshire is the UK's leading charity providing support services for more than 21,000 disabled people. Many of the residential homes offer **Opportunities For Volunteers** , who assist disabled residents with social activities.

Board, lodging and pocket money is provided. Period of placement from 6 to 12 months. Volunteers must be able to speak good English.

Apply online.

RIDING FOR THE DISABLED ASSOCIATION: Lavinia Norfolk House, Avenue R, Stoneleigh Park, Warwickshire CV8 2LY (☎0845-658 1082; fax 0845-658 1083; e-mail cd-hols@rda.org.uk; www.rda.org.uk).
The RDA is a registered charity consisting of some 530 member groups throughout the UK. Providing holidays for disabled people is one of the many services it offers to its members.
Volunteer Helpers required to help on RDA holidays throughout the summer months, providing 24 hour care and supervision for between 3 and 7 days. Living expenses are provided along with free accommodation at some venues. Volunteers are needed for a minimum of 3 days between May and September. A knowledge of horse riding is preferable along with a first aid/medical qualification and work experience with disabled people. Suitably qualified foreign applicants are welcome. Minimum age 16.

To *apply* and for details of the holidays being run, contact the above address from January.

THE 3H FUND: 147a Camden Road, Tunbridge Wells, Kent TN1 2RA (☎01892-547474; fax 01892 524703; e-mail info@3hfund.org.uk; www.3hfund.org.uk).
The fund organises subsidised group holidays for physically disabled children and adults with the support of volunteer carers, thus affording a period of respite for regular carers.
Volunteers (approx. 90) are asked to provide as much help as they feel comfortable with. This could range from assisting with cutting up a guest's food, to helping with lifting and pushing a wheelchair. Full training is provided. Holidays are usually for one week and take place between May and September. A caring nature, the willingness to ensure that a disabled guest has an enjoyable holiday and the ability to co-operate as a team member are essential qualities. Board and accommodation are provided in venues such as holiday centres but a financial contribution (50% for students) is requested. Advice can be given on raising this by sponsorship.

Each holiday has an experienced leader, co-leader and nurse as well as other supportive volunteers. Applicants must be over 17 years of age and have a reasonable level of physical fitness.

Contact Lynne Loving at the above address as soon as possible for further information.

VITALISE (formerly Winged Fellowship Trust): Shap Road, Kendal, Cumbria LA9 6NZ (☎0845-345 1970; fax 01539-735567; e-mail volunteer@vitalise.org.uk; www.

vitalise.org.uk).
Vitalise is a leading UK charity providing holidays for disabled people and breaks for carers.
Volunteers needed for one or two weeks at a time, to help trained staff enhance the holiday atmosphere for the guests. Holidays are available at purpose-built centres in Essex, Nottingham, Cornwall, Merseyside and Southampton, where guests can enjoy a break with or without their regular carer. Volunteers are provided with free accommodation and meals in exchange for their time. Overseas applicants with good English welcome.

For an *application form* please contact the team at the above address.

Social and Community Schemes

L'ARCHE: 10 Briggate Silsden, Keighley, West Yorkshire BD20 9JT (☎01535-656186; fax 01535-656426; e-mail info@larche.org.uk; www.larche.org.uk).
Seeks to reveal the particular gifts of people with learning disabilities who belong at the very heart of their communities and who call others to share their lives. There are L'Arche communities in Kent, Inverness, Ipswich, Liverpool, Lambeth, Bognor, Brecon, Edinburgh and Preston where people with and without learning disabilities share life in ordinary houses.
Volunteer Assistants required to share life and work with people with learning disabilities in an ecumenical Christian-based community. Volunteers receive £43 per week and free B & L. Assistants required all year, usually for 6 months. Volunteers should be aged 18 and over. After completing the application form candidates are invited to visit the community and interviews are held. Overseas applicants in possession of the necessary work visas are welcome.

Applications to the above address.

CSV: CSV National Team, 5th Floor Scala House, 36 Holloway Circus, Queensway, Birmingham B1 1EQ (☎0800-374991; fax 0121-643 7690; e-mail volunteer@csv.org.uk; www.csv.org.uk/fulltimevolunteering).
Volunteers go away from home for 4-12 months and volunteer on a range of social care and community projects in Britain. You could support children with special needs, homeless people, mentor young offenders, or enable someone with a disability to lead an independent life. You gain valuable work experience by volunteering with CSV.
All volunteers receive free accommodation and food (or a food allowance of £37.60 per week), all expenses and a living allowance of £31 per week. You can start a placement at any time of the year. Support is provided to all volunteers. No qualifications are required and volunteering with CSV is available to everyone aged 16 and over. Placements are only open to UK and EU nationals who are living in the UK.

Applications are welcome at any time. Further details from the above address or freephone number.

COTTAGE & RURAL ENTERPRISES LTD: Gray's Court, Blagdon Hall, Seaton Burn, Newcastle-upon-Tyne NE13 6DD (☎01670-789802; fax 01670-789725; e-mail carenorth@freeuk.com).
CARE provides support to people with a learning disability through the provision of residential accommodation work and other day-care facilities, offering each person the opportunity to live a full and purposeful life.
Volunteers work alongside staff, assisting people with learning disabilities in CARE's communities around England. Approximately 40 hours work a week. Volunteers

receive an allowance and board and lodgings. A minimum commitment of 4 weeks is expected at any time of the year. Must have good communication skills.

Applications to Gary Richardson, Director of Fundraising and Corporate Affairs, at the above address.

THE PRINCE'S TRUST: 18 Park Square East, London NW1 4LH (☎020-7543 1234; fax 020-7543 1200; webinfops@princes-trust.org.uk; www.princes-trust.org. uk).

The Prince's Trust is the UK's leading youth charity. It helps young people overcome barriers and get their lives working.

Volunteers for the Team programme, a 12-week course enabling young people to develop essential life skills of benefit to future employment. Some 10,000 people take part each year. The programme involves team building activities, an outdoor residential week away, work experience and projects in the community. They take place in over 300 different locations throughout the UK.

For further *information* call the above number or visit the website.

TOC H: The Stable Block, The Firs, High Street, Whitchurch, Aylesbury, Buckinghamshire HP22 4JU (☎01296-642020; fax 01296-640022; e-mail info@ toch.org.uk; www.toch.org.uk).

Toc H offers short residential volunteering opportunities throughout the year in Britain, lasting usually from a weekend up to two weeks. **Project Work** undertaken can include: work with people with different disabilities; work with children in need; playschemes and camps; conservation and manual work. These projects provide those who take part with opportunities to learn more about themselves and the world we live in.

Minimum age 16; there is no upper age limit. The Toc H events programme is published yearly and can be viewed on their website.

There is no closing date for *applications*.

Workcamps

ATD FOURTH WORLD: 48 Addington Square, London SE5 7LB (☎020-7703 3231; e-mail Atd@Atd-uk.org; www.atd-quartmonde.org/accueil-uk.html).

ATD Fourth World is an international voluntary organisation which adopts a human rights approach to overcome extreme poverty. It supports the effort of very disadvantaged and excluded families in fighting poverty and taking an active role in the community. Founded in a shanty town on the outskirts of Paris in 1957, it now works in 27 countries on 5 continents.

ATD Fourth World organises work camps, street workshops and family stays in London and Surrey in the UK and other European countries. The work camps are a combination of manual work in and around ATD's buildings and conversation and reflection on the lives and hopes of families living in extreme poverty and on the aims and objectives of the organisation.

The street workshops bring a festival atmosphere to underprivileged areas. **Voluntary Artists, Craftsmen** share their skills with the children and their parents. These street workshops for painting, crafts, computing and books etc. take place in the streets of deprived areas and make it possible to break down barriers allowing freedom of expression and building confidence.

The family stays allow families split up by poverty, perhaps with children in care, to come together for a break. The volunteers assist ATD Fourth World workers to give the families a holiday to grow together and learn new skills. The camps, street workshops and family stays take place from July to September. Most last two weeks. Participants pay their own travel costs plus a contribution to the cost of food and accommodation. ATD is willing to take on foreign applicants.

For *further information* volunteers should see the ATD international website, or for UK opportunities, contact the above address.

CONCORDIA: 19 North Street, Portslade, Brighton, East Sussex BN41 1DH (☎01273-422218; fax 01273-421182; e-mail info@concordia-iye.org.uk; www concordia-iye.org.uk).
Concordia is a small not-for-profit charity committed to international youth exchange. Its International Volunteer Programme offers young people the opportunity to join an international team of **Volunteers Working On Community-Based Projects** ranging from nature conservation, restoration and construction to more socially based schemes; they last for 2-3 weeks with a main season running from June to September, although there are some spring and autumn projects. In general no special skills or experience are required but real motivation and commitment are essential.
Volunteers pay a registration fee of approx. £110 for UK projects and must fund their own travel. Board and accommodation are available free of charge. Volunteers aged 20 or over are also required to act as group co-ordinators in the UK, for which training is required and expenses are paid. Volunteers can also apply for long term volunteer projects through the EVS programme. Please note that foreign applicants must apply through a voluntary organisation in their own country; if necessary Concordia can pass on details of partner organisations.

Applications should normally be made to the above address. Details of all projects can be found on the website from March/April.

INTERNATIONAL VOLUNTARY SERVICE (IVS): IVS-GB South, Old Hall, East Bergholt, Colchester CO7 6TQ (☎01206-298215; e-mail ivssouth@ivs-gb.org. uk); IVS-GB North, Oxford Place Centre, Oxford Place, Leeds LS1 3AX (☎0113-246 9900; fax 0113-246 9910; e-mail ivsnorth@ivs-gb.org.uk); IVS-Scotland, 7 Upper Bow, Edinburgh EH1 2JN (☎0131-226 6722; fax 0131-226 6723; e-mail Scotland@ ivs-gb.org.uk; www.ivs-gb.org.uk).
IVS is the British branch of Service Civil International (SCI), a peace organisation working for international understanding and co-operation through voluntary work. IVS organises some 25 projects in Britain each year as well as sending volunteers to projects in 45 countries overseas.
Volunteers work for two to four weeks in an international team of 6-20 people, living and working together. The project types include work with children, disabilities, disadvantaged, peace, anti-racism, environment and arts and culture.

Most projects run between April and October. Some winter and long-term opportunities are available. Volunteers pay their own travel costs and a registration fee (abroad £145/£120, in UK £95/£50), which includes annual membership. Accommodation and food are provided by the project. Volunteers must be over 18 to go abroad, or 16 for projects in the UK. Applicants from overseas should apply for IVS Projects through partner organisations in their own country, see www.sciint.org for a full list of offices.

For more information, *contact* one of the regional addresses above. The listing of summer projects is available from April on the website and in brochure form.

NATIONAL TRUST WORKING HOLIDAYS: c/o Working Holidays Booking Office, Sapphire House, Roundtree Way, Norwich NR7 8SQ (☎0870-429 2429; www. nationaltrust.org.uk; enquiries@thenationaltrust.org.uk).

A charity dependent on volunteers which cares for more than 248,000 hectares of outstanding countryside, almost 600 miles of unspoilt coastline, and over 200 historic houses and gardens.

The National Trust organises more than **400 Working Holidays** in outdoor conservation work, biological surveying, archaeology, construction and various other interests. These take place on National Trust properties in England, Wales and Northern Ireland throughout the year. Each project involves 12 or so volunteers and lasts for 1 week to 10 days. There are also some weekend projects.

Volunteers pay from £60 per week to help cover the cost of board and lodging, and are responsible for their own travel expenses. Accommodation varies from purpose-built hostels to converted barns; volunteers supply bedding or sleeping bags. Minimum age 18. Overseas applicants welcome but must be over 18 and have good conversational English.

For a brochure, *please telephone, e-mail* or *write* using the above contact details.

PILGRIM ADVENTURE: South Winds, Culver Park, Tenby, Pembrokeshire SA70 7ED (☎01834-844212 ; e-mail Pilgrim.adventure@virgin.net; www.pilgrim-adventure.org.uk).
An ecumenical Christian organisation founded in 1987. Provides an annual programme of 'Pilgrim Journeys' on foot and by boat through Celtic Britain and Ireland.
Volunteer Team Members to help lead all age groups of 10 to 25 people taking part in Pilgrim Adventure's annual programme of Pilgrim Journeys within the UK and Ireland. Staying in hostels, monasteries, tents and small hotels. Team members should be able to co-lead at least one Pilgrim Journey of about 7 days each year, and take an active part in the planning of Pilgrim Journeys throughout the year. Training will be provided. Applicants must have a sense of adventure and Christian commitment.
Applications to Mr David Gleed at the above address.

Vacation Traineeships & Internships

Accountancy, Banking and Insurance

BARCLAYS BANK PLC: Graduate Recruitment, 2nd Floor, 54 Lombard Street, London EC2M 3XA (www.barclays-graduates.co.uk).
Barclays is much more than just high street banking for personal customers. The Group is also a leading provider of financial services to high net worth clients, small and medium businesses, multinational corporations and financial institutions.
Barclays' Summer Business Placements are designed to give penultimate year students quality work experience and provide a taste of what it is like to work for Barclays on the graduate programme. Students will have the opportunity to gain practical commercial experience and to develop skills at the heart of an international organisation.

An allowance of c. £350 per week is provided. Placements last for 8 weeks, commencing in July with a short induction course. This includes presentations from senior people, team activities and social events. After induction, placement students will join their team for the summer within their chosen business area. Placements exist in Barclays Corporate or Retail banking businesses or within a specialist function such as Marketing, Human Resources, Finance or IT. If students perform well during their placement and show the potential to make a valuable contribution to the business, they will be considered for a place on the graduate programme for September.

Applicants must be penultimate year students expecting a 2:1 degree and holding a minimum of 300 UCAS points.

Applications are on-line only and full details will be available on the website from September. Deadline for applications is 31 December.

DELOITTE: (☎0800-323333; e-mail gradrec.uk@deloitte.co.uk; www.deloitte. co.uk/graduates).

Leading professional services firm with exciting summer vacation opportunities in offices across the UK.

Deloitte's **Summer Vacation Scheme** will give you an insight into the UK's fastest growing professional services firm. You will experience the work carried out by Deloitte's professionals, have exposure to a variety of prestigious clients and have the possible opportunity to travel abroad. You will be given real responsibility and support and have the chance to work alongside trainee and qualified professionals. Most vacation students go on to accept full time positions with Deloitte on completion of their degree.

Placements are open to penultimate year students with 300 UCAS tariff points and a predicted 2.1 degree in any discipline. Deloitte also run a number of other programmes, including Insight Days and Open Days for all years, offering specific programmes for those in their first year of study.

For *further information*, events on campus, and to apply online, visit www.deloitte. co.uk/graduates.

ERNST & YOUNG: Graduate Recruitment, Becket House, 1 Lambeth Palace Road, London SE1 7EU (☎freephone 0800-289 208; e-mail gradrec@uk.ey.com; www. ey.com/uk/graduate).

Ernst & Young is one of the world's largest professional services firms dedicated to helping their clients identify and capitalise on business opportunities throughout the world. They help businesses and organisations to improve their effectiveness and achieve their objectives via a range of expert services, from auditing to tax, corporate finance to entrepreneurial business development, economic analysis to IT advice.

Most of the 21 offices in the UK offer students in their penultimate year at university the opportunity to work for a period of up to six weeks in the summer vacation. The scheme consists of a one-week induction course followed by **practical work experience in a specific business unit/office** for the remainder of the programme. The programme provides a real-life experience of working within Ernst & Young and their culture, enabling you to obtain a better understanding of what a career with them would involve. Applicants should have a minimum of 24 UCAS points (excluding general studies) and possess the determination to build a successful business career.

For *further information* and to apply on line, visit www.ey.com/uk/graduate.

HSBC: 8 Canada Square, London E14 5HQ (☎0800-289 529; www.hsbc.co.uk). The HSBC group is one of the largest banking and financial service organisations in the world. Their Corporate, Investment Banking and Markets business provides tailored financial solutions to a range of international clients.

First Year Internships. Approximately **50 Internships** are offered every year to first year undergraduates (or second years on a 4 year course). Wages are £350 per week. Interns work either with retail or commercial customers, learning the basics of personal or commercial banking. Interns are part of a team, gaining hands-on experience of the core business. A dedicated line manager will take care of the day-to-day training.

Penultimate Year Internships. Approximately **37 Internships** are offered to those students about to commence their final year at university. Wages are £355 per week.

Interns attend a 2-day induction course at HSBC's Group Management Training College to learn about the bank. They will also receive guidance on completing their own business project for which there exists a broad range of possibilities. For example, you could be asked to identify opportunities to cross-sell to existing business customers and attract new business.

Both Internships last for 7 weeks from July to August. The bank tries to locate interns at convenient branches across the UK. Accommodation is not provided. Overseas applicants are welcome to apply, provided they have the relevant documentation.

Applications should be made online at the Graduate Careers pages of the above website. The deadline for applications is 31 March.

KPMG: 1-2 Dorset Rise, London EC4Y 8EN (☎freephone 0800-664 665; www. kpmgcareers.co.uk).
KPMG is one of the world's leading firms of business advisers, providing a huge variety of clients with audit, tax and advisory services that are based on deep industry knowledge. They are part of an international network with almost 100,000 people across nearly 150 countries.
KPMG runs **Vacation Programmes** offering an insight into the workings of a leading business advisory firm; it shows both the opportunities available to graduates and how a major international firm operates. KPMG offers on a national basis, vacation experience to students of any degree discipline in their penultimate year at university. The length of the programmes vary and they may include work shadowing partners, managers and both qualified and trainee business advisers.
Visit the above website for further details and to apply.

PRICEWATERHOUSECOOPERS: Cornwall Court, 19 Cornwall Street, Birmingham B3 2DT(☎0800-100 2200; e-mail recruitment@pwc.com; www.pwc. com/uk/careers).
PricewaterhouseCoopers is the world's largest professional services organisation, providing a full range of business advisory services including auditing, business advisory, tax and actuarial services.
The eight week **Summer Internship Programme** gives students an insight into what the company does, the way it works and its company culture. The programme runs in all the national offices, in a range of business areas: Actuarial, Advisory, Assurance, Tax and Legal Services and Professional Services. Students are given a combination of business training and work experience similar to that of a graduate. Working with teams, students are able to make a direct contribution to the work of the firm while developing their own personal skills. Wages are £200-£400 a week. There are **200 positions** throughout the country. Placements last for 8 weeks from the first week of July. Accommodation is provided in the first week only; beyond that, it is up to the applicant.
PricewaterhouseCoopers are looking for outstanding penultimate year undergraduates of any degree discipline. As competition for places is fierce you will need a strong academic record, expecting at least a 2:1, with a minimum of 280 UCAS points, and should be able to demonstrate excellent communication and interpersonal skills.
Apply online at www.pwc.com/careers between October and 31 March 2007. Early applicants stand a better chance of gaining a position in their area of preference.

SAINSBURY'S SUPERMARKETS: 169 Union Street, London.
For **Finance Positions** see Sainsbury's under *Business and Management* below.

WATSON WYATT WORLDWIDE: Terra Firma, 86 Station Road, Redhill, Surrey (☎01737-241144; e-mail graduate.recruitment@eu.watsonwyatt.com; www. watsonwyatt.com/graduatecareers).
A global consulting firm focused on human capital and financial management.
Actuarial and Investment Consulting Summer Scheme (approx. 20). Wages of approximately £250 per week. Placements last for 6 weeks. Applicants should be penultimate year students, expecting a 2:1 degree or have 24 UCAS points. No accommodation is available but assistance may be given in finding some.
Applications should be made by 28 February 2006 on-line using the above website address.

Business and Management

BELAF STUDY HOLIDAYS: Banner Lodge, Cherhill, Calne, Wiltshire SN11 8XR (☎01249-812551; fax 01249-821533; e-mail enquiries@belaf.co.uk; www.belaf. com). An agency founded in 1975 that organises work traineeship placements in Southern England, London and the surrounding regions, Wiltshire, Dorset, Hampshire, Gloucestershire and Somerset.
Work Placements (40). Mainly unpaid. Placements last from 4-8 weeks and are available throughout the year, except in July and August. Placements available in sectors including tourism, catering, engineering and education. Minimum age 17 years; applicants must have a reasonable standard of English.
Applications from January-May to Carole Browne at the above address.

DIALOGUE DIRECT LTD: (☎0845-458 3901; email jobs@dialoguedirect. co.uk; www.funjobs4u.co.uk.)
A successful international fundraising agency working on behalf of charities and NPOs (not-for-profit organisations) such as Amnesty International, Greenpeace, Mencap. Raising donations *face-to-face* for well-known charities all over the UK, in mobile teams. Work available year-round with main campaign in the summer months.
Dialoguers. OTE £212.10 to £450 per week. (avg £250/wk for those without previous training/experience). All candidates start as face-to-face fundraisers, communicating directly with the public. Teams live together and travel throughout the UK, accommodation and transport is provided. Contracts are flexible after initial 5 week commitment. Must have a positive and flexible attitude towards work and team-life, excellent communication skills and an energy and passion to succeed and represent good causes.
Team Guides. Fast progression to Team Guide for the right candidate: opportunity to gain management skills. DialogueDirect has in-house training with a yearly seminar for Team Guides from across DD Europe.
All candidates must be over 18 years and available to work away from home. No maximum age limit. Overseas applicants with fluent English and a working visa welcome, particularly those from New Zealand, Australia, America and South Africa. Also ideal for students, graduates and gap year students.
Apply directly via the website www.funjobs4u.co.uk.

L'OREAL (UK) LTD: 255 Hammersmith Road, London W6 8AZ (☎020-8762 4000; fax 020-8762 4001; e-mail HR@uk.loreal.com; www.loreal.co.uk). A market leader in cosmetics, L'Oreal has a presence in 130 countries. The company has been in the UK for over 70 years and are leaders in many sectors of the health and beauty market. Their leading brands can be found in 9 out of 10 UK homes.
L'Oreal offers **80 Internships** every year to penultimate year students. They are

available in nearly all their functions, but most predominantly in Commercial, Marketing, Logistics, Finance, Manufacturing, PR and Market Research and can take place in either London, Manchester or Wales. During the placement, interns will work on a real life project that allows them to focus on a particular discipline whilst gaining an insight into the overall business. Interns are expected to make a real contribution to the day-to-day operations of their team. Wages are competitive. Interns are expected to work 39 hours per week. Internships last for 10 weeks from July to September. Accommodation is not available. Overseas applicants are welcome to apply; help can be given in gaining work permits.

Applications should be made online at the above website. An interview will be necessary, as well as assessment centre tests.

JOHN LEWIS: 171 Victoria Street, London SW1E 5NN (☎020-7592 6310; fax 020-7592 6301; e-mail careers@johnlewis.co.uk; www.jlpjobs.com).
The John Lewis Partnership offers **2 Placements**, lasting 6 weeks, to penultimate year university students of any discipline. Successful candidates gain an overall view of working in John Lewis. They gain experience of customer service standards, stock handling methods and everything else involved in working in a large retail business. This is backed up by insights into selling support functions and work a project focusing on a commercial aspect of the business. Trainees receive £230-£240 per week. While no accommodation is provided, efforts are made to place trainees in branches close to where they live. You should have good written and verbal communication skills as you will be working with senior management, colleagues on the shop floor and customers and you will also make a presentation based on your project.
Applications should be made online at www.jlpjobs.com.

SAINSBURY'S SUPERMARKETS: 33 Holborn, London EC1N 2HT (☎0845-241 4927; e-mail sainsburys@reed.co.uk; www.sainsburys.co.uk/graduates).
Summer Placements are available in Finance and Buying. The positions are open to anyone at either undergraduate or graduate level who is looking to broaden their business experience. Salary is £15,000 per annum pro rata. The placements last for 6 to 8 weeks during the summer months and are based in our Retail Support Centre in London.
Applications should be made online via the above website.

TRIDENT TRANSNATIONAL: The Smokehouse, Smokehouse Yard, 44-46 St John Street, London EC1M 4DF (☎020-7014 1420; fax 020-7336 8561; e-mail info. transnational@trid.demon.co.uk; www.trident-transnational.org).
International division of the Trident Trust, an educational charity and organiser of work experience programmes for overseas nationals in the UK.
As part of a nationwide charity, Trident's London-based office has access to a large network of potential employers for work placements and summer jobs; they offer **Work Experience and Working Holiday Schemes** for young people aged 18-35 from the EEA. Since 2006 they have a Work Experience Parliament Programme with which they organise internships with MPs for students with an interest in politics. They send applicants' CVs to relevant companies in the UK. Work placements are accredited with a certificate issued by the University of Cambridge Local Examinations Syndicate. Placements last between 6 weeks and 12 months and are available all year round. The scheme costs £250 for work experience placements (£300 for parliament placements) and £195 for working holiday placements. It is occasionally possible to find placements for non-European students who must obtain a Training and Work Experience Scheme permit for the UK. Accreditation and English courses are available as part of their programmes.

Applications should be made at least 2 months in advance by e-mail to info. transnational@trid.demon.co.uk.

WESSER AND PARTNER: The White House, Argyle Way, Stevenage, Hertfordshire SG6 2TA (☎01438-356222; fax 01438-356444; e-mail joinus@wesser.info; www. wesser.co.uk). Wesser and Partner specialises in door to door charity fundraising by talking to members of the public and promoting the charity, St. John's Ambulance. **Charity Fundraisers (50)** required to raise donations. Wages approximately £300 per week. Full-time hours (maximum of 40 per week). Minimum period of work 4 weeks between May and September. Accommodation is available in a 5-bedroom team house, charged at £40 per week. Minimum age 18. No previous experience necessary. Overseas applicants are welcome to apply, provided they speak English to the same level as a native speaker.

Applications should be made online between March and May at the above website. An interview will be necessary.

The Law

ADDLESHAW GODDARD: 150 Aldersgate Street, London EC1A 4EJ (☎020-7606 8855; fax 020-606 4390; e-mail grad@addleshawgoddard.com; www. addleshawgoddard.com/whatif).

Addleshaw Goddard is a leading national law firm with international capability. Ranked 16th largest law firm in the UK, as well as in The Sunday Times 2006 "100 Best Companies to Work For", Addleshaw Goddard has four major divisions: Contentious and Commercial, Corporate, Finance and Projects, and Real Estate. The firm currently has nearly 180 partners, over 400 associates and a total of 1,200 employees.

Addleshaw Goddard offer a **Two Week Summer Vacation Scheme**. The scheme provides opportunities to experience work within legal departments and is supplemented by a number of presentations and exercises. The scheme is currently remunerated at a rate of £180 per week in the North and £250 per week in London. The scheme is open to all those who would be in a position to commence a training contract with the firm in September 2009 or March 2010. Placements are located in the Firm's London, Manchester and Leeds offices.

Applications will only be considered via the firm's online application form, which can be found along with further information at www.addleshawgoddard.com. The closing date for applications is 31 January 2007.

DLA PIPER: Victoria Square House, Victoria Square, Birmingham B2 4DL (☎0121-262 5675; fax 0121-262 5793; e-mail recruitment.graduate@dlapiper.com; www. dlapiper.com).

One of the world's largest law firms offering around **200 Vacation Placements** throughout their UK offices: Birmingham, Edinburgh, Glasgow, Leeds, Liverpool, London, Manchester and Sheffield. The placements are 2 weeks long and involve shadowing a current trainee solicitor, attending talks, a visit to court, as well as social events.

Wages in London are £230 per week, £180 per week outside London. The scheme is open to undergraduates and graduates who are able to apply for training contracts; i.e. second year law students, final year non-law. Applicants are expected to have at least 3 Bs at A Level, with an expected or attained 2:1 degree. Accommodation is not provided, but advice given if necessary.

Applications should be made on the company's online application form before 31 January.

PINSENT MASONS: Dashwood House, 69 Old Broad Street, London EC2M 1NR (☎020-7418 7000; fax 020-7418 7050; e-mail graduate@pinsentmasons.com; www. pinsentmasons.com).
Pinsent Masons is one of the most highly regarded specialist law firms in Europe and the Asia Pacific region with 7 UK offices, as well as alliances in Spain, the US and Dubai. Masons provides a complete legal structure to clients operating in construction and engineering, energy and infrastructure industries and to users and suppliers of information and technology.
The **Summer Vacation Scheme** placements run for two weeks between mid-June and the end of August. The placements are designed to provide a real flavour of Pinsent Masons' culture whilst improving your skills and knowledge. Students have the opportunity to spend time in 2 areas doing real work, as well as mixing with other students and staff through skills workshops, business presentations, group exercises and much more. Pinsent Masons is looking for bright, motivated 2nd year Law students or final year non-Law students who are expected to achieve at least a 2:1 as their final degree classification and have a minimum of 24 UCAS points.
Applications should be made online by 31 January at the above website.

NABARRO NATHANSON: Lacon House, 84 Theobalds Road, London WC1X 8RW (☎020-7524 6000; fax 020-7524 6524; e-mail graduateinfo@nabarro.com; www.nabarro.com).
Nabarro Nathanson is one of the country's leading commercial law firms offering a broad range of legal services to major national and international clients across a range of practice areas. Offices in London and Sheffield. There are **50** places available in the **Summer 2007 Vacation Scheme** in London and **8** in Sheffield. Each placement is for a period of 3 weeks. Applicants must be in at least their penultimate year of a law degree or final year of a non-law degree (Mature Graduates, GDL, and LPC students are also welcome to apply). Students should submit an application form between 1 November 2006 and mid-February 2007.
Apply online at www.nabarro.com or via www.cvmailuk.com.

Media
INDEPENDENT TELEVISION:
A limited number of work experience placements are sometimes available with the 12 regional ITV companies. Vacancies are rarely known in advance and demand constantly outstrips supply.
Applicants must be students on a recognised course of study at a college or university; their course must lead to the possibility of employment within the television industry (ideally, work experience would be a compulsory part of the course); and the student must be resident in the transmission area of the company offering the attachment, or in some cases, attending a course in that region. However, opportunities may occasionally exist for students following computing, librarianship, finance, legal, administrative or management courses. Suitably qualified applicants from overseas are considered.
Placements vary in length from half a day to several weeks, depending upon the work available and the candidate's requirements. Students do not normally receive payment from the company, although those on courses of particular relevance to the industry may be paid expenses. Students from sandwich courses who are on long-term attachments may be regarded as short-term employees and paid accordingly.
Applications should be sent to the Personnel Department of the applicant's local ITV Company. General information and a careers handbook on the television

industry can be obtained from Skillset, the Sector Skills Council for the Audio Visual Industries via their website (www.skillset.org). You can also contact Skillset Careers, the specialist media careers advice service on 0808-0300 900 for more information on work experience.

Public Sector

THE ARMY: Freepost (LON15445), Bristol BS38 7ME (☎0845-730 0111; ; e-mail suni@aca.mod.uk; www.armyofficer.co.uk).

Although the Army does not offer vacation training as such, it does run the **Gap Year Commission**, which is open to students who wish to take a year out after leaving school and before taking up a firm place at University. It is aimed at students of high academic ability who demonstrate a responsible and mature attitude and show leadership potential.

Successful candidates attend a 3-week course at Sandhurst and are commissioned into their chosen Corps or Regiments as 2nd Lieutenants, on a special rate of pay of £13,970-£15,221 per annum. They serve for a minimum of four months and a maximum of 18 months. There is no subsequent obligation to serve in the Army.

As a first step, *applications* can be made online or by calling the above number.

THE CIVIL SERVICE: (www.careers.civil-service.gov.uk). As one of the UK's largest employers, with over 100 government departments and agencies, we offer unparalleled challenge, stimulation and career development options. Opportunities for work experience depend on the individual department's current business needs.

For further information on vacancies and departmental HR contracts visit www. careers.civilservice.gov.uk.

Science, Construction and Engineering

CORUS: Ashorne Hill Management College, Leamington Spa CV33 9PY (☎01926-488025; fax 01926-488024; e-mail recruitment@corusgroup.com; www. corusgroupcareers.com).

Corus is a customer focused, innovative, solutions driven company. It manufactures, processes and distributes metal products as well as providing design, technology and consultancy services.

Every year Corus offers **Summer Placements and 12-month Placements** around the UK in the following areas; engineering, manufacturing and operations management, metallurgical and technical services, research development and technology, commercial (sales and marketing), supplies, logistics, finance and human resources. Salary is based on £13,000 per year pro rata. Help can be given in finding accommodation. These positions are suitable for students in their first or second year at university.

Register online at www.corusgroupcareers.com. Registration takes 5 minutes. A full application will then be invited by Corus should a vacancy arise matching your requirements.

COUNTRYSIDE PROPERTIES PLC: Countryside House, The Drive, Brentwood, Essex CM13 3AT (☎01277-260000; fax 01277-690503; e-mail careers@cpplc.com; www.countryside-properties.com/careers).

A specialist development company recognised in particular for the development of sustainable communities and urban and rural regeneration. The Group's highly skilled, professional team is dedicated to maximising returns and profitability while creating developments of outstanding quality which add real value to communities

and to the environment.
Countryside Properties offers a **Work Experience/Sponsorship Training Programme** to university students for a period of 6 weeks over the summer vacation, linked and followed by sponsorship through university. The scheme provides work experience in land, development, construction, project management, surveying, buying and estimating departments. Trainees receive £250 per week for the six-week placements. Traineeships are located in their Brentwood or Warrington offices. Applicants ideally will be studying a related degree and have an interest in the industry.
Applications should be sent to Kim Brumley at the above address no later than December.

EXXONMOBIL: Recruitment Centre, MPO2, ExxonMobil House, Ermyn Way, Leatherhead, Surrey KT22 8UX (☎0845-330 8878; e-mail uk.recruitment@ exxonmobil.com; www.exxonmobil.com/ukrecruitment).
ExxonMobil is a worldwide leader in the petroleum and petrochemicals business, with both global and local customers ranging from major airlines to individuals visiting 45,000 service stations worldwide.
Around **20 eight-week Summer Placements** during July and August are offered for degree students in the Production and Development Department in Aberdeen and London, for students of any engineering discipline; and in Manufacturing and Distribution, in Fawley, for students of Chemical Engineering.
The summer placements are open to penultimate year students and salaries will be a minimum of £16,125 (pro-rata). All students will be given a project to complete (based on a real business scenario), receive some skills training and attend a two-day outdoor team-building course. During the placement, students will have the opportunity to go through the graduate recruitment process, with the possibility of securing a graduate job before their final year of study.
Apply via www.exxonmobil.com/ukrecruitment or call 0845-330 8878 for a brochure. Closing date is 10 December, but apply early as interviews start in October.

FABER MAUNSELL: Marlborough House, Upper Marlborough Road, St Albans AL1 3UT (☎020-8784 5736; fax 020-8784 5937; e-mail jacqui.brown@fabermaunsell. com; www.fabermaunsell.com).
An international multi-disciplinary buildings, transportation and environmental consultancy. Offices throughout the UK. One of the *Sunday Times* '100 Best Companies to work for' in 2006.
Work placements/Sponsorships/Industrial Placements. Open to students looking to pursue a career within the industry. Competitive salary package offered. Applicants considered who have the right to live and work within the UK.
Applications online via careers at www.fabermaunsell.com. Interview required.

GIFFORD: Carlton House, Ringwood Road, Woodlands, Southampton SO40 7HT (☎023-8081 7500; fax 023-8081 7600; e-mail recruitment@gifford.uk.com; www. gifford.uk.com).
Gifford is an award-winning consultancy, offering a comprehensive service in engineering and design. Prime disciplines cover civil, structural and building services engineering, together with complementary support from geotechnical, environmental, survey, transportation and archaeological departments. With more than 50 years in the industry, 550 staff worldwide and 8 UK offices, Gifford values creativity, clarity and the ability to appreciate the problem from the client's perspective, and pride themselves on their reputation for providing technically innovative engineering solutions.
Summer Vacation Traineeships for 15 to 20 students to work at offices located in

Southampton, Chester, York, Leeds, London, Oxford, Manchester, and Birmingham. Student engineers work with a design team within a multi-disciplinary consultancy environment. A summer placement will usually last between 10-12 weeks and Gifford welcomes applications from students studying any of the above disciplines.
Apply by submitting a letter of application and CV online at www.gifford.uk.com/recruitment or by post to the above address.

IMI PLC: Lakeside, Solihull Parkway, Birmingham Business Park, Birmingham B13 8RR (☎0121-717 3700; fax 0121-717 3751; www.thesearch-imiplc.com).
Employing more than 13,000 people in more than 30 countries worldwide, IMI is a diverse group of businesses which operate in highly specialised and growing markets, primarily in the fields of fluid controls (pneumatics, severe service values and indoor climates) and retail dispense (beverage dispense and merchandising systems). All are linked by one common aim: to provide smart, value-added engineering based solutions to major global customers. IMI operate globally and in many different areas.
Each year IMI offers a number of **Vacation Placements (approx. 12)** to penultimate year students studying for a degree in Mechanical, Manufacturing or Electrical and Electronic Engineering. On completion of a successful placement, students will be offered sponsorship through their final year at university and a place on the IMI's Global Graduate Development. Placements can be overseas depending on individual language skills and availability. Successful candidates should be able to work for a period of 8-12 weeks.
Apply online at www.thesearch-imiplc.com. Closing date for applications is 28 February 2007.

MOTT MACDONALD: St Anne House, 20-26 Wellesley Road, Croydon CR9 2UL (☎020-8774 2176; fax 020-8681 5706; e-mail human.resources@mottmac.com; www.mottmac.com).
The firm is a multi-disciplinary engineering consultancy engaged in development touching many facets of everyday life from transport, energy, water and the environment to the building and communications industries.
Vacation Placements (50+) are offered throughout the UK, for civil, mechanical, building, electrical, transportation, water and environment, and energy services. Trainees receive £230-£240 per week; placements occur during the summer vacation and last for 8-12 weeks. Overseas applicants are welcome. Where possible they will try and place you in an office near your home.
Applications should be made via an online application form at www.careers.mottmac.com.

NIAB: Huntingdon Road, Cambridge CB3 0LE (☎01223-342203; fax 01223-342206; e-mail jobs@niab.com; www.niab.com).
Vacation Work involving working in fields and laboratories is offered to about 30 applicants a year, at regional trial centres and the head office. £9,716 p.a. pro rata for experienced applicants and £8,311 p.a. pro rata for other applicants. Accommodation not provided although lists of accommodation are available.
Applications from April/May for summer work to the People and Professional Development Office at the above address.

ROLLS-ROYCE PLC: PO Box 31, Derby DE24 8BJ (☎01332-244344; e-mail peoplelink@rolls-royce.com; www.rolls-royce.com/university).
A global company operating in four dynamic markets: civil and defence aerospace, energy and marine.
Although an engineering business, **Summer Internships** are offered in purchasing,

logistics, finance and human resources, operations management, as well as engineering. They are ten-week placements, with a structured programme and set objectives. They are designed for undergraduates in at least their second year of study. **Full Internships** are placements that last anywhere from four to twelve months, usually as part of a degree course. They typically run from the end of June and last for one year, although it is possible to accommodate both shorter and longer placements. The internships are designed for students in the their second year of study so that they can apply knowledge gained from their course.

To *apply*, visit the above website.

SCOTT WILSON: Scott House, Basing View, Basingstoke, Hampshire RG21 4JG (☎01256-310200; fax 01256-310201; www.scottwilson.com).
A dynamic multi-disciplinary international consulting group involved in engineering, transportation planning and environmental planning projects throughout the UK, Europe, and world markets.
The company has a regular requirement for Civil Engineering students who have completed at least one year of their University course to undertake **Summer Vacation Work** based in their Basingstoke offices and occasionally at their other offices. Opportunities are available within their Maritime, Highways and Transportation sections.
Applicants should have a genuine interest in their subject, be adaptable, and show initiative. Duties and duration of placement may vary considerably depending on the workload at the time.
Applications should be made in April to the Personnel Department at the above address.

SKANSKA CIVIL ENGINEERING: Maple Cross House, Denham Way, Maple Cross, Rickmansworth, Hertforshire WD3 2AS (☎01923-423124; fax 01923-423209; e-mail hr.ukce@skanska.co.uk; www.skanska.co.uk).
Trainee Positions (30) working in the positions of civil engineer, quantity surveyor, land surveyor or in construction management. Placements are nationwide and site-based. Wages are subject to previous experience. Ideally to work over the summer vacation and for a minimum period of 8 weeks or for 12 months in the industrial placement year. University or College degree students (HNC or HND) or pre-university gap year students considered. Some assistance with accommodation available.
Applications should be made before May to HR Manager, Skanska Civil Engineering at the above address. Interview required.

SHELL STEP PROGRAMME: PO Box 8749, Nottingham NG1 9AT (☎0845-950 8321; fax 0115-950 8321; e-mail enquiries@step.org.uk; www.step.org.uk).
The Shell Step Programme offers around **1,200 Work Experience Placements** to undergraduates in small to medium sized businesses and community organisations throughout the UK. Projects last from 4 to 12 weeks. Applicants must be second and penultimate year undergraduates registered on a full time UK university degree course. Students are paid in the region of £185 per week (tax and national insurance free).
Applications can be made throughout the year. For summer projects, mid-June is the deadline. To apply, complete an online application form at www.shellstep.org.uk.

Travel and Tourism

THISTLE TOWER HOTEL: De Vere Gardens, London W8 5AF (☎020-7937 8121; fax 020-7937 6626; www.thistlehotels.com).

Student Vacation Traineeships are offered in the following areas:
Human Resources Trainee for work involving recruiting, selecting and interviewing.
Kitchen Staff required to work with a team of chefs preparing food.
Housekeeping Staff for work involving supervising, cleaning and the maintaining of bedrooms to hotel standard.
Receptionist/Cashier for a customer service position, checking guests in and out of the hotel.

The placements are paid or unpaid depending on the department worked in and last from 3 months to 1 year. Experience is not always necessary as training is provided. Applicants from overseas with proper work documents are welcome.

Applications should be sent to recruitment@thistle.co.uk.

London and Home Counties

Prospects for Work.
London: if you want to move to London to work during the summer season, think first about where you are going to live. While rented accommodation is not difficult to find the price is likely to be high and staying for only a short period may prove difficult. However, there are several youth hostels, and you may be able to find a cheap deal among the 'Accommodation to Rent' columns of the city's many newspapers and magazines. In addition to numerous local papers there are several publications which are not associated with any particular area. The main ones to look out for are: *TNT, Metro* and *Southern Cross* (free), the *Evening Standard* (daily), *Time Out* and *Loot*. These publications also carry job advertisements. Vacancies arise most commonly in retail, secretarial, hotel, restaurant and domestic work. The chance of finding a job will be increased if you are flexible as to where you can work, so consult the local paper in several different districts.

All Jobcentre Plus offices in London have Jobpoints where temporary work can be found. Some branches of Jobcentre Plus (☎0845-606 0234; www.

jobcentreplus.gov.uk; www.worktrain.gov.uk) keep lists of vacancies with the local Borough Council – these tend to be clerical and administrative posts. There are also hundreds of private employment agencies, especially along Oxford Street. Drake International (branches at 20 Regent Street, SW1; ☎020-7484 0800; 44 South Molton Street, W1Y; ☎020-7629 4129) covers a range of fields, including secretarial, industrial, driving and catering, for both permanent and temporary positions. Many such agencies advertise in *TNT* magazine.

Prospects for finding vacation traineeships and internships are particularly good in London, as it is the location of many big companies' head offices. The diversity of business in London means that opportunities in virtually any area of industry could be available.

Home Counties: in the comparatively prosperous Home Counties (those counties surrounding London), job prospects can be fairly good over the summer. In particular, there is a demand for staff among marquee erectors and events organisers. The Jobcentre Plus in Reading displays jobs at Ascot and Windsor racecourses, Henley Regatta, music festivals and other events both in the town and elsewhere in the region through its Jobpoint system. Epsom, Newbury and Sandown are the other main racecourses in the area; it is worth contacting these at any time of year.

Reading is a major source of longer-term summer employment in the Home Counties. Office, domestic, retail and catering work tend to be the most common, though it is worth approaching the local authority, which runs various summer programmes. Vacancies tend to be most numerous in the earliest months of the year. Try looking in the *Reading Evening Post* (daily), the *Reading Chronicle* (weekly) and the *Newbury Weekly News*.

Windsor is a busy tourist town all year round, but especially over the summer. Temporary work may be available at the Leisure Pool as well as at the local hotels and river boat companies. McDonalds is among the largest employers of temporary staff. The Jobcentre Plus offices in Maidenhead and Slough have a wide range of vacancies, both full and part time, permanent and temporary, and in a variety of occupations. The weekly *Maidenhead Advertiser* (on Fridays) has job pages.

In Luton, north of London, there is demand for factory workers, who may need forklifting qualifications. In addition, a large number of vacancies exist within the service sector, including retail work which is steadily increasing due to the expansion of the airport. Various other types of work are also available, including manual labour, caring, and catering.

Business and Industry

ALLSORTS: 45 Victoria Road, South Woodford, London E18 1LJ (☎020-8491 7000). An agency specialising in the placement of television and film extras.
Television and Film Extras needed all year round. Hopeful extras must register first for a fee of around £15. Expect, if used, to receive between £30 and £90 a day; more if you are required to have a haircut. The agency will require at least one recent professional quality 8x10 photo.

For further *information*, contact the agency at the above address.

THE BIG BUS COMPANY: 48 Buckingham Palace Road, London SW1W ORN (☎020-7233 9533; fax 020-7828 0638; e-mail bb_recruitment@bigbustours.com; www.bigbustours.com). Sightseeing tours of London.
Tour Bus Drivers to drive open top sightseeing buses in London in the summer. Wages £10.17 per hour. To work 40-50 hours per week. Applicants need a PCV

qualification.
Sightseeing Representatives to sell tickets for open-top sightseeing tours of London and to guide tours on buses. Minimum 40 hour week on rota working weekends. Applicants must be aged at least 18 with good communication and customer care skills; full training given.
Applications to Andy Sutherland at the above address.

CATCH 22: 199 Victoria Street, London SW1E 5NE (☎020-7821 1134; e-mail london@c22.co.uk; www.c22.co.uk). Employment agency covering the whole of the London area.
General Industrial Staff for temporary jobs such as furniture moving, driving, warehouse, message-running and cleaning. Flexible hours but usually 8 hours a day and preferably 5 days a week. Possibility of overtime. Work available all year round. Minimum period of work 3 months. No accommodation available. Minimum age 18. Must be adaptable to different environments and have a good level of English.
Apply by phone when in the UK to the above number.

HARRODS LTD: Knightsbridge, London SW1X 7XL (☎020-7730 1234; e-mail recruitment@harrods.com; www.harrods.com). One of London's premier retail outlets with a staff of 5,000.
Sales, Administrative and Support Staff to work throughout the Summer Sale and between October and January for the Christmas period and for the January Sale. Applicants must be a minimum of 18 years old and be eligible to work in the UK. Fluent spoken English and some retail experience would be an advantage.
Interested applicants should e-mail their CV to recruitment@harrods.com

MOVES: 141 Acton Lane, London NW10 7PB (☎0870-010 4410; fax 020-8267 6003; e-mail colinc@moves.co.uk; www.moves.co.uk). A north London removals/ distribution firm that is sympathetic to erratic habits of people working for relatively short periods to fund travel, for instance.
Removals Drivers/Assistants required year-round. Work available Monday to Friday or at weekends; good rates of pay. Especially good for students during the long holiday, since this is the company's peak-time. No accommodation available.
For further *information*, contact Colin at the above address.

PHOENIX RECRUITMENT CONSULTANTS LTD: First Floor, Brooke House, Market Square, Aylesbury, Buckinghamshire HP20 1SN (☎01296-422499; fax 01296-423300; e-mail info@phoenixmed.co.uk; www.phoenixmed.co.uk).
Temporary Staff required for on-going positions in the following recruitment areas: office support, sales and marketing, customer services and telesales, accountancy and finance, construction and industrial, technical and IT, legal, human resources, retail, and management. Previous experience preferable for all positions. Accommodation occasionally provided. Overseas applicants with valid work permits and visas, and fluent English welcome.
Applications at any time to Niamh Ginger at the above address. Interview or telephone interview required.

VAUXHALL AFTERSALES: Griffin House, Osborne Road, Luton LU1 3YT (☎01582-426077; fax 01582-426446; siobhan.mears@uk.gm.com; www.vauxhall. co.uk).
Warehouse Operatives (50). Duties include picking and packing in a parts distribution warehouse. Wages, plus shift premium if applicable. To work 38 hours a week. Staff

needed from mid-July for 7 weeks. No accommodation provided. Applicants must be over 18.

Applications to the Personnel Dept. (TW4) before the end of February, for a 7-week contract commencing on mid-July 2007.

WETHERBY STUDIOS: 23 Wetherby Mansions, Earls Court Square, London SW5 9BH (☎020-7373 1107; e-mail mikearlen@btopenworld.com).
Male Photographic Models. Wages £100 cash for 2-hour sessions. Dozens needed throughout the year. No accommodation available. Should be aged 18-40 years, but physique is more important than age. While more than half the models used are slim, it can be difficult to find men who have worked on their chest and arm definition, which is required if picture sessions promoting leisure wear are planned. Moustaches and beards permissible. No modelling experience necessary. Applicants must supply snapshots to show how they photograph facially and physically. Follow-ups are frequent, depending on the photographers' reactions to the first test shots. Overseas applicants and all colours more than welcome, but must speak fluent English.
Applications to Mr Mike Arlen, Director, Wetherby Studios.

Children

ADVENTURE & COMPUTER HOLIDAYS LTD: PO Box 183, Dorking, Surrey RH5 6FA (☎01306-881299; e-mail info@holiday-adventure.com; www.holiday-adventure.com). A small, friendly company with 22 years experience in running activity holidays for children aged 4-13. Based at Belmont School, Holmbury St Mary, near Dorking, in Surrey.
Camp Leaders, Teachers required for day camps. £180 to £200 per week. To work 8am-6pm. Minimum period of work 1 week. Work available every half-term and school holiday throughout the year (mostly July to August). Qualifications or experience with children preferred. Staff need to live in London or Surrey area. Minimum age 19.
Applications any time to Su Jones, Director, at the above address. Interview required.

CREATIVE KIDS PARTIES: 51 Fotherley Road, Mill End, Rickmansworth, Hertfordshire WD3 8QQ (☎01923-462684; www.creativekidsparties.co.uk/jobs). A family entertainment business catering for kids' parties and community and corporate events.
Children's Party Entertainers (2). Wages start at £6.50 per hour once trained. To work 10 to 20 hours per week including weekends and evenings. Staff required all year round but no accommodation available. No experience necessary as training is given in all aspects of the work but applicants should be friendly and enthusiastic. They should also be car owners and drivers and available to work evenings and weekends.
Apply to Judith Jones at the above address as soon as possible.

CROSS KEYS, MINI MINORS AND EXPERIENCE UK: 48 Fitzalan Road, Finchley, London N3 3PE (☎020-8922 9686; fax 020-8343 0625; www.campsforkids. co.uk).
Group Leaders and Group Assistants (20) to work at a residential children's activity camp (XUK) based in Norfolk. Duties involve being responsible for junior or senior children aged 6-17 and include the care of children and the planning and running of activities and supervising trips. Wages of c. £150 per week plus accommodation, food and drink. Period of work July-August.
Day Camp Group Leaders, Group Assistants (20) to work in a daytime children's

activity camp in north London. To work as part of a team of three adults per 24 children running games and activities within a school environment. Wages of £150-£200 per week depending on position and experience. Working hours generally 8.30am-3.30pm but may vary slightly. Should have an interest/background in childcare. Camps take place in all school holidays; summer camps will take place July-August.

Applicants for either camp must be enthusiastic team workers and aged at least 18. Full in-house training will be given. Possession of lifeguard/first aid qualifications would be an advantage.

Applications to Richard on 020-8371 9686 or go to 'staff zone' on the above website.

CROYDON PLAY PLUS: 2nd Floor, Day Lewis, 324-340 Bensham Lane, Thornton Heath CR7 7EQ (☎020-8239 7189; fax 020-8239 7196; e-mail play.plus@virgin. net). Charity providing play and care for primary school age children in four centres across the Croydon area.
Holiday Playworkers (10+) needed for the summer. Wages £5.35 per hour. To work 5 hour shifts per day for 3 to 6 weeks in Croydon area. To assist with play activities and to accompany children on outings. The many duties include preparing play activities and clearing away, preparing and clearing snacks, helping with collection of children from school and generally participating in all the activities involving children and supervising safety. Children aged 4 to 11 years. Minimum age 18 with childcare experience.

For *applications* contact Jean Bellinfantie, Accounts Officer at the above address. Must be police checked, give two references and be able to attend an interview in June.

GEOS ENGLISH ACADEMY LONDON: 16/20 New Broadway, Ealing, London W5 2XA (☎020-8566 2188; fax 020-8566 2011; e-mail info@geos-london.co.uk; www.geos-london.co.uk).
Activity Leaders for junior summer school. Wages to be arranged. To work from end of June to the end of August. Minimum age 18. Some experience with children required, though no formal qualifications necessary.
Applications to Jane Flynn, Principal at the above address.

MRS J. MARBER: 27 Ham Farm Road, Ham Common, Richmond, Surrey TW10 5NA (☎020-8546 9457; e-mail jmarber@waitrose.com).
Au Pair required for an adult family. Duties to include light housework, ironing, washing up and walking the dog. Own bedroom and bathroom provided. To work 5 hours a day/5 days a week. Minimum stay 3 months. Position most suitable for a female student: aged 17-25, non-smoker, with a good knowledge of English. Public transport is available in the area.
Applications, including a recent photograph and s.a.e. or IRC, to Mrs J. Marber at the above address.

NORTH HERTFORDSHIRE DISTRICT COUNCIL: Council Offices, Gernon Road, Letchworth, Hertfordshire SG6 3JF (☎01462-474550 24-hour helpline; fax 01462-474559; www.north-herts.gov.uk).
Playworkers for summer playschemes. Duties include general supervision, health and safety, planning of activities and creating a fun and happy environment to play in. Wages from £7.39 to £11.02 per hour. All staff work 35-40 hours a week, Monday to Friday. To work 23 July to 24 August, depending on summer holidays. Applicants must be over 18. Experience of working with children aged 5-11 is essential. Teacher/

Nursery nurse/play training qualifications are an advantage. Accommodation not provided.
Applications to HR Administration.

MRS PEREIRA: 511 Activity Club, Tottenham Sports Centre, 701-703 Tottenham High Road NI7 8AD (tel/fax 020-8801 1400). After school and school holiday programme for entertaining children; the club caters for 45-52 children aged 3-11. **Child Supervisors (11).** Duties include local school pick-up, art, craft and cookery activities, some cleaning, and child supervising. Wages start from minimum national wage. To work Monday to Friday; for 20-25 hours per week in term time and 25 to 30 hours in holidays. Minimum period of work negotiable. Playworker positions are available around the year. No accommodation available. Applicants need a childcare qualification and a first aid certificate; only those who are reliable, motivated and trustworthy need apply.
Applications to Mrs Liz O'Brien at the above address from November. Interview necessary.

PGL TRAVEL LTD: Alton Court, Penyard Lane, Ross-on-Wye, Herefordshire HR9 5GL (☎0870-401 4411; e-mail recruitment@pgl.co.uk; www.pgl.co.uk/recruitment). PGL recruit around 2,000 staff each year to assist with the running of their children's activity centres throughout the UK, including Devon, the Isle of Wight, Lincolnshire, the south coast, Surrey, Shropshire, Perthshire and Wales. Europes' largest provider of adventure holidays for children has offered outstanding training and work opportunities to seasonal staff for almost 50 years. PGL jobs provide a break from the 9-5 routine. If you are enthusiastic, energetic and looking for real experience and responsibility in a stimulating environment, PGL could have the job for you.
Activity Instructors in canoeing, sailing, windsurfing, fencing, archery, motorsports, pony trekking and more. Qualifications not essential for all positions as full training will be provided. Minimum age 18.
Group Leaders also needed to take responsibility for groups of children, helping them to get the most out of their holiday. Previous experience of working with children is an advantage. Minimum age 18.
Support Staff to assist the catering, domestic and maintenance teams.
Wages from £70-£100 per week plus free B & L. Positions available from February-November, for the full season, as little as eight weeks, or any period in between, although there are very few summer-only vacancies.
Applications can be made online, downloaded from the website, or call for an information pack.

STONY STRATFORD CHILDRENS CENTRE: London Road, Stony Stratford, Milton Keynes MK11 1JQ (tel/fax 01908-562485; e-mail stony.childrens.centre@ milton-keynes.gov.uk).
Playworkers (4-6) required to supervise and instigate play activities, perform domestic duties and participate in trips etc. Wages from £170 to £190 per week. To work 39 hours per week, from Monday to Friday. Minimum period of work is 6 weeks. Positions available mid-July to September. Must be keen and have sports/craft skills and interests. Must relate well to children. Suitable foreign applicants considered providing police check can be carried out. Fluent English essential. Minimum age 18. No accommodation available.
Applications should be made from May to Linda Kehoe.

Holiday Centres and Amusements

BRITISH AIRWAYS LONDON EYE: County Hall, Westminster Bridge Road, London SE1 7PB (☎0870-443 9187; fax 0870-990 8882; e-mail recruitment@ba-londoneye.com; www.ba-londoneye.com). The Eye is one of the tallest structures in London, standing 135 metres high on the south bank of the Thames, opposite Big Ben and the Houses of Parliament. It provides stunning views over central London and beyond.

Guest Service Assistants. Wages from £7.28 per hour. Very busy working environment with some outdoor positions.

To work approx. 40 hours, 5 days out of 7 per week, on a rota basis including weekends and bank holidays. All positions are for the full season from the beginning of June to the end of September. Holiday will be paid at the end of the contract. Applicants must be 18 or over and have a minimum of 1 year's customer service experience. No qualifications are necessary, but the right attitude is. Foreign applicants must be available for an interview, have a relevant working visa and speak fluent English.

Applications to Gayle Catt, Recruitment Manager, from April onwards. Keep an eye on the website for more details. Interview required.

CATAMARAN CRUISERS/BATEAUX LONDON: Embankment Pier, Victoria Embankment, London WC2N 6NU (☎020-7925 2215; fax 020-7839 1034; e-mail info@bateauxlondon.com; www.bateauxlondon.com). London sightseeing and restaurant boat company operating on the River Thames, providing sightseeing cruises with commentary and refreshments. Lunch and dinner restaurant cruises.

20-30 positions in retail, hosting, ticket agency, pier supervision, and waiting staff. Wages from £5.35 per hour. Contracts available April to October. Applicants must have experience of dealing with the public in front line situations and preferably some retail experience, a positive attitude and a happy smile. Second language an advantage. Foreign applicants with reasonable English welcome. No accommodation available.

Applications to the above address from March onwards. Interview necessary.

CHESSINGTON WORLD OF ADVENTURES: Chessington, Surrey KT9 2NE (☎01372-731541; fax 01372-731570; www.chessington.com). One of the most popular family theme parks in the south of England. Located off Junction 9 & 10 of the M25 and accessible via trains from Waterloo to Chessington South.

Rides, Retail, Food & Beverage, Cleaning, Photography, Admissions, Games and Warehouse are just a few of the departments that recruit for the busy summer periods. Rates of pay range from £5.20-£7.00 per hour, plus benefits. These include free uniform, free parking, staff restaurant, social club, and regular staff events and parties, and up to 40 complimentary tickets to any Tussauds attractions. Flexible hours are available. Enthusiastic, fun and friendly people of all ages are required to join the teams.

To apply visit the website, or call the recruitment line on the above number.

EUROPEAN WATERWAYS LTD: 35 Wharf Road, Wraysbury, Middlesex TW19 5JQ (☎01784-482439; fax 01784-483072; e-mail sales@gobarging.com; www. gobarging.com). Owners and operators of luxury hotel barges cruising rivers and canals in England, Scotland and France.

Deck Hands, Housekeepers, Chefs, Boat Pilots, Tour Guides. Wages £160 to £350 per week plus accommodation and meals. Applicants must be available for the whole season, which runs from early April until the end of October.

All positions require applicants to hold a valid driving licence and be aged 23 or over. Chefs must be fully qualified, with experience and boat pilots need to have experience on rivers. Foreign applicants with a working visa, who are able to drive in the UK and have good English are welcome. Some knowledge of French is helpful.

Applications should be sent to Isabelle Price at the above address by February. Interview required.

GLL: Middlegate House, The Royal Arsenal, Woolwich, London SE18 6SX (☎020-8317 5000 ext. 4020; fax 020-8317 5021; e-mail recruitment@gll.org; www.gll.org.uk). The largest leisure centre operator in London, with over 50 centres. As a worker-owned and controlled organisation GLL offers opportunities and benefits that far exceed the rest.

Leisure Assistants and Lifeguards (many). National Pool Lifeguard qualification an advantage but not essential; training is given.

Kids Activity Instructors (many). Coaching qualifications and experience of working with children required.

Wages of £5.65 and over per hour for up to 39 hours work per week. Minimum period of work 10 weeks. Positions are available from June to September. Foreign applicants welcome with appropriate permits, must have a good command of the English language. Minimum age 18. Subsidised training courses are also offered to those who want to build a career in the leisure industry. All employees must undergo a CRB check.

Applications should be made from early May onwards to the Human Resources Department, at the above address. Interview necessary.

LEGOLAND WINDSOR: Winkfield Road, Windsor, Berkshire SL4 4AY (Human Resources Department, ☎01753-626143; fax 01753-626142; e-mail jobs@LEGOLAND.co.uk; www.LEGOLAND.co.uk/jobs). LEGOLAND Windsor is a theme park dedicated to the imagination and creativity of children of all ages. Staff are employed in the following positions:

Admission Assistants, Food and Beverage Assistants, Retail Assistants, Rides and Attractions Assistants, Environmental Services Assistants, Security Guards. Wages start at £5.35 per hour (2006 figure), with benefits offered. Applicants will work an average of 40 hours over 5 days (variable, including weekends) and must be available for a minimum period of 8 weeks. Part time positions are also available in the above areas. The operating season lasts from March to October. Help is available to find accommodation. Fluent English essential. Minimum age of 16. No previous experience necessary; training will be given in all departments.

Applicants must have a passion for serving others, an exuberant personality and a natural affinity with children. To be part of the LEGOLAND team staff need to be willing to work hard and have fun whatever the weather (many positions involve working outside).

Apply online at the above website from January.

LONDON ZOO: Regent's Park, London NW1 4RY (☎020-7722 2333; fax 020-7586 5743; e-mail hr@zsl.org; www.zsl.org). The largest zoo in terms of species and staff in Britain.

Keepers are taken on during the summer months (April to September). Wages by arrangement. Some weekend work is required, but expect two days off per week. Applicants must have experience of working with animals.

To *apply*, visit www.zsl.org during February and March when the seasonal recruitment takes place.

THE SHERLOCK HOLMES MUSEUM: 221B Baker Street, London NW1 6XE (☎020-7738 1269; fax 020-7738 1269; e-mail info@sherlock-holmes.co.uk; www. sherlock-holmes.co.uk).
Victorian Maids (2) to receive visitors attending the museum. Knowledge of other languages would be an asset.
Sherlock Holmes Lookalike to dress up as Sherlock Holmes and give out promotional literature to tourists. Must be slim, at least 6′ tall and well spoken.
Wages by arrangement; no accommodation available. Period of work from May to September.
Applications to Grace Riley, Manager, at the above address.

THORPE PARK: Human Resources Department, Thorpe Park, Staines Road, Chertsey, Surrey KT16 8PN(☎01932-577302; www.thorpepark.com). One of the top theme parks in the South, located off junction 11/13 of the M25 and accessible via trains from Waterloo to Staines; a short bus ride will take you to the park.
Staff for food and beverage, cleaning, rides and attractions, shops, security admissions, warehouse and photography. Rates of pay £5.20 to £7.00. Flexible hours available. Benefits include free uniform, free parking, staff canteen, social nights, discounted merchandise and 20 complimentary tickets to any Tussauds group attraction. Enthusiastic and friendly people of all ages are required to join the teams.
Applications via the online form at the above website from January.

MADAME TUSSAUDS LONDON: Marylebone Road, London NW1 5LR (☎0870-999 0046; www.madame-tussauds.com). The Tussauds Group is one of Europe's largest operators and developers of visitor attractions with over 10 million guests a year.
Customer Service and Retail Positions are available within the central London site from late June to mid-September. Experience in a customer-focused environment and a positive and energetic attitude is crucial for these fun roles.
Please *apply online* at www.madame-tussauds.co.uk/aboutus_jobs.asp.

Hotels and Catering

AA APPOINTMENTS: St Claire House, 30-33 Minories, London EC3N 1PQ (☎020-7480 7506; fax 020-7480 5467; e-mail london@aaappointments.com; www. aaappointments.com). In business for 23 years, placing candidates in the travel industry, mainly in the UK and Ireland.
General Staff required year-round for jobs in such areas as hotels, groups and conferences, business travel and tour operators. Experience is preferred. Wages dependent upon job taken.
For further *information*, contact the Agency at the above address.

ALL VARIETY CATERING: Farnham Golf Club, Park Road, Stoke Poges, Buckinghamshire SL2 4PJ (☎01256-889100).
Bar/Kitchen Assistant for Golf Club to work in the bar, help chef, cleaning etc. Wages of £80 per week with free accommodation and gas, water and electricity. To work 35 hours per week. Overtime not available. Positions from June to September. Hours are by arrangement. Minimum 18 years old.
Applications to Natasha Bye, Director at the above address.

ADMIRAL GROUP: 55 Eastcastle Street, Oxford Circus, London W1W 8EF (☎020-7580 8446; fax 020-7580 8447; e-mail westend@admiralgroup.com; www. admiralgroup.com). A recruitment agency specialising in catering and hospitality. The Group requires top quality **Chefs, Events Service Staff, General Assistants, Kitchen Porters, and Corporate Waiting Staff** for immediate temporary bookings in central London. Staff are paid on a weekly basis and can expect to earn: Chefs £7.50-£11.00, waiters £5.05-£6.00 and kitchen porters/general assistants £5.05-£5.50 per hour plus holiday pay. Fabulous personal presentation, excellent English language ability, flexibility, bubbly personalities, and experience in a catering environment required. Applicants must be eligible to work in the UK and own uniform is required.
Call for an interview.

THE BERKELEY: Wilton Place, Knightsbridge, London SW1X 7RL (☎020-7201 1645; fax 020-7201 1643; e-mail recruitment@the-berkeley.co.uk). A five-star deluxe hotel on the corner of Knightsbridge and Wilton Place and has achieved the 'Investor in People' status. Opened in 1972, it has 214 luxurious bedrooms.
Day Room Attendants (5). Wages approximately £12,000 per annum, pro rata; to work 40 hours per five-day week. To clean 8 to 11 rooms a day. Good command of English and experience as a room attendant is desirable.
Commis Chefs (4). Wages approximately £11,000+ per annum pro rata; to work 45 hours per five-day week. Duties include assisting other chefs in preparation and service of food, maintaining high standards of hygiene and ensuring tidiness and cleanliness of designated sections.
Other jobs may also be available, including waiting work. Previous experience is required. Minimum period of work is 6 months. Overseas applicants with excellent spoken English are welcome. An interview is required. All candidates must demonstrate a high standard of personal presentation.
Applications from March to the above address.

BRAY LAKE WATERSPORTS: Monkey Island Lane, Windsor Road, Maidenhead, Berkshire SL6 2EB (☎01628-638860; fax 01628-771441; e-mail info@braylake.com; www.braylake.com). Set next to a 50-acre lake, ideal for beginners and intermediate windsurfers, sailors and canoeists. Caters for both adults and juniors. Has a good range of equipment for teaching, hire and demo.
Kitchen Manager needed to run small coffee bar and be in charge of stock and health and safety. Wages negotiable, between £25-£40 per day. The ideal candidate would have an interest in water sports, and be looking to use the time to gain water sports experience and eventually become an instructor. Some catering experience preferable.
Applications should be sent to Lindsay Frost, Centre Manager at the above address.

THE CROWN HOTEL: 7 London Street, Chertsey, Surrey KT16 8AP (☎01932-564657; fax 01932-570839; e-mail crownhotel@youngs.co.uk; www.crownchertsey. co.uk). The hotel dates back to Queen Victoria's reign.
Chefs (3), Bar Staff (4), Waiting Staff (3), Receptionist (2), Night Porter (2). Pay negotiable depending on experience. Work is 5-days split shifts, 39 hours per week. Both live-in and live-out jobs are available.
Applications to Tony and Sian O'Brien, General Managers.

EUROCOM: Suite 45, Surbiton Business Centre, 46 Victoria Road, Surbiton, Surrey KT6 4JL (☎020-8390 4512; post@europeancommunications.com). An employment agency specialising in placing seasonal staff in the hospitality industry. **All Staff** needed for placement in 4 and 5 star hotels. Minimum contract is 6 months out of every year. Wages dependent upon job taken.

Contact the Agency at the above address for further *information*.

FULLER, SMITH & TURNER: The Griffin Brewery, Chiswick Lane South, Chiswick, London W4 2QB (☎020-8996 2000; fax 020-8996 0230; www.fullers.co.uk). UK pub/bar/hotel group.

Bar and Catering Staff. Wages at least at national minimum rate. Hours by arrangement. Positions available all year round. Accommodation sometimes available. Vacancies mainly in the London and South East areas of the UK. Minimum age 18. Foreign applicants with permission to work in the UK and good command of spoken English welcome. Up-to-date vacancy list located on website.

For *applications* see the website, or contact using the details above.

GREAT FOSTERS HOTEL: Stroude Road, Egham, Surrey TW20 9UR (☎01784-433822; fax 01784-472455; www.greatfosters.co.uk). A privately owned historic hotel with period bedrooms and superb banqueting facilities. Close to London with excellent train links.

Summer Staff required for all areas of the hotel: banqueting, terrace, bar, housekeeping, portering and pool. Wages TBC. B & L available subject to availability.

Applications to Cathy Nolan, Deputy Manager, at cathy@greatfosters.co.uk.

HILTON LONDON METROPOLE: 225 Edgware Road, London W2 1JU (☎020-7402 4141; fax 020-7724 8866; www.hilton.co.uk/londonmet). The largest conferencing and banqueting centre in Europe. A cosmopolitan four-star hotel with 1,058 bedrooms, 40 meeting rooms and three ball rooms to cater for 3,000 guests.

Waiting Staff. Wages from £200 per week. Must have excellent communication skills and waiting experience.

Bartenders. Wages from £200 per week. Must have excellent communication skills and experience of bar work.

Communication Service Agents to deal with guests' enquiries and requests. Wages from £200 per week. Must have excellent communication skills and customer service experience.

Benefits include free meals on duty and free dry cleaning of uniform. To work 39 hours per week. Staff required all year round. No accommodation available. Minimum period of work 6 months. Minimum age of 18 for all positions.

Applications at any time to the Human Resources Department, FAO The Recruitment Manager.

HILTON COBHAM: Seven Hills Road South, Cobham, Surrey KT11 1EW (☎01932-864471; fax 01932-867067; www.hilton.co.uk/cobham). A four-star hotel with 158 bedrooms, 13 function rooms and a leisure club facility. Set in 27 acres of woodland in Surrey; half an hour from London by train.

Food and Beverage Servers to work in the Café Cino Bar, Zuccotta Restaurant or Conference & Banqueting Operations. Wages £5.05 per hour (live in). Some experience preferred.

Room Attendants. Wages £5.05 per hour.

All positions are based on 39 hours per week and for a minimum of 12 months. Accommodation is subject to availability and charged at £130 per month. A good level of English is important for all front line positions. A telephone interview is sufficient if applicants enclose a photo with their CV as well as references.

Applications should be addressed to Becky Clark, Human Resources Department.

THE IMPERIAL LONDON HOTELS LTD: 6 Coram Street, Russell Square, London WC1N 1HA (☎020-7278 3922; fax 020-7278 9318; e-mail personnel@imperialhotels. co.uk; www.imperialhotels.co.uk). Group of 6 prestigious hotels based in Russell Square (Central London) area. Multi-national staff and clientele. Family run company since 1830s.
Waiting Staff, Chamber Staff, Bar Staff, Porters. Wages £133.50 per week plus B & L. To work a 40 hour week. Minimum period of work 3 months between the end of May and the beginning of September. Applicants must be over 18. Experience preferred. Foreign applicants with valid work documents welcome. Good level of English required for porters, bar staff and dining room staff.
Applications should be made from April onwards to the Personnel Department. Interview required for UK residents.

KENSINGTON CLOSE HOTEL: Wrights Lane, Kensington, London W8 5SP (☎020-7937 8289; fax 020-7937 8170; e-mail hr@kensingtonclosehotel.com; www. kensingtonclosehotel.com). A 550-bedroom hotel serving international professional clients located in central London.
Waiting Staff. Wages and hours to be arranged. Minimum period of work 3 months between June and September. No accommodation available. Overseas applicants welcome.
Applications from May to the Personnel Officer. Interview necessary.

L&G RECRUITMENT: 6 Minories, London EC3N 1BJ (☎020-7481 1475; fax 020-7481 4951; e-mail consultants@lgrecruitment.co.uk; www.secsinthecity.co.uk). In business for 14 years.
Temporary Waiters and Waitresses, Stewards and Bar Staff needed for venues and functions in London such as Livery Halls, museums, Guild Hall, riverboat cruises, royal functions, film premieres, fashion shows etc. No qualifications, only previous experience is necessary. Minimum age is 18. Non-UK citizens considered if they have a good grasp of English and a valid work permit. Wages £4.80-£6 per hour.
To *apply*, contact Bob Fortt, the Catering Manager. Interviews are essential, along with copies of your passport, visa and references.

LONDON HOSTELS ASSOCIATION LTD: 54 Eccleston Square, London SW1V 1PG (☎020-7834 1545; fax 020-7834 7146; www.london-hostels.co.uk; e-mail ngrant@london-hostels.co.uk). Established in 1940, recruits residential staff for 11 London hostels run for young employed people and full-time bona-fide students.
General Domestic Staff to do housework and help in kitchens. Wages by arrangement, paid monthly with B & L provided. To work an average of 30-39 hours per week (mornings and evenings). Minimum period of work 3 months throughout the year. Work available all year round, long stays welcome. Opportunities to attend courses and improve English skills.
Voluntary Jobs also available, working only 20 hours per week in exchange for board and lodging. Minimum stay 8 weeks.
Common sense and willingness to tackle a variety of jobs required. Foreign applicants with permission to work in the UK are welcome.
Applications should be sent 2 months before date of availability to the Personnel Manager, London Hostels Association, at the above address.

HAMILTON MAYDAY TEMPORARY CATERING STAFF: 2 Shoreditch High Street, London E1 6PG (☎020-7377 1352; fax 020-7434 2168) (City); 21 Great Chapel Street, Soho, London W1F 8FP (☎020-7432 7000) (West End). Arranges temporary and permanent catering jobs to suit all levels of experience. Excellent benefits.
Chefs. Wages from £8.00 per hour.
Waiting Staff, Deli Assistants. Wages from £5.35 per hour.
Bar Staff. Wages from £5.35 per hour.
Kitchen Porters and Catering Assistants. Wages from £5.35 per hour.
Silver Service. Wages from £5.35 per hour.
Temporary and permanent positions available all year round. Overtime is available for evening and weekend work and employees are paid weekly.

Applicants should telephone any of the offices listed above to arrange an appointment from Monday to Thursday between 10am and 3pm. All applicants must have a valid work permit and references.

MICHAEL WISHER AND ASSOCIATES: Unit 14, Silver Road, London W12 7SG (☎020-8740 3100; fax 0115-984 6001; e-mail ripesh@michaelwisher.co.uk; www.michaelwisher.co.uk). Specialises in providing temporary hospitality staff to major corporate and sporting events across the UK.
Bar Staff (50), Plate Waiting Staff (50), Box Staff (50). Wages from £5.51 per hour. Hours of work are variable depending on the event and venue. The work is flexible so staff can choose hours to suit. Work is available throughout the year, however the summer months are the busiest period with many sporting events taking place over this time. Transport is always provided, free of charge, to and from the venues. No experience necessary. Applicants should be 18 and over. Overseas applicants with fluent English, relevant work permits and documentation are welcome to apply.

Application forms should be downloaded from the above website and returned to Ripesh at the above address. Successful applicants must attend an informal induction session.

NATIONAL TRUST ENTERPRISES: c/o Polesden Lacey, Dorking, Surrey RH5 6BD (☎01372-455033/4; fax 01372-452023; e-mail sue.knevett@nationaltrust.org. uk; or louise.doe@nationaltrust.org.uk; www.nationaltrust.org.uk).
Catering Assistants to work in 17 National Trust properties catering to the general public in West Sussex, East Sussex, Kent and Surrey. Wages vary from property to property but will be at least in line with the recommended minimum wage rates. Accommodation not available. Do not apply if accommodation is required. Working hours vary but may include working over weekends and bank holidays. Experience of working in the catering industry and basic food hygiene are desirable but not essential; full training will be given.

Those interested should *contact* Sue Knevett, Catering Operations Manager, or Louise Doe at the above address who will refer them to an appropriate property.

NORFOLK PLAZA HOTEL: 29/33 Norfolk Square, London W2 1RX (☎020-7723 0792; fax 020-7224 8770; e-mail melanie@norfolkplazahotel.co.uk; www. norfolkplazahotel.co.uk). An 87 bedroom, three-star hotel by Paddington Station in London W2. The majority of clients are Europeans on short leisure breaks in London, with a mixture of local UK Corporate customers. The hotel employs approximately 40 staff.
Hotel Receptionists. Wages £50 (gross) per 8-hour shift, with 5 shifts per week, plus weekly tips. Uniforms and other benefits provided free. Period of work June to end of September. Minimum age 20. Applicants must be able to speak fluent English;

knowledge of another Western European language would be an advantage. Experience of working on a computer database system and telephone switchboard essential. Overseas applicants welcome. Two weeks' training will be provided for successful applicants. No accommodation available.

Applications should be sent to Melanie Scholtz, Front Office Manageress at the above address, or to melanie@norfolkplazahotel.co.uk.

PEPPERMINT EVENTS: 19 Pensbury Street, Battersea, London SW8 4JL (☎0845-226 7845; fax 0845-094 1679; e-mail jobs@peppermintevents.co.uk; www.peppermintevents.co.uk). An event and bar management company that caters for events such as Henley Royal Regatta, Skandia Cowes Week and various music festivals in London and the South East.

Bar Staff, Trained Bartenders, Catering Staff and Cashiers (approx. 100) required for both paid and unpaid positions. Wages depend on position and experience of applicant. Unpaid staff are reimbursed with free entry tickets to festivals, crew camping, plus a free meal and two free drinks per shift in exchange for two shifts per event. Staff usually needed to work 6 to 8 hour shifts from June to September, but recruitment is ongoing. Camping accommodation provided at festivals only. Applicants should be 18 or over. Experience of bar work is preferred, but not essential (except for trained bartender positions). Overseas applicants are welcome to apply provided they have the relevant documentation and speak English to the same level as a native speaker.

Applications should be made to Adam Hempenstall at the above address, or via the website.

PHOENIX RECRUITMENT CONSULTANTS LTD: First Floor, Brooke House, Market Square, Aylesbury, Buckinghamshire HP20 1SN (☎01296-422499; fax 01296-423300; e-mail info@phoenixmed.co.uk).

Temporary Staff required for on-going hotel, catering and hospitality positions. Previous experience preferable. Accommodation occasionally provided. Overseas applicants with valid work permits and visas, and fluent English welcome.

Applications at any time to Niamh Ginger at the above address. Interview or telephone interview required.

THAMES LUXURY CHARTERS LTD: 6 Minories, 6 Putney Common, London, SW15 1HL (☎020-8780 1562; fax 020-8788 0072; e-mail operations@ thamesluxurycharters.co.uk; www.thamesluxurycharters.co.uk).

Silver Service and Bar Staff (20) required to work on board vessels on the Thames for corporate hospitality events. Hours of work are variable, but mostly evening work; wages from £5.50 per hour plus tips. Applicants must have previous experience, a good command of English and like boats.

Applications to HR Manager.

THISTLE KENSINGTON PARK AND PALACE HOTELS: De Vere Gardens, London W8 5AF (☎020-7937 8121; fax 020-7937 6626; www.thistlehotels.com).

Food/Beverage Assistants to work in the restaurant or bar. Wages at national minimum rate.

Conference and Banqueting Assistants to set up conference and banqueting rooms and help guests. Wages at national minimum rate.

Front Office Assistants for reception/switchboard/concierge/reservations work. Wages at national minimum rate. Fedelio/Delphi experience necessary.

Applicants are expected to work 39 hours over a 5 day week. Minimum period of

work 4 months.
Applications should be sent to recruitment@thistle.co.uk.

THISTLE TOWER HOTEL: De Vere Gardens, London W8 5AF (☎020-7937 8121; fax 020-7937 6626; www.thistlehotels.com).
Waiting Staff and Bar Person required throughout the year. Wages from national minimum rate. Minimum age is 18 years for bar work.
Applications to HR Dept at the above address.

THISTLE VICTORIA: De Vere Gardens, London W8 5AF (☎020-7937 8121; fax 020-7937 6626; www.thistlehotels.com). A 4-star hotel in the heart of Victoria, near Buckingham Palace and the West End. 364 bedrooms, a bar, restaurant, lounge and seven conference rooms.
Front of House and Food and Beverage Staff with excellent customer service skills needed. Wages from national minimum rate. Applicants must be 18 and ideally have leisure and tourism experience (but not essential). Minimum stay 1 year and all nationalities welcome. The hotel has an Equal Opportunities Policy.
Applications to the HR Dept at the above address.

Language Schools

DISCOVERY SUMMER: 20 Queensbury Place, London SW7 2DZ (☎020-7823 8484; fax 020-7823 9070; e-mail mary@discoverysummer.co.uk; www.discoverysummer.co.uk). Organises summer courses for students learning English as a Foreign Language.
Activity Leaders (25) required to supervise sports, arts and craft activities, parties and excursions for students aged 9 to 15. Wages are £225 per week. Staff are required for a minimum of 2 weeks between July and mid-August, with one day off per week. Accommodation is provided. Applicants must be 18 and over. Experience of sports coaching or teaching/supervising children is desirable.
Applications should be made from April to June to Mary Pincham, Manager, via e-mail to the above address.

EJO: Passfield Business Centre, Lynchborough Road, Passfield, Surrey GU30 7SB (☎01428-751933; fax 01428-751944; steve@ejo.co.uk; www.ejo.co.uk). An established TEFL school with 35 centres around the United Kingdom.
TEFL Teachers (85-90). Needed around the UK at the school's peak time of July. To work a minimum of two weeks to one month. Wages are £185 to £270 per week. Accommodation is available at one of the three residential schools owned by the organisation. Relevant qualifications necessary.
For further *information*, contact the Education Department at the above address.

ENGLISH IN LONDON: 27 Delancey Street, London NW1 7RX (☎020-7388 6644; fax 020-7387 7575; e-mail london@skola.co.uk; www.skola.co.uk/london). Long established language school; also runs CELTA teacher training courses.
EFL Teachers to teach classes of 15 adults or 20 children. Wages starting at £11.55 per hour. To work Monday to Friday, 15 hours (part-time) or 25 hours (full-time). Minimum period of work of 4 weeks. Positions are available from late June to early September. CELTA or Trinity certificate required. Experience preferred but not essential. No accommodation available.
Applications to Andrew Cossee at the above address from Easter onwards. Interview necessary.

ENGLISH LANGUAGE & CULTURAL ORGANISATION: Lowlands, Chorleywood Road, Rickmansworth, Herts WD3 4ES (☎01803-299691; fax 01923-774678; e-mail efl@elco.co.uk; www.elco.co.uk). A group of ARELS accredited TEFL centres.
TEFL Teachers (20-30). Needed to work at three locations in the south of England during the summer. Accommodation is provided. Wages on request. Relevant qualifications will be necessary.
Contact Tony Thompson, the Director, at the above address.

EXCEL ENGLISH LANGUAGE SCHOOL: 8 Muswell Hill, London N10 3TD (☎020-8365 2485; e-mail liz@excelenglish.co.uk; www.excelenglish.co.uk). Excel English is a well-established, British Council accredited school in North London.
Activities Assistants (3). Wages £180 to £200 per week. Required for residential junior school and non-residential adult school.
Activities Organiser (1). Wages £250 to £325 per week. Required for residential junior school.
Course Director (1). Wages £350 to £425 per week. Required for residential junior school. Must have previous academic or other management experience and a TEFL or PGCE qualification.
Teaching Staff (6). Wages £240 to £330 per week. Required for residential junior school. Must have CELTA or PGCE qualification.
All staff are required to work 2 out of 3 sessions per day (morning, afternoon and evening) for a minimum of 3 weeks from mid-July to mid-August. Accommodation is provided free of charge. Activities assistants should be undergraduates or new graduates with experience in youth work or creative activities. All applicants must be able to demonstrate a responsible attitude. Overseas applicants are welcome but must have native speaker fluency in English.
Applications should be made to Liz Granato, Vice Principal, at the above address. An interview will be necessary, but can be conducted over the phone.

FRANCES KING SCHOOL OF ENGLISH: 77 Gloucester Road, London SW7 4SS (☎020-7870 6533; fax 020-7341 9771; e-mail info@francesking.co.uk; www. francesking.co.uk). A large language school located on 2 sites in central London. Students come from all over the world, particularly Italy and Spain during the summer months.
EFL Teachers (30). Pay on an hourly basis. To teach up to 30 hours per week at various centres, plus optional leading of groups and taking part in activities with students. Period of work from the first week of July to the last week of August. Must hold RSA/Cambridge TEFL certificates and have a minimum of one year's experience.
Applications to Drew Hyde, Director of Studies, at the above address.

GEOS ENGLISH ACADEMY LONDON: 16/20 New Broadway, Ealing, London W5 2XA (☎020-8566 2188; fax 020-8566 2011; e-mail info@geos-london.co.uk; www. geos-london.co.uk).
EFL Teachers (15). Wages on application. To work from end of June to the end of August. Teaching duties are for 3 hours per day Monday to Friday, helping with the social programme in the afternoons. Applicants must have RSA, CTEFLA/CELTA, or Trinity College TESOL.
Applications to Jane Flynn, Principal, at the above address.

HAMPSTEAD SCHOOL OF ENGLISH: 553 Finchley Road, Hampstead, London NW3 7BJ (☎020-7794 3533; fax 020-7431 2987; e-mail info@hampstead-english.

ac.uk; www.hampstead-english.ac.uk). The school has an average of 350 foreign students, and enjoys a reputation for excellence. Staff pride themselves on treating each student as an individual.

Student Group Leaders to guide foreign language students around London and take care of them while on route to and during their evening engagements. Wages of £7.00 per hour (negotiable); flexible hours ranging from 15 to 40 hours over mainly afternoons and evenings. Work would suit undergraduates aged 19 and over who have successfully completed at least one year of a university course. Work is available from last week of June to early September. Applicants should be energetic, enthusiastic and like dealing with people. No accommodation provided.

Applications to Jill Sieff, Principal, at the above address. Applicants must be available for interview.

HARVEN SCHOOL OF ENGLISH: The Mascot, Coley Avenue, Woking, Surrey GU22 7BT (☎01483-770969; fax 01483-740267; e-mail info@harven.co.uk; www. harven.co.uk). A private organisation providing full-time intensive courses in English as a foreign language with a comprehensive social programme for adults and juniors in pleasant surroundings.

Qualified EFL Teachers (10), Sports/Social Assistants (2) to work for an English language school in June, July and August. Salary according to qualifications and experience. To work from Monday-Friday or Saturday from 9.30am-4pm approx. and some evenings for the social programme. No accommodation provided. Applicants should have relevant qualifications and experience.

Applications to the Director of Studies, at the above address.

INTERNATIONAL COMMUNITY SCHOOL: 4 York Terrace, Regent's Park, London. NW1 4PT (☎020-7935 1206; fax 020-7935 7915; e-mail admissions@ics. uk.net; www.skola.co.uk/ics).

EFL Teachers (10-15) to work between the start of June and the end of August. Hours of work are full-time, 9am-4.30pm, for wages of £310-£360 per week. Staff should have CELTA/DELTA/PGCE and preferably experience of teaching young learners.

Applications to the Director of Studies at the above address.

INTERNEXUS: Regent's College, Inner Circle, Regent's Park, London NW1 4NS (☎020-7487 7489; fax 020-7487 7409; e-mail london-academics@internexus.to; www.internexus.to). Small, friendly and professional British Council accredited English language school in the heart of Regent's Park.

Part and Full-Time EFL Teachers (2-5). Minimum CELTA qualification needed. **Business English Teachers (1-2).** 2 years' experience preferred.

Wages £11 to £15 per hour. Applicants for both positions are required to work 3 to 6 hours per day. Teachers should be available to work for a minimum period of 2 weeks from mid-June to the end of September. B & L is not provided. Only applicants who can speak English at the same standard as a native speaker need apply.

Applications should be made approximately 4 weeks in advance of the proposed start date to Mark Holloway or Steve Phillips, either by e-mail or to the above address.

KING'S SCHOOL OF ENGLISH (LONDON): 25 Beckenham Road, Beckenham, Kent BR3 4PR (☎020-8650 5891; fax 020-8663 3224; e-mail info@kingslon.co.uk; www.kingslon.co.uk). The only all year round recognised school in Beckenham. Takes around 150-250 students from all over the world and specialises in teaching general English to international groups of adult learners. Established in 1966 and British Council

accredited.
EFL Teachers (approx 10) to work from mid-June to end of August for 20 to 28 lessons per week programmes (minimum 4 weeks) for learners aged 16 and over. Only UCLES CELTA/DELTA qualified applicants to apply from January.
Applications to the Principal at the above address.

LINGUACENTRE LTD: Trafalgar House, Grenville Place, Mill Hill, London NW7 3SA (☎020-8959 5081; fax 020-8959 5088; e-mail info@linguacentre.co.uk; www. linguacentre.co.uk).
Teachers for TESOL/TEFLA work from July to August. To teach approximately three hours per morning from Monday to Friday or approximately 6 hours per day for 2 to 3 days per week. Part time work also available. TEFLA, TESOL or similar qualifications are needed.
Teachers for teenage classes from July to August. Classes for three hours per morning from Monday to Friday. TESOL/PGCE or similar qualifications necessary, or relevant experience. Extra hours are possible on some days.
Wages by arrangement. No accommodation available.
Applications to Louise Magnus, Principal, at the above address.

LANGUAGE LINK: 21 Harrington Road, London SW7 3EU (☎020-7225 1065; fax 020-7584 3518; e-mail recruitment@languagelink.co.uk; www.languagelink. co.uk). Language Link is accredited by the British Council and is a member of English UK. Located in the borough of Kensington and Chelsea, it is open all year, with a friendly, family atmosphere.
EFL Teachers (20). Pay is dependent on qualifications and experience. Monday-Friday. To work from end of June to the end of August. Applicants must be Cambridge, Trinity or equivalent TEFLA certified. This 4-week CELTA qualification can be taken at Language Link (e-mail teachertraining@languagelink.co.uk).
Applications from May to the Director of Studies at the above address. An interview is required.

MALVERN HOUSE INTERNATIONAL: 1-17 Shaftesbury Avenue, London W1D 7EA (☎020-7440 1790; fax 020-7440 1799; e-mail luke@malvernhouse.co.uk; www.malvernhouse.co.uk). Malvern House consists of 3 young and sociable colleges in central London, catering for TEFL and business English courses, Cambridge exams and pre-university courses, to students from all over the world.
EFL Teachers (8) required to teach general and specific English to mixed-nationality groups of up to 18 students, aged 16 and over. Wages from £9.00 per hour depending on qualifications and experience. Part and full-time positions are available, with hours ranging from 15 to 30 per week. Teachers required for a minimum of 4 weeks from June to September. No accommodation is available. Applicants must be graduates with a minimum CELTA/TESOL qualification.
Applications should be made from mid-May to Luke Simmons, Director of Operations, at the above address. An interview will be necessary.

OISE YOUTH LANGUAGE SCHOOLS: Oise House, Binsey lane, Oxford OX2 0EY (☎01865-258300; fax 01865-244696; e-mail younglearners@oise.net; www. oise.net). Work available throughout Britain.
EFL Teachers required to teach small groups of foreign students. Must be qualified and have experience.
Academic Directors. Qualified EFL teachers with organisational ability.
Period of work Easter and June, July, August. Applicants must be graduates and speak

English to the level of a native speaker.
Details from the Recruitment Administrator, OISE.

OXFORD HOUSE COLLEGE: 28 Market Place, Oxford Circus, London W1W 8AW (☎020-7580 9785; fax 020-7323 4582; e-mail dos@oxfordhouse.co.uk; www. oxfordhousecollege.co.uk). A leading British Council accredited college in central London providing English, Computing, Travel and Tourism and Teacher Training courses.
EFL Teachers and EFL Teacher/Trainers required to work for a minimum period of 2 weeks or throughout the year. Applicants must be TESOL/TEFL certified.
Applications at any time to the Director of Studies at the above address.

PROJECT INTERNATIONAL: 20 Fitzroy Square, London W1T 6EJ (☎020-7916 2522; fax 020-7916 8586; e-mail tim@projectinternational.uk.com; www. projectinternational.uk.com).
Teaching/Activity Staff (50) to teach English and supervise activities at a residential summer school. Wages of £190-£350 per week plus full board. Staff needed for up to 6 weeks from early July. Possession of TEFL and PGCE qualifications an advantage but not essential.
Applications to Tim Precious, Operations Manager, at the above address.

SELS SCHOOL OF ENGLISH: 64-65 Long Acre, Covent Garden, London WC2E 95X (☎020-7240 2581; fax 020-7379 5793; e-mail english@sels.co.uk; www.sels. co.uk). Located in fashionable Covent Garden near the Opera House, the school teaches English at all levels to foreign adults in groups of 5-9 and on a one-to-one basis.
Assistant to work in the tea room and clean premises. Wages £5.50 per hour. To work 3-6 hours per day, Monday to Friday and alternate weekends. Period of work by arrangement. Knowledge of Portuguese, Spanish or Italian useful.
Clerks/Secretaries. £6.00 to £7.00 per hour. To work approximately 20-40 hours per week. Must have word processing skills and some secretarial experience.
Applications to Mr Y. Raiss, Sels School of English, at the above address.

SUPERSTUDY UK: 1-3 Manor Parade, Sheepcote Road, Harrow HA1 2JN (☎020-8861 5322; e-mail superstudy.london@btinternet.com; www.superstudy.com). Teaches English to all nationalities, from elementary level to advanced, specialising in general English and conversation in a friendly atmosphere. Five minutes walk from Harrow-on-the-Hill Underground station. Also provides IELTS classes.
EFL Teachers (2-4). Wages from £12.54 per hour, exact hours of work to be arranged. Minimum period of work 2 to 4 weeks between 1 July and 31 August. Accommodation not available. RSA/UCLES, CELTA and first degree required.
Applications as early as possible to Anna Marsal at the above address.

TASIS ENGLAND AMERICAN SCHOOL: Coldharbour Lane, Thorpe, Surrey TW20 8TE (☎01932-565252; e-mail dwest@tasis.com; www.tasis.com). Set in 35 acres; approximately 30 minutes train journey from London, the school runs a summer programme for American and International students.
Counsellors to supervise sports and activities such as visits and trips all over England, and act as teaching aides. Driving licence necessary.
Teachers to teach English as a foreign language and traditional high school maths and English courses. Must be familiar with the American educational system. Wages according to relevant experience. Room and board provided. Applicants must have a standard of English as high as that of a native speaker and have completed at least one year at university.

Applications, including CV, should be sent by 14 March to Mr David West, Director of Summer Programmes, at the above address.

THAMES VALLEY CULTURAL CENTRES: 13 Park Street, Windsor, Berks SL4 1LU (☎01753-852001; fax 01753-831165; e-mail recruit@thamesvalleycultural. com; www.thamesvalleycultural.com). A summer school which has several centres in prestigious locations in the south-east. TVCC provides English language courses and activities for young learners from all over the world during the months of July and August.
Senior Managers and Pastoral Staff (up to 50), TEFL Teachers (up to 80), Specialised Recreation Teachers, Sports Instructors and Administrative Staff required for all centres. Staff should have appropriate skills, experience and qualifications relevant to the position. There are residential (free full board and accommodation) and non-residential positions.
Applications, including CV, should be made to the above address. Recruitment begins at the end of April for positions starting at various times in July.

Medical

ALLIED HEALTHCARE GROUP: The Old Chapel House, Bryants Bottom Road, Great Missenden, Buckinghamshire HP16 0JS (☎01494-488040/1; fax 01494-488650; e-mail highwycombe@alliedhealthcare.com). Nursing agency.
Health Care Assistants needed for work in the community, hospitals and nursing homes. Wages £5.35-£14.20 per hour, depending on the situation.
Support Workers to work with children and adults with learning disabilities. Base wage of £7.67 per hour.
Positions are available all year. Minimum period of work 6 weeks. Overseas applicants with fluent English and valid work permits or student visas welcome.
Applications should be made to Mrs Vanessa Cracknell. Interview necessary.

AMBITION 24 HOURS: Sentinel House, 16-22 Sutton Court Road, Sutton, Surrey SM1 4SV (☎020-8288 9071; fax 020-8288 8993; e-mail info@ageny-nursing.co.uk). Specialists in the provision of qualified nurses and healthcare staff for temporary placement with hospitals, nursing homes and HM Prison Service. They have also recently started a construction industry supplier, which specialises in electricians, plumbers, builders etc. on a temporary or permanent basis.
Healthcare Assistants, Domiciliary Carers. Wages £7.00-£10.00 per hour.
Domestic Assistants. Wages £5.50-£7.00 per hour.
All positions ongoing. Flexible hours to suit. Applicants must have at least 6 months experience or must enrol on a 3 day Ambition Care Course and then complete a 30-hour placement.
To *register* call 08718-733 333. Interview required.

CARE ASSOCIATES: Unit 207 Down House, 3-9 Broomhill Road, Wandsworth, London SW18 4JQ (☎020-8871 5075; fax 020-8874 3111; e-mail care_associates@ yahoo.co.uk). Recruiters of domiciliary care workers for one-to-one home care, mostly within central London.
Live-in Home Carer (3). Wages £375 before tax per week. To work 7 days a week.
Night Workers (3). Wages £60-£65 before tax per night. To work casually.
Day Care (3). Wages from £7.00 before tax per hour. To work casually.
All applicants must be over 24, with a relevant NVQ or 2 years care experience. Free board and food available only for live-in work; minimum period of work 3 months.

Staff required from June until September. Fluent English or good communication skills necessary; suitably qualified non-UK citizens will be considered.

Apply to Gavin Gilligan at the above address. An interview will be required, although this can be done over the telephone with written applications.

COMPLETE CARE CENTRE LTD: 6 Lind Road, Sutton, Surrey SM1 4PJ (☎020-8288 0902). A care agency supplying staff to private care homes and local authorities.

Care Assistants. Wages of £5.00-£7.00 per hour.
Support Workers. Wages of £8.00-£10.00 per hour.
All positions involve shift work. Staff required all year round, with no minimum period of work. Applicants should be over 18, have experience as a care assistant (preferably two years) and a Moving and Handling Certificate. Suitably qualified foreign applicants with fluent English welcome. No accommodation available. NVQ Level 2 in Care pass required or equivalent. CRB checks apply.

Applications should be made at any time to Sam, Lesley or Dawn at the above address. Interview required.

ENA CARE AGENCY LTD: Smallford Lane, St Albans AL4 0SA (☎01727-825000; fax 01727-825005; e-mail jobs@ena.co.uk; www.ena.co.uk).
Live-in Care Assistants to work one-to-one as a live in carer in the home of one of our clients who are all over 18 years old. ENA specialize in providing care for clients with active lifestyles. They care for about 120 clients who all live in their own homes in the south of England, who are physically disabled but who live independent lifestyles with the help of their carer. Work involves helping with outdoor visits, going to work, university, swimming, shopping, going to the pub, visiting friends etc.. Assistants also help with personal care, light household duties, shopping and cooking. The company takes care to get to know care assistants before placing them, aiming to match personalities and interests.

Wages from £360-£400, board and accommodation included. Minimum period of work 3 months, with 4 day free training course for successful applicants. A maximum working day of 6 to 8 hours. Positions are available all year. Applicants should be 21 years and over and able to drive. Previous care experience is useful but not essential.

Applications should be made at any time to Recruitment at the above address. Interviews held in London every Thursday.

KELLS NURSES BUREAU: 43 The Grove, London N13 5LQ (☎020-8886 6589; fax 020-8886 6168; e-mail kellsnursing@tiscali.co.uk).
Care Assistants (30-40) to work with elderly and frail people in local authority residential homes in North and Central London. Wages from £7.00. Shifts are from 7.30am to 2pm and from 1.30 to 9pm. Period of work May to September. Minimum age is 20 and experience of working in a similar post for at least 6 months is essential; the work is particularly suitable to nursing and medical students.

Applications should be sent to Michael Ganeski, the Manager.

PHOENIX HEALTHCARE: First Floor, Berkeley House, Walton Street, Aylesbury, Buckinghamshire HP21 7DS (☎01296-422499; fax 01296-423300; e-mail info@ phoenixmed.co.uk; www.phoenixmed.co.uk). Medical and healthcare recruitment specialists providing a quality, reliable service for positions across the UK.
Temporary Staff required for on-going medical and pharmaceutical positions. Previous experience preferable. Accommodation occasionally provided. Overseas applicants with valid work permits and visas, and fluent English welcome.

Applications at any time to Jill Frew or Melanie Garside at the above address. Interview or telephone interview required.

SOPHISTICARE LTD: Unit 16, Galaxy House, The Enterprise Centre, New Greenham Park, Newbury, Berks RG19 6HR (☎01635-817401; fax 01635-817412; e-mail julie.evans@sophisticare.co.uk; www.sophisticare.co.uk).
Support Care Workers (any number) to offer home care support of elderly people and adults with physical and learning difficulties. The job involves giving assistance with personal care, housework, shopping, pension collection etc. in the Newbury, Thatcham, Hungerford, Kintbury, Compton and Lambourn areas of Berkshire. Wages start at £6.50 per hour Monday-Friday and £6.68 per hour Saturday-Sunday increasing to £7.21 and £7.35 per hour respectively following training. Up to £250 per month in expenses, £10 per month mobile phone allowance and holiday pay also provided. Part- and full-time work available, including weekend work, between the hours of 7am and 9.30pm. Period of work by arrangement; vacancies ongoing around the year.
Applicants must be aged over 17; no previous experience required but own transport essential.
Applications to Julie Evans, Director, at the above address.

STRAND NURSES BUREAU: Brettenham House, 1 Lancaster Place, London WC2E 7RN (☎020-7836 6396; fax 020-7240 6324; e-mail strand@advantagehealthcare. com; www.advantagehealthcare-strand.com). An agency specialising in temporary positions in all work areas, including private and NHS hospitals, GP practices/clinic, occupational health and private homecare.
Staff constantly required for all areas of healthcare assistance. No minimum period of work. Accommodation advice available. Fluent English is essential; non-UK qualified nurses and experienced healthcare assistants considered.
Apply at any time via e-mail or look at vacancies on the above website. An interview will be necessary.

VKL NURSING AND HEALTHCARE SERVICES LTD: 108-112 (2ⁿᵈ Floor), Shenley Road, Borehamwood, Herts WD6 1EB (☎020-8381 6254; fax 020-8327 0165; e-mail enquiries@vklnursing.co.uk; www.vklnursing.co.uk). Recruiters of qualified nurses and healthcare assistants for private and NHS Hospitals.
Qualified RMN/RGN Nurses. Wages from £12.73-£29.33 per hour. Must be registered with the NMC.
Healthcare Assistants. Wages from £7.65-£16.39 per hour. Intensive training courses are run for healthcare assistants.
Applications to Moira Fullagar at the above address.

Outdoor

BUCKS WIGWAMS: Ibstone, High Wycombe, Buckinghamshire HP14 3XT (☎01491-638227; fax 01491-638233; e-mail richard@buckswigwams.freeserve. co.uk; www.buckswigwams.com).
Marquee Erectors (5) wanted for the summer period until the end of November to put up marquees in the Thames Valley area. Wages from £5.00 to £7.00 per hour according to age and experience. Working hours are 8am to 5pm with some overtime and weekend work. Minimum age 18. Must have own transport and be physically fit.
Applications should be made in writing to Mr W.M. King, Manager.

DIALOGUE DIRECT LTD: (☎0845-458 3901; email jobs@dialoguedirect. co.uk; www.funjobs4u.co.uk.) A successful international fundraising agency working on behalf of charities and NPOs (not-for-profit organisations) such as Amnesty International, Greenpeace, Mencap. Raising donations *face-to-face* for well-known charities all over the UK, in mobile teams. Work available year-round with main campaign in the summer months.
Dialoguers. OTE £212.10 to £450 per week. (avg. £250/wk for those without previous training/experience). All candidates start as face-to-face fundraisers, communicating directly with the public. Teams live together and travel throughout the UK; accommodation and transport is provided. Contracts are flexible after initial 5-week commitment. Must have a positive and flexible attitude towards work and team-life, excellent communication skills and an energy and passion to succeed and represent good causes.
Team Guides. Fast progression to Team Guide for the right candidate; opportunity to gain management skills. Dialogue Direct has in-house training with a yearly seminar for Team Guides from across DD Europe.
   All candidates must be over 18yrs and available to work away from home. No maximum age limit. Overseas applicants with fluent English and a working visa welcome, particularly those from New Zealand, Australia, America and South Africa. Also ideal for students, graduates and gap year students.
   Apply directly via the website www.funjobs4u.co.uk.

CLAREMONT MARQUEES: Fishers Hill House, Hook Heath Road, Woking, Surrey GU22 OQE (☎01483-720472; fax 01483-724714; e-mail robertatkins@ tiscali.co.uk; www.claremontmarquees.com).
Marquee Erectors/Labourers (5). Wages from £6.00-£7.00 per hour. Flexible working hours, normally approximately 8 to 10 hours a day. Period of work 1 April to 1 October; minimum period of work is one week. Applicants must be fit and strong. No accommodation available.
   Applications to Robert Atkins, Owner, at the above address from the start of April.

INTENTS MARQUEES CO: Laplands Farm, Ludgershall Road, Brill, Aylesbury, Buckinghamshire HP18 9TZ (☎01844-238466; fax 01844-238870; e-mail enquiries@ intents-marquees.co.uk; www.intents-marquees.co.uk). A family-run group operating up to around 50 miles from the base hiring and erecting marquees and equipment for weddings, parties and corporate functions.
Marquee Erectors (2). Wages £6.00 per hour, for minimum 8 hours per day. Staff are needed from April to October for a minimum of 1 week. Applicants must be over 18, strong and fit, preferably with a driving licence. Must be active, willing to travel and flexible regarding working hours. Foreign applicants are welcome but must speak English and have a valid work permit.
   Applications to Mr Rowan Cope from 1 January at the above address.

MARQUEE MAGIC: 45 Packmores Road, London SE9 2NA (☎0870-085 1405; fax 020-8859 4089; e-mail marqueemagic@tiscali.co.uk; www.marqueemagic. co.uk).
Marquee Installers (3). Wages at £6 per hour. To work 10 hours a day, from June to early September. Must have own transport within local area for early morning start.
   Applications to Tony Bourke at the above address.

SAVOIR FAIRE (MARQUEES) LTD: 1 Woodside Terrace, Cadmore End, High Wycombe, Buckinghamshire HP14 3PE (☎01494-883663; fax 01494-883553; e-

mail party@savoirfaire.co.uk; www.savoirfaire.co.uk).
Marquee Erectors (up to 10). Wages from £5.00 per hour with occasional tips. To work Monday to Friday from 8am to 5pm or 6pm plus occasional weekend work at time and a half. Required from April to September. Must be sociable, work well in a small team, preferably strong and at least five feet eight inches in height. No accommodation available.

Applications to Richard Hall, Managing Director, at the above address.

Sport

BRAY LAKE WATERSPORTS: Monkey Island Lane, Windsor Road, Maidenhead, Berkshire SL6 2EB (☎01628-638860; fax 01628-771441; e-mail info@braylake.com; www.braylake.com). Set next to a 50-acre lake ideal for beginners and intermediate windsurfers, sailors and canoeists. Caters for both adults and juniors. Has a good range of equipment for teaching, hire and demonstration.
Seasonal Watersports Instructors (8) to teach windsurfing, sailing and canoeing. Wages dependant on qualifications. Required from June/July to September to instruct adults and juniors in windsurfing, sailing and canoeing for 5 days a week. Instructors should hold RYA Windsurfing, RYA Sailing or BCU Canoeing Instructor's Certificates. Some static caravan accommodation available on-site.

Applications should be sent to Lindsay Frost, Centre Manager at the above address.

CONTESSA RIDING CENTRE: Willow Tree Farm, Colliers End, Ware, Hertfordshire SG11 1EN (☎01920-821792/496; fax 01920-821496; e-mail contessariding@aol.com; www.contessa-riding.com). Riding school and competition yard with a particular interest in dressage. Set rurally 30 miles north of London; easy access to Cambridge and Stansted Airport.
Stable Helpers to perform general yard duties including mucking out, grooming, tack cleaning and horse handling. Horses range from novice to grand prix standard. Pocket money, riding and self-catering accommodation are provided.

To work from 8am-5pm (beginning at 8.30am on two days) over 5½ days per week, throughout the year, especially around the holiday periods. Minimum period of work 2½ months. Applicants must be aged 17 or over; qualifications and experience preferred. Applicants should ideally be available for an interview and must apply with CV and references. Brochures available.

Applications are welcome year round to Tina Layton at the above address.

FMC: All England Lawn Tennis and Croquet Club, Church Road, Wimbledon, London, SW19 5AE (☎020-8971 2465; fax 020-8944 6362; e-mail resourcing@ fmccatering.co.uk; www.fmccatering.co.uk). FMC is one of the largest outdoor event caterers in Europe. Its varied agenda covers some of the most prestigious events in the society calendar including The Championships at Wimbledon, Chelsea Football Club, the Harlequins Rugby Club at the Twickenham Stoop Ground and the Brit Insurance Oval, Kennington, as well as numerous other outdoor and private catering events.
Staff of all categories, including Management and Chefs are required to work at events. The Championships at Wimbledon require 1,600 staff between Saturday 23 June and Sunday 8 July inclusive. Hours of work and rates of pay are by arrangement. Applicants must be able to supply photocopied proof of their right to work in the UK with applications and provide the original on the date of their first assignment. Applicants for all events should be people who are outgoing and fun loving with good communication skills.

For an *application* pack and more information about the Championships and all our other events please contact the FMC Personnel Department at the above address.

FRENCH BROTHERS LTD: The Clewer Boathouse, Clewer Court Road, Windsor, Berks SL4 5JH (☎01753-851900; fax 01753-832303; e-mail sales@boat-trips.co.uk; www.boat-trips.co.uk). French Brothers is a prestigious Thames passenger boat operator.
Boat Crew, Bar Staff and Caterers required at any time, though work is usually seasonal. Minimum period of work 6 weeks. Foreign applicants with sufficient English to understand the safety conditions of the business are welcome.
Applications should be made to Chris Brace, Operations Manager, at the above address. Interview required.

GREEN LANE RIDING TUITION LTD: Green Lane, off Garth Road, Lower Morden, Surrey SM4 6SF (☎020-8337 3853; fax 020-8337-8383; e-mail greenlanetuition@yahoo.co.uk; www.greenlaneridingtuition.com). A BHS approved riding school. Lots of school riding activities and thriving pony club, with the opportunity to ride young horses.
Riding Teacher (1). Work involves mostly teaching and general yard duties; riding is available. Wages are according to experience; to work either full-time or part-time. Applicants must either have BHSAI qualification or be very experienced with children.
Applications should be sent to the Secretary at the above address.

Voluntary Work

Archaeology

SILCHESTER ROMAN TOWN LIFES PROJECT: Reading University, Department of Archaeology, Whiteknights, PO Box 227, Reading, Berkshire RG6 6AB (☎0118-931 8132; fax 0118-931 6718; e-mail archaeology@rdg.ac.uk; www.silchester.rdg.ac.uk).
Situated midway between Reading and Basingstoke, a major long-term excavation of the industrial and commercial area of a Roman town.
Volunteers are required for July and August to work on the excavation. The project is suitable for both beginners and those with more experience. Minimum age 16. The cost is approximately £200 per 6-day week, which includes food and campsite facilities with hot showers, although volunteers must provide their own camping equipment.
Visit the above website for further information, or contact Amanda Clarke at the above address.

Children

CHILDREN'S COUNTRY HOLIDAYS FUND (CCHF): Stafford House, 91 Keymer Road, Hassocks, West Sussex BN6 8QJ (☎01273-847760; e-mail enquiries. cchf@staffordhouse.org.uk; www.childrensholidays.org.uk).
CCHF provides residential activity holidays and weekends for London children in need who have no other chance of a holiday. CCHF runs action-packed Activity Holidays that last for 7 days during the school summer holidays, and Activity Weekends that run throughout the year, based at countryside children's centres.

Volunteers are responsible for the care and welfare of 4 children, within a larger group under the guidance of an experienced Leader. Volunteers choose the amount of weeks/weekends they volunteer. High quality training is provided, as well as accommodation and food. All expenses paid. Minimum age 18. UK residents only.
Applications between January and May only. CRB check required.

THE OK CLUB: Christian Holt House, Denmark Road, Kilburn, London NW6 5BP (☎020-7624 6292; fax 020-7372 6598; e-mail keith@okclub.org.uk; www.okclub. org.uk).
Christian organisation carrying out a wide variety of work with young people and children.
Volunteers (40) required to engage in work with children, young people and young adults, or related administration. Part time and full time opportunities available. Reasonable expenses and travel provided for part time volunteers; pocket money and food allowance for full time. Accommodation is available free to full-time staff and at a low cost to part-time staff. No minimum period of work for part time volunteers; full time positions are for one year minimum and applicants should be committed Christians. Volunteers required all year round.
Applicants should preferably have experience in youth/children's work or skills such as sports/art/IT. Foreign applicants with appropriate permits welcome.
Applications should be made to Keith Lunn, Director, by e-mail or at the above address.

Conservation and the Environment

CORAL CAY CONSERVATION LTD: 40-42 Osnaburgh Street, London NW1 3ND (☎0870-750 0668; fax 0870-750 0667; e-mail info@coralcay.org; www.coralcay. org).
Coral Cay Conservation sends Volunteers to the Caribbean and Asia-Pacific to take part in community-based coral reef and tropical forest conservation projects.
Volunteer Marketing Assistants are required to help manage Volunteer recruitment campaigns.
The above is needed to work for Coral Cay Conservation (CCC), a not-for-profit organisation established in 1986 to provide support for the conservation and sustainable use of marine and terrestrial resources. CCC maintains full-time expedition projects in the Philippines, Trinidad and Tobago and Fiji.
Assistants are required to work at CCC's London offices on a voluntary basis. For applicants able to commit to approximately 900 hours, a free four week placement on a CCC expedition will be awarded. This offer excludes the costs of flights, insurance and other costs not included in the standard CCC Expedition Fee.
Applications at any time to the above address.

ENVIRONMENTAL INVESTIGATION AGENCY: 62-63 Upper Street, London N1 0NY (☎020-7354 7960; fax 020-7354 7961; e-mail ukinfo@eia-international. org; www.eia-international.org).
The EIA is an independent, international campaigning organisation committed to investigating and exposing environmental crime.
Volunteers needed to help the small team of staff in various areas, including general office administration, assisting with fundraising, and aiding campaigns with research. Volunteers are required for anything from a few hours per day through to full time; lunch and travel expenses are usually covered.
Enquiries to Rachel Noble at the above address.

LONDON AND WEST MIDDLESEX NATIONAL TRUST VOLUNTEERS:
c/o Hughenden Manor, High Wycombe, Buckinghamshire HP14 4LA (e-mail bookings@lwmntv.org.uk; www.lwmntv.org.uk).
The largest regional volunteer group of the National Trust, with more than 250 members from all over the UK. Members carry out practical conservation all over the country.
Volunteers to repair paths, build bridges, clear scrub, repair dry stone walls and carry out other general land management and access work. Volunteers participate in weekend programmes, staying in Basecamps, usually dormitory style accommodation with basic facilities. Volunteers work all day Saturday, until lunchtime on Sunday.
Basecamps are supervised by National Trust wardens who provide safety equipment and tools. The group is open to anyone over 16. Volunteers need enthusiasm and old clothes. The weekends have leaders who organise catering and travel. Membership of the group costs £6.00 per year. A typical weekend will cost around £10 for food, accommodation and travel.
Contact the above address for an information pack or visit the website for full details on the group.

SAVE THE RHINO INTERNATIONAL: 16 Winchester Walk, London SE1 9AQ (☎020-7357 7474; fax 020-7357 9666; e-mail henry@savetherhino.org; www.savetherhino.org).
A London-based charity raising funds for projects protecting rhinos in Africa and Asia. Save the Rhino raises funds through endurance challenges, applications to trusts and foundations, marathons, donations, merchandise and membership.
Office and Event Volunteers needed to assist in general office work or occasionally help out at events. Office work includes data entry, managing mailings, research and administration, while event help can be anything from manning the merchandise stall, running in a rhino costume or marshalling a race. Volunteers work from 10am to 6pm with lunch and travel expenses provided.
Applications to Henry French at the above address.

Heritage

ALEXANDER FLEMING LABORATORY MUSEUM: St. Mary's Hospital, Praed Street, London W2 1NY (☎020-7886 6528 fax 020-7886 6739; e-mail kevin.brown@st-marys.nhs.uk; www.st-marys.org.uk/about/fleming_museum.htm).
The museum has been designated an International Historic Chemical Landmark and visitors come from all over the world. Situated close to Paddington Station, with good transport links.
Volunteer Guides needed all year round to conduct visitors around the Alexander Fleming Laboratory Museum, which is based on a reconstruction of the laboratory in which Fleming discovered penicillin. The job includes making a short presentation and retail duties in a small museum shop. Full training will be supplied: knowledge of the subject matter is not required. Hours from 10am to 1pm from Monday to Thursday. In addition the museum offers a summer placement working as a volunteer in the archives of St Mary's Hospital and as a guide, offering experience in archives and museums. Hours from 10 am to 5pm from Monday to Friday. Minimum age of 16. The museum lacks disabled access.
Applications to Kevin Brown, Trust Archivist and Museum Curator.

THE ALICE TRUST: Waddesdon Manor, Aylesbury, Buckinghamshire HP18 0JH (☎01296-653307; fax 01296-653212; e-mail liz.wilkinson@nationaltrust.org.uk;

www.waddesdon.org.uk).
Waddesdon Manor, a National Trust property, is a magnificent French Renaissance-style chateau, home to the Rothschild Collection of 18th century French furniture and decorative arts, with acclaimed Victorian gardens.
Volunteer Gardeners required for a diverse range of maintenance tasks, alongside the team of professional gardeners. A limited number of full-time residential internships are available, normally for a period of up to 6 months. Rent-free accommodation and some assistance with food expenses may be available. Commitment and reasonable fitness are required and experience is preferred but not essential. Overseas English speaking applicants are considered. Early application advised.
Other volunteer opportunities may sometimes be available within the Collection; contact the above address to find out more.
Applications with CV and references to Liz Wilkinson (ref SJ7) at the above address.

THE FORGE MUSEUM AND VICTORIAN COTTAGE GARDEN: High Street, Much Hadham, Hertfordshire SG10 6BS (tel/fax 01279-843301; e-mail cristinaharrison@btopenworld.com; www.hertsmuseums.org.uk/forge).
The Forge Museum is owned by the Hertfordshire Building Preservation Trust. It is situated in the picturesque village of Much Hadham, and houses displays about blacksmithing and village life.
Volunteer Museum Assistants (2). These positions are aimed at those interested in gaining museum work experience. To work at least 2 days a week and up to 5 days a week. Applicants must be over 16. No previous experience is necessary.
Volunteer Conservation Assistants (10). These positions are aimed at anyone interested in gaining experience of conservation work in museums. No previous experience is necessary as training will be given. To work between 1 and 5 days per week.
Volunteers are required from July to the end of August for a minimum period of 1 week.
Applications should be addressed to Cristina Harrison and sent to the above address from May onwards.

Physically/Mentally Disabled

INDEPENDENT LIVING ALTERNATIVES: Trafalgar House, Grenville Place, London NW7 3SA (☎020-8906 9265; e-mail enquiry@ILAnet.co.uk; www.ILAnet.co.uk).
Volunteers required to provide support for people with disabilities, to enable them to live independently in their own homes. The work involves helping them get dressed, go to the toilet, drive, do the housework, and so on. Volunteers receive £63.50 a week plus free accommodation, usually in the London area or in Cumbria. ILA offers a chance to learn about disability issues and see London at the same time. No qualifications required, except good English. Vacancies arise all year round.
Applications should be sent to Tracey Jannaway at the above address.

INDEPENDENT LIVING SCHEMES: Lewisham Social Care and Health, John Henry House, 299 Verdant Lane, Catford, London SE 6 1TP (☎020-8314 7239: 24 hours; fax 020-8314 3013; e-mail ken.smith@lewisham.gov.uk).
Part of a local government body which assists disabled people. Very close to central London.
Volunteers (3 at any one time) to help disabled people living independently. Duties

include dealing with the personal care and assisting with the leisure and social activities of independent people with severe disabilities (lifting is involved). Allowances of £60 per week and an additional £15 per month are paid, plus free, shared accommodation with all bills covered. To work on a rota basis with other volunteers; usually 24 hours on (sleeping in) followed by 48 hours off.

Volunteers are needed around the year; six-month commitment required. Applicants should be aged 16 or over and should have a commitment to civil rights for disabled people. Good command of spoken English is preferred.

Applications to Kenneth Smith, Project Worker, at the above address. An interview in London is usually required before an offer can be made.

KITH & KIDS: The Irish Centre, Pretoria Road, London N17 8DX (☎020-8801 7432; fax 020-8885 3035; e-mail projects@kithandkids.org.uk; www.kithandkids. org.uk).
A self-help organisation that provides support for families of children with a physical or learning disability.
Volunteers needed to take part in social development schemes working on a two-to-one basis with disabled children and young people, helping them with everyday skills and community integration. Hours of work 9.30am-5pm daily. Minimum period of work 2 consecutive weeks in August or a week at Christmas/Easter. There is also a 3-day training course before each project. Lunch and travel expenses within Greater London provided. Minimum age 16. No experience necessary, but lots of enthusiasm essential. No accommodation available. The organisation does also run a one-week camping holiday in August with accommodation for volunteers.
For *further details* contact the Volunteer Organiser at the above address.

SHAD (WANDSWORTH): Volunteer Manager, SHAD Wandsworth, 5 Bedford Hill, London SW12 9ET (☎020-8675 6095; e-mail volunteering@shad.org.uk; www. shad.org.uk).
SHAD (Support and Housing Assistance for people with Disabilities) is a voluntary organisation that aims to enable independent living to severely physically disabled people who would otherwise need to rely on their families or residential care.
Volunteers are required to act as Personal Care assistants for disabled people. Volunteers receive £60 per week personal allowance, expenses, free flat share with other volunteers, support, training, excellent work experience and generous time off. No experience is necessary but a minimum commitment of 4 months or more is required. All nationalities are welcome but a good standard of English is essential.
For an information pack and application form *contact* the above address.

WOODLARKS CAMP SITE TRUST: Kathleen Marshall House, Tilford Road, Farnham, Surrey GU10 3RN (☎01252-716279; e-mail enquiries@woodlarks.org.uk; www.woodlarks.org.uk).
Woodlarks Camp Site Trust provides a setting for people of all ages with disabilities to expand their capabilities and have fun. This small-scale camping site and woodland activity area has facilities including a heated outdoor swimming pool, an aerial runway, a trampoline, archery and more. A dining/recreation room, disabled-friendly toilet block and some indoor sleeping accommodation are alongside the camping area. Woodlarks is staffed and maintained entirely by volunteers.
Camps are held weekly from May to September. Six open camps accept individual disabled campers and require **Volunteer Carers/Enablers**. Volunteers are normally taken on for one camp lasting a week, though some help on more. Tent accommodation provided. Helpers pay a modest fee to cover the cost of food, outings.

Written *applications* to the Honorary Secretary, Kathleen Marshall House, at the above address, enclosing an s.a.e or IRC.

Social and Community Schemes

BATTERSEA DOGS & CATS HOME: 4 Battersea Park Road, London SW8 4AA (☎020-7622 3626; fax 020-7622 6451; e-mail jobs@dogshome.org; www.dogshome. org).
Probably Britain's best-known and largest dog home, also with two country re-homing centres at Old Windsor and Brands Hatch in Kent.
Volunteers are needed at all three centres to walk the dogs and socialise with dogs and cats throughout the year.
For further *details*, visit the website, or send applications to the above e-mail address.

DOGS TRUST: 17 Wakley Street, London EC1V 7RQ (☎020-7837 0006; fax 020-7833 2701; e-mail jobs@dogstrust.org.uk; www.dogstrust.org.uk).
The UK's largest dog charity, founded in 1891 to protect dogs from abuse of every kind.
Volunteers are always needed to help the kennel staff with their duties and for dog walking. Volunteers must be at least 16 in order to comply with Dogs Trust's insurance terms. For further details of local centres, visit the website.
Some of the larger re-homing centres can offer **Work Placements**. Applicants should make their requests and give reasons in writing.
To *apply* for either opportunity, contact your local re-homing Centre Manager.

THE GRAIL CENTRE: 125 Waxwell Lane, Pinner, Middlesex HA5 3ER (☎020-8866 0505; fax 020-8866 1408; e-mail waxwell@compuserve.com).
The Grail is home to a community of Christian women. The Elizabethan house has modern extensions and is set in 10 acres of wooded garden, which contain several hermitages for individual retreats.
2-3 Volunteers are needed throughout the year to live alongside the resident community and help maintain the house and garden. Much of the work is manual. Duties are arranged on a flexible basis and volunteers are required to be available for 7½ hours daily. There is one full day off a week and one day's holiday per 2 weeks worked. Those who need a well-defined timetable/fixed hours would find this pattern unhelpful. Volunteers are offered board, their own room and an allowance for necessary expenses. Minimum age 20; no upper limit. No special skills are required, but good will and sense of humour are essential.
Overseas applicants pay their own fares and arrange the correct immigration clearance but an invitation letter is provided on request. EU applicants should be familiar with medical cover arrangements between their country and the UK. Others should be insured or prepared to pay the cost of any treatment they may require. Applicants must have enough spoken and written English to function in this very busy household. In-house lessons can be arranged for those interested. Religious observance is not a requirement.
Send a letter, CV and a recent photograph to the Volunteer Co-ordinator at the above address. Early applications are likely to be more successful. All applications must include a s.a.e. or an IRC.

HACKNEY INDEPENDENT LIVING TEAM: Richmond House, 1a Westgate Street, London E8 3RL (☎020-8985 5511 volunteer hotline ext. 222; fax 020-8533

2029; e-mail volunteers@hilt.org.uk; www.hilt.org.uk).

Helps adults with learning disabilities in Hackney to live in the community as independently as possible, and to continue to develop their independence and personal identity. Based in North East London.

Independent Living Support Volunteers (30). Volunteers may be involved in all projects and activities of HILT. Some of the ways in which volunteers have supported service users include sports, leisure and social activities, arranging and accompanying on holidays and in assessing education and training opportunities. Volunteers support service users in personal development and achieving goals. Living allowance of £60 per week, plus weekly zones 1-2 Travelcard and free accommodation.

Applicants must be committed to enabling people with learning difficulties to have as much control over their lives as possible. They should also help provide a service which reflects the cultural, racial and religious needs of service users, and promote anti-discriminatory practice. They should have a willingness to understand service users' emotional needs, and attend regular meetings with supervisors and staff and communicate ideas and suggestions.

To provide 35 hours a week support on a shift basis. Minimum period of work 4 months at any time of the year. Applicants must be over 18. All volunteers have their own furnished room, including all bills apart from telephone. Food allowance is incorporated into weekly allowance. Overseas applicants must have a good level of conversational English, and the right to enter the UK. Interview necessary.

Applications as far in advance of intended start date as possible to the Volunteer Co-ordinator.

HEALTHPROM: Star House, 104-108 Grafton Road, London NW5 4BD (☎020-7284 1620; fax 020-7284-1881; e-mail healthprom@healthprom.org; www.healthprom.org).

Healthprom works in partnerships to improve healthcare for the most vulnerable in Eastern Europe and Central Asia.

Some ongoing **Voluntary Opportunities** exist in administrative, research, communications and fundraising areas. Excellent experience is to be gained by committed and reliable volunteers with an interest in international development work. Local travel and lunch expenses will be paid.

Applications, including CV, to the Business Manager, at the above address.

HOLY CROSS CENTRE: Holycross Church, The Crypt, Cromer Street, London WC1H 8JU (tel/fax 020-7278 8687; e-mail cmt@hcct.org.uk; www.hcct.org.uk).

Social centre in the Kings Cross area of London with mental health issues and drug/alcohol problems, some of whom may be homeless.

Part-Time Volunteers (40) needed to run the centre, befriending clients, catering and offering peer support in a friendly and informal atmosphere, with the possibility of teaching arts and crafts and computing. Volunteers work 5 hours per week. Minimum commitment 3 months. In return they receive travel expenses and a meal for each session. Training and support provided.

Applications to M.Willett, Centre Management Team, at the above address.

SIMON COMMUNITY: Office F2, 89-93 Fonthill Road, London N4 3JH (☎020-7561 8270; fax 020-7619 3589; e-mail info@simoncommunity.org.uk; www.simoncommunity.org.uk).

The Simon Community is a community of volunteers and homeless people living and working with those for whom no other provision exists.

Volunteers are expected to help run its projects, including two residential homes, as well as participate in group meetings, regular outreach work and campaigning and fund raising. The community also conducts tea runs round London and other outreach work.

B & L are provided plus £33 per week pocket money. A small amount is also saved for volunteers when they leave. Volunteers are required throughout the year for a minimum of 6 months. All applicants should be aged 19 or over, have a mature and responsible attitude and a good command of the English language.

Initial enquiries to the above address.

SOUTHWARK HABITAT FOR HUMANITY: 93 Gordon Road, London SE15 3RR (☎020-7732 0066; fax 020-7732 6060; e-mail administrator@shfh.org.uk; www.southwarkhfh.org.uk).

Volunteer Construction Workers to work with an innovative community self-help group, building homes to provide affordable housing for people with low incomes. Southwark HFH is part of HFH Great Britain.

The construction programme is continuous throughout the year so help is needed on weekdays and Saturdays; volunteers can help for as little as one day. Volunteers must pay for their own transport but lunch and hot and cold drinks will be provided. Applicants should be aged over 18; no building skills or experience are needed as skilled supervisors direct the work.

If interested, *call* the above telephone number.

Vacation Traineeships & Internships

Accountancy, Banking and Insurance

ABN AMRO: 250 Bishopsgate, London EC2M 4AA (☎020-7678 7874; fax 020-7678 2588; www.graduate.abnamro.com).

One of the world's leading financial institutions. With more than 3,000 branches and approx. 100,000 employees in 59 countries. It serves major corporations and institutions and operates in three distinct customer segments: Wholesale Clients, Consumer and Commercial Clients, Private Clients and Asset Management.

Summer Internship Programme available in Wholesale Clients in London to penultimate-year graduates – a 10 to 12-week structured programme. 100 interns to be recruited worldwide across London, Amsterdam, Paris, Frankfurt, New York, Hong Kong, Sydney and Sao Paolo. Also offers a range of internship opportunities lasting from 2-6 months depending on location.

Visit www.graduate.abnamro.com for more details, entry requirements, and how to apply. Check website for deadlines in other locations .

BANK OF ENGLAND: Threadneedle Street, London EC2R 8AH (☎020-7601 5577; fax 020-7601 5460; e-mail recruitment@bankofengland.co.uk; www.bankofengland.co.uk/jobs).

Central bank of the United Kingdom; at the centre of economic policy making and implementation.

Summer Placements available to penultimate year undergraduates reading any subject and final year/ graduates about to take an MSc in Economics and/ or Finance. Applicants must have an interest in economics and finance and be expecting a minimum 2:1 degree. Placements are based in London and will last 6-8 weeks in summer 2007. For further information refer to the website.

Applications should be made via the online form at www.bankofengland.co.uk/ jobs by 8 December 2006.

BLOOMBERG L.P.: City Gate House, 39-45 Finsbury Square, London EC2A 1PQ (fax 020-7661 5809; http://careers.bloomberg.com or www.bloomberg.co.uk).
Approx. 120 Internships in most areas of the business including Sales, Broadcast and Broadcast Operations, HR, IT Support, Global Data and R & D.
The internships would suit university students or graduates but anyone can apply. Looking for people with proven interest in Finance. A fluency in a second European language is a bonus. Internships last 10 weeks and the wage is dependent on experience. No accommodation is provided. Overseas students with a UK work permit are welcome.
Applications must be made via the website.

EUROMONEY INSTITUTIONAL INVESTOR PLC: Nestor House, Playhouse Yard, London EC4V 5EX (☎020-7779 8888; fax 020-7779 8842; e-mail people@ euromoneyplc.com; www.euromoneyplc.com).
Euromoney Institutional Investor plc is an international publishing and events company based in central London. It often has vacation and work experience placements available for university undergraduates or gap year students with excellent grades and an interest in finance. The work available includes research or project work for our editorial teams, or telesales and data entry work for our sales and marketing teams. Length of placements and wage vary depending on the work available. Accommodation is not provided. Students of any discipline are considered, with economics, law and languages particularly useful. Qualified overseas applicants who hold a relevant work permit are welcome to apply.
For further information about these employment opportunities, visit the employment section of the company's website.
Applications, including CV and covering letter should be sent by e-mail to people@ euromoneyplc.com or by post to Sarah Widdicombe at the above address.

FINANCIAL SERVICES AUTHORITY: 26 The North Colonnade, Canary Wharf, London E14 5HS (☎020-7066 3568; 020-7066 1019; e-mail fsa.graduates.gov.uk; www.fsa.gov.uk/careers). The FSA ensures integrity in the UK financial markets and protects consumer interests.
The FSA **Summer Internship** is available to 30 students in their penultimate year at university. Wages are approximately £400 per week. The placements last for 10 weeks between June and August. Interns spend their time getting to know how the FSA upholds the highest standards and how that impacts on the world of business. Through project-based work in one department, interns will have the chance to gain a unique insight into the UK financial system.
Candidates should have a minimum 300 UCAS points, be expecting a 2:1 degree and be able to show a keen commercial awareness. Candidates must have the unrestricted right to work in the UK.
Applications should be made online via the FSA website. An interview and assessment centre test will be required.

GOLDMAN SACHS INTERNATIONAL: 133 Fleet Street, London EC4A 2BB (☎020-7552 1738; www.gs.com/careers).
Goldman Sachs is an international global investment, banking, securities and investment management firm.
Summer Analyst Placements are available for **250-350** students in their penultimate

year at university who have a proven interest in Finance. Wages are competitive and depend on experience. The placements last for 10 weeks between June and September. Accommodation is not available. Overseas applicants of any nationality are welcome to apply, provided they speak fluent English.

Applications should be made online via the above website before 30 December. An interview will be necessary.

INSTITUTE FOR FISCAL STUDIES: 7 Ridgmount Street, London WC1E 7AE (☎020-7291 4800; fax 020-7323 4780; e-mail mailbox@ifs.org.uk; www.ifs.org. uk).

IFS is an independent research institute which specialises in the economic analysis of public policy, especially in the fields of tax and benefit policy, the public finances and public spending. It aims to bridge the gap between purely academic research and issues of practical policy. The research is largely orientated towards microeconomic analysis, and has a strong quantitative flavour.

The institute makes use of major UK surveys of households, individuals and firms in order to analyse the impact of taxation and other public policies on individuals' and companies' behaviour. Research is disseminated through conferences and publications. IFS aims to provide impartial information from a politically independent standpoint and to inform public debate.

IFS offers approx. **5 Placements** which last for 6 weeks in the summer in London. Trainees can expect to work for a research team on a particular project. Tasks involve the preparation and analysis of data, the conducting of literary searches and writing up research findings. Applicants should have a minimum of 2 years undergraduate experience in Economics or a closely related subject (or 3 years if following a 4-year course). The salary in 2006 was £290 per week. No accommodation is provided, paid travel expenses to interview within the UK only. Overseas applicants entitled to work in the UK are considered.

Application details, including the closing date, will be posted on the IFS website (www.ifs.org.uk) each autumn. Interviews take place in London.

JP MORGAN: 10 Aldermansbury, London EC2V 7RJ (www.jpmorgan.com/ careers).

Investment banking is a complex industry, so whilst working with JP Morgan for the summer, you'll gain an insight into how one of the world's largest financial institutions works.

200 Summer Internships are available within the investment banking department. Applicants are given full responsibility from day one, so whilst they have the opportunity to learn from those around them, they'll also have a job as a fully contributing member of the team. The work can be intense, so JP Morgan are looking for students with impressive academic qualifications, outstanding personal qualities and a good deal of ambition. Wages are highly competitive. Internships last for 10 weeks between June and September. Overseas applicants are welcome to apply, provided they speak English to the same level as a native speaker.

Applications should be made online via the website. The application process lasts from 1 September to 21 January. An interview will be necessary.

MERRILL LYNCH EUROPE PLC: Merrill Lynch Financial Centre, 2 King Edward Street, London EC1A 1HQ (☎020-7996 3528; ml.com/careers/europe).

110 Summer Internships are available within the following departments: Global Markets, Investment Banking, Research and Technology. Internships are aimed at penultimate year university students. There are no required degree disciplines but students should have outstanding academic achievement and be able to demonstrate quantitative and analytical problem solving skills.

Compensation is competitive. Internships start in June and last 10 weeks. No accommodation is provided, although advice on how to find accommodation may be offered. Foreign applicants are welcome but all applicants must possess a valid work permit. Further details about the departments where internships are available are available on the website.

All *applications* must be made online at ml.com/careers/europe by 5pm on 12 January.

Business and Management

DAVY'S WINE MERCHANTS: 44-46 Tooley Street, London SE1 2SZ (☎020-7716 3300; e-mail cdt@davy.co.uk; www.davy.co.uk).
Wine merchants and operators of Davy's Wine Bars and Restaurants. They also operate several 'Bar Café Bars'.

Davy's offer eight paid **Work Experience** placements with both on and off job training for people looking to enter the wine bar industry. The placements also include courses on Basic Food Hygiene, Introduction to Wine and First Aid. Placements last from 6 to 12 months. Applicants should be at least 18 years old and have a basic understanding of hospitality, as well as a strong sense of team spirit and a commitment to providing excellent customer service. Good spoken English and documented evidence confirming the right to work legally in the UK essential. Some accommodation is available.

Written applications or *e-mails* should be sent to the Recruitment Administration Officer at the above address.

Charity Work

BRITISH RED CROSS: 44 Moorfields, London EC2Y 9AL (☎020-7877 7077; e-mail mkemsley@redcross.org.uk; www.redcross.org.uk). The British Red Cross helps people in crisis, whoever and wherever they are. They are part of a global network of volunteers, responding to natural disasters, conflicts and individual emergencies.

They offer **15 to 20 Internships** at their central London office. The internships are unpaid but reasonable travel expenses are reimbursed and lunch is provided. Interns should expect to work for 2 to 3 days per week for 8 to 10 weeks from July to September. Each internship has its own role description. However, all interns should be enthusiastic, committed and interested in pursuing a career in the voluntary sector. The internships are aimed at university students, school leavers or those in further education. They also accept applications from those changing career path. Overseas applicants are welcome to apply, provided they have the relevant documentation and funding.

Applications should be made from May via the above website. An interview will be necessary.

CANCER RESEARCH UK: 61 Lincolns' Inn Fields, London WC2A 3PX (☎0845-009 4290; e-mail internships@cancer.org.uk; www.cancerresearchuk.org/internships). One of the world's leading independent organisations dedicated to cancer research. They support research into all aspects of cancer through the work of more than 3,000 scientists, doctors and nurses.

Cancer Research UK is looking for approximately **50** high-calibre individuals looking to gain experience in the fields of fundraising, marketing, retail, communications and campaigning for their **Internship programme**. Interns work on real projects that will make a difference to the charity. They are also provided with a thorough induction to the charity, as well as given mid-internship training on CV writing and interview techniques.

Internships are unpaid, but travel and lunch expenses are provided. Applicants are required to work normal office hours for a period of 12 weeks from July to September. No accommodation is available. Applicants are usually undergraduates, graduates or professionals looking for a career change. Overseas applicants are welcome to apply provided they have the correct documentation to work in the UK and speak English to the same standard as a native speaker.

Applications should be made to the Internship Executive via e-mail to the above address. For more information, visit the Cancer Research website from April. An interview will be necessary.

THE YOUNG FOUNDATION: 18 Victoria Park Square, Bethnal Green, London E2 9PF (☎020-8980 6263; e-mail lilli.geissendorfer@youngfoundation.org.uk; www. youngfoundation.org.uk).
A centre for social innovation that identifies and understands unmet social needs and develops practical initiatives to address them. They work in many fields, including health, education, housing and cities, and bring together research and action, including the creation of new enterprises.
Research, Launchpad and Transforming Neighbourhood Internships (up to 10). Interns' tasks usually include: background project research; literature searches and reviews; drafting briefings, articles, speeches and presentations; participation in project meetings; arranging, conducting and transcribing research interviews and helping to organise and run events.

Internships are unpaid, but a £5 lunch expense and travel expenses (within London zones 1-6) are provided daily. Required to work 3 days a week for 2 months between May and September. No accommodation available. All applicants should be 18 or over, and must be able to show a commitment to progressive social change. Foreign applicants are welcome to apply, provided they have the relevant work permits.

Applications should be made from February to Lilli Geissendorfer at the above address. An interview will be necessary, but phone interviews are possible.

Law

ALLEN & OVERY: One Bishops Square, London E1 6AO (☎020-7330 3000; fax 020-7330 9999; e-mail graduate.recruitment@allenovery.com; www.allenovery.com/careeruk).
Allen & Overy is an international legal practice comprising Allen & Overy LLP and its affiliated undertakings. It has over 450 partners and some 4,800 staff working in 25 major centres on three continents serving business, financial institutions, government and private individuals. Expertise in a wide range of areas, including corporate and commercial, banking, capital markets, real estate, litigation, tax, employment, anti-monopoly and I.T. With a network of offices, Allen & Overy respond quickly and effectively on a co-ordinated worldwide basis.

Allen & Overy offers three-week **Summer Placements** to penultimate year university students (law and non-law) interested in a career in law. The schemes take place in the London office and the salary is £250 per week. Students spend time in two departments, seeing how the business functions by working with lawyers and participating in a wide range of training and social events. During the three weeks, students will carry out legal research and observe lawyers in action; training will be given in skills such as negotiation and interview techniques. Students will also be invited to social events with other vacation students, trainees, associates and partners.

Application forms are available online at www.allenovery.com/careeruk from 1 November. For paper applications, please contact Graduate Recruitment at the above address.

ASHURST: Broadwalk House, 5 Appold Street, London (☎020-7638 1111; fax 020-7859 1800; e-mail gradrec@ashurst.com; www.ashurst.com).

International City law firm with 175 partners, around 550 solicitors and a total staff of 1,600. Main areas of practice are in: Corporate; Employment, Incentives and Pensions; Energy; Transport and Infrastructure; EU and Competition,; International Finance; Litigation; Real Estate; Tax and Technology and Commercial.

Ashurst offers **65 Placements in the Summer and 25 at Easter**. During the schemes, students are placed in a different department each week and share an office with a solicitor or partner. The main aim is that students become involved in the solicitor's daily workload by completing 'real' tasks such as letter writing, drafting, legal research and attending client meetings. In addition, a series of lectures, workshops and social activities are arranged.

Penultimate year law degree students and final year non-law degree students are eligible. Wage is £250 per week. No accommodation is provided but help in finding some can be given. Foreign applicants who speak fluent English are welcome.

Applications should be made online to Stephen Trowbridge, Graduate Recruitment, by 31 January.

AS LAW PRACTICE SOLICITORS: 119 Kenton Road, Kenton, Harrow, Middlesex HA3 0AZ (☎020-8907 9896; fax 020-8909 1377; e-mail angelawyer@onetel.com). Offering **1-3 Work Experience** positions. Reasonable travelling expenses will be paid by arrangement. Positions are available throughout the year including the Summer, Christmas and Easter vacations; they will take place at Head Office. Accommodation is not provided but inform the company if required as arrangements can be made at your own cost; applicants must preferably be second year law students or higher qualification. Non-UK citizens are considered as long as they are law students with adequate English.

To *apply*, contact Mr Sumeray, Practice Manager, at the above address.

S.J. BERWIN LLP: 10 Queen Street Place, London EC4R 1BE (☎020-7111 2268/2393; fax 020-7111 2000; e-mail graduate.recruitment@sjberwin.com; www. sjberwin.com).

S.J. Berwin offer up to **60 Placements** on their vacation training schemes, each lasting 2 weeks. Attendees receive £270 per week. The placements are open to second year law students (and above) and third year non-law students (and above) who are expecting or have gained a 2:1 degree. Participants spend 2 weeks working in a department ideally suited to them, gaining hands-on experience in a wide range of legal tasks during the summer. While accommodation is not provided suggestions on good hostels and university halls can be made. Suitably qualified applicants from abroad who do not require a work permit are considered.

Applications should be completed online at www.sjberwin.com/gradrecruit. The deadline is 31 January 2007.

CHARLES RUSSELL LLP: 8-10 New Fetter Lane, London EC4A 1RS (☎020-7203 5241; fax 020-7203 5307; e-mail graduate.recruitment@charlesrussell.co.uk; www.charlesrussell.co.uk).

Charles Russell is a top 50 UK legal practice, providing a full range of services to UK and international companies, organisations and individuals. 75% of work carried out is corporate commercial, whilst the other 25% is for private clients.
They offer **16 Vacation Scheme Placements,** each one lasting 2 weeks between June and July. Interns will be paid £200 per week and will be expected to work for 35 hours per week. Attendees will spend the placement in two different departments. In addition to gaining an insight into the practice, interns will participate in a number of structured activities including a "mock trial". Each candidate will be nominated a mentor (a recently qualified solicitor) as well as working closely with the current trainees.

Charles Russell are looking for candidates who have or are expected to achieve a 2:1 degree, with good A Level and GCSE results and who are eligible to start a training contract in 2009 or sooner. Overseas applicants are welcome to apply, although a good command of English is required.

Applications should be completed online at the Graduate Recruitment pages of the website. The application process lasts from 1 December 2006 to 31 January 2007.

CMS CAMERON McKENNA: Mitre House, 160 Aldersgate Street, London EC1A 4DD (☎0845-300 0491; fax 020-7367 2000; e-mail gradrec@cms-cmck.com; www. grad.law-now.com).
CMS Cameron McKenna, an international city law firm, offers **Two-Week Placements** to students during Easter, Summer and Christmas. Positions are open to second year law students or final year non-law students who expect to achieve at least a 2:1 degree. The firm is distinctive, unstuffy and approachable, and is looking for creative, bright, commercially aware, committed people who have the potential to contribute to its future success.

To apply visit the firm's online application form or call 0845-300 0491 for an information pack. The closing date for the Easter and Summer schemes is 16 February 2007.

CLIFFORD CHANCE: 10 Upper Bank Street, Canary Wharf, London E14 5JJ (☎020-7006 1000; fax 020-7006 5555; e-mail contacthr@cliffordchance.com;www. cliffordchance.com/gradsuk).
Clifford Chance is a truly global law firm operating as one organisation throughout the world, aiming to provide the highest quality professional advice by combining technical expertise with an appreciation of the commercial environment in which clients work. The range of work performed by the firm worldwide can be divided into six main areas of business: Banking and Finance, Capital Markets, Corporate, Litigation and Dispute Resolution, Real Estate and Tax, Pensions and Employment.
Vacation Placements (85). Students will be given a broad overview of Clifford Chance, through being involved in live projects within a close-knit team environment. The work will be demanding, but support is always close at hand; your colleagues will ensure your experience is as rewarding as possible. You will also be involved in project work, skills sessions and pro bono activities as well as attending seminars on the firm's main practice areas.

During Christmas, there are two-day workshops (13/14 December 2006; 20/21 December 2006; 3/4 January 2007); at Easter, a two-week placement (26 March-5 April 2007); in Summer, two four-week placements (25 June-20 July 2007; 23 July-17 August 2007). The placements are held in London, with the opportunity to spend two weeks at one of the European offices for those with relevant language ability.

Wages £270 per week; accommodation not provided; information pack gives details to assist with the search for accommodation. Penultimate and final year Law and non-Law students with an excellent and consistent academic record and a strong 2:1 degree required. Must be highly driven individuals who can demonstrate a clear commitment to their career. Applicants must also be able to communicate accurately and fluently.

Apply online at www.cliffordchance.com/gradsuk.

CLYDE & CO: 51 Eastcheap, London EC3M 1JP (☎020-7623 1244; fax 020-7623 5427; e-mail theanswers@clydeco.com; www.clydeco.com/graduate).
Clyde & Co, the City law firm, offers **20 Summer Placements** in their London and Guildford branches. Time will be spent being supervised by a Partner, whilst attending organised talks and skills sessions.
Wages are £250 per week; no accommodation can be provided. These placements will be two weeks long, throughout June and July. The placement is open to penultimate-year law students, final year non-law students and graduates. Only EU candidates, or those who do not require a work permit, will be considered. Those who are suitable will attend an assessment morning, where they will have an interview with a member of Graduate Recruitment, undertake a written exercise, a verbal reasoning test and also a personality profile.
Apply on-line, via the above website, before 31st January.

DUNCAN LEWIS & CO: 17-19 Peterborough Road, Harrow, Middlesex HA21 2AX (☎0800-740 8081; fax 020-8515 3649; e-mail recruitment@duncanlewis.co.uk; www.duncanlewis.co.uk).
Paralegal Vacancies (8-10). Expenses paid. To work for one to four weeks in the summer, or one week at Easter at the Head Office in Hackney or at Harrow-on-the-Hill. Applicants must be university students with a law degree or equivalent. Suitably qualified non-UK applicants will be considered.
Apply to the above address by March.

LINKLATERS: 1 Silk Street, London EC2Y 8HQ (☎020-7456 2000; fax 020-7456 2222; e-mail graduate.recruitment@linklaters.com; www.linklaters.com/careers/ ukgrads).
Linklaters is a law firm which specialises in advising the world's leading companies, financial institutions and governments on challenging transactions and assignments.
Vacation Placements (110). Salaries are £275 per week. 80 placements for either four-week or two-week schemes are offered in the summer predominantly for law students (although penultimate year non-law students are welcome to apply), and 30 two-week placements are offered at Christmas for final year non-law students. Placements give students the opportunity to experience the real work of a trainee solicitor in a large, international law firm.
Applications should be made online at www.linklaters.com/careers/ukgrads. Deadline for the summer scheme: 19 January 2007.

MACFARLANES: 10 Norwich Street, London EC4A 1BD (☎020-7831 9222; fax 020-7831 9607; e-mail gradrec@macfarlanes.com; www.macfarlanes.com).
Macfarlanes is a leading law firm based in the City of London with a strong international outlook. Areas of work include corporate, property, litigation & dispute resolution and private clients.
Macfarlanes runs a **Summer Placement Scheme** that offers those seeking a training contract the opportunity to gain hands-on experience of life in a City law firm. There are **44 Positions** available for the 2 week scheme, open to candidates with a strong academic record at both A-level and degree level. Candidates receive a wage of £250

per week.
Applications by 28th February to Louisa Hatton, Graduate Recruitment Officer, at the above address.

PRITCHARD ENGLEFIELD: 14 New Street, London EC2M 4HE (☎020-7972 9720; fax 020-7972 9722; e-mail isilverblatt@pe-legal.com; www.pe-legal.com).
Student Placements (20). Two-week placements, running between the end of June and the end of August, to assist legal advisers in a variety of tasks. To work in the office in London; travel expenses will be paid. Applicants must be undergraduates or graduates who are fluent in French or German.
Apply to Mr Ian Silverblatt between 1 January and 31 March.

RICHARDS BUTLER: Beaufort House, 15 St. Botolph Street, London EC3A 7EE (☎020-7247 6555; fax 020-7247 5091; e-mail gradrecruit@richardsbutler.com; www.richardsbutler.com).
Richards Butler is a premier international law firm with its head office in the City of London and 10 other offices worldwide.
Richards Butler offer three 2-week **Vacation Schemes** during the summer to both law and non-law students in their 2nd Year or above. Students partake in skills training, presentations and work-shadowing during the two weeks. Trainees receive £250 per week and will need to arrange their own accommodation. Foreign applicants eligible to work in the UK are welcome.
Applications between November and February should be submitted online via the website by 6 February 2007.

SIMMONS & SIMMONS: City Point, One Ropemaker Street, London EC2Y 9SS (☎020-7628 2020; fax 020-7628 2070; e-mail recruitment@simmons-simmons.com; www.simmons-simmons.com/traineelawyers).
Simmons & Simmons lawyers provide high quality advice and a positive working atmosphere in their 20 international offices. The firm offers their clients a full range of legal services across numerous industry sectors. They have a particular focus on the world's fastest growing sectors that include: Financial Institutions; Energy and Infrastructure; and Technology. They provide a wide choice of service areas in which their lawyers can specialise. These include Corporate and Commercial; Communications; Outsourcing and Technology; Dispute Resolution; Employment and Benefits; EU & Competition; Financial Markets; IP; Projects; Real Estate; Taxation and Pensions.
Simmons & Simmons' **Summer Internship** is one of their primary means of selecting candidates for a career at the firm. It provides them with the chance to test suitability for a training contract. It is also a unique opportunity to get to know them and decide if they are the best firm for you..
Undergraduates usually apply for internships in their penultimate year. However, Simmons and Simmons are also happy to offer internships to final year students, graduates, mature students, international students and those changing career.
Applications should be marked for the attention of Vickie Chamberlain, Graduate Recruitment Manager from 1 November.

STEPHENSON HARWOOD: One, St Paul's Churchyard, London EC4M 8SH (☎020-7329 4422; fax 020-7329 7100; e-mail cemail@shlegal.com; www.shlegal.com).
Stephenson Harwood is an international City law firm with 7 overseas offices across Europe and Asia. A medium-sized law firm based in a spectacular location opposite

St. Paul's Cathedral, with a friendly culture and international practice. Their main areas of work are: Corporate, Employment, Pensions and Benefits, Banking and Asset Finance, Dry and Wet Shipping Litigation, Commercial Litigation, Real Estate, and Property and Insurance and Reinsurance.

Stephenson Harwood offer 18 students the opportunity to spend **2 weeks work-shadowing** solicitors. Students spend 1 week each in 2 different departments. Applicants must be second year Law undergraduates or third year non-Law undergraduates. Salary is £250 per week.

Each of the placements last 2 weeks and take place in June and July in the firm's St Paul's Office. No accommodation is provided.

Applications by online application form only to the Graduate Recruitment Department. Visit the above website for details of application dates. The application form can also be found at www.cvmailuk.com/shlegal.

TROWERS AND HAMLINS: Sceptre Court, 40 Tower Hill, London EC3N 4DX (☎020-7423 8000; fax 020-7423 8104; e-mail hstallabrass@trowers.com; www.trowers.com).

Trowers and Hamlins offers **30 Vacation Placements** for penultimate year law students and final year non-law students. Students assist solicitors and trainee solicitors for a period of two weeks during which time they rotate around two different departments. A week is spent in two different departments. Real work is given to successful applicants, for example, attending court and client meetings.

Salary at £225 a week. Successful applicants should have a minimum of 320 UCAS points and a 2:1 or above at degree level (predicted or obtained). Placements will take place in the firm's Head Office in London and also at the Manchester office. Accommodation cannot be provided.

Applications to Heather Stallabrass, Graduate Recruitment Officer, by 1 March.

WHITE & CASE: 5 Old Broad Street, London EC2N 1DW (☎020-7532 1000; fax 020-7532 1001; e-mail trainee@whitecase.com; www.whitecase.com/trainee).

White & Case is a leading global law firm with more than 2,000 lawyers in 36 offices in 24 countries. The firm works with international businesses, financial institutions, and governments worldwide on corporate and financial transactions and dispute resolution proceedings. Clients range from some of the world's longest established and most respected names to many start-up visionaries.

White and Case run two **Vacation Placement Programmes** per year – one week placements are available at Easter for 20 people, and two week placements are available during the summer for 40 people. Our programmes provide a real opportunity to discover what working in a global law firm is really like. Students will work with lawyers on a daily basis and attend organised presentations, training events and social activities.

Applicants must either be in their penultimate year of a law degree or final year of a non-law degree, and interested in pursuing a career as a solicitor. Foreign applicants are considered.

To apply for a placement in 2007, complete the online application form available on the website and submit it by 31 January 2007.

Media and Marketing

BIRDS EYE VIEW FILM FESTIVAL: Unit 310a Aberdeen Centre, 22-24 Highbury Grove, London N5 2EA (☎020-7704 9435; e-mail rosiestrang@birds-eye-view.co.uk; www.birds-eye-view.co.uk). Birds Eye View presents the new generation of talented women filmmakers from across the globe. Through London-based festivals and UK touring programmes, they entertain audiences with innovative films, including shorts, features and documentaries.

A number of **Internships** are available across the office, including project assistant, office management, research assistant and marketing assistant positions. All internships are voluntary, but travel expenses are paid. Hours are flexible, but interns must commit to a minimum of two days per week over two months. Staff required until October. No accommodation is available. All applicants must be over 18. Office experience is preferred. Overseas applicants are welcome, but must speak good English.

Applications should be made from October to Rosie Strang, Project Manager, at the above address.

BRUNSWICK ARTS: 16 Lincoln's Inn Fields, London WC2A 3ED (☎020-7396 5309; fax 020-7936 1299; e-mail lwilliams@brunswickgroup.com; www. brunswickgroup.com).

A leading public relations firm specialising in the arts. Promotes capital projects, organisations and individual activities, festivals and exhibitions.

Brunswick Arts have an ongoing programme of **Internships**, to work as a Press Assistant, assisting with the day-to-day running of a busy press office, supporting all team members. Role also includes researching for new business pitches and assisting with administrative tasks. Approximately 7 to 10 positions offered each year, to work in the head office in London for a period of 2 weeks. Positions are unpaid and travel expenses are not covered but interns receive a written reference as well as invitations to key London parties and openings, a good opportunity for long-term networking.

The internships are open to university students from all years but not school leavers or college students. Applicants should be high academic achievers with good communication skills, interested in getting a taster of the world of art and communications. Foreign applicants welcome but fluent English essential. No accommodation available.

To apply send a CV along with an outline of your availability to Louisa Williams at the above address.

GLOBE EDUCATION: Shakespeare's Globe, International Shakespeare Globe Centre, 21 New Globe Walk, Southwark, London SE1 9DT (☎020-7902 1400; fax 020-7902 1401; e-mail alex@shakespearesglobe.com; www.shakespeares-globe. org).

Restored Shakespearean theatre on the banks of the Thames with exhibition, lecture programme and workshop. Caters for 70,000+ students each year.

Administration Work Experience Placements (30). To work in the main areas of operation, including exhibitions, fundraising, communications, research, stage management, corporate events and front of house. Some stewarding and special events work will also be available in the summer.

Positions are unpaid, and expenses cannot be provided. Hours by arrangement. Minimum period of work 3 months. Positions available all year round. Applicants must be 18 years and over. Foreign applicants with fluent English welcome to apply.

Applications should be made to Alexandra Massey, Courses Manager, at the above address. Internship descriptions and an application form for each placement is available within the education section of the website. Interview required.

MERIDIAN RECORDS: PO Box 317, Eltham, London SE9 4SF (☎020-8857 3213; fax 020-8857 0731; e-mail mail@meridian–records.co.uk).

Meridian Records is a small record company specialising in the recording and production of classical records.

In 2007 the company will be seeking **One or Two Candidates** who can demonstrate motivation and a keen interest in music. No other particular qualifications are required, although applicants should have a general interest in all aspects of running a record company. An ability to read music is useful but not essential. The successful candidate(s) will participate in a wide variety of tasks including the preparation of artwork, accounting, recording, editing and the maintenance of machines, buildings and grounds.

The traineeships are unpaid, though the company may be able to offer accommodation on its premises. The placements run for a varying number of weeks during any of the three main vacations. Overseas applicants will be considered. It is the policy of Meridian Records only to employ non-smokers.

Applications should be sent to Mr Richard Hughes, Director, at the above address.

PROUD GALLERIES GROUP: Proud Galleries, 5 Buckingham Street, The Strand, London WC2N 6BP (☎020-7839 4942; fax 020-7839 4947; e-mail info@proud. co.uk; www.proudgalleries.co.uk).

The most popular private photographic gallery in Europe, with up to 10,000 paying customers per show. Launched in autumn 1998 to bring affordable high quality photography to a mainstream market by exhibiting accessible shows with popular themes. Owns two London venues.

Internship. Involves general assistance with the running of the gallery, organising/ planning of launch nights, hanging and wrapping of prints, customer service, research for future exhibitions, maintaining press books and more. Ideal for anyone interested in learning more about every aspect of the industry, including production, management and sales. Internships last for a minimum of 4 weeks. Positions available all year round. Expenses cannot be provided. Minimum age 18, qualifications important but not essential. Fluent English essential.

Applications should be made at any time to the above address.

ROYAL OPERA HOUSE EDUCATION: Covent Garden, London WC2E 9DD (☎020-7212 9410; fax 020-7212 9441; e-mail education@roh.org.uk; www. royaloperahouse.org).

The Royal Opera House offers **Work Placements/Internships** for students with an interest in ballet or opera, though not necessarily in performance. Placements offered across the organisation but predominantly in technical and production areas. Both the period of work and the duration of the placement to be mutually agreed. Minimum age 18.

Contact Joanne Allen, Work Placement Co-ordinator for further information.

Public Sector

CIVIL SERVICE: Cabinet Office, 67 Tufton Street, London SW1P 3QS (☎020-7276 1619; fax 020-7276 1502; www.faststream.gov.uk/diversity).

Summer Development Programme For Ethnic Minorities. A 6 to 8-week programme designed to introduce the varied work of the UK Civil Service. Includes a formal residential training course. A training allowance of £285 (London) £245 (elsewhere) per week is provided. The course is open to undergraduates/graduates of any discipline; applicants must be UK nationals from an ethnic minority with an expected/achieved 2:2. Must be able to demonstrate effective communication skills, creativity, resilience and motivation.

For further details please see our website. *Application forms* can be downloaded from the 27 November 2006 to 24 January 2007.

GOVERNMENT ECONOMIC SERVICE: HM Treasury, 1 Horse Guards Road, London SW1A 2HQ (☎020-7270 4577; fax 020-7270 4862; e-mail rob.more@ hm-treasury.gov.uk; www.ges.gov.uk). The Government Economic Service is the UK's largest recruiter of economists with over 1000 professionals in more than 30 departments. The GES gives you access to a wide range of economist career options. **50 Economist Summer Vacation Placements.** Interns are expected to provide support to professional economists dealing with a range of issues affecting Government policy. Wages are £16,000 to £17,000 pro rata for a 35-hour week. Placements last for 6 weeks between July and August. Applicants must be studying for a degree in economics, or, if it is a joint degree, economics must comprise at least 50% of the total course (including macro and micro economics). They should also be either UK nationals, Commonwealth citizens, Swiss nationals or members of the European Economic Area.

Applications should be made from January 2007 to Rob More, at the above address.

Science, Construction and Engineering

BLACK & VEATCH: Grosvenor House, 69 London Road, Redhill, Surrey RH1 1LQ (☎01737-774155; fax 01737-772767; www.bvl.bv.com). Black & Veatch is a multidisciplinary engineering service provider who undertake both infrastructure and non-infrastructure projects in water and waste water, often as part of an integrated co-located team. As part of the Black & Veatch Group, we can draw on the experience and expertise of more than 6000 professionals and specialists worldwide. Of these, nearly 1000 are part of Black & Veatch Water, Europe region.

The organisation offers **2 or 3 placements** over the summer to undergraduate students of Civil Engineering. These traineeships last for up to 10 weeks and take place in the company's Environmental Management or Water Utilities departments.

Applications should be sent to hrdept@bv.com by Easter.

DATA CONNECTION LTD: 100 Church Street, Enfield EN2 6BQ (☎020-8366 1177; e-mail recruit@dataconnection.com; www.dataconnection.com). Founded in 1981, Data Connection is one of the world's most successful computer technology companies with a worldwide reputation for developing complex high quality products. Customers include some of the biggest names in the IT industry, such as Cisco, Microsoft, IBM and BT. The company has over 350 employees and is based in North London, with offices in Edinburgh, Chester, San Francisco and Washington DC. They offer outstanding students the chance to develop their computing skills at the cutting edge of technology.

Vacation Work is offered to exceptional students with an interest in the development of complex software. Data Connection provides complex and challenging programming assignments, with help and support. A salary of £1,300 per month and subsidised accommodation in the Company House is offered. Successful applicants typically have all A grades at A level. Many vacation students go on to join Data Connection as full-time employees; some receive sponsorship while still at University.

Interviews are held all year round. However, as vacancies are limited it is best to apply in the autumn term.

For more details *contact* Charmaine Gudge at the above address, send your CV to the above email address or apply on-line following the links from the website.

M.W. KELLOGG LTD: Kellogg Tower, Greenford Road, Greenford, Middlesex UB6 0JA (☎020-8872 7000; fax 020-8872 7272; e-mail info@mwkl.co.uk; www. mwkl.co.uk).
M.W. Kellogg Ltd is a world leader in the design, engineering, procurement, construction and project management of process plants within the oil, gas and petrochemical industries. Client base includes all the major oil companies.
Traineeships offered during the summer vacation mainly for **Engineering and IT Positions.** Main degree subjects of interest are chemical engineering, mechanical engineering or computer science or other related degree. Other possible areas include, Purchasing and Supply, Construction, Civil and Structural, Business, CAD, Electrical, Instrumentation, Process Control and Materials. Excellent facilities and a work environment conducive to enthusiastic innovative team players are offered.
Trainees will be paid around £7.00 per hour. Placements take place at the head office in Greenford. Help is usually given with finding accommodation, but students must pay for their own board and lodging.
Applications should be sent from April to the Recruitment Officer at the above address.

SIR ROBERT MCALPINE LTD: Eaton Court, Maylands Avenue, Hemel Hempstead, Hertfordshire HP2 7TR (☎01442-233444; fax 01442-230024; e-mail careers@sir-robert-mcalpine.com; www.sir-robert-mcalpine.com).
Sir Robert McAlpine Ltd is one of the UK's major building and civil engineering contractors, undertaking projects such as industrial plants, marine works, power stations, hospitals, offices, theatres, leisure and retail complexes.
University students reading degrees in construction-related subjects, or 'A' Level students considering such degrees, are offered **Summer Placements** lasting a minimum of 8 weeks. Students assist site engineers and quantity surveyors working on various major construction sites throughout the country. The salary varies according to experience and qualifications and assistance in finding lodgings is provided. The maximum number of vacancies is 35.
Applications should be made to the Human Resources Department, at the above address, or via the above website.

Sport

BRAY LAKE WATERSPORTS: Monkey Island Lane, Windsor Road, Maidenhead, Berkshire SL6 2EB (☎01628-638860; fax 01628-771441; e-mail info@braylake. com; www.braylake.com).
Set next to a 50-acre lake, ideal for beginners and intermediate windsurfers, sailors and canoeists. Caters for both adults and juniors. Has a good range of equipment for teaching, hire and demonstration.
Work Experience/Trainee Positions available for people with some watersports experience, who are keen to pursue this interest, with a view to possibly becoming a watersports instructor. Positions are unpaid or low paid but offer the opportunity to spend a lot of time on the water in order to gain experience and ultimately qualifications. Bray Lake may offer to subsidise the right candidate through the costly watersports instruction training course. Opportunities to supplement income are also available by helping out around the centre. Positions available from June to September.
Applications should be sent to Lindsay Frost, Centre Manager at the above address.

The West Country

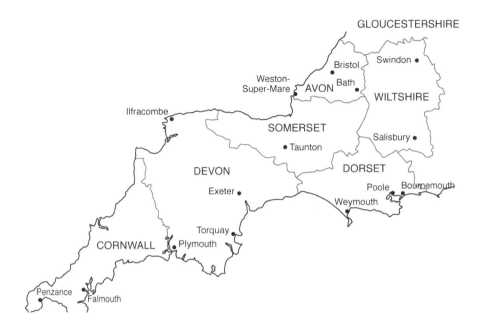

GLOUCESTERSHIRE

Bristol Swindon •

Weston-
Super-Mare AVON Bath

WILTSHIRE

Ilfracombe

SOMERSET

Salisbury •

• Taunton

DEVON DORSET

Exeter • Poole Bournemouth
Weymouth

Torquay •
CORNWALL • Plymouth

Penzance
Falmouth

Prospects for Work.
The coasts of Dorset, Devon, Somerset and Cornwall are scattered with hotels
which need staffing during the summer season. Bournemouth alone has 20,000 hotel
rooms, the largest number outside London. The largest employers of temporary
staff are the many holiday camps in the region: Pontins has several centres in the
South West, Butlins has its refurbished Family Entertainment resorts and there are
a further two camps in St Ives and Hayle. The Jobcentre Plus in Penzance recruits
for local caravan parks during both Easter and summer, as well as for employers
on the Scilly Isles. The Scilly Isles' particularly long summer season runs from
early March to November and as a result recruitment begins in late November. In
and around Penzance there are often vacancies for chefs, kitchen/service staff, and
summer food processors.

There may well be a demand for agricultural workers, flower pickers and fruit
pickers at the strawberry farms around Camborne or in Penzance, home to one of
the largest bulb farms in the area.

Vacancies in Taunton in Somerset are mainly for administration, retail and the
hospitality and leisure industry. There is also a need for temporary fruit pickers
and production workers, mainly recruited through employment agencies, although
this is predominantly in the Bridgewater and Chard area more than in Taunton
itself. It is important to apply early as the demand is high among students. Some
temporary jobs are advertised in the *Somerset County Gazette* and vacancies in the

region and nationwide can also be accessed on the Jobcentre Plus website, www. jobcentreplus.gov.uk, or telephone Jobseeker Direct on 0845-606 0234. Temporary jobs are also advertised in the town's two colleges. Bristol is one of the few other areas away from the coast where there is an extensive demand by retailers for more staff over the summer; again, the number of students vying for jobs makes it sensible to apply early.

The Bristol area also has a high number of tourism vacancies over the summer months. For more information on this, visit the Tourism Taskforce website: www. tourismskillsnetwork.org.uk. As the largest city in the South-West, Bristol is currently undergoing a huge transformation. Work has already begun on its city centre regeneration programme. The £500 million pound project involves the creation of a new city quarter at the entrance to Bristol, comprising around 1 million square feet of retail and leisure space, bringing substantial investment and thousands of new jobs.

Business and Industry

GLEN LYN GORGE: Glen Lyn Gorge, Lynmouth, Devon EX35 6ER (☎01598-753207; www.theglenlyngorge.co.uk). A visitor attraction with self-catering holiday accommodation.
Staff to work from April to September. Wages £200 to £300 per week; hours are dependent upon the weather. No experience required, just enthusiasm. Work to include being part of a boat crew, gardening and looking after the accommodation. Accommodation is available at a minimal price. Non-UK residents with suitable qualifications will be considered.
Apply to Matthew Oxenham at the above address from February for further information. An interview will be required.

ROCHESTERS EVENT HIRE LTD: Deer Park Farm, Marshwood Vale, Bridport, Dorset DT6 5PZ (☎01308-868743; fax 01308-868086).
Delivery Driver needed June to August/September. Wages £5.35 per hour. Hours to be agreed with applicant. Up to 60 hours a week if wanted. Clean driving licence essential.
Washing Machine Loaders (2) also to check orders and pack. Wages £5.35 per hour. Positions available from June to September. Sense of humour and common sense required.
Apply to Trevor Richards, Director.

TORBAY LANGUAGE CENTRE: Conway Road, Paignton, Devon TQ4 5LH (☎01803-558555; fax 01803-559606; e-mail tlc@lalgroup.com; www.lalgroup. com). A large school with good resources and a CELTA training centre.
Office Assistant for Teaching Department. To work either 8am to 4pm or 10am to 6pm Monday to Friday. Full training given. Applicants should be over 18 and have basic computer skills.
Tuck Shop Assistants (2). To work 9.30am to 1pm, Monday to Friday. Training given. Applicants should be 16 or over, have some shop counter experience and be good with money.
Customer Services Assistants (3). To work 6 days a week from 8am to 6pm. Applicants should be 18 or over, have good organisational and computer skills and be able to multi-task.
Wages at national minimum rate depending on age. No accommodation available. Staff required during June and August.
Applications to the Director of Studies at the above address.

Children

MOORLAND HALL: Brentor Road, Mary Tavy, Tavistock, Devon PL19 9PX (☎01822-810466; fax 01822-810661; e-mail info@moorlandhall.co.uk; www. moorlandhall.co.uk). Offers residential summer language and activity courses to children aged 9 to 16 years. Located on the western boundary of Dartmoor National Park, Moorland Hall is a beautiful Victorian house with a swimming pool.
House Mother/Supervisor. Wages approximately £200 per week. To work flexible hours. Previous experience required.
Applications should be sent to Mr Jo Farrington at the above address.

RICHARD LANGUAGE COLLEGE: 43-45 Wimborne Road, Bournemouth, Dorset BH3 7AB (☎01202-555932; fax 01202-555874; e-mail clas@rlc.co.uk; www.rlc.co.uk).
Leaders/Social Organisers (3) to work 8 hours a day interacting with language students, plus Saturday excursions to Oxford, Bath, Stonehenge etc. Wages of £115 a week with accommodation provided. Period of work from June to August. Applicants must be aged at least 21 and have sports qualifications.
Applications to C. Leclerc, Marketing, at the above address.

TORBAY LANGUAGE CENTRE: Conway Road, Paignton, Devon TQ4 5LH (☎01803-558555; fax 01803-559606; e-mail tlc@lalgroup.com; www.lalgroup. com).
Activity Leaders to organise activities for children aged 10-18 including leading sports, trips to theme parks, city tours, discos and transfers to and from the airport.Wages are set at national minimum rate. Flexible working hours including day, evening and weekend work; an average working week would be 40 hours but overtime is available. Period of work by arrangement between June and September. Accommodation is not provided, help provided with finding accommodation Applicants must be aged at least 18, good with children and enjoy the outdoor life.
Applications to Simon Nelson, Head of Leisure Management, at the above address.

Holiday Centres and Amusements

ALLNATT CENTRES: 35 Ulwell Road, Swanage BH19 1LG (☎01929-421075; e-mail bookings@allnatt.co.uk; www.allnatt.co.uk). Residential outdoor centres providing education, inspiration and play through adventure activities and environmental education to schools, youth and overseas groups.
Duty Managers, Centre Assistants, Teaching Staff and Catering Staff. Inspirational people required to fill these positions in year round operations at Swanage and on the Isle of Wight. Live-in, work for the season or just a couple of months. Applicants must have an interest in educating young people and a passion for working and playing in the outdoors. More information available from the above address.
Applications to the Manager at the above address. Interviews carried out in person or over the phone.

COLLIFORD LAKE PARK: St Neot, Cornwall PL14 6PZ (☎01208-821469; e-mail info@cheapwatersports.com; www.collifordlakepark.com).
General Assistant to provide general help around the park, helping in the shop, café and at reception. Wages £100 per week plus food and board. To work 8 hours per day, 5-6 days a week from June to September. Applicants need to speak English; experience of either outdoor work with animals or outdoor maintenance would be

helpful. Must be over 19 and able to drive, preferably with own vehicle. *Applications* to Charlotte Bricknell at the above address.

CREALY ADVENTURE PARK: Clyst St Mary, Exeter, Devon EX5 1DR (☎0870-116 3333; fax 01395-233211; e-mail fun@crealy.co.uk; www.crealy.co.uk).
Retail Assistants (10-15) in the Guest Services Department. Pay dependent on age and experience. Flexible hours to suit. Required for Easter and Summer holidays. Experience in till operation an advantage. Minimum age 16.
Catering Assistants (20) for fast food outlets during the summer holidays. Flexible hours to suit. Experience not essential. Minimum age 16.
Play Supervisors & Ride Operators (15) for summer work. Must have outgoing personality and be able to adhere to strict working practices to comply with health and safety best practice. Minimum age 16.
Staff can expect full training and benefits.
Please *apply* to the Personnel Officer at the above address.

EXMOUTH FUN PARK: Queen's Drive, The Seafront, Exmouth, Devon EX8 2AY (☎079-7048 2236; e-mail chriswrighty@lineone.net). Family-based amusement park, situated opposite the beach. Friendly holiday atmosphere.
Assistant Fun Park Manager (1), Fun Park Assistant (2). Negotiable wage depending on age and experience. To work 30-50 hours per week. Minimum period of work July and August. Positions are available from April to mid-September. These seasonal positions are paid for hours worked which may mean fewer hours than expected as the site is weather dependent. Good level of English required. Rugby players particularly welcome. Accommodation not available.
Applications should be made from March onwards to Mr C. Wright. Interview necessary.

K'S ENTERTAINMENT CENTRES: Warren Road, Minehead, Somerset TA24 5BG (☎01643-704186; fax 01643-702134; e-mail info@ks-entertainment-centres. co.uk; www.ks-entertainment-centres.co.uk). Operates three family entertainment centres on the south-west coast of England.
General Assistants (16+). Wages at national minimum rate, dependent on age and experience. To work 48 hours per week. Minimum period of work 6 weeks. Positions available from 1 April to 31 October. Accommodation available. Foreign applicants with permission to work in the UK considered.
Applications should be made to June Campbell at the above address.

OCEANARIUM: Pier Approach, West Beach, Bournemouth BH2 5AA (☎01202-311990; fax 01202-311990; e-mail info@oceanarium.co.uk; www.oceanarium. co.uk).
Front Of House/Retail Assistants. To serve customers, operate tills, stock up and for light cleaning, selling guide books, and leafleting.
Catering Assistants. To prepare food, work tills, clean, serve customers and clean tables. Minimum age 18.
Welcome Hosts/Hostesses to greet customers, entertain and give talks.
All positions are from July to September. Minimum age 16.
For *applications,* contact, the Personnel Manager at the above address.

PARK RESORTS: Bideford Bay Holiday Village, Bucks Cross, Bideford, Devon EX39 5DU (☎01237-431331; fax 01273-431624; www.park-resorts.com/recruitment).

Lifeguards. Wages on application. Must hold National Pool Lifeguard qualification.
Catering Assistants, Bar Assistants. Wages on application.
All staff to work 39 hours a week. Posts occur between Easter and end of October. An ability to deal with people is essential. Accommodation available at a small charge. Overseas applicants with good English and eligibility to work in the UK will be considered. Minimum age 18 years.
Applications from January to the Personnel Manager, Park Resorts.

PERRAN SANDS HOLIDAY PARK: Haven Holidays, Perranporth, Cornwall TR6 0AQ (☎01872-573551; www.havenholidays.com).
Bar team, Catering Team, Lifeguards (200). Wages NMW.
Reception Staff (10) for general holiday park duties, meeting and greeting customers. Wages NMW.
Shop Staff (50). Wages NMW.
Positions available from March to October. To work 5 to 6 days per week. Minimum age 18. Limited accommodation available at a charge of 57p per hour worked. Foreign applicants with fluent English and visa welcome.
Applications from February to the HR Department at the above address.

WESTERMILL FARM HOUSE: Exford, nr Minehead, Somerset TA24 7NJ (☎01643-831238; info@westermill.com; www.westermill.com). Campsite, six self-catering cottages and farmhouse cottage on 500-acre working hill farm by a river in the middle of Exmoor National Park.
Farm Campsite Assistants (1). Wages on application. Large caravan provided, meals with family. Long hours, with 1 day off a week. Duties include signing people in and out, cleaning shower and loo block, working in the small farm shop, checking and cleaning cottages, log cottage painting and some domestic jobs including cooking.
Must be non-smokers, conscientious, intelligent and hard working, with a practical nature. Help required during July and August. Overseas applicants welcome.
Applications and further details (enclosing letter, CV, and passport-sized photo) from January to Mrs O.J.C. Edwards at the above address.

Hotels and Catering

ABBOTSBURY OYSTERS: Ferrymans Way, Ferrybridge, Weymouth, Dorset DT4 9YA (☎01305-788867; fax 01305-760661). A friendly, busy seafood bar connected to a working oyster farm.
Waiting Staff (3). Will also involve some kitchen work. Wages on application; to work 6 to 25 hours a week. Applicants must possess empathy, responsibility, consistency and efficiency.
Staff are required from Easter to September. Accommodation is not available.
Applications should be sent at any time to the Manager at the above address.

BATH HOTEL: Lynmouth Street, Lynmouth, North Devon EX35 6EL (tel/fax 01598-752238; e-mail bathhotel@somersetriviera.com; www.somersetriviera.com/bathhotel). A family-run seasonal hotel with approximately 14 members of staff during the season.
Chamber Person (1). Wages £160 per week, live-in; to work 37 hours over 6 days. Must be over 18.
Waiting Staff (2), Bar Person (1), Kitchen Porter (1). Wages £160 per week, live-in; to work 37 hours per week over 5½ days. Must be over 18.

Staff required from March-October for a minimum period of 6 months. Foreign applicants with a good level of English are welcome.
Applications, from March to June, to Sharon Hobbs at the above address.

BOURNEMOUTH HIGHCLIFF MARRIOTT HOTEL: St Michael's Road, Westcliff, Bournemouth, Dorset BH2 5DU (☎01202-557702; fax 01202-292734; e-mail hr.bournemouth@marriotthotels.co.uk; www.mariotthotels.co.uk). Following £5.6 million of refurbishment by Whitbread, they consider this the premier hotel in Bournemouth.
Restaurant Staff (5), Pool Bar Staff (3), Leisure Club Staff (2), Kitchen Porters, Chamber Maids, Commis Chef, Chef de Partie, Night Porter.
All wages from national minimum rate, depending on age and experience. Limited accommodation available. Full training, leisure club membership and excellent staff facilities are provided. To work 39 hours over 5 days per week (30 to 40 for pool attendant). Minimum period of work of 2 months between June and September. Good level of English required. Pool staff should be RLSS/National Pool Lifeguard qualified.
Applications should include a referee and be made to the HR Manager at the above address from March onwards. Interview in person or by phone will be required.

CAMELOT CASTLE HOTEL: Atlantic Road, Tintagel, Cornwall PL34 0DQ (☎01840-770202; Fax 01840-770978; e-mail annette@camelotcastle.com; www. camelotcastle.com).
Chamber Staff, Waiting Staff, Kitchen Staff, Front of House, Reception and Bar Staff to work in busy hotel. Wages £3.50 per hour with accommodation, breakfast and dinner provided. To work 6 hours a day, 6 days a week from May to the end of October. Minimum age 19. Applicants must be willing to do any aspect of hotel work. Foreign applicants with appropriate visas and sufficient English welcome.
Applications to Irina Mappin at the above address or by e-mail from March.

COLLAVEN MANOR HOTEL: Sourton, Devon EX20 4HH (☎01837-861522; fax 01837-861614; e-mail collavenmanor@supanet.com; www.collavenmanor.co.uk). A small AA two-star silver award country house hotel with 9 bedrooms. Situated in a rural location amidst lovely scenery; the hotel is recommended in the *Good Hotel Guide*.
Waiting Staff (1). Wages at national minimum rate.
Kitchen Assistant (1). Wages at national minimum rate.
Accommodation is provided free of charge. Period of work June to September. All staff must be adaptable and flexible, and prepared to assist in the general running of the hotel. Applicants must be over 16. Overseas applicants who speak English considered.
Applications from December to Mrs J. Mitchell. References must be provided if an interview is impossible.

THE CHINE HOTEL: 25 Boscombe Spa Road, Bournemouth, Dorset BH5 1AX (☎01202-396234; fax 01202-391737; e-mail enquiries@chinehotel.co.uk; www. fjbhotels.co.uk/chine).
Waiting Staff (4) needed for restaurant and pool service; some silver service. Wages £4.25 per hour plus tips. To work 40 hours per 5-day week; some casual work available. Period of work mid-June to early September. Live out. Food hygiene certificate, previous experience and references needed.
Chamber Staff (3) needed to clean bedrooms and public areas. £4.25 per hour. 30-40

hours work per 5-day week. Period of work mid-June to early September. Live out. Previous experience and references required.
Applications to the Hotel Manager.

CROWN HOTEL: Exford, Exmoor, Somerset TA24 7PP (☎01643-831554; fax 01643-831665; e-mail info@crownhotelexmoor.co.uk; www.crownhotelexmoor. co.uk). Award-winning seventeenth century coaching inn set in the heart of beautiful Exmoor National Park. Internationally-renowned cuisine.
General Assistants needed for waiting in the restaurant, bar work, cleaning rooms and washing-up duties. Wages £200 per week minus B & L. To work 39 hours per week. Minimum period of work of 2 months. Positions are available from April to September inclusive. Fluent English essential. Minimum age 19. B & L available, cost to be arranged. Suitably qualified foreign applicants welcome.
Applications should be as soon as possible to Mr Chris Kirkbride at the above address.

THE CROWN HOTEL: Blockley, Gloucester GL56 9EX (☎01386-700245; fax 01386-700247; e-mail reservations@crown-hotel-blockley.co.uk).
Dining Room Staff (2), General Assistants (2) for the summer period June to October. Wages at national minimum rate plus tips and accommodation. 40 hour week split shifts. Some experience preferred. Minimum age 18 years.
Applications to the Manager at the above address.

DEVON COAST HOLIDAYS: Grosvenor Hotel, Belgrave Road, Torquay TQ2 5HG (☎01803-294373; fax 01803-291032; e-mail info@grosvenorhoteltorquay. co.uk; www.grosvenor-torquay.co.uk).
Chef, Waiting Staff (3), Bar Staff, Housekeeping Staff (3), Reception Staff, Nightporter. Wages £5.00 per hour; to work 3-6 days per week. Suitably qualified non-UK citizens will be considered; fluent English is not required among housekeeping staff. Staff receive meals on duty and use of the leisure facilities.
Apply to Gemma Balaam at the above address.

THE EAST CLOSE COUNTRY HOTEL: Lyndhurst Road, Hinton St Michael, Christchurch, Dorset BH23 7EF (☎01425-672404; fax 01425-674315; e-mail enquiries@eastclosehotel.co.uk; www.eastclosehotel.co.uk). Beautiful 18th Century manor house sitting in 7 acres on the south west edge of the New Forest. In easy reach of Bournemouth and Southampton.
Waiting Staff (3), Chamber Assistant. Must be aged at least 17.
Bar Assistant. Must be aged at least 18.
All the above for restaurant and function work, including weddings. Wages of £145 per week plus tips and accommodation. Period of work by arrangement from May.
Applications to the above address.

ENGLISH HOLIDAY CRUISES LTD: 2D Pillar & Lucy House, Merchants Road, Gloucester GL1 2PB (☎0845-601 7895; fax 0845-601 7897; e-mail recruitment@ englishholidaycruises.co.uk; www.englishholidaycruises.co.uk). Operates Britain's largest inland riverboat hotels.
Stewards/Stewardesses (5). Wages £250 and over per week. Required to work 50 hours over 6 to 7 days. Minimum period of work 4 months between May and September. Live-in positions only. Accommodation is charged at £30 per week; food is included free of charge. Applicants must be 18 and over, preferably with previous

bar or restaurant experience. Overseas applicants are welcome, but must be able to speak English to the same standard as a native speaker and have the right to live and work in the UK.

Applications should be made at any time to Jay Clements, Operations Manager, at the above address.

FAIRHAVEN SEA FRONT HOTEL AND RESTAURANT: 37 The Esplanade, Weymouth, Dorset DT4 8DH (☎01305-760200; fax 01305-760300; e-mail fairhaven@kingshotels.co.uk; www.kingshotels.co.uk/fairhaven). The Hotel is part of a family owned group of hotels and restaurants in Weymouth. Weymouth is a holiday resort on the South coast with a sandy beach and 17th century harbour.
Waiting Staff (5), Chefs and Grill Cooks (3), Kitchen Assistants (2). Wages by arrangement plus tips. Meals provided and accommodation may be available. To work 6 days a week. All staff must be available from the end of May to September. Some jobs are suitable for overseas students wishing to perfect their English.

Send *applications* (with photograph) from March onwards to the Manager, Fairhaven Hotel.

THE HOOPS: Horns Cross, Bideford, Devon EX39 5DL (☎01237-451222; fax 01237-451247; e-mail sales@hoopsinn.co.uk; www.hoopsinn.co.uk). A 13th century 3-star historic inn and hotel with 12 rooms, close to the coastal path. Renowned for its cooking and traditional coaching inn atmosphere.
General Assistants for duties including waiting, housekeeping and kitchen. To work 40-45 hours per week. Minimum age 18. Experience preferred.
Chefs also needed. Experience essential.

Staff required for spring, summer and winter seasons. Local accommodation available.

Applications, including recent photograph, to Mrs Gay Marriott at the above address.

KNOLL HOUSE HOTEL: Studland Bay, near Swanage, Dorset BH19 3AH (☎01929-452233/450450; fax 01929-450423; e-mail staff@knollhouse.co.uk; www. knollhouse.co.uk). A country house holiday hotel superbly located in a National Trust Reserve overlooking Studland Bay. Independent and family run, it has a reputation for service and care of its guests, many of whom return annually.
Waiting Staff (6-10) for dining room including wine service. Pay above national minimum wage.
Housekeeping Staff (6-10). Pay above national minimum wage. No experience required.
General Assistants (2-3) to care for children. Pay above national minimum wage.
Kitchen Assistants (2-3). Washing up and helping in kitchens. Pay above national minimum wage.
Chefs (4). Salary dependent on experience. 706/1 or equivalent not always necessary.

All staff to work 38 hours. Positions available for a minimum of 6 weeks between March and October. Easter and summer vacation positions also available, as well as further positions for the entire season. Deduction made for B & L, available in single rooms. A happy disposition and a good attitude are more important than experience. Minimum age 17 years. EU applicants with good spoken English welcome. Interview is not always necessary.

Applications from the start of the year to the Staff Manager, Knoll House Hotel.

LAND'S END AND JOHN O'GROATS COMPANY: Land's End, Sennen, Penzance, Cornwall TR19 7AA (☎0870-458 0099; fax 01736-871812; e-mail info@ landsend-landmark.fsnet.co.uk; www.landsend-landmark.co.uk). A leading tourist attraction in Cornwall located in a spectacular setting. It comprises various exhibitions and trading units operating throughout the year. In winter the operation is reduced.

Catering Personnel and Retail Staff for various jobs at Land's End from spring to early autumn. Wages by arrangement; hours depend on the level of business. Applicants should be aged over 16, those with previous experience preferred.

Applications to Personnel at the above address.

LUNDY COMPANY: The Lundy Island Shore Office, The Quay, Bideford, Devon EX39 2LY (☎01237-423233; fax 01237-477779; e-mail admin@lundyisland.co.uk; www.lundyisland.co.uk). Lundy is an island off the North Devon coast owned by the National Trust with 23 letting properties, a pub and a shop.

Tavern Staff (4) to help run the pub. Wages are variable, with free B & L; to work a 5-day week. Staff are required from April to September. Applicants must have previous bar/kitchen experience.

Applications from January to Derek Green at the above address. Interview necessary. Also see under *Heritage* in the Voluntary Work section.

MR & MRS I.S. MACDONALD: The Flat, 1 Barton Road, Woolacombe, North Devon (☎01271-870752). Fish and chip takeaway in a popular surfing resort, a few minutes' walk from the sea.

Counter Assistants (3) to serve takeaway food, plus some general cleaning and hygiene. Wages £220-£230 per week, on an hourly basis. Free B & L in comfortable flat with excellent facilities. To work 40-48 hours per 6-day week. Period of work negotiable for May to October season. Certificate advantageous but not essential. Must be reliable, have a pleasant appearance and a sense of humour. Excellent English essential.

Applications (enclosing s.a.e. and photograph) from March to Mr & Mrs I. S. MacDonald at the above address.

MOORLAND LINKS HOTEL: Forestdale Hotels, Yelverton, Devon PL20 6DA (☎01822-852245; fax 01822-855004; e-mail moorland.links@forestdale.com; www.moorlandlinkshotel.co.uk). Moorland Links Hotel is set in 9 acres of Dartmoor National Park, 7 miles from the historic city of Plymouth.

Banquet/Restaurant Staff (4) to serve breakfast, lunch and dinner for weddings, conferences and banquets. Wages at national minimum wage rate. To work a 40-hour week over 5 days on a 7-day rota of split and straight shifts. Some late night work involved. Minimum period of work 3 months between June and October. Applicants must be over 18, flexible, friendly and conscientious with good communication skills. Board and accommodation are available at a cost of £20 per week. Foreign applicants with an intermediate level of English welcome.

Apply to Nicole Quinn, General Manager at the above address from April.

MOUNTAIN WATER EXPERIENCE: Courtlands, Kingsbridge, Devon TQ7 4BN (tel/fax 01548-550675; e-mail mwe@mountainwaterexp.demon.co.uk; www. mountainwaterexperience.com).

General Assistant needed for April-November. The work involves general kitchen and housework duties plus bar work. No qualifications are required, but candidates need to be over 18 and have a good sense of humour.

For *applications* and for details of wages and hours please contact Mark Agnew, Operations Manager, at the above address.

THE NARRACOTT HOTEL: Beach Road, Woolacombe, Devon EX34 7BS (☎01271-870418; e-mail reservations@narracott.co.uk; www.narracott.co.uk). Seafront 79-bedroom hotel with extensive leisure facilities situated in a small coastal village near a surfing beach surrounded by National Trust land, and overlooking Woolacombe Sands.

Waiting Staff, Porters, Kitchen Staff and Room Staff. Wages specified on application. Minimum period of work 3 months, for an 11-month season between February and January.

Applications, including details of work experience and photo, to Mr Wyld, The Narracott Hotel.

NORFOLK ROYALE HOTEL: Richmond Hill, Bournemouth, Dorset BH2 6EN (☎01202-551521; fax 01202-299729; norfolkroyale@englishrosehotels.co.uk; www. englishrosehotels.co.uk). A luxury four-star hotel owned by the English Rose Hotels Group.

Bar Staff, Waiting Staff. Wages on application. Part-time and full-time work available for both positions. Previous experience helpful.

Chamber Staff. Wages on application. Full-time and part-time work available.

No accommodation is available. Staff are required for periods of 12 weeks or longer (although shorter time will be considered). Overseas applicants with work permits are considered.

Applications at any time to Personnel. Interview necessary.

THE OLD STOCKS HOTEL: The Square, Stow on the Wold, Gloucester GL54 1AF (☎01451-830666; fax 01451-870014; e-mail info@oldstockshotel.co.uk). A small 18 bedroom family run hotel with a friendly team of caring staff. Located in the highest point of the Cotswolds, a Grade II listed building.

Housekeepers (2), Waiting Staff (2), Kitchen Assistants (2), Bar Staff (2). Wages approximately £180 per week for 40 hour, 5 day week. Minimum period of work one month between April and November. Accommodation available. Previous experience not necessary as full training will be provided.

Applications should be sent to Helen E. Allen, Proprietor at the above address.

PENKERRIS: Penwinnick Road, St. Agnes, Cornwall TR5 0PA (tel/fax 01872-552262; e-mail info@penkerris.co.uk; www.penkerris.co.uk). Attractive detached house with garden in unspoiled Cornish village. Dramatic cliff walks, beaches and good surfing nearby.

Guesthouse Assistant required, to work on an *au pair* basis. Accommodation provided. Pocket money according to duties and season. Afternoons free to visit the beach or explore the cliff walks. The guesthouse is open throughout the winter. Min. work period 3 months; much longer preferred, but 3 weeks acceptable over Christmas and Easter. Overseas applicants welcome: the job is ideal for students wishing to perfect their English as they can study at Truro College nearby. The owner can also help with English as she has years of experience in EFL teaching

Applications a.s.a.p. to Mrs Dorothy Gill-Carey at the above address.

QUEEN'S HALL: The Queen's Hall, Warren Road, Minehead, Somerset TA24 5BG (☎01643-703044; fax 01643-702134; e-mail mk@queenshall.info; www.queenshall. info). A food-led family pub.

Bar Staff/Waiting Staff (10). Wage meets with NMW. To work 40 hours per week, all year around. Minimum period of work is six months; accommodation is available at a charge of £40 per week. Applicants must be over 18 years old, and have at least

an intermediate level of English.
Applications should be made, at any time, to Marcus at the above address. An interview may not be required.

RIVIERA HOTEL: Burnaby Road, Alum Chine, Bournemouth, Dorset BH4 8JF (☎01202-763653; fax 01202-768422; e-mail info@rivierabournemouth.co.uk; www. rivierabournemouth.co.uk). A large family holiday orientated hotel based 20 minutes' walk from the centre of Bournemouth and 2 minutes walk from the beach.
Waiting Staff (2). Wages on application, plus tips. To work 36 hours over 6 days per week. Experience required.
Chamberperson. Wages on application, plus tips. To work 36 hours over 6 mornings per week. Experience preferred.
Wages may be increased depending on experience. Accommodation is available. Min. work period 3 months between March and November. Minimum age 18. All applicants must have a friendly personality. Overseas applicants eligible to work in the UK welcome.
Send *applications* with s.a.e. in February to the General Manager, Riviera Hotel.

ROSKARNON HOUSE HOTEL: Rock, Wadebridge, Cornwall PL27 6LD (Tel/fax 01208-862785).
General Assistant (1/2). Minimum of £100 for working 40 hours basic a week, plus overtime. To work 6 days per week. Any catering or housekeeping knowledge useful.
Assistant Cook, Kitchen Porter. Wages and hours negotiable. Free B & L provided. Min. period of work 6 weeks from 25 May to 12 October. Work also available for 2 to 4 weeks at Easter. Overseas applicants eligible to work in the UK welcome.
Applications in late March to Mr Veall at the above address.

THE ROYAL CASTLE HOTEL: 11 The Quay, Dartmouth, Devon TQ6 9PS (☎01803-833033; fax 01803-835445; e-mail enquiry@royalcastle.co.uk; www. royalcastle.co.uk). A busy three-star hotel which employs around 50 staff.
Waiting Staff (4-6), Bar Staff (4-6). Wages from £5.35 per hour. To work 40 hours over 5 days a week. Work available all year round. Accommodation is available at a cost of approx. £37.50 per week. No experience necessary, just a bright personality, the right attitude, and the ability to work hard and play hard.
Applications about 3 weeks prior to desired start to the Duty Manager. Interview sometimes required.

THE ROYAL YORK AND FAULKNER HOTEL: The Esplanade, Sidmouth, South Devon EX10 8AZ (☎01395-513043; fax 01395-577472; e-mail work@ royalyorkhotel.net; www.royalyorkhotel.net). Regency resort hotel occupying a superb position on the Esplanade of Sidmouth, a charming coastal resort. 70 rooms. Family business.
Waiting Staff. Wages at national minimum rate. To work 40 hours per week.
Bedroom Cleaners/Dining Room Relief. Wages at national minimum rate. To work approx. 40½ hours per week.
Accommodation and full board offered. Open February to December inclusive. Minimum period of employment 4 months.
Applications to Miss Sara Hook.

SANDBANKS HOTEL: 15 Banks Road, Poole, Dorset BH13 7PS (☎01202-707377; fax 01202-709272; e-mail enquiries@sandbankshotel.co.uk; www.fjbhotels.

co.uk/sandbanks). AA 3-star hotel. 116 bedrooms. Situated on beautiful Blue Flag beach. Excellent service and food.
Waiting Staff (4). Wages £4.25-£4.85 per hour. To work 5 days out of 7, split shifts, 40 hours or casual, overtime available. Good level of English.
Room Attendants (4). Wages £4.25-£4.85 per hour. To work 5 days out of 7, straight shifts, 37½ hours or casual.
Porter, Bar Staff. Wages £4.25-£4.85 per hour. To work 40 hours per week; must be aged 18 or over.
Minimum period of work of 2 months. Positions are available from May to October. Applicants should be 18+, previous experience is necessary for all positions – those without experience will in no way be considered. Overseas applicants welcome as long as they have a good understanding of English.
Applications should be made to the Human Resources Manager. Interview necessary.

TJM TRAVEL: 40 Lemon Street, Truro, Cornwall TR1 2NS (☎01872-272767; fax 01872-272110; e-mail jobs@tjm.co.uk; www.tjmtravel.co.uk). A trendy surf lodge in the lively town of Newquay.
Assistants. To work 4-6 hours per week, six days a week, from April until September. Minimum period of work is two weeks. B & L is included. Wages on application. Conversational English is required.
Apply, from 1 February, to the above address.

TORS HOTEL: Lynmouth, North Devon (☎01598-753236; fax 01598-752544; e-mail Torshotel@torslynmouth.co.uk; www.torslynmouth.co.uk). A 3-star, 4-crown, 31 bedroom hotel situated on the North Devon coastline with stunning sea views across the Bristol Channel to Wales.
Silver Service Waiting Staff. £169 a week. Experience or the ability to learn required. 39 hours, 5 days; split shifts. Wages dependent on experience.
Chamber Person, Porters, Kitchen Porters. £169 a week. To work 39 hours a week. No experience needed. Wages dependent on experience.
All staff work 5 days a week. Free B & L provided. Season lasts from March to January. Period of work must be for the whole period from April until September, applicants only available for summer vacation need not apply. Bonus paid on completion of season.
Send *Applications* with details of previous experience and photograph a.s.a.p. to the Manager, the Tors Hotel.

TOWNGATE PERSONNEL LTD: 3 Alum Chine Road, Westbourne, Bournemouth, Dorset BH4 8DT (☎01202-752955; fax 01202-752954; e-mail enquiries@towngate-personnel.co.uk; www.towngate-personnel.co.uk). A recruitment agency specialising in recruitment within the hotel and catering industry.
Short-term Live-in Assignments available in hotels in the west country and throughout England.
Hotel Receptionists (20). Wages £200 to £250 per week; to work 8 hours a day, 5/6 days a week. Hotel reception experience essential.
Silver Service Waiting Staff (30). Wages £200 to £250 per week; to work split shifts, 6 days a week. Silver service experience essential.
Chefs (30). Wages £200 to £500 per week; to work split shifts, 6 days a week. Must have relevant experience.
All positions are in 3 or 4-star hotels in the Channel Islands. Accommodation is available at a cost of approximately £40 per week. Staff are required from March

to October for a minimum of 6 months. Applicants from the EU/EEA and others on working holiday visas considered.
Applications from February to James Tucker, Operations Manager, at the above address. Telephone interview required.

TRESCO ESTATE: Tresco, Isles of Scilly, Cornwall TR24 0QQ (☎01720-424110; fax 01720-422807; e-mail personnel@tresco.co.uk; www.trescojobs.co.uk). Private island holiday resort, 28 miles off the Cornish coast. No cars, discos, or street lights, just silver beaches and a mild climate.
Waiting Staff (18), Housekeeping Staff (18), Bar Staff (4), Chefs – All Levels (18), Kitchen Assistants/Porters (4), Retail Assistants (8), Receptionists (5), Cottage Cleaners (6), Maintenance person (1), Tractor/Transport Driver (1), Housekeeping Supervisors (2), Restaurant Supervisors (3) needed to cover all duties in one of the Estate's three luxury hotels, the island stores, the holiday cottages department, or the Abbey Gardens Shop and Cafe. Wages for 2007 start at £5.35 per hour with live-in accommodation and meals deducted from your wages at a charge of approximately £55 per week. Tips for hotel staff are split at the end of the season for all who complete their contract.
To work 40 hours or over per week, generally split shifts over 5 to 5½ days per week. Period of work from February to November with further vacancies mid season. Applicants must be over 18 and have a valid work permit. Applicants will not be considered mid-season unless able to work a minimum of 10 weeks to include all of July and August.
Applications at any time, by post, fax or e-mail (as above), stating the position you are interested in, and why you consider yourself suitable.

TREYARNON BAY HOTEL: Treyarnon Bay, St Merryn, Padstow, Cornwall PL28 8JN (☎01841-520235; fax 01841-520239).
Kitchen Porter to work 6 to 8 hours per day providing general kitchen clean-up and help with preparing vegetables and starters. Applicants must have a basic hygiene certificate.
Chef/Cook to work 8 to 10 hours per day preparing, breakfast, lunch, dinner and for the overall running of a clean kitchen. Must have a Basic/Intermediate food hygiene certificate or NVQ.
Bar Staff (3-4) for general bar duties 6 to 8 hours per day, experience preferred but not essential.
Housekeeper/Room Cleaner (1-2) to clean rooms and some hotel areas for 5 to 6 hours per day, there is also some laundry work (although most of it is sent out). All staff are required from July to September, and must be over 18, wages are from the minimum rate according to age and experience, except for the chef whose wages will be £6.00-£7.00 per hour with accommodation available.
To apply *contact* Jennifer Kenley at the above address.

THE VICTORIA & BELMONT HOTELS: The Esplanade, Sidmouth, Devon, EX10 8RX (☎01395-512555/512651; fax 01395-579101; e-mail info@victoriahotel. co.uk; www.brend-hotels.co.uk). 4-star hotels with a relaxed atmosphere and a young and enthusiastic team. Located on the beautiful Devon coastline in Sidmouth, famous for its International Folk Festival.
Room Attendants (2) to service guests' rooms. Wages £135/£150 per week, dependent on age, (plus gratuities) to include all meals and accommodation. To work 5 days per week, mostly straight shifts 7am-3pm or 8.30am-4.30pm. Required for a minimum of 3 months to include September. Full training given.

Silver Service Waiting Staff (2) to serve breakfast, dinner and three lunches. Wages £150/£180 per week, dependent on age, plus gratuities, to include all meals and accommodation. To work 5 days per week. Required for a minimum of 3 months to include September. Full training given.

Candidates should be of smart appearance, with a pleasant outgoing personality and sense of humour and must be over 18 years old. Must be EU citizens or possess UK work permit.

Applications to Mrs A.M. Taylor, Personnel and Training Manager, at the above address.

WATERSMEET HOTEL: Mortehoe, Woolacombe, Devon EX34 7EB (☎01271-870333; fax 01271-870890; e-mail info@watersmeethotel.co.uk; www.watersmeethotel.co.uk). A 3-star high quality country house hotel with 25 bedrooms set on the National Trust's North Atlantic Coastline and overlooking a sandy beach. **Restaurant/Bar Staff (2), Housekeeping Staff (2), Kitchen Staff (2).** Live-in to include B & L. To work 40-42 hours per week over 6 days. Minimum period of work 3 months between May and October. Minimum age 18 years. Experience an advantage.

Applications, with CV and photograph, from January to Mr Michael James at the above address.

THE WINDMILL RESTAURANT: Salisbury Road, Marten, Marlborough, Wiltshire SN8 3SH (☎01264-731372; fax 01264-731284).
Kitchen Assistant (2). Wages £6.00-£7.00 per hour, plus accommodation. Will be required to do basic food preparation and cleaning.
Assistant Manager (1). Wages £8.50-£11 per hour, plus accommodation. Restaurant skills necessary.
Waiting Staff (2). Wages £6.50-£7.50 per hour, plus accommodation. Restaurant skills necessary.
Assistant Chef (1). Wages £7.50-£8.50 per hour. Food preparation skills necessary. All positions to work 9:30am-2pm and 6pm-10pm, 5½ days per week, from 1 February until the 31 October. Minimum period of work is 4 weeks.

Apply at any time by phoning Chris Ellis on the above telephone number.

WOOLACOMBE BAY HOTEL: Woolacombe, Devon EX34 7BN (☎01271-870388; fax 01271-870613; www.woolacombe-bay-hotel.co.uk). A family hotel situated near 3 miles of golden sands and a surfing beach.
Waiting Staff, Room Staff, Kitchen Staff, Bar Staff, Porters. £5.35 per hour (live-in). To work 44 hours per week. Minimum period of work 6 months between Easter and October. Staff are also required over Christmas and New Year (approximately 22 December to 2 January). Minimum age 18.

Applications from March to the Manager, Woolacombe Bay Hotel.

Language Schools

BOURNEMOUTH TEACHING SERVICE: 139 Charminster Road, Bournemouth BH8 8UH (☎01202-521355; fax 01202-521355; e-mail bts@englishinbournemouth.co.uk; www.englishinbournemouth.co.uk). A school specialising in teaching English to classes of multi-national adult students.
EFL Teachers (2). To teach classes of up to 10 students. Wages are £200 to £300 per week. To work 15 to 22 hours per week for a minimum of four weeks between July and August. No accommodation is provided. Applicants should have fluent English,

an RSA TEFL Certificate and relevant experience.
Contact Steve Laughton from May at the above address. An interview will be required.

CHANNEL SCHOOL OF ENGLISH: Country Cousins Ltd., Bicclescombe, Ilfracombe, Devon EX34 8JN (☎01271-862834; fax 01271-865374; e-mail help@ country-cousins.com; www.country-cousins.com). Situated on the beautiful North Devon coast, the school offers a range of English courses with 12, 15 or 21 hours of lessons per week to those aged 7 to adult.
EFL Teachers (15). Wages £10.20 per hour; to work 24 hours per week, July-August. Must have TEFL qualification and should have experience with the age range 11-18.
Social Organisers to work July and August, supervising children and young adults on the school's sports and excursion programme. Wages £5.00 per hour. Ideally candidates would be trainee teachers.
Applications to John Swan at the above address.

EAGLE INTERNATIONAL SCHOOL: Tiami, 55 Elms Avenue, Lilliput, Poole, Dorset BH14 8EE (tel/fax 01202-745175; e-mail eaglesch@aol.com).
Teacher/Leaders needed to work with overseas students in the 11-17 age range. Wages £220 per week. Work available over the Easter and Summer vacations. Duties will involve giving classes in English conversation and supervising students on the activity programme. Preference given to B.Ed and P.G.C.E. Modern Languages and English/Sport/Drama students.
Applications to J. Rees, Principal.

EF INTERNATIONAL LANGUAGE SCHOOLS: 24 Braidley Road, Bournemouth, Dorset BH2 6KX (☎01202-296234; e-mail matt.llewillin@ef.com; www.ef.com).
EFL Teachers required for July and August to work full-time. Wages vary according to location and experience. Candidates should have at least a first degree and CELTA.
Applications with CVs should be sent to the School Director at the above address.

EF INTERNATIONAL LANGUAGE SCHOOLS: Castle Road, Torquay, Devon TQ1 3BG (☎01803-297606; e-mail dean.rollings@ef.com; www.ef.com).
EFL Teachers required for July and August to work full-time. Wages vary according to location and experience. Candidates should have at least a first degree and CELTA.
Applications with CVs should be sent to the School Director at the above address

HARROW HOUSE INTERNATIONAL COLLEGE: Harrow Drive, Swanage, Dorset BH19 1PE (☎01929-424421; fax 01929-427175; e-mail info@harrowhouse. co.uk; www.harrowhouse.com). A 37 year-old international language college set in the Purbecks in the heart of Dorset, which teaches English to students from over 60 countries.
English Language Teachers (15-20) required to teach children from age 8 upwards. Wages £330 per week. To work six days per week. Applicants must possess a CELTA qualification or equivalent.
Residential Sports/Activities Teachers (19-24). Wages £200 per week plus full board and accommodation. Required to work six days per week. Must have relevant experience and qualifications.
Drama/Art Leaders (2). Wages £330 per week. Required to work 6 days per week. Relevant experience and qualifications required.

Activities Co-ordinator required to provide students with a full leisure programme. Wages £330 per week. Could be a residential position. Relevant qualifications and experience required.

Staff required for a minimum of 6 weeks from approximately 16 June until the end of August. Where accommodation is not included as a part of the wage, it is available at a cost of £70 per week. Foreign applicants are welcome to apply, but must have a level of English appropriate to the position.

Applications from February onwards to Sharon Patterson for the posts of English teachers and drama/art leaders, and to Paul Yerby for the posts of sports and activities teachers, at the above address.

KING'S SCHOOL OF ENGLISH: 58 Braidley Road, Bournemouth BH2 6LD (☎01202-293535; fax 01202-293922; e-mail info@kingsgroup.co.uk; www.kingsgroup.co.uk). A private school of English for overseas students. Offers courses for all ages, but much of their work is with teenagers and children. The school is located 5 minutes from the centre of Bournemouth. It has a very busy summer period, offering a fun, vibrant but hard-working atmosphere.

EFL Teachers (40). Wages from £200-£350 per week, to give 20-40 lessons per week. Must have TEFL certificate or diploma, and preferably a degree and relevant experience.

Social and Sports Supervisors (20). Wages from £150-£250 per week, working full time 5-6 days per week. Must have relevant sports and social activities experience/qualifications.

Administrative Assistants (10). Wages from £150-£225 per week, working full time 5-6 days per week. Must have good computer, organisational and interpersonal skills.

Course Directors (4). Wages from £300-£375 per week, working full time. Must have a diploma in TEFL, university degree and considerable TEFL experience.

Minimum period of work 2 weeks. Positions are available between 1 July and 31 August. Foreign applicants may be considered for positions other than teaching posts. Fluent English absolutely essential. All applicants must be enthusiastic, versatile and enjoy working with young people. Accommodation not usually available, but included for teachers on residential courses.

Applications should be made from April onwards to the School Principal at the above address. Interview required.

RICHARD LANGUAGE COLLEGE: 43-45 Wimborne Road, Bournemouth, Dorset BH3 7AB (☎01202-555932; fax 01202-555874; e-mail acadman@rlc.co.uk; www.rlc.co.uk).

EFL Teachers (20). £252 to £270 per week depending on qualifications and experience. Hours 8.30am to 4.30pm, Monday to Friday. Teaching 6 or 7 lessons of 45 minutes per day to adults of mixed levels and different nationalities, in classes of about 10 students. Minimum work period 2 weeks between 1 June and 30 August. Must have first degree and RSA Prep. Certificate in TEFL.

Help cannot be given in finding accommodation. All serious applicants will be considered. Longer-term year-round placements for suitable applicants.

Applications from 28 February to the Academic Manager, Richard Language College.

SCANBRIT SCHOOL OF ENGLISH: 22 Church Road, Bournemouth BH6 4AT (☎01202-428252; fax 01202-428926; e-mail info@scanbrit.co.uk; www.scanbrit.co.uk). Scanbrit School is a British Council accredited school situated adjacent to the

beach in a suburb of Bournemouth.
EFL Teachers (10). Wages between £10 and £12 per hour. To teach for 20 to 30 hours a week from 9am to 4pm, Monday to Friday over the summer. Applicants should have some teaching experience and a minimum RSA Certificate TEFL qualification.
Applications with CV to the above address.

SEYMOUR INTERNATIONAL LANGUAGE SERVICES: 86 Plymouth Road, Plympton, Devon PL7 4NB (☎01752-202094; fax 01752-202096; e-mail c.seymour@ btinternet.com).
Sports Teachers (4). Wages £8 per hour. Must hold a first aid certificate.
English Teachers (15). Wages £42 per day; to work from 9.30am to 4.45pm Monday to Friday. Should be a TEFL graduate; car necessary.
  Period of work July-August.
Applications to Mr Seymour at the above address.

SOUTHBOURNE SCHOOL OF ENGLISH: 30 Beaufort Road, Bournemouth BH6 5AL (☎01202-422300; fax 01202-417108; e-mail paul@southbourneschool. co.uk; www.southbourneschool.co.uk). A family run school, working for 40 years teaching English as a foreign language. British Council accredited and a member of English UK.
EFL Teachers (20). Wages minimum £10.30 per hour; to work 15-30 hours per week. Must have one of the following qualifications; PGCE, B.ed., Cert Ed., RSA Cert EFL, RSA Diploma EFL, TESOL, Trinity Diploma.
Residential Teachers for junior courses required for 4 weeks. Wages £325 per week. To start work in July.
Sports Organisers/Assistants (8). Wages £180-£300 per week. To work 40-50 hours a week. Sports training useful. Minibus driver useful, with category D1 licence or minibus licence.
  Free accommodation on residential courses. Staff required from mid June-end August.
Applications from Easter to the Director of Studies at kathryn@southbourneschool. co.uk.

STUDY VACATIONS: The Old Bakery, Jews Lane, Landsdown View, Bath BA2 3DG (☎01225-443261; fax 01225-420585; e-mail recruitment@elac.co.uk; www. elac.co.uk).
EFL Teachers (17) required to teach foreign students aged 13 to 17 in Bath, East Sussex, Nottingham and Camarthen. £9-£11 per hour. Required to teach for 5-8 hours per day. Three and four week contracts June/July. Residential or non-residential. Some posts also for Director of Studies (£350 per week plus accommodation).
Applications to Tim Cooke, Operations Manager at the above address.

SUL LANGUAGE SCHOOLS: 31 Southpark Road, Tywardreath, Par, Cornwall PL24 2PU (☎01726-814227; fax 01726-813135; e-mail efl@sul-schools.com; www. sul-schools.com). A well-established business that provides language holiday courses in Cornwall, Devon, Somerset, Midlands, Ireland and Scotland for foreign teenagers. Courses run for 2-4 weeks from April to September.
EFL Teachers. Wages dependant on experience and qualifications but are usually from £26 per morning of 2½ hours. To work mornings and possibly afternoons, supervising activities. Teachers required from April-August for a minimum period of 2 weeks. Applicants should be TEFL qualified or hold a languages degree or teaching qualification. Accommodation is available at some centres.

Applications from January to the Director of Studies at the above address. Interview usually required.

TORBAY LANGUAGE CENTRE: Conway Road, Paignton, Devon TQ4 5LH (☎01803-558555; fax 01803-559606; e-mail tlc@lalgroup.com; www.lalgroup. com). A large school with very good resources. CELTA training centre so there is excellent teacher support and guidance. Maximum class size of ten students. Also runs a small residential centre in North Devon.
EFL Teachers. Wages around £9.50 per hour; to teach between 15-30 hours per week. Teachers required from last week of June until late summer for minimum of 4 weeks. Must be CELTA or equivalent or PGCE with TEFL experience. Accommodation list available from the school.
Application pack available at the above address.

TWIN ENGLISH CENTRE SALISBURY: The Duchess of Albany Building, Ox Row, Salisbury, Wiltshire SP1 1EU (☎01722-412711; fax 01722-414604; www. twinuk.com). Small but expanding language school in the centre of Salisbury. Offers English tuition to groups of international students in a friendly work environment.
Part Time EFL Teachers (5). Wages £11 per hour minimum, depending on experience. To work mornings and some afternoons. Applicants must be TEFL qualified with experience teaching multi-lingual groups.
Part Time Social Activity Organisers (4). Wages from £5.00 per hour. To work mornings, afternoons and some weekends.
Staff required from June to September. Board and accommodation is not provided. Enthusiasm and energy needed.
Applications from March to the Principal at the above address.

Medical

ALTOGETHER CARE: 21 Glendinning Avenue, Weymouth, Dorset DT4 7QF (☎01305-784518; fax 01305-206145; e-mail info@altogether-care.co.uk; www. altogether-care.co.uk).
Carers, Live-in Carers, Agency Carers. Wages are competitive, all hours to suit. Staff are required all year long. Qualifications are not always necessary, since the chance of furthering skills exists within the company. The minimum period of work is 6 months; accommodation could be provided, if demand requires it, at £70 per week. Fluent English is essential, but non-UK citizens with the relevant skills will be considered.
Apply to the address above all year around. An interview will be needed.

ELITE CARE NURSING AGENCY: PO Box 165, Barnstaple, Devon EX32 8HJ (☎01271-346666; enquiries@ecna.co.uk; www.ecna.co.uk).
Qualified Nurses (30). Must be RGN/RMN to work in local nursing homes and hospitals.
Care Assistants (30) to work in clients' own homes, also required to work in local nursing homes and hospitals. Must be experienced. Will require CRB disclosure (Police check).
Work available all year round.
Applications to Mrs Linda Bland at the above address.

LIVING AWARENESS: 1 The Green, East Knoyle, Salisbury SP3 6BN (tel/fax 01747-830504; e-mail live.aware@virgin.net; www.livingfocus.net). Michael, a disabled teacher of movement and dance, needs help from a team to manage a project from his own home. Active interests in meditation, exercise and diet essential. Assist with dance events/sessions for people with learning difficulties and mental or physical impairments. Visits to the Green House can be made by appointment. Enquiries always welcome or visit a small summer camp held once a year.
Carers/Personal Assistants (2) to run the house and be part of an organised team in order to enable an active and disabled person to live a creative and healthy alternative lifestyle. Also train to assist in the community with exercises. Wages negotiable. Full board and accommodation. To work variable hours. Enquiries/applications invited all year round, especially mid-June, September and spring. Fluent English required.
Applications and enquiries should be made as soon as possible to Michael Mitchell at the above address or by e-mail.

NEWCROSS HEALTHCARE SOLUTIONS: 9th Floor Colston Tower, Colston Street, Bristol BS1 4XE (☎0117-934 0640; fax 0117-925 4971; e-mail karen. underwood@newcrosshealthcare.com). A nursing agency providing trained and untrained staff to the NHS, private care homes and local authority establishments.
Healthcare Workers. Wages from £7.00 per hour. Must be 18 or over with a minimum of 6 months' experience.
Registered Nurses. Wages from £13.50 per hour. Must have a minimum of 3-6 months' experience.
Vacancies are on-going, with flexible hours to suit. Accommodation is not available.
Apply, by phone, to Karen Underwood.

NEWCROSS HEALTHCARE SOLUTIONS LTD: Waterside, Berry Pomeroy, Totnes, Devon TQ9 6LH (☎01803-867800; fax 01803-867218; e-mail hg@ newcrosshealthcare.com; www.newcrosshealthcare.com). Part of nationwide suppliers of staff throughout the healthcare industry, from the NHS and Trust Hospitals to home caring.
RGNs (500), RMNs (500). At least 1 year's experience. To work 37 hours and over per week. Wages are high.
HCA (Carers) (1,000). 3 to 6 months' experience. To work 37 hours and over per week. Wages are high.
Homecare Buddies (1,000), Ancillary Staff (500). To work 37 hours a week. Must be 16 or over; no experience necessary.
No minimum period of work. B & L not available. Non-UK citizens with suitable qualifications will be considered.
Applications should be sent to the above address. Interviews will be necessary.

THORNBURY NURSING SERVICES: 7 & 9 Whiteladies Road, Clifton, Bristol BS8 1NN (☎0845-120 5252; fax 0845-120 5270; e-mail tnsrecruitment@tnsltd. com).
Registered and Auxiliary Nurses to work nationwide carrying out day and night-shift agency nursing work in NHS and private hospitals and nursing homes. Wages are from £22.00 per hour for registered nurses, or from £11.50 per hour for auxiliary nurses, with holiday pay included in this rate. Candidates must have 6-12 months experience (dependent on specialism) within the last two years of clinical nursing and NMC Registration for qualified nurses. All applicants must pass an interview prior to being accepted.

To obtain positions *contact* the agency at the above address.

WESTBOURNE CARE SERVICES: Claire Court, 8 Church Street, Yeovil, Somerset BA20 1HE (☎01935-472486; e-mail westbournecare@hotmail.com). A care agency sending competent and trustworthy workers to care for elderly and disabled individuals.
Care Assistants (2), Experienced Care Assistants (2), Trained and Experienced Care Assistants (2), NVQ Trained Care Assistants (2). Wages from £6.00 to £10 per hour according to experience, competence, qualification and past records on suitability, reliability, good health and trustworthiness. To work Monday to Sunday, various shifts available.
Senior Care Assistants for example qualified, enrolled nurses for home care positions. Wages on application.
Work involves caring for elderly or disabled individuals either in their own home or in a registered home environment. Positions available all year round. Minimum age 21. Applicants should be in good health (a health screening is done as part of the recruitment process) and should preferably hold Criminal Records Bureau vetted certificates and 2 references. A CRB check is imperative if applicants do not already hold certificates. Foreign applicants who have been trained as auxiliary nurses and are fluent in English welcome.
Contact Westbourne Care Services at the above number at any time for an application form. Interview required.

Outdoor

BOLDSCAN LIMITED: Unit 4 Tonedale Business Park, Wellington, Somerset TA21 OAW (☎01823-665849; fax 01823-665850). Manufactures marquees and hires them out to the event industry.
Marquee Erectors (15-20). Work involves the erection of marquees for local events, weddings and shows. Wages at national minimum rate. Required to work 40 to 60 hours per week. Applicants must be at least 18 years old. Period of work from 1 April to 30 September for a minimum of 4 weeks. Accommodation not available.
Applicants should *apply* from mid-February to Mr P.Cornish at the above address. Interview necessary.

M & S BROOKING: Stokely Farm Shop, Stokenham, Kingsbridge, Devon TQ7 2SE (tel/fax 01548-581010; info@stokeley.co.uk; www.stokeley.co.uk).
Fruit and Vegetable Pickers (3). £5.35 per hour. Required to work 20 hours per week (including some weekends). Extra hours may be available. From June to September. Must be over 18 years of age.
Applications to J H Tucker, Farm Manager at the above address.

BURNBAKE CAMPSITE: Rempstone, Corfe Castle, Wareham, Dorset BH20 5JJ (☎01929-480570; e-mail info@burnbake.com; www.burnbake.com). Long-established campsite.
Campsite Assistants (3) to handle enquiries, serve the shop, help with cleaning and rubbish collection and carry out general site maintenance and customer service duties. Wages of £180 per week with free mobile accommodation. To work 8am-12pm and 5pm-7pm over a 6 day week. One assistant required 29 April to 17 September, two assistants needed 8 July to 9 September.
For *applications* or further details, contact Tim Bircham at the above address.

CHARLTON ORCHARDS: Creech St. Michael, Taunton, Somerset TA3 5PF (tel/fax 01823-412959; e-mail sally@charlton-orchards.co.uk; www.charltonorchards.com). Family run fruit farm, growing apples, pears and plums, close to the town of Taunton. **Fruit Pickers (5-6)** to pick and pack plums and apples in August, September and October. Payment at basic agricultural rate and occasional opportunities for piece-rate; campsite accommodation available at no charge. To work approximately 8 hours per day, Monday to Friday. Must be aged 16 and over: it would be helpful if applicants are not red/green colour blind.

Applications to Duncan Small, Partner, at the above address.

J.F. COLES: Stephens Farm, Spaxton, Near Bridgwater, Somerset TA5 1BU (☎01278-671281; fax 01278-671530). **Pea and Bean Pickers (20).** Piece-work rates, hours from 7am-4pm. Minimum period of work 6 weeks between June and September. Own tents required for accommodation, but water and portaloos are available. No experience necessary. Overseas applicants welcome.

Applications from end of May to Mr and Mrs Coles at the above address.

K.S. COLES: Chelston House Farm, Chelston, Wellington, Somerset TA21 9HP (☎01823-664244; fax 01823-660325; e-mail kscoles@btinternet.com). Situated in one of the most attractive areas of England, K.S. Coles have been trading for more than 30 years and now supply several of the major multiples with fresh produce. **Pea Pickers (60 or more).** Piecework rates apply. Period of work approximately mid-June to the end of August. Hours from 6am to 4.30pm. Minimum age 18.

Applications to Mrs C.M. Coles, Partner, or Miss S. Coles, at the above address.

CUTLIFFE FARM: Sherford, Taunton, Somerset TA1 3RQ (☎01823-253808). The farm is within easy walking distance from Taunton town centre, with all the facilities available in a large country town. **Fruit Pickers (30+)** required to pick strawberries, raspberries and runner beans. Wages at piece work rate plus bonuses. Period of work late May to mid-July. Some accommodation may be available in caravans. Minimum age 18. Overseas applicants welcome, provided they have obtained the necessary work visa.

Applications to A.P. & S.M. Parris at the above address.

DANCO INTERNATIONAL PLC: The Pavilion Centre, Frog Lane, Coalpit Heath, Bristol BS36 2NW (☎01454-250222; fax 01454-250444; e-mail elisa@danco.co.uk; www.danco.co.uk). **Marquee Erectors (10-15)** to put up marquees around the UK. Wages £5.35 per hour plus a £10 night out allowance when on site. To work 50 to 60 hours per week. 7 day weeks are required, with days off once job is complete. Basic accommodation provided but applicants need sleeping bag, pots, pans, cutlery and plates in addition to wet weather gear and steel toe-capped boots. **Warehouse Operatives** to load and unload trailers and pick orders. Wages £5.70 per hour; to work 50-60 hours per week, including weekend work. Basic accommodation provided on site.

Period of work from May to September. Applicants should be aged 20 years upwards; those with driving licences preferred.

Applications to Elisa Lunt, Personnel Manager, at the above address.

THE DORSET BLUEBERRY COMPANY: Littlemoors Farm, Ham Lane, Hampreston, Wimborne, Dorset BH21 7LT (☎01202-891426; fax 01202-874737;

e-mail info@dorset-blueberry.co.uk; www.dorset-blueberry.com). Britain's primary producers of fresh blueberries for major supermarkets. **Pickers and Packers** required. Wages are calculated by kg performance and good workers can earn high wages. Positions available from July to September.
Applications only accepted through the above website.

GRAND WESTERN HORSEBOAT CO: The Wharf, Canal Hill, Tiverton, Devon EX16 4HX (☎01884-253345; e-mail info@horseboat.co.uk; www.horseboat.co.uk). One of only five horsedrawn barges in England and the last one in The West Country. This family-run business operates horsedrawn barge trips along the Grand Western Canal, a designated country park and local nature reserve.
Crew Member for the horsedrawn barge. Will include working with heavy horses, steering, roping and team work. Pay meets national minimum wage. From 4 days per week, longer in high season. Position available from May to September. Must be reliable, adaptable, fit, polite and of clean appearance. Applicants should be 25 and over and hold a driving licence. Accommodation not available.
Applications should be made to Mr P.R. Brind from 1 April at the above address.

HAYLES FRUIT FARM LTD: Winchombe, Cheltenham, Gloucestershire GL54 5PB (☎01242-602123; fax 01242-603320; e-mail jobs@hayles-fruit-farm.co.uk; www.hayles-fruit-farm.co.uk). A very friendly family run mixed fruit farm in a beautiful rural location in the Cotswolds.
Fruit Pickers (10) to work approximately 8am to 4pm, picking soft fruit, apples, pears, plums and nuts. Piece work rates, approximately £30-£50 per day. Minimum period of work 3-5 weeks between August and end of September. Minimum age 21 years. Some accommodation provided and campsite available. A subsidised hot meal can be provided every evening for people staying in tents. No experience necessary. Foreign applicants must have a work permit, or reside in the EU.
Applications from 1 May to Mr Martin Harrell at the above address.

J.G. MARQUEES: Nettwood Farm, East Harptree, Bristol BS40 6DA (☎01761-221366; e-mail jeremy_griffin@btconnect.com).
Marquee Erectors. Wages from £5.35 to £6.50 per hour. To work 8.30am to 5.30pm, Monday to Friday. Positions are available from May to October. Applicants must be able to drive to get to work.
Applications should be made to Jeremy Griffin, Proprietor, at the above address.

MANOR FARM: Shepton Beauchamp, Ilminster, Somerset TA19 OLA (☎01460-240221; fax 01460-240544; e-mail lize@tesco.net).
Fruit Packers/Shop Assistants (3) needed for a pick-your-own farm producing strawberries, raspberries and runner beans. Wages of £6 per hour, more for weekend work; no accommodation available. To work in the shop 9am to 5pm during the week, plus alternate Saturdays/Sundays in June and July (August not so important); packing hours 7.30am to 1 or 2pm. Period of work from June to September.
    Applicants should be aged at least 18 with common sense and a good sense of humour. For work in the shop applicants must like old people and children, be patient and able to add up. The job will involve working with the owner and overseas students.
Applications to E.B. England, Partner, at the above address.

SHULDHAM SOFT FRUIT GROWERS LTD: East Stoke House, Stoke-sub-Hamdon, Somerset TA14 6UF (☎01935-822300; fax 01935-824596; e-mail shuldham@btconnect.com). Set in beautiful countryside in southeast Somerset. Nearby towns for good shopping and nightlife. Excellent transport links. Family business, small and friendly.

Pickers/General Farm Hands (8) needed from 20 May to 31 August to pick soft fruits including strawberries, blackberries, tayberries, gooseberries, loganberries, raspberries and redcurrants, weather permitting during harvest. After the harvest, to carry out general husbandry of the farm and land. To work up to 6 days a week; 6-8 hours per day. May involve early starts (6am-6.30am) usually finishing at about midday. Some late afternoon picking. Minimum of £5.00 per hour., up to £6.00/£7.00 per hour possible. No accommodation provided but camping with own gear if necessary at nearby campsites. Applicants should be strong, determined, conscientious and versatile in approach. Foreign applicants with appropriate permits or visas, secured by themselves, are welcome.

Applications to Simon Shuldham, Managing Director.

SOUTH DEVON ORGANIC PRODUCERS LTD: Wash Barn, Buckfastleigh, Devon TQ11 0LD (tel/fax 01803-762100; e-mail sdop@farmersweekly.net). Organic vegetable growers.
Casual Field Staff (10-20). To weed, plant and harvest organic field scale vegetables. Minimum agricultural wage. To work 39 hours plus overtime; flexible hours. Positions are available from June to September/October. No previous experience necessary. Foreign applicants with necessary work permits welcome; fluent English not essential. Minimum age 17. No accommodation available. Transport is essential.

Applications should be made from the end of May onwards to Mrs Vanstone at the above address. Telephone interview sufficient.

SOUTH WEST MARQUEES LTD: Brook Farm, Whatley, Frome, Somerset BA11 3JX (☎01373-836999; fax 01373-836088; e-mail info@southwestmarquees.co.uk; www.southwestmarquees.co.uk.
Drivers/Marquee Erectors (1-3). Duties to include erecting and dismantling marquees, yard duties and cleaning of carpets. Wages of £4.50-£6.00 per hour depending on skill, with basic accommodation provided. To work 30-60 hours a week, with overtime at time and a half once over 40 hours per week. To normally work 6 days per week Monday-Sunday, with Saturdays normally off. Period of work from May to September.

Applicants should be aged over 18, strong and hard working. Those with a clean driving licence preferred; being able to drive a 7½ ton lorry a real bonus.

Applications to Chris White, Director, at the above address.

STUART LINE CRUISES: 5 Camperdown Terrace, Exmouth, Devon EX8 1EJ (☎01395-279693; fax 01395-279693; e-mail info@stuartlinecruises.co.uk; www. stuartlinecruises.co.uk). Passenger boat operator in Devon.
Boat Crew (2). Wages from £100-£150 per week. Flexible hours. Positions available for the summer. Fluent English helpful. No accommodation available. No experience necessary as full training is given. Minimum age 16.

Applications should be made to Ian Stuart at the above address. Interview required.

VIP MARQUEES: 30 Sercombes Gardens, Starcross, Exeter EX6 8SB (☎01392-833924; fax 01392-833987; e-mail sales@vipmarquees.com).
Labourers/Drivers (3-6) to erect and dismantle marquees in Devon and Cornwall. Wages at national minimum rate, to work 48 hours and over for 6 or 7 days a week

from June to August. Working days can be long, from between 6am and 7am until the job is complete. Drivers must be aged 25+ for insurance purposes.
Applications to D. Clements, Manager, at the above address.

Sport

GREENBANK SWIMMING POOL: Wilfrid Road, Street, Somerset BA16 0EU (☎01458-442468; e-mail greenbankpool@btinternet.com; www.greenbankpool. co.uk). A very busy, privately-run open-air swimming pool with more than 1,000 bathers during hot periods.
Lifeguards (3) to supervise and clean the pool and premises. Wages from £5.35 per hour. To work a minimum of 35 hours per week on a rota basis. Standby required during busy periods. Minimum period of work May to September. Royal Life Saving Society's National Pool Lifeguard Qualification expected. No accommodation available.
Applications, including a reference, should be made from between 1 March and the end of April to Mr D. Mogg, Pool Manager, at the above address. Interview necessary.

KNOWLE MANOR & RIDING CENTRE: Timberscombe, Minehead, Somerset TA24 6TZ (☎01643-841342; fax 01643-841644; e-mail info@knowlemanor.co.uk; www.knowlemanor.co.uk). Knowle Manor is a residential riding holiday centre based in Exmoor National Park. Set in 80 acres of grounds with indoor heated swimming pool, trout lake, croquet and badminton areas.
Riding Instructor (1) to work 5 days a week. Salary according to qualifications. Applicants must have B.H.S.A.I.
Ride Leaders (2) to work approximately 42 hours a week. Wages by the hour and according to the national minimum wage. Tax and National Insurance deductions. Experience with horses essential. Recommended B.H.S. Riding and Road Safety. First Aid Certificate needed. Mature outlook also needed. Minimum age 18. Staff training is undertaken. If living in, staff accommodation is £27.30 per week.
In-House Helpers (3) to perform all household duties in the hotel, including cleaning and waiting. Wages as above. To work approximately 35 hours a week. No experience necessary but applicants must be cheerful.
Minimum period of work for all positions is July to end of August or preferably September to October. Suitably qualified foreign applicants welcome.
Applications from January onwards to Ruth and Kevin Lamacraft at the above address.

MENDIP OUTDOOR PURSUITS: The Warehouse, Silver Street, Congresbury, Somerset BS49 5EY (☎01934-820518; e-mail info@mendipoutdoorpursuits.co.uk; www.mendipoutdoorpursuits.co.uk). A multi-activity mobile centre established in 1987 for clients aged 8 years and above. Training available in safety, education, technical skills and NVQs.
Instructors. Wages from £245 per week. Minimum age 21.
All instructors to work 5 days per week. Must hold qualifications in outdoor pursuits. Freelance and full-time work between May and September. Overseas applicants able to communicate well in English welcome. All candidates must be available for interview.
Applications to Dave Eddins at the above address.

ROCKLEY WATERSPORTS: Enefco House, Strand Street, Poole, Dorset BH15 1HJ (☎0870-777 0541; fax 0870-777 0542; e-mail personnel@rockleywatersports.

com; www.rockleywatersports.com). Based in beautiful Poole Harbour and South-West France, Rockley teach watersports to all abilities and ages and are one of Europe's most highly regarded watersports centres.

Watersports Instructors (75). Experienced instructors, senior instructors and sailing managers required.

Couriers/Entertainment Team (30). Duties include assisting with general site duties, and delivering the entertainments package.

Driver/Handyman (4). Responsible for transfers, hospital and shopping runs. Duties also include general maintenance. This is a senior position.

Residential Assistants (2). Responsible for the pastoral care of up to 100 residential children. Experience preferred.

The jobs offer the opportunity to gain watersports experience and use all the centre facilities. Staff required for the summer season, from March to October. All successful applicants must complete a CRB check.

For an *application form* contact Richard Percy at the above address.

WEST-ANSTEY FARM EXMOOR: Dulverton, Somerset TA22 9RY (☎01398-341354). A working farm and stables adjoining open moorland four miles from Dulverton, the nearest town. Lovely riding county, moorlands, fields and woods.

Riding Assistants (2). Must be able to take out rides and lead beginners when necessary. Hours vary depending on schedule of activities. Must be fairly light, a good rider and with experience of going on riding holidays or of conducting treks and caring for ponies, horses and people. Sense of fun, helpfulness and a cheerful disposition essential. Must also be willing to help indoors when necessary.

Pocket money plus B & L provided. Applicants must be non-smokers and able to get on with both adults and children. Accommodation only available for females. Work available all year round. Minimum work period of 8 to 10 weeks. Minimum age of 16. First Aid certificate required. Riding certificates desirable. Applicants are required not to have face piercings.

Applications with a contact phone number and photograph a.s.a.p. to the Proprietor, West-Anstey Farm Exmoor.

Voluntary Work

Conservation and the Environment

CHURCHTOWN OUTDOOR ADVENTURE: Churchtown Farm, Lanlivery, Bodmin, Cornwall PL30 5BT (☎01208-872148; e-mail bookings@vitalise.org.uk; www.vitalise.org.uk).

Churchtown Farm provides outdoor, environmental and adventurous training courses accessible to everyone, regardless of degree of special need. As well as the more traditional courses, in ecology and outdoor pursuits, a new development is the provision of personal development programmes which concentrate on personal growth, encouraging a positive image of self, and promoting self-confidence. In-service courses for teachers and carers can be organised and opportunities exist for team building and development courses, suitable for all staff groups. The Centre is attractively converted and well equipped with an indoor swimming pool, farm, nature reserve and pleasant grounds. Sailing and canoeing takes place on the nearby River Fowey and the Centre is only five miles from the coast. Help is available with care requirements and a qualified night staff is on call on site throughout the night.

Up to 16 **Volunteers** are needed at a time to support the professional staff. Accommodation is in a shared house adjacent to the main Centre. Applications are invited from anyone who feels they have an empathy with special needs people. Whilst a background in environmental, outdoor or medical areas would be an advantage, volunteers are welcome regardless of academic qualifications. Currently an allowance of £25 per week is payable, provided that volunteers stay for longer than three weeks.

Those interested should apply to the Head of Care at the above address.

THE CORNWALL WILDLIFE TRUST: Five Acres, Allet, Truro, Cornwall TR4 9DJ (☎01872-273939; fax 01872-225476; e-mail cwt@stgeorgeslooe.fsnet.co.uk and info@cornwt.demon.co.uk; www.cornwallwildlifetrust.org.uk).

St. George's Island lies half a mile off the Cornish coast and comprises twenty-two and a half acres of rough grassland, scrub, woodland, beaches and cliffs. It is one mile in circumference and rises to 150 feet at its highest point. The island is open to day visitors, and their landing fees and other income generated go towards the island's conservation and upkeep. Volunteers on working holidays greatly assist the Island's conservation projects.

About 20-30 **Volunteers** are taken on between Easter and October, usually for periods of one or two weeks, and they carry out tasks according to their enthusiasms, skills and abilities. This could include gardening, wood and track clearing, fencing, log-cutting, general conservation, general DIY and decorating. Volunteers live in a shared, self-catering chalet for which they buy their own food for the period. There is a charge of £5 for the boat from Looe.Volunteers are also required to meet and assist day visitors arriving by boat. As post is delivered and collected from the island every two or three weeks, please allow at least three weeks for a reply to enquiries by post.

Applications should be sent by e-mail to the above address.

THE MONKEY SANCTUARY: Looe, Cornwall PL13 1NZ (☎01503-262532; e-mail info@monkeysanctuary.org; www.monkeysanctuary.org).

Home to a colony of Woolly Monkeys and Rescue Centre for ex-pet Capuchins. The Sanctuary is a community dedicated to conservation, sustainable living and animal welfare. Education of the public in these areas is their main summer activity. **Volunteers** are required to work 40 hours per week in the sanctuary, and are essential in allowing the team of keepers to care for the colony. Help is needed in the kiosk, and with cleaning while the sanctuary is open to the public between April and September; during the closed season (October to March) volunteers assist with general maintenance work and cleaning. No qualifications are necessary but workers must have an interest in animal welfare and conservation.

Food and accommodation are provided, and volunteers are asked to make a voluntary donation to the Monkey Sanctuary Trust (suggested £45 per week waged, £35 per week students/unwaged). Minimum age 18. Overseas applicants with a good standard of English welcome.

Applications, four or five months in advance, should be made to Volunteer Co-ordinator at the above address, enclosing stamped s.a.e. or International Reply Coupon.

NATIONAL BIRDS OF PREY CENTRE: Newent, Gloucestershire GL18 1JJ (☎01531-820286; fax 01531-821389; e-mail kb@nbpc.co.uk; www.nbpc.co.uk).

A centre involved in the conservation and captive breeding of about 80 species of birds of prey.

Volunteers are welcome year-round, to help carry out habitat conservation tasks, including hedge planting, pond maintenance and clearing woods. Those who volunteer for longer lengths of time do get the chance to be involved with the birds and their handling.

For further *details*, contact the Centre at the above address.

THE NATIONAL SEAL SANCTUARY: Gweek Nr. Helston, Cornwall TR12 6UG (☎01326-221361; fax 01326-221210; e-mail seals@sealsanctuary.co.uk; www. sealsanctuary.co.uk).

The Sanctuary is a well-known marine animal rescue centre.

Volunteers are taken all year around to help with the Sanctuary's work, including caring for seals and sea lions. Volunteers must be over 18 and must be able to work for two weeks.

Apply to Marianne Fellows at the above address.

WILDFOWL & WETLANDS TRUST: Slimbridge, Gloucester GJ2 7BT (☎01453-891900; e-mail enquiries@wwt.org.uk; www.wwt.org.uk).

WWT is a charity aiming to promote the conservation of wildfowl and their wetland habitats as well as increasing the public's knowledge of these birds. The Centre has the world's largest collection of wildfowl.

The WWT depends on help from **Volunteers**. At Slimbridge, volunteers assist throughout the grounds and centre including the Visitor Services, Education, Aviculture and Horticulture departments. Grounds volunteers assist the wardens in their daily duties and gain practical conservation knowledge and experience. Volunteers working in visitor information usually live locally and work one day a week on a regular basis. Duties include manning the information desk, guiding school parties and the public and assisting with the development of educational material.

Full-time and part-time opportunities are available but some placements do require volunteers to commit to a minimum of 2 months at the centre to allow time for training. Limited on-site accommodation is available. Volunteers must be 16 or over. No previous experience or qualifications are required, only plenty of enthusiasm, a willingness to help and a capacity to learn.

For further *details* contact the Slimbridge office. Other WWT centres also welcome the assistance of volunteers – contact the centre you are interested in for information.

Festivals and Special Events

CHELTENHAM FESTIVAL OF LITERATURE: Town Hall, Imperial Square, Cheltenham, Gloucestershire GL50 1QA (☎01242-263494; fax 01242-256457; e-mail clair.greenaway@cheltenham.gov.uk).

The Cheltenham Festival of Literature will be in its 58th year in 2007 and is the largest and most popular of its kind in Europe. There is a wide range of events including talks and lectures, poetry readings, novelists in conversation, creative writing workshops, exhibitions, discussions and a literary festival for children.

Festival Volunteers (25) to look after both the authors and the audience as well as helping with the setting up of events, front of house duties, looking after the office and assisting the sound crew. To work for 10 days from 8-17 October; the hours at the festival are fairly long, the festival day runs from 10.00am- midnight. Applicants should be graduates over 18, with an interest in literature, arts administration or events management.

Volunteers are given free accommodation, travel expenses and food and drink. Free entry to all events is also provided. Overseas applicants are welcome but must have a very high standard of spoken and written English.

Applications should be sent to Clair Greenaway, Festival Manager, from May onwards to the above address.

Heritage

LUNDY COMPANY: Lundy Island, Bideford, North Devon EX39 2LY (☎01721-863636; fax 01237-431832; e-mail warden@lundyisland.co.uk; www.lundyisland. co.uk).
Lundy is an island off the North Devon coast managed by the Landmark Trust with 23 letting properties, a pub and a shop.
Volunteer Positions. There are various outdoor positions available involving conservation and farm work and general island duties. The jobs are variable according to the time of year. Volunteers need no experience but must have lots of enthusiasm. Basic, self-catering accommodation is provided free of charge and there is a reduced fare on boat trips. Volunteers are required from April to October for a minimum of 1 week.
Applications should be sent to the Warden at the above address from January onwards.

Social and Community Schemes

LEE ABBEY COMMUNITY: Personnel, Lee Abbey, Lynton, Devon EX35 6JJ (☎01598-752621; e-mail personnel@leeabbey.org.uk; www.leeabbey.org.uk).
A Christian conference, retreat and holiday centre on the north Devon coast, run by a 90-stong international community with a vision to renew and serve the church.
Volunteers. Board, lodging and pocket money provided. Minimum stay is 3 months. Minimum age is 18. Volunteers must be committed Christians. No qualifications necessary. Foreign applicants with fluent English welcome.
Applications should be made using the application form obtainable from the above address.

Vacation Traineeships & Internships

Law

BURGES SALMON SOLICITORS: Narrow Quay House, Narrow Quay, Bristol BS1 4AH (☎0117-902 2766; fax 0117-902 4400; e-mail katy.edge@burges-salmon. com; www.burges-salmon.co.uk).
Based in Bristol, Burges Salmon is one of the UK's leading commercial law firms offering an exceptional quality of life combined with a concentration of legal talent unsurpassed by any other firm in the country. Burges Salmon provides national and international clients with a full commercial service through 6 main departments: Corporate and Financial Institutions (CFI), Commercial, Property, Tax and Trusts, Commercial Disputes and Construction (CDC), and Agriculture, Property Litigation & Environment (APLE). Specialist areas include: Banking, Competition, Corporate Finance, Employment, IP and Technology, and Transport. The firm is ranked top tier by Chambers and Partners for 18 of its practice areas.
40 two-week placements for 2007. Remuneration £250 per week. Full fees are paid for both the GDL and LPC. Also pay maintenance grants of £6,000 to LPC students and £12,000 to students studying both the GDL and LPC (£6,000 p.a). Closing date for applications 31 January 2007. 20 training contracts for September 2009.

Applications and queries to Miss Katy Edge, Graduate Recruitment Manager, at the above address.

Science, Construction and Engineering

RENISHAW PLC: New Mills, Wotton-under-Edge, Gloucestershire GL12 8JR (☎01453-524433; fax 01453-524404; e-mail recruitment@renishaw.com; www. renishaw.com).

A British engineering company specialising in metrology, which designs and manufactures high precision metrology equipment and systems, and exports account for over 90% of its sales. Employs around 1,700 people in 24 countries.

Work Placements. Wages from £200-£260 per week. Placements last between 6 and 13 weeks. Available to undergraduates currently studying towards a degree in engineering or physics. Placements are based in rural Gloucestershire, so students must have their own transport. Students who spend time working in the company are considered for sponsorship through university.

Applications should be made in January to the above address, e-mailed in Microsoft Word format or made online. Interviews take place in mid-February.

The South Coast & Channel Islands

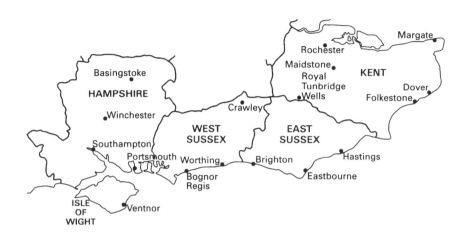

Prospects for Work.

Hotel and catering jobs should not be too hard to come by along the southern coast as long as you begin your search in good time. In Hastings, for example, many hotels open just for the holiday season and vacancies are generally for unskilled workers. Early enquiries are advisable in view of the likely difficulties in finding accommodation. Holiday camps in the area, such as the Combe Haven Holiday Park or Pontins at Camber Sands, always need seasonal summer staff. For details of work in the Hastings area visit Hastings Jobcentre Plus, telephone Jobseeker Direct on 0845-606 0234 or visit www.jobcentreplus.gov.uk.

Eastbourne has roughly ten times as many hotels as Hastings and throughout the season all types of hotel and catering vacancies are available. A large number of seafront kiosks also need staffing throughout the summer. Eastbourne hosts an annual Airborne week that attracts hundreds of thousands of visitors and staff are required to sell programmes, act as stewards and clean up afterwards. Eastbourne Jobcentre Plus has, in the past, operated a student register throughout the summer that endeavours to match students to suitable vacancies, and may continue to do so, despite the large merge with the Eastbourne Benefits Centre. Anyone wanting to look for work in the area can contact Jobseeker Direct on 0845-606 0234; for the price of a local telephone call, staff can complete a comprehensive jobsearch of vacancies locally or nationwide. You can also search for yourself at www.worktrain.gov.uk or www.jobcentreplus.gov.uk.

Holiday camps in West Sussex always need seasonal staff too. Bognor Regis Jobcentre Plus is the main contact for Butlins, the largest employer in the region. Butlins is just one of the many holiday camps along the South Coast; others include Sussex Beach Holiday Village, Sussex Coast Holiday Village, Church Farm Holiday Village and Pontins Ltd in Combe Sands, near Rye. Most of these provide live-in accommodation as well.

As well as work connected with the tourist industry, southern England is a good area for agricultural work, particularly in the hop fields and orchards of Kent (the 'Garden of England') during September. Around Ramsgate on the south Kentish coast casual agricultural workers are required for the harvesting of potatoes and cauliflowers. Thanks to technology and new crops, it is possible to find agricultural work at any time of year. Wages are not bad, but be prepared for an early morning start. Some seasonal jobs of this kind are advertised in the Ramsgate Jobcentre, although note that the amount of advertised work has reduced. Employers tend to employ the same people year after year, so you need to start looking reasonably early. It is probably best to contact the employers directly.

The South Coast is one of the principal areas for English language schools, which require teachers, youth leaders and supervisors. The majority of schools can be found at coastal resorts: Hastings, Bexhill, Eastbourne, Brighton, Hove and Bognor Regis, and in Tunbridge Wells, Thanet and Canterbury inland.

Sporting activities, like Cowes Week on the Isle of Wight (end of July/beginning of August) generate a short-term requirement for staff to help with catering, marshalling and car parking. The Southampton Boat Show, which takes place in mid-September, creates temporary vacancies for canvassers in the weeks running up to it, and for cleaners and caterers during the event. Southampton Jobcentre Plus keeps information regarding these jobs.

Both Jersey and Guernsey have thriving tourist industries, and thus a huge number of opportunities for temporary work, for example, in hotels, hire car companies, tour operators, ferry operators and watersports.

The fact that Jersey is exempt from VAT, capital gains tax or inheritance tax means that financial services thrive there, although there are very few vacancies for temporary staff in this sector. You can also check the local newspapers, the *Jersey Evening Post* and *Guernsey Press and Star*. Potential jobseekers should be aware that Jersey retains the right to deport non-UK Nationals; even EEA/EU citizens need a work permit before they can be employed in the Channel Islands.

Business and Industry

CHILSTONE GARDEN ORNAMENTS: Victoria Park, Fordcombe Road, Langton Green, Kent TN3 0RE (☎01892-740866; fax 01892-740249; ornaments@chilstone. co.uk; www.chilstone.com). Manufacturers of reconstituted stone architectural items and garden ornaments, close to Tunbridge Wells, in a beautiful woodland setting.
Workshop Helpers (5) to help with the mixing, making and general labouring. Must be strong and energetic.
Office Assistant to help with general office duties. Typing would be an advantage.

Wages and hours by arrangement. Interesting and varied work available throughout the year. Applicants need to find own accommodation, although some is available with the workshop foreman for a reasonable rate.
Applications to Mrs G. Gilbert at the above address.

LE COCQS STORES: 15 Le Hurst, Alderney, Channel Isles GY9 3TR (☎01481-824646; fax 01481-824189; e-mail shop@lecocqs.com; www.lecocqs.com).
Staff (4) to operate the check out, fill the shelves, deliver and warehousing duties. Wages of £5.50-£5.82 per hour. Flexible working hours. Period of work from June to September. Cheap local accommodation available on campsite by the beach. Minimum age 20.
Applications to Dave Thomas, Manager, at the above address.

PREMIER CARE NURSING AGENCY: 9 High Pastures Barn, Graywood Road, East Hoathly, East Sussex BN8 6QL (☎01825-873003; fax 01825-873373). An employment agency supplying temporary staff to a wide variety of clients throughout Sussex.
Temporary Care Workers (20), Temporary Support Workers (20). Wages £6.75 to £8.25 per hour.
Temporary Kitchen Staff (20), Temporary Domestics (20). Wages £6.25 to £7.25 per hour.
To work 10 to 40 hours per week. Must be over 18 and a car driver. Minimum period of work is one week; temps are paid weekly. Accommodation is not available. Fluent English is essential. Positions are ongoing.
Applicants should apply to the address above. An interview will be required.

PURE VACATIONS LIMITED: Suite 8, Wilson House, 119-120 John Wilson Park, Whitstable, Kent CT5 3QY (☎01227 264264; e-mail debbie@purevacations.com; www.purevacations.com).
Office Administrators (2), Sales Executives (2) to follow booking enquiries, assist in ticketing, general basic administration duties. Salary will be based on experience and hours worked and agreed. Hours will vary but very sociable and as required. All days of the week are optional and working conditions are good. Based in Whitstable, Kent (no accommodation provided). Applicants should be 16 and upwards with a general interest in the travel industry and adventure travel, especially in outdoor activities including surfing, ranching, golf etc. Outgoing, fun, active but professional person. Any qualifications to do with activities including surfing will be advantageous but not necessary. Foreign language would be an advantage but again not necessary. Must be professional. Job may lead to a good future career with a market leader.
Applications to Debbie Nel, General Manager at the above address.

REGENT LANGUAGE HOLIDAYS: 40-42 Queens Road, Brighton BN1 3XB (☎01273-718620; fax 01273-718621; e-mail holidays@regent.org.uk; www.regent. org.uk). Regent operates four residential centres in Southern England. They specialise in summer language holidays combining English language tuition with a range of activities and excursions.
Administrators (4). £250-£300 per week. Full board and accommodation provided. Graduate preferred, proven accounting/banking experience/skills.
Applications at any time to Recruitment at the above address.

SATURDAY VENTURE ASSOCIATION: (Disability Awareness UK), PO Box 9, Chichester, West Sussex PO20 7YD (tel/fax 01243-513464; e-mail sva@talk21. com; www.satven.org). A national registered charity promoting disability awareness in the community through talks in schools, demonstrations and drama workshops, employing disabled speakers and occupational therapists. The association operates in West and East Sussex, Hampshire, Dorset and Croydon.
Project Workers (2). Involves research, correspondence and fund raising. Wages from £5.00 per hour. To work 15 to 20 hours weekly. Must have current driving licence, own transport and be a non-smoker. A Level plus and graduates preferred. Can help with accommodation. Public speaking a plus.
Positions are available from January 2007.
Applications should be made as soon as possible to Sarah at the above address.

SYSTEMSOLID LTD: The Sanderson Centre, 15 Lees Lane, Gosport, Hampshire PO12 3UL (☎02392-524331; fax 02392-510287; sales@sanderson-centre.co.uk).

Decorator/Handy Person (1) needed from 1 July to 30 September to perform general decorating and other manual duties. Hours from 9am to 5pm. Wages on application. *Contact* Mr A.C. Smith, Director.

TONY FRESKO ICE CREAM LTD: Warren Farm, White Lane, Ash Green, Aldershot, Hampshire GU12 6HW (☎01252-315528; fax 01252-334537; e-mail joesawyer@btconnect.com; www.fresco.com). Mobile ice-cream outlet, with a fleet of 15 vans.
Drivers (25) for mobile ice cream sales at various shows and fetes and on rounds of industrial and housing estates. Wages from £6.00 to £10 per hour. To work approximately 11am to 9pm, 7 days of the week available. Minimum period of work of normally 6 weeks. Positions are available from March to October. Full driving licence required. Foreign applicants with appropriate work permits and acceptable spoken English welcome. No accommodation available.
Applications should be made from February onwards to Mr J Sawyer at the above address. Interview necessary.

Children

CALSHOT ACTIVITIES CENTRE: Calshot Spit, Fawley, Southampton SO45 1BR (☎023-8089 2077; fax 023-8089 1267; e-mail carol.oneill@hants.gov.uk; www.calshot.com). Hampshire County Council-run outdoor activity centre providing dinghy sailing, windsurfing, canoeing, power boating, rock climbing, track cycling, skiing, snowboarding and archery.
Summer Activity Supervisors (4) required to help run the centre. Duties include: providing pastoral care for the children outside activity times; organising games and activities; supervising pre-bed drinks; organising roll calls; assisting with the supervision of some off site activities; ensuring children are up and attending breakfast. Required to work an average of 42 hours per week, from 18 July to 31 August. B & L can be provided at a charge.
Applicants should be 18 years or over. Experience of working with children is an advantage, but a responsible and mature attitude and the ability to work as part of a close-knit team are just as important. Overseas applicants are welcome to apply as long as they have relevant work permits.
Applications should be made to Carol O'Neill, at the above address, from April.

HOLIDAY CLUB 4KIDS: Vinalls Business Centre, Neptown Road, Henfield, West Sussex BN5 9DZ (☎01273-494455; fax 01273-494451; info@holidayclub4kids. com).
Activity Coaches. Wages from £36 per day. Hours 8.30am to 5.30pm. To run a range of activities for children aged 4 to 13 years including sports, art and crafts, dance, drama and music. Teaching qualifications useful, but not essential. Must like children and have some experience of working with them. Minimum age 17. No accommodation provided.
Programme Managers for management of holiday club's team of coaches. From £55 per day. Childcare or teaching qualifications required.
All positions available from mid-July to mid-August.
Apply to Lyn Povey at the above address.

JUNIOR CHOICE ADVENTURE: 14 Queensway, New Milton, Hampshire BH25 5NN (☎0870-5133773; fax 0870-5133774; e-mail jcajobs@travelclass.co.uk; www. juniorchoiceadventure.co.uk). Provider of fun experiences for school children, with

stunning locations throughout the south-west.
Activity Instructors (120). Wages £260 per month plus B & L. No experience required as full training and qualifications are provided, including a Modern Apprenticeship.
Senior Instructors (13). Wages on application. Needs industry experience, as will be leading a team of instructors, as well as giving necessary training.
Centre Managers (13). Wages on application. Excellent communication, organisational and managerial skills necessary; responsible for the day-to-day running of the activity centre.
Watersports Positions (10). Competitive wages. Various watersports qualifications necessary; details on application.
All positions average 40 hours work per week, 5 or occasionally 6 days a week from March to July. B & L is available.
To *apply*, contact the above address.

LEISURE SERVICES: Council Offices, Rushmoor Borough Council, Farnborough Road, Farnborough, Hampshire GU14 7JU (☎01252-398745; fax 01252-524017; www.rushmoor.gov.uk).
Playleaders needed every school holiday to help organise a daily programme of activities and events for children aged 4-11. Wages £5.50 per hour. Accommodation is not available. Hours 8.30am-5.30pm (with a break for lunch) from Monday to Friday. Period of work every school holiday except Christmas. Two day training course provided. Minimum age 18. Applicants should have experience of working with children and be good organisers. Playwork qualifications or experience would be an advantage, as would sports and games, arts and crafts and drama and music.
Applications all year round to D.A. Wall at the above address.

LTC INTERNATIONAL COLLEGE: Compton Park, Compton Place Road, Eastbourne, East Sussex BN21 1EH (☎01323-727755; fax 01323-728279; e-mail info@geos-ltc.com; www.geos-ltc.com). A friendly private language school running residential courses for young learners. Set in a mansion house in its own park, 20 minutes walk from Eastbourne town centre.
Residential Social Organisers (4). Wages £220 per week for 40 hours per week; must be flexible as hours not 9 to 5. Free board and lodging. Would suit people interested in sport and/or music who like working with young students aged 10-16.
Contact the above address for further details.

VILLAGE CAMPS: Personnel Office, Department 809, Rue de la Morache 14, 1260 Nyon, Switzerland (☎+41 22-990 9405 (English); fax +41 22-990 9494; e-mail personnel@villagecamps.ch; www.villagecamps.com/personnel). Exciting opportunity to work with children in an international environment.
Activity Instructors needed for Village Camp's summer residential camp held at the historic Hurstpierpoint in the foothills of the South Downs of south-east England. Brighton is just 15 minutes away.
Nurses, Receptionists, TEFL Teachers, House Counsellors also required for the same programme. Agreement periods vary from 3 weeks.
B & L provided, along with accident/liability insurance and a net weekly allowance. Allowances are paid in local currency. Applicants must be a minimum of 21 years old (18+ for house counsellors) and have relevant experience and/or qualifications. A second language is desirable. A valid first aid and CPR certificate is required whilst at camp. Recruitment starts in December. There is no deadline to submit applications but positions are limited. Interviews are by telephone. Please specify department 809 on application.

For *information* on dates, locations and positions available and to download an application form, visit our www.villagecamps.com.

Holiday Centres and Amusements

ATHERFIELD BAY HOLIDAYS: Sherpherds Chine, Chale, Ventnor, Isle of Wight PO38 2JD (☎01983-740307; fax 01983-740022; e-mail info@atherfieldbay.co.uk; www.atherfieldbay.co.uk). Small family owned holiday centre providing holidays for school parties, families and the over 50s. Situated 8 miles from Ventnor on a cliff top, in 14 acres of grounds, and on own foreshore.
Waiting Staff (8), Kitchen Porters (2), Bar Staff (2), Snack Bar Assistants (4), Stillroom Assistants (2). Basic weekly wage £90. Free B & L.
All staff to work approx. 36 hours a week. Employment from 5 May to early October. Min. period of work 8 weeks. Experience not essential but must have friendly personality. Use of camp facilities when off duty. Minimum age for girls is 16, boys 17. Training given.
Applications, which must include a s.a.e. for a quick reply, from 15 March to Mrs Alexandra Walker, Atherfield Bay Holidays.

HARBOUR PARK LTD: Seafront, Littlehampton, West Sussex BN17 5LL (☎01903-721200; fax 01903-716663; e-mail fun@harbourpark.com; www.harbourpark.com). A family entertainment centre situated right on the sea front with rides and attractions for all ages including a coffee bar, burger bar and ice cream parlour.
Ride Operators and Catering Staff. Wages at national minimum rate, depending on age, plus accommodation. To work 5 to 6 days per week including weekends. Period of work June to September. Must be able to work July and August. Minimum age 18 years. Overseas applicants eligible to work in UK welcome.
Applications must be received by end of June.

HOBURNE NAISH: Christchurch Road, New Milton, Hampshire BH25 7RE (☎01425-273586; fax 01425-282130; e-mail naish@hoburne.com; www.hoburne.com/park_naish). Holiday park with 1,000 units of accommodation for holidaymakers, second home owners and residents, situated midway between Bournemouth and Southampton. Overlooks the Isle of Wight and Christchurch Bay.
Bar and Amusement Arcade Staff (12), Waiting Staff (6), Kitchen Staff (4), Receptionists (1) to work mainly evenings and weekends.
Lifeguards (12) for daytime and weekend work. Lifesaving qualification required.
Wages from minimum rate for all positions. To work 40 hours per week from 1 June to mid-September. No accommodation available. Foreign applicants with fluent English welcome.
Applications from 1 April to the General Manager, at the above address. Interview required.

SAUSMAREZ MANOR: St Martin, Guernsey, Channel Islands GY4 6SG (☎01481-235571; fax 01481-235572; e-mail sausmarezmanor@cwgsy.net; www.sausmarezmanor.co.uk). House and show garden open to the public with Sculpture Park, seen on TV and in national print media. Good beaches and a busy nightlife are nearby.
Housekeeper to do housework on a regular basis and clean the Manor House which is open to the public. Wages £100 per week plus free food and own bedroom. To work 3 full days and 3 half days a week with most evenings free. Period of work May to October although it is understood that one person may not be able to work the entire

period. Should ideally have experience of working en famille.
Gardener/Handyman also welcomed to work with the groundsman in sculpture park/ garden for some/all the summer. Wages at £100 per week plus food and own bedroom. Working hours are 3 full days and 3 half days per week, with the opportunity for extra work if desired at around £8 an hour.

Overseas applicants welcome. Interview necessary, but can be conducted by phone. Early application is advised and appreciated because applicants generally either come back the following year or send a friend because they enjoy it so much.

Apply from January to Peter de Sausmarez at the above address.

VECTIS VENTURES LTD: Blackgang Chine, Ventnor, Isle of Wight PO38 2HN (☎01983-730330; fax 01983-731267; e-mail info@blackgangchine.com or info@ robinhill.com). Blackgang Chine and Robin Hill Country Park (Down End, near Arreton, Isle of Wight PO30 2NU; ☎01983-527352; fax 01983-527347) are 2 visitor attractions on the Isle of Wight with a range of family amusements. Open daily throughout the summer, attractions include a small number of rides and also activity play areas.
General Park Assistants (15) to work on rides, in retail outlets and catering facilities and for gardening and car parking. Wages £4.95 per hour, to work 5-6 days a week. Staff are required from April to September/October and must work from July to August a minimum period of 6 weeks. Applicants should be over 18 years old. No experience is necessary but applicants should be friendly and outgoing.

Overseas applicants are welcome but must have reasonable English. No accommodation available.

Applications should be sent to Mr. Simon Dabell, Managing Director, at the above address between January and March. Interview necessary.

WIGHT CITY LEISURE PLC: 37 Culver Parade, Sandown, Isle of Wight PO36 8AT (☎01983-405302; fax 01983-406115; e-mail info@bogeys.co.uk; www.bogeys.co.uk).
Arcade Assistants (6). Wages £5.35 per hour. To work flexible shifts 9am-6pm or 6-11pm, 5 or 6 days a week.
Bar Staff (6). £5.50 per hour. To work flexible shifts 10am-6/7pm or 7pm-1/2 am.
Disco Bar Staff (4). Wages £6.50 per hour. To work 10pm-2am or 9pm-3am.

Applicants must be aged at least 18 and speak good English.

Applications to Paul Green, Director, at the above address.

Hotels and Catering

APPULDURCOMBE HERITAGE: Appuldurcombe House, Wroxall, Isle of Wight PO38 3EW (☎01983-852484; fax 01983-840188; e-mail enquiries@appuldurcombe. co.uk; www.appuldurcombe.co.uk). The Isle of Wight owl and falconry centre, and historic Appuldurcombe House.
Shop Assistant, Café Assistant. Wages from £5 per hour. Hours to be agreed; minimum period of work is two months, from June until the end of September. Must be flexible about working days, including weekends. Accommodation could be provided. Fluent English is essential. Suitably qualified non-UK citizens will be considered. Applicants must be over 18. Experience in tourism preferred.

Applications to Jane or John Owen from Easter at the above address. An interview may be necessary.

BALMER LAWN HOTEL: Lyndhurst Road, Brockenhurst, Hampshire SO42 7ZB (☎01590-623116; fax 01590-623864; e-mail info@balmerlawnhotel.co.uk; www.

balmerlawnhotel.co.uk). A friendly hotel situated in the heart of the New Forest with leisure facilities available. Approximately 20 minutes from Southampton and Bournemouth by train.

Waiting Staff (2-4) to work 39 hours per week, including weekends, serving breakfast 6.30am-11am, lunch 11am-3pm, and dinner 6.30-11pm, on a shift basis.

Wages on application minus £20 for accommodation. Applicants should be over 20 years old and preferably have previous experience of the hotel industry, though training will be given.

Applications to Mark Albray, General Manager at the above address.

CAREYS MANOR HOTEL: Lyndhurst Road, Brockenhurst, New Forest, Hampshire SO42 7RH (☎0870-751 2305; fax 0870-751 2306; e-mail info@careysmanor.co.uk; www.careysmanor.co.uk). An attractive 3-star hotel in the beautiful countryside of the New Forest with 79 bedrooms, 2 restaurants, with a brand new spa. The hotel employs 120 staff.

Restaurant Staff and Kitchen Staff. Wages of approximately £200 per week. Board and lodging is available for £35 per week. To work a 50 hour week. Minimum period of work 1 July to 15 September. Applicants must be over 16 and have qualifications. Overseas applicants considered.

Applications from April to the HR Manager.

COURTLAND'S HOTEL: 3-5 Wilmington Gardens, Eastbourne, East Sussex BN2 4JN (☎01323-723737; fax 01323-732902; e-mail enquiry@courtlandseastbourne. com; www.courtlandseastbourne.com).

Room Assistants (2) to work from 8am to 2pm.

Day Porters (2) to work from 10am to 2pm and 5pm to 9pm.

Restaurant Staff (2) to work from 8 to 11am and 6.30 to 9pm.

All wages at national minimum rate. Staff needed to begin work as soon as possible.

Applications to the Manager at the above address.

GOODWOOD HOUSE: Goodwood Estate Company, Goodwood, Chichester, West Sussex PO18 0PX (☎01243-755000; e-mail careers@goodwood.co.uk; www. goodwood.co.uk). The home to the Dukes of Richmond for over 300 years, Goodwood House has long been famous for both its natural beauty and its legendary hospitality.

Casual Waiting Staff (approx. 60) required to join the prestigious catering team who provide a renowned service for events in the State Apartments. Wages at £5.80 per hour. Hours of work are flexible, but most shifts last for a minimum of 5 hours. Staff required all summer from June to September. Accommodation is not provided. Previous experience is preferable, but not necessary. Ideally, candidates should be willing to learn and be of smart and neat appearance. Overseas applicants are welcome to apply, as long as they have relevant documentation and speak English to the same standard as a native speaker.

Application forms should be downloaded from the Careers page of the above website and sent to either David Edney or Ryan Grant at the above address. CVs will not be accepted. An interview will be necessary.

GRAND HOTEL: Grand Parade, St Leonards, Hastings, East Sussex TN38 0DD (☎01424-428510; fax 01424 428510).

General Hotel Worker (1) to clean bedrooms and work in the laundry and kitchen. Wages NMW. Accommodation available for one person only. Work available all year round. Overseas applicants welcome.

Applications to Mr Peter Mann at the above address.

GRANGE MOOR HOTEL: St Michaels Road, Maidstone, Kent ME16 8BS (☎01622-677623; fax 01622-678246; e-mail reservations@grangemoor.co.uk; www. grangemoor.co.uk). A 50-bedroom family run hotel with banquet room seeks staff for office Christmas dinners/parties.

Waiting Staff (10), Washers Up (6). Wages from £5.50 per hour, cash paid weekly. To work hours to suit between 1 and 23 December for lunches and evening meals. Christmas Day work available between noon-5pm at £15 per hour. Waiting staff required to provide plated service for Christmas dinners, full training will be given, applicants must be over 17, friendly, helpful and polite. No accommodation available.

Applications to Mrs Christine Sedge, at the above address.

HOTEL L'HORIZON: St Brelade's Bay, Jersey, Channel Islands JE3 8EF (☎01534-494404; fax 01534-494450; e-mail rearls@handpicked.co.uk or lhorizon@handpicked. co.uk). A 4-star 106-bedroom hotel, located on one of the island's beautiful beaches. Hotel L'Horizon offers a unique work experience for employees who prove themselves to be dedicated, responsible and efficient, with further employment prospects after the seasonal contracts terminate.

Food and Beverage Service Attendants, Room Attendants, Kitchen Porters, Commis Waiting Staff/Chef de Rangs. To work a 5-day week.

All applicants must be presentable, have excellent customer care skills and have worked within a similar environment before. Uniform and meals on duty and accommodation provided. Overseas applicants who have good English considered.

Applications should be made by application form available together with further information from the above address and website.

HOTEL REX: St Saviours Road, St Helier, Jersey JE2 4GJ (☎01534-731668; fax 01534-766922; e-mail enquiries@hotelrex.co.uk; www.hotelrex.co.uk). Established 40 years ago, the hotel is 5 minutes from St Helier.

Receptionists (2). Wages £210 per week plus bonus. Must have computer experience.

Waiting Staff (4). Wages £210 per week plus bonus. Must have silver service experience.

Kitchen Porter. Wages £190 per week plus bonus.

All staff work 42 hours a week. Accommodation is available at a cost of £50 per week. Staff share accommodation, with a maximum of 2 per room. Uniforms are supplied by the hotel. Minimum period of work 6 months between April and October. French and Italians are encouraged to apply.

Applications from 1 March to David Burton, Hotel Manager. Interview necessary.

LAKE HOTEL: Shore Road, Lower Bonchurch, Ventnor, Isle of Wight PO38 1RF (☎01983-852613; e-mail richard@lakehotel.co.uk; www.lakehotel.co.uk). A small hotel (20 rooms) in a quiet, peaceful location. Very busy and a high standard of service and cleanliness. Family run. Close to beach.

Chamber Staff (2). To work 39 hours a week. Shifts: 7.30am-12.30pm and 6.30pm-8.30pm.

Waiting Staff (2). To work 40 hours a week. Shifts as above.

All staff work 6 days for £160 a week, plus free B & L. Min. period of work 3½ months between April and end of October. No replies will be made for shorter availability. Some experience required, and applicants should have a sense of humour, be tidy and polite, and be able to work quickly and under pressure. Overseas applicants with good English welcome.

Applications from January to Mr Wyatt, Lake Hotel.

LONSDALE, SMITH'S, EDEN AND PALM COURT HOTELS: 51-61 Norfolk Road, Cliftonville, Margate, Kent CT9 2HX (☎01843-221053; fax 01843-299993). A family run group of private hotels. Hotels have indoor heated swimming pools and sports facilities. All rooms are en suite and have telephones, colour TVs and tea and coffee making facilities. Seaside location, half an hour from Dover and Canterbury, and 1½ hours from London.
Restaurant Staff /Room Attendants (4). Wages at national minimum rate, less £42 for food and accommodation.
Chefs. Pay on application.
To work 40 hours over 5 days a week (usually on split shifts) with no overtime. Must be over 18. Minimum period of work 3 months all year round. Overseas applicants welcomed.
Applications from January to Mrs Ann Smith. Interview not necessary.

LUCCOMBE HALL HOTEL: Luccombe Hall Hotel, Luccombe Road, Shanklin, Isle of Wight PO37 6RL (☎01983-869000; fax 01983-863082; e-mail enquiries@ luccombehall.co.uk; www.luccombehall.co.uk). Luccombe Hall Hotel is on a popular beach with squash, indoor and outdoor pools, gym, sauna.
Kitchen Staff (1-2), Waiting Staff (1-2), Room Attendants (1-2) for the school holidays. Live in or out. Pay £80 per week while training, and £100 per week thereafter (live-in); or £4.25 per hour (live out). Split shifts, 5/6 days per week. Hotel will train if no previous experience: applicants should be cheerful, reliable and sober.
Applications to Miss Claire Wells, General Manager.

THE MASTER BUILDERS HOUSE HOTEL: Buckler's Hard, Beaulieu, Hampshire SO42 7XB (☎01590-616253; fax 01590-616297; e-mail res@themasterbuilders. co.uk; www.themasterbuilders.co.uk).
Commis Waiting Staff to work in the 2-rosette Riverview Restaurant. Serve at breakfast, lunch, afternoon teas, dinner and conference set-up.
Bar Staff in the bar and galley to serve drinks and pub food.
Chamberstaff servicing guestrooms and evening turndown.
Wages £4.60-£5.00 per hour plus tips. Accommodation may be available; single room (£30 per week), shared (£25 per week), including 3 meals daily. Positions available from end April/May to end August/September. Applicants need good English, a pleasant outgoing personality, to enjoy the countryside and be good team players in an international team.
Applications to Sam Brinkman, General Manager, at the above address.

MORVAN FAMILY HOTELS: 57 Rouge Bouillon, St Helier, Jersey JE2 3ZB (☎01534-722153; fax 01534-722153; e-mail recruitment@morvanhotels.com). A company in operation for 50 years which runs 6 hotels on the picturesque island of Jersey.
Staff required for various posts ranging from head chefs through to chamber staff. Wages by arrangement; accommodation is available at a cost of approx. £60 per week, plus meals. Minimum period of work 6 months between March and October. Overseas applicants considered.
Applications from January to Mary Healy, Group Personnel Manager. Interview not necessary.

NATIONAL TRUST ENTERPRISES: The Restaurant, Chartwell House, Mapleton Road, Westerham, Kent TN16 1PS (☎01732-866368).

Catering Assistants (8). Wages on application. Hours negotiable.
Applications at any time to the above address.

OCKENDEN MANOR HOTEL: Ockenden Lane, Cuckfield, Haywards Heath, West Sussex RH17 5LD (☎01444-416111; fax 01444-415549; e-mail ockenden@ hshotels.co.uk; www.hshotels.co.uk/o-manor).
Commis Waiting Staff to work in the restaurant and bar and at functions. Wages of at least £170 per week plus tips and accommodation; to work split shifts over a 5-day week.
Period of work by arrangement around the year for a minimum of 12 months. Applicants must be aged at least 18 and have restaurant experience; silver service experience desirable.
Applications to Adam Smith, Manager, at the above address.

PAYNE AND GUNTER: Goodwood Racecourse, Goodwood, Chichester, West Sussex PO18 0PS (☎01243 774839, Fax 01243 784490). Payne and Gunter are the official caterers at Goodwood Racecourse and Festival of Speed and Goodwood Revival, supplying all catering staff .
Waiting Staff, Catering Assistants, Bar Staff, Table Clearers etc (200-1,200 per event) required from March to October. Wages are £5.45 per hour with lunch provided. Applicants must be 18 years of age.
Apply for an application pack at the above address or e-mail staffing.goodwood@ compass-group.co.uk.

THE PRIORY BAY HOTEL: Priory Drive, Seaview, Isle of Wight PO34 5BU (☎01983-613146; fax 01983-616539; e-mail enquiries@priorybay.co.uk; www. priorybay.co.uk).
Kitchen Porters, Waiting Staff, Bar Staff, Room Attendants, Chefs (many vacancies). Wages by arrangement plus tips. To work up to 48 hours per week. To work the summer season, beginning in May/June. All applicants should have experience in the catering or hospitality trade and a working knowledge of English. Accommodation may be provided.
Applications should be sent to the Personnel Department, at the above address.

ROYAL BEACH HOTEL: South Parade, Southsea, Portsmouth, Hants PO4 0RN (☎02392-731281; fax 02392-817572; e-mail enquiries@royalbeachhotel.co.uk; www.royalbeachhotel.co.uk). A three-star, 124-bedroom, seafront hotel commanding stunning views over to the Isle of Wight.
Waiting Staff (3) to serve breakfast, lunch and dinner and functions as required.
Room Attendants (2) to be responsible for cleaning guest bedrooms, bathrooms and corridors.
Wages at national minimum rate plus tips. Accommodation available plus meals/ uniform. To work 5 days per week in shifts. Minimum period of work 12 weeks. Overseas applicants welcome.
Applications to the Personnel Manager at the above address.

ROYAL ESPLANADE HOTEL: Ryde, Isle of Wight PO33 2ED (☎01983-562549; fax 01983-563918). Seafront hotel open all year round.
Waiting Staff, Kitchen Porters, Chamber Staff, Bar Staff. From £5.35 per hour plus tips. Free B & L. To work 39 hours per week. All staff work 6 days per week. No experience needed. Full in-house training is given.
Applications enclosing photograph to the General Manager at the above address.

SOUTHERN WORK EXPERIENCE: 12 Eversfield Road, Eastbourne, East Sussex BN21 2AS (☎01323-638523; e-mail info@theardmoregroup.com; www. theardmoregroup.com). An employment agency specialising in placing seasonal staff in the hospitality industry.
General Staff for hotel and industry work places lasting between 2 and 3 months. Wages dependent upon job taken.
Contact the Agency at the above address for further information.

STOCKS ISLAND HOTEL: Sark, via Guernsey, Channel Islands GY9 0SD (☎01481-832001; fax 01481-832130; e-mail personnel@stockshotel.com; www. stockshotel.com). Sark is a beautiful and remote rural island 20 miles from France; fishing, farming and eco-tourism provide the main local employment. There are no motor cars and no airport. Stocks is a traditional old farmhouse and home of the Armorgie family, located in a wooded valley in the centre of the island.
Restaurant Waiting Staff for general waiting and some cleaning duties in an award-winning restaurant. Must possess silver-service skills, a pleasant personality and caring attitude.
Kitchen Porter for general kitchen cleaning duties and some vegetable preparation in a high quality kitchen with a brigade of qualified chefs. Must work extremely cleanly, efficiently and quickly. Overseas applicants considered.
General Assistants for housekeeping plus general waiting and cleaning duties. Must have a pleasant personality and very good references. The ability to work quickly, cleanly and efficiently are essential.
Wages £130 per week, tax-free with no deductions. B & L provided. Private medical health cover provided. To work an average of 50 hours per week over 6 days. Fifteen members of staff required to work from April until October, with two additional workers between June and September. Overseas applicants welcome but must speak the standard of English of a native. Preferred age group 20-35.
For further details *contact* Mr Paul Armorgie, Stocks Island Hotel and Restaurants.

THISTLE BRIGHTON HOTEL: Kings Road, Brighton BN1 2GS (☎0870-333 9129; fax 0870-333 9229; e-mail brighton@thistle.co.uk; www.thistlehotels. com). Award-winning hotel company whose policy is to put its guests at the heart of everything it does. 56 hotels nationwide – discounted staff accommodation scheme.
Waiting Staff required to provide food service in the hotel's restaurant. Wages at national minimum rate. To work between 5 and 39 hours a week in shifts (6.30am to 3pm, 10am to 5.30pm, 3pm to 11.30pm).
Bar Person needed to serve in a Mediterranean style cafe-bar. Wages at national minimum rate plus tips. To work between 5 and 39 hours per week. Applicants must be over 18 years of age.
Room Attendants wanted to carry out housekeeping and room cleaning work. Wages at national minimum rate. Hours of work 9.30am to 4.30pm.
Concierge/Hall Porter wanted for front reception, guest liaison and to carry luggage. Wages at national minimum rate. To work a 39 hour week, either 7am to 3.30pm or 3pm to 11.30pm. Applicants must be over 21 for insurance purposes.
Night Guest Services Porter. Wages at national minimum rate plus tips. To work 39 hours per week, 11pm to 7.30am. Tasks include general setting up duties, some food preparation and hotel security. Applicants must be over 25.
All remuneration schemes include a company benefits package.
Applications or requests for further details should be made to the above address.

THE WESSEX HOTEL: Paternoster Row, Winchester, Hampshire SO23 9LQ (☎0870-400 8126; fax 01962-849617; e-mail wessex@macdonald-hotels.co.uk; www.macdonaldhotels.co.uk/wessex). Four-star, 94 bedroom hotel adjacent to Winchester Cathedral and close to the city centre.
Receptionist. Wages £5.35 per hour. To work 30 hours over 5 days per week. Minimum period of work 6 months. Must be Fidelio trained.
Waiter, Waitress, Bar person, Room Attendant. Wages £5.35 per hour. To work 30 hours over 5 days per week.
Chef. Wages £5.35 per hour. To work 30 hours over 5 days per week.
  Minimum period of work 3 months between April and December. Board and lodging may be available at a cost of £50 per week. Applicants should have excellent customer service skills, be enthusiastic, and work well in a team. Experience preferred but not essential. Minimum age 18.
  Applications to Dawn Chemoun or Christine Howton at the above address from January onwards. Interview required.

THE YEW TREE INN: Chalvington, Near Hailsham, East Sussex BN27 3TB (☎01323-811326; fax 01323-811170).
Bar Staff; Waiting/Kitchen Assistant. Wages of £6 per hour, with no accommodation available. To work 6 to 8 hour shifts with flexibility required; both positions would involve weekend shifts, with some free time during the week. Period of work by arrangement over the summer. Applicants should be aged at least 18 and English speaking.
  Applications to Clare Fripp at the above address.

Language Schools

CICERO LANGUAGES INTERNATIONAL: 42 Upper Grosvenor Road, Tunbridge Wells, Kent TN1 2ET (☎01892-547077; fax 01892-522749; e-mail enrolments@cicero.co.uk; www.cicero.co.uk). A small, friendly and professional language school accredited by the British Council and a member of English UK. Students are mainly in their 20s and 30s, from more than 70 countries.
EFL Teachers to teach students of many nationalities (average age 25). Salary £11-£13 per hour. Hours of work variable. Period of work late June to start of September. Accommodation is not available. Applicants must have a degree and TESOL/CELTA qualifications. Experience also important. Punctuality and a professional attitude are essential.
  Applications from April to Carrie Reay, Cicero Languages International.

CONCORDE INTERNATIONAL SUMMER SCHOOLS LTD: Arnett House, Hawks Lane, Canterbury, Kent CT1 2NU (☎01227-451035; fax 01227-762760; e-mail info@concorde-int.com; www.concorde-int.com). Concorde International has been organising summer schools for over 33 years in the south of England. They have a high return rate of international students and teachers.
EFL Teachers (approx. 150) required to teach in summer schools for full or part time positions. An average working week consists of 15 hours tuition and 5 social activities, but weeks vary according to individual programmes. Both residential and non-residential positions are available. Applicants should have the RSA CELTA or Trinity College certificate TESOL or equivalent or PGCE in an appropriate subject, and some summer school experience.
Course Directors (approx. 5) to ensure the smooth running of the centre and liaise with Head Office, the local host family organiser and the group leaders. Other duties

include holding staff meetings and weekly in-house training sessions, briefing teachers and standing in for them if required. To work 48 hours per week. Both residential and non-residential positions are available, depending on the centre. Applicants must hold a RSA Dip. TEFL or Trinity College diploma in TESOL and have a minimum of 5 years' summer school experience.
Assistant Directors of Study (approx. 5) required to ensure the smooth running of the centre, liaise with Head Office, oversee the daily routine and give support to staff, in addition to 15 hours' tuition a week. To work 35 hours per week. Positions are residential and non-residential. Applicants should hold DELTA/Dip. TEFL or Trinity College London Diploma preferred, but CELTA and experience will be considered.
Centre Managers (approx. 5) required to ensure the smooth running of the social programme and take care of the students' health and welfare. Other duties include checking transfer arrangements, liasing with Head Office, and regular staff at the centres. Positions are residential. To work 48 hours per week. Applicants should preferably hold a qualification in leisure management although other management qualifications/experience will be considered.
Social Assistants (25). Experience preferred but not essential.
Social Organisers (5). To work 48 hours per week. Qualifications and experience an advantage.
    Wages by arrangement. Minimum period of work 1 week; the centres are open in June, July and August. EU nationals preferred but non-EU applicants with necessary work permits/visas considered. Fluent English is essential.
    Applications as soon as possible to the Vacation Course Director at the above address or by e-mail. Interview required.

EASTBOURNE SCHOOL OF ENGLISH: 8 Trinity Trees, Eastbourne, East Sussex BN21 3LD (☎01323-721759; fax 01323-639271; e-mail english@esoe.co.uk; www. esoe.co.uk). Runs language courses for students aged 16 and over from all around the world. The freetime programme is lively and varied.
Assistant Social Organiser (1). Wages £185 per week. Responsible post suiting someone energetic, enthusiastic and reliable. Some experience with overseas students an advantage. Minimum age 20. To work 6 days per week (flexi-time). Required from mid-June to mid-September. Accommodation not available. Interview necessary.
    Applications with a CV to Graham White, Principal, from early 2007 at the above address.

EF INTERNATIONAL LANGUAGE SCHOOLS: 1-2 Sussex Square, Brighton, East Sussex BN2 1FJ (☎01273-571780; e-mail sarah.williamson@ef.com; www. ef.com).
EFL Teachers required for July and August to work full-time. Wages vary according to location and experience. Candidates should have at least a first degree and CELTA.
    Applications with CVs should be sent to the School Director at the above address.

EF INTERNATIONAL LANGUAGE SCHOOLS: Palace Court, White Rock, Hastings, East Sussex TN34 1JP (☎01424-428458; e-mail hastings@ef.com; www. ef.com).
EFL Teachers required for July and August to work full-time. Wages vary according to location and experience. Candidates should have at least a first degree and CELTA.
    Applications with CVs should be sent to the School Director at the above address.

EJO LTD: Passfield Business Centre, Lynchborough Road, Passfield, Liphook Hampshire GU30 7SB (☎01428-751933; e-mail steve@ejo.co.uk; www.ejo.co.uk). **Course Directors, Senior EFL Teachers, EFL Teachers** required for residential and non-residential courses. Course Directors and Senior Teachers need to be TEFL qualified with a good degree (MA or TEFL/TESOL Dip preferred) and 2 or more years of teaching experience. Teachers need to have CELTA/Trinity TESOL qualification. **Activity Staff** required for non-residential and residential courses, to work 5 to 6 days per week. Applicants should be studying towards or graduates in a sports or arts qualification.
Qualified Lifeguards and First Aiders required for residential centres.
Staff are required for Easter, June, July and August. Pay varies according to qualifications and experience.
Applications to The Education Department at the above address.

EMBASSY CES: Gensing Manor, Dane Road, St Leonards on Sea, East Sussex TN38 0QN (☎01424-464820; fax 01424-464821; e-mail hastings@embassyces.com; www.embassyces.com). All year round language school with large summer centre.
EFL Teachers wanted for July and August to teach adults and children; to also assist with a programme of social activities/excursions. Cambridge CELTA certificate required. Applications from January to the above address.
Sports & Social Activity Organisers required during July and August. Graduates and Undergraduates, minimum age 20. Qualifications in sports coaching, first aid, arts and crafts an advantage. Accommodation available. Work includes running a full activity programme: discos, excursions, sports, local visits. Applicants should have common sense and a good sense of fun. Overseas applicants with a sufficient knowledge of English considered.
Apply from February onwards either online (click on www.embassyces.com/jobs and follow the summer jobs links) or contact the Recruitment Department for an application pack. Interview necessary, usually by telephone.

HASTINGS ENGLISH LANGUAGE CENTRE (HELC): St Helens Park Road, Hastings, East Sussex TN34 2JW (☎01424-437048; fax 01424-716442; e-mail english@helc.co.uk; www.helc.co.uk). Adult only British Council accredited school.
EFL Teachers (10). £150-£264 for 15-24 hours per week. Degree and CELTA (or equivalent) required. Staff wanted from June to October. Minimum period of work 4 weeks. Accommodation not available.
Applications from February to Hastings English Language Centre at the above address.

KENT SCHOOL OF ENGLISH: 3 Granville Road, Broadstairs, Kent CT10 1QD (☎01843-874870; fax 01843-860418; e-mail chris.mcdermott@kentschool.co.uk; www.kentschoolofenglish.com). A medium sized school specialising in short courses for groups from 21 countries; a dynamic, energetic, enthusiastic and friendly place to work.
EFL Teachers (30) and Social Activity Assistants (6). £180-£270 per week. To work 30-35 hours per week from Monday to Saturday. Minimum period of work of 4 weeks. Positions available mid-June to mid-September. Applicants should be over 18 and teachers require the relevant TESOL or CELTA certificate.
Applications welcome from 1 March to Chris McDermott at the above address.

LTC INTERNATIONAL COLLEGE: Compton Park, Compton Palace Road, Eastbourne, East Sussex BN21 1EH (☎01323-727755; fax 01323-728279; e-mail

info@geos-ltc.com; www.geos-ltc.com). A friendly private language school running courses for adult students and residential courses for young learners. Set in a mansion house in its own park, 20 minutes walk from Eastbourne town centre.
EFL Teachers (5). Wages from £240 per week, with free B & L. To teach 20 lessons per week; includes evening and some weekend social and residential duties. Minimum of RSA/Cambridge CELTA or Trinity Cert. TESOL required.
Residential Welfare Officers (4). Wages from £220 per week, with free B & L. To work 40 hours per week, including evenings and weekends. Would suit a student. First Aid an advantage.

Staff required from end of June to mid-September. Overseas applicants for teaching posts must have an advanced level of English (IELTS 9 or equivalent).

Applications from February to Alisdair Goldsworthy, Director of Studies, at the above address.

PILGRIMS ENGLISH LANGUAGE COURSES: 4-6 Orange Street, Canterbury, Kent CT1 2JA (☎01227-762111; fax 01227-459027; e-mail gary.luke@pilgrims. co.uk; www.pilgrims.co.uk).
EFL Teachers (25). £290 per month plus full board and accommodation. Required to work from late June to August. Must have recognised TEFL qualification. For details of working conditions see www.pilgrimsrecruitment.co.uk.
Programme Staff (25) required to lead sports, drama, art and music. £265 plus full board. Required to work same work period as above. For full working conditions see the website www.pilgrimsrecruitment.co.uk.

Applications to Gary Luke, Director of Training, at the above address.

REGENCY SCHOOL OF ENGLISH: Royal Crescent, Ramsgate, Kent CT11 9PE (☎01843-591212; fax 01843-590300; e-mail reception@regencyschool.co.uk).
Temporary EFL Teachers (15). Wages approx. £10 per hour. Guaranteed 14 hours of teaching per week, but up to 28 hours usually available. Must hold at least a Trinity College or RSA Certificate.
Activity Leaders (3). Approximately £100 per week for 20-30 hours' work. Must be sporty and enthusiastic.

Minimum period of work 6 weeks between June and September. Overseas applicants with a standard of English as high as that of a native speaker considered. The school has hotel accommodation but this is often full during the summer.

Applications from April to Ian Dickie, General Manager, Regency School of English.

REGENT LANGUAGE HOLIDAYS: 40-42 Queens Road, Brighton BN1 3XB (☎01273-718620; fax 01273-718621; e-mail holidays@regent.org.uk; www.regent. org.uk). Regent operates four residential centres in Southern England. They specialise in summer language holidays combining English language tuition with a range of activities and excursions.
EFL Teachers (40). Wages from £295-£350 per week for 15 hours tuition and 6 afternoon or evening sessions. Will assist in social programme. RSA/Trinity qualified.
Centre Managers (4). Wages from £500-£550 per week. Graduate, preferably Masters/RSA/Trinity qualified with appropriate management experience and a proven and successful track record.
Activity Leaders (4). Wages from £230-£270 per week. Graduate preferred, preferably with sports/coaching qualifications or experience.

Full board and accommodation provided.

Applications at any time to Recruitment at the above address.

RICHARD LEWIS COMMUNICATIONS: Riversdown House, Warnford, Hants SO32 3LH (☎01962-771111; fax 01962-771050; e-mail steve.allison@rlcglobal. com; www.crossculture.com). An international company committed to providing training solutions in the areas of language, cross culture and communication skills. The company operates in 5 continents, and offers career opportunities to travel.
EFL Teachers. Wages from approximately £280 per week depending on experience/ qualifications, with food and accommodation provided. To teach from 9am-5pm; teachers will also be expected to attend dinner daily and perform one evening duty, such as escorting a trip to the pub or theatre per week. Applicants should have a university degree, RSA/Trinity TEFL certificate and at least 1 year's teaching experience.
Applications to Steve Allison, Director of Studies, at the above address.

SCHOOL OF ENGLISH STUDIES FOLKESTONE: 26 Grimston Gardens, Folkestone, Kent CT20 2PX (☎01303-850007; fax 01303-256544; e-mail info@ses-folkestone.co.uk; www.ses-folkestone.co.uk). Founded in 1957, the School of English Studies Folkestone is a serious, professional and successful language school.
EFL Teachers (25). Wages £300-£400 per week; to work 35 hours per week. Applicants must have a UK degree and a TEFL qualification.
Sports & Activities Co-Ordinators (12). Wages £225-£350 per week; to work 35 hours per week. Applicants must be 21 or over and have some appropriate qualifications.
Both positions available involve working with students of English from overseas. Accommodation is not available in Folkestone; however, it is available at residential Summer Centre in Ashford. Staff are required from 29 June to 27 August for a period of 2 to 8 weeks.
Applications to Simon Himbury, Principal at the above address from January 2007 onwards.

STAFFORD HOUSE SCHOOL OF ENGLISH: 19 New Dover Road, Canterbury, Kent CT1 3AH (☎01227-452250; fax 01227-453579; e-mail info@staffordhouse. com; www.ceg-uk.com/staffordhouse_english/index.html). The summer school has mixed nationality classes with a maximum of 15 students per class. Ages 12 to adult. Emphasis is on productive skills and fluency-based activities.
EFL Teachers (20). TEFL qualifications such as RSA/Trinity Certificate or RSA/Trinity Diploma required.
Activity Organisers (10). Reliability, energy and enthusiasm essential.
Rates of pay on application. Minimum period of work 1 week between June and September.
Applications from February, to Naomi Cooper (teachers) or Laura Kay (activity organisers) at the above address. Interview required.

UNIVERSAL LANGUAGE SERVICES ENGLISH SCHOOL: 43-45 Cambridge Gardens, Hastings TN34 1EN (☎01424-438025; fax 01424-438050). A medium-sized professional, language school situated in the centre of Hastings and accredited by the British Council.
EFL Teachers. All applicants must have Trinity College Cert. TESOL or RSA CELTA: £151 for 15 hours per week, £240 for 24 hours per week. Applicants with Trinity College Diploma TESOL or RSA DELTA: 15 hours per week – £170, or 30 hours per week – £340. Some residential positions available. Minimum period of work 1 week, between 20 June and 16 September.
Apply by sending an e-mail to the above address.

WARNBOROUGH COLLEGE (UK): International Offices, 8 Vernon Place, Canterbury CT1 3WH (☎01227-762107; fax 01227-762108, e-mail wu@ warnborough.edu, www.warnborough.edu or www.warnborough.ac.uk). Certificates, Diplomas, Professional Development and Corporate Training. Learning centres in the UK and around the world or via Distance Learning.

Mentors, EFL Teachers, Tour Guides, Translators, Activity Organisers regularly sought. Payments depend on teaching qualifications/experience. Other employment offered. Please see website for all openings.

Apply on line (registrar@warnborough.edu) or by fax/post to the Registrar.

Medical

ACQUA DORIA LTD: 3 Oriel Court, Omega Park Alton, Hampshire GU34 2QE (☎01420-85202; fax 01420-84974; e-mail admin@acquadoria.wanadoo.co.uk). Small, friendly care agency providing assistance to elderly/disabled people living in their own homes.

Home Care Assistants/Health Carers to assist with personal and domestic care for the elderly. Wages £6.25 per hour with flexible hours and days. Work available throughout the summer. Accommodation not normally available but they are happy to provide assistance in finding appropriate lodgings. Experience in care preferred. Foreign applicants with the appropriate visa and work permit welcome.

Apply to Mrs S. Stamp or Mrs A. Withey at the above address. Interview and criminal record disclosure required.

BELVADERE CARE LTD: 12 Windsor Road, Worthing, West Sussex BN11 2LX (☎01903-537499; fax 01903-521654).

Care Assistants required for agency work in nursing and rest homes and to work with people with learning/physical disabilities. Wages are between £5.70 and £6.90 per hour. Applicants must be over 18.

Applications to Celia Madgwick, Director, at the above address.

EVERYCARE (EASTBOURNE): 8 Hyde Gardens, Eastbourne, East Sussex BN21 4PN (☎01323-430762; fax 01323-430764; e-mail everycare.eastbourne@ btopenworld.com).

Care Assistants needed for ongoing positions in nursing homes and residential homes. Wages start at £7.26 per hour with holiday pay and a mileage allowance. Working hours to suit; days and nights available. Applicants must be over 18, with at least 6 months experience in a care setting.

Applications to Angela Fuller or Susan Wood at the above address. Interviews and enhanced CRB check required.

HOME COMFORTS COMMUNITY CARE LTD: Suite 6, Quarry House, Mill Lane, Uckfield, East Sussex TN22 5AA (☎01825-762233; fax 01825-762234; e-mail marie@hcccltd.fsnet.co.uk). Care agency/employer with clients all over Sussex. Established 1995.

Full Time/Part Time Care Workers (15-20) to work various shifts in nursing homes, residential homes and homes for adults with learning disabilities in East Sussex, West Sussex and Kent. Some personal care: washing, dressing. Wages £7.00 basic per hour plus travel expenses (average inclusive hourly earnings £9.25 per hour); own transport essential. Positions available at all times of year. Applicants must be aged at least 18. Basic training will be given in first aid and manual handling; a caring nature would be useful for this work. Foreign applicants with fluent English

and eligibility to work in the UK welcome.
Applications to Marie Ingram, Human Resources Director, at the above address.

HOME HELP UK: Old Forest Barn, Kiln Lane, Buriton, Petersfield, Hampshire GU31 5SL (☎01730-236950; fax 01730-710164; e-mail enquiries@homehelpuk. co.uk; www.homehelpuk.co.uk).
Care Workers. To look after elderly/vulnerable people in their own homes, helping to dress and get up/get ready for bed and social support. Wages £6.00+ per hour. Flexible hours to suit worker; generally mornings and evenings (including weekends). Needed all summer and other holiday periods. Minimum age 18. Experience not needed as training given. Own transport essential.
Applications to Julia Hedley, Operations Director, at the above address.

OPTIONS TRUST STAFF RECRUITMENT: 4 Plantation Way, Whitehill, Bordon, Hampshire GU35 9HD (☎01420-474261, e-mail optionstrust@pvm.ndo.co.uk). A non-profit making organisation, set up and run by a number of disabled people who employ personal assistants to enable them to live in their own homes, in the community.
Personal Assistants (10-12) to carry out personal care, domestic duties and driving. £100-£200 a week plus free B & L. Minimum period of work 6 months at any time of year. Minimum age 18. Driving licence required but no previous experience is necessary.
Applications to Mrs V. Mason at the above address.

Outdoor

2 IN TENTS MARQUEE HIRE: Romayne, Bridge Road, Brabourne Lees, Ashford, Kent TN25 6QQ (☎01303-812700; fax 01303-812999; e-mail sales@2intents.co.uk; www.2intents.co.uk). Supplier and installer of quality marquees for weddings and special occasions.
Marquee Erectors, Labourers, Drivers (Up to 20). Wage NMW plus bonuses. Staff required every day of the week to suit, between April and September. Minimum period of work 1 month. Drivers require a clean licence. Fluent English essential, but non-UK citizens who have suitable skills will be considered. Applicants must be smart in appearance. Accommodation is not provided.
Apply to J Childs at the above address. An interview will be necessary, but can be done over the telephone.

AMBERVALE FARM: North Common Lane, Sway, Lymington, Hampshire SO41 8LL. New Forest farm five minutes away from the sea by car.
Live-In Assistant to help with horses and manual work on the farm; tidying, gardening and building. All accommodation, home cooked meals included as well as horse riding and swimming.
Experienced All-Round Builder (1-2) to work on the farm. Food, wage and mobile home accommodation provided.
Applications enclosing a s.a.e. to Mrs C.M. Nicholson-Pike at the above address.

ARM MARQUEES LTD: North Farm, London Road, Washington, West Sussex RH20 4BB (☎01903-877456; fax 01903-877464; e-mail robert@armmarquees.com; www.armmarquees.com).
Labourers (4) and Driver (1) required to put up and take down marquees and clean and store equipment. Paid at hourly rate. Required from mid-June to August.

Accommodation possible. Minimum ages: 17 and over for labourers; 21 and over for driver (with clean licence).

Applications to T Costelloe, Company Secretary, at the above address.

S.C. AND J.H. BERRY LTD: Gushmere Court Farm, Selling, Faversham, Kent ME13 9RF(☎01227-752205). A family-run farm in a beautiful area of Kent, which grows a range of crops to sell to supermarkets, wholesalers and brewers.
Apple Pickers/Hop Pickers (15). Wages at standard Agricultural Wages Board Rates. Apple picking mostly paid at piece work rates. To work a standard 39 hours per week, plus up to 16 hours overtime. Workers are needed for the entire period between 25 August and 28 September. Work cannot be guaranteed during wet weather. Self-catering accommodation in caravans available for approximately £15 a week: blankets, pillows and separate kitchen, lounge and shower facilities are provided, as well as TV room and various sporting facilities. Applicants should bring their own sleeping bags, towels, as well as wellington boots and waterproof clothing.

Applicants should be students over 18 years old. EEA applicants considered. Possession of a driving licence would be an advantage.

Applications (with s.a.e. or IRC) should be sent from 1 May to Mr J.P.S. Berry at the above address.

BRAMSHOT HOUSE: Fleet, Hampshire GU51 2RT (☎01252-617304; e-mail duckworth@namedmugs.com). A family who need help with their large garden, chickens, ducks, general repairs and maintenance. Would suit anyone wanting a working holiday. Bramshot House is 45 minutes by train from London. The helper may often be taken along on trips to places of interest with the family.
Gardeners/Painters/Carpenters (1-2). £20 pocket money per week. Flexible working arrangement averaging 3-5 hours per day. Plenty of free time for sightseeing. Self-contained fully furnished flat provided, also produce from the garden when available and use of bicycle, tennis court and swimming pool. Some skill in painting, gardening or carpentry essential. Overseas applicants welcome.

Applications to Mrs P.A. Duckworth at the above address.

JOHN M. CARTER LTD: Industrial Estate, Winchester Road, Basingstoke, Hampshire RG22 4AB (☎01256-324434; fax 01256-816209; e-mail info@ johnmcarterltd.co.uk; www.johnmcarterltd.co.uk). Hire out traditional marquees and aluminium structures.
Marquee Erectors (15). Wages upon application. To work Sunday to Friday, 8am until late, from May until October. Minimum period of work is between 2 and 3 months. Non-UK citizens are considered; fluent English is preferable.

To *apply*, contact Mrs P. Payen at the above address. An interview will be required.

CHANDLER & DUNN LTD: Lower Goldstone, Ash, Canterbury, Kent CT3 2DY (☎01304-812262; fax 01304-812612; e-mail jobs@chandleranddunn.co.uk; www. chandleranddunn.co.uk). Farm in East Kent between the historic towns of Sandwich and Canterbury.
Fruit Pickers (numbers variable) for periods between early June and the end of September; mostly for apples in September. Most picking is piecework so opportunity for fast pickers to earn more. Daily paid casual fruit picking Monday to Saturday from 8am to 4pm approximately.

No accommodation on farm but campsite very close. Must be aged at least 16 and be entitled to work in the UK; please note that the farm does not use the Seasonal Agricultural Workers Scheme (SAWS).

Applications by e-mail, fax or post, as above.

S.H. CHESSON: Manor Farm, Oldbury, Ightham, Sevenoaks, Kent TN15 9DG (☎01732-780496; fax 01732-780509). Situated approximately 40 miles from London. About a mile from station and shops.
Fruit Pickers (20) to work 6 days per week picking strawberries (June-Sept) and apples/pears (Sept/Oct). Piecework rates in the region of £200 to £250 per week. Hours of work vary depending on the nature of the job. Start time 6.30am to 8.00am; finish 2 to 5pm. Day off alternate Sat/Sun. Minimum work period 4 weeks between June and mid-October. Campsite charges £11.20 per week; kitchen, showers, laundry, tv/video room, canteen, outdoor recreations, outings and entertainment provided. Bring your own tent. Minimum age 18. EU/EEA citizens welcome. Non EU/EEA citizens must apply for necessary work permit through Concordia.
Apply in writing for an application form, from 1 March to Mr A.T. Chesson at the above address. All applicants must enclose a s.a.e.

EWELL FARM: Edward Vinson Ltd., Graveney Road, Faversham, Kent ME13 8UP (☎01795-539452; fax 01795-539509; e-mail students@edwardvinson.co.uk; www.edwardvinson.plus.com). A friendly fruit growing company with several farms.
Fruit Pickers to work June to October. Wages at piecework rates; £30 to £50 per day possible depending on ability. No accommodation available. Hours flexible, but typically 7am-3pm; weekend work available but time off as needed without restrictions. Applicants should be at least 16 and reasonably healthy.
Applications to Kristina Isand, at the above address.

GREENWAY FRUIT FARM: Herstmonceux, Eastbourne, East Sussex BN27 4PP (☎01323-833118; fax 01323-833118). 45-acre farm producing dessert apples and pears for UK supermarkets, farmers markets and local outlets.
Fruit Thinners (6). Wages at national minimum rate. To work up to 9 hours a day, 6 days per week. One month's work in June. Manual dexterity required.
Fruit Pickers (12). Wages at piece-work rate with bonus. To work 6-7 days a week, up to 12 hours a day. Workers required for September and October, but must sign a contract for an agreed work period at the time of hiring. 10% of wages are lost if this contract is breached. Applicants should be physically fit and have a light touch.
Board and accommodation are available at a cost of £15 per week. Foreign applicants with an understanding of English welcome.
Apply to Graham Love at the above address from May (for the thinning work) or from June (for picking work). Telephone interview required.

H.E. HALL & SON LTD: Little Pattenden, Marden, Kent TN12 9QL (☎01622-831376; fax 01622-831654; peter.hall@targetfarm.co.uk).
Fruit Pickers (10). Paid piece work based on minimum wage. Required for work from 8am to 3pm, Monday to Friday, but flexible hours and days dependent on weather and crop. Minimum period of work 1 day between mid-August and mid-October. Basic self-catering accommodation available at no cost. Minimum age 20. No previous experience necessary but it is useful. Overseas applicants considered if work authorisation is in order and English is spoken.
Applications from July onwards to Peter Hall by telephone.

HILL FARM ORCHARDS: Droxford Road, Swanmore, Hampshire SO32 2PY (☎01489-878616; e-mail hifol@eur-isp.com). Pleasantly situated between Portsmouth and Southampton, with shops and pubs nearby. Packing apples and

pears for high class outlets.
Fruit Pickers (10) to work from September to October.
Fruit Packers (5). Period of work October to March.
Pruners (5). Period of work January to April.
Pay as set by Agricultural Wages Board and piecework rates at the height of the seasons. To work 8am to 4.30pm Monday to Friday, with occasional weekends. Minimum period of work 1 month. Min. fee accommodation available. Applicants must be eligible to work in the UK and have a moderate level of English. Minimum age 20.
Applications by e-mail (or post) to Mr Paul Roberts, Farm Manager, at the above address.

TIM HOARE: Adsdean Farm, Funtington, Chichester P018 9DN (☎01243-575464; e-mail tim.hoare@farming.co.uk).
Tractor Driver/Livestock: to work from June to Sept. 39 hours per week plus overtime. Must have driving licence. Minimum age 18.
Applications to Tim Hoare at the above address.

JERSEY CYCLETOURS: 2 La Hougue, Mauger, St. Mary, Jersey JE3 3AF (☎01534-482898; fax 01534-484060; e-mail jerseycycletours@hotmail.com). The company's bikes (Trek, Giant, Dawes) are the best maintained and equipped hire bikes in Jersey; they need people who are keen and able to maintain their standards.
Cycle Mechanic, Bike Issuer needed from April to the end of September. Mechanic must have experience in bike building and repair. Issuer should be clear headed and enjoy cycling and helping people. Wages are aae. Working week 20-40 hours per week.
Contact **Daniel Wimberley at the above address.**

LAUREL TREE FRUIT FARM: Boar's Head, East Sussex TN6 3HD (☎01892-661637 or 01892-654011; mobile ☎077-6898 0308; fax 01892-663417).
Pickers (20) for top fruit picking (apple and pear). Wages meet the national minimum rate; to work 6 hours per day. Period of work depends on harvest, but probably 20 days between 25 August and 30 September (approx). No accommodation available, but limited camping is permitted. Overseas applicants with valid working visas welcome. No interview necessary.
Applications from 20 August onwards to Robert Booker (mobile phone 077-6898 0308) or evenings at the above number.

F.W. MANSFIELD & SON: Nickle Farm, Chartham, Canterbury, Kent CT4 7PL (☎01227-731441; fax 01227-731795).
Fruit Pickers And Packers (50-100) to pick and pack apples, pears, strawberries, plums and cherries. National minimum wage or piecework rates; to work variable hours a week, plus overtime - as they wish. Accommodation in caravans for £25 per week with communal kitchen and washing facilities. Cash daily during harvest. Workers needed from May to November, must be aged at least 18, fit and hard working.
Applications to the Farms Manager at the above address.

MOODIES: Unit A, Station Road Industrial Estate, Liphook, Hampshire GU30 7DR (☎01428-644310; fax 01428-661620; e-mail moodies@btinternet.com; www. moodies.co.uk).

Marquee Erectors (4) required to assist with putting up and taking down marquees from June to October. £5.35-£8 per hour depending on age and experience. Must be available to work weekends and bank holidays.
Applications to D. Moodie, Director, at the above address.

A.R. NEAVES & SONS: Little Sharsted Farm, Doddington, Near Sittingbourne, Kent ME9 OJT (☎01795-886263; fax 01795-886470; e-mail arneaves@btconnect. com). A friendly family-run business which has been running for sixty years and supplies fruit to the supermarkets.
Strawberry Pickers (20) for casual work. Wages on a piecework basis, to work 8 hours a day Monday to Saturday. Applicants must be over 18; no experience is necessary. Pickers are required from 1 June to July or August for a minimum of 6 weeks, however as there are other fruits (cherries, plums, apples), there could be up to 3 months work available.
Overseas applicants with a valid work permit are welcome. Accommodation is available at a charge of £25 per week.
Applications should be sent to Sarah Neaves from the beginning of May onwards at the above address.

NEWMAFRUIT FARMS LTD: Howfield Farm, Howfield Lane, Chartham, near Canterbury, Kent CT4 7HQ (☎01227-730048; fax 01227-732476; e-mail enquiries@newmafruit.co.uk). Newmafruit is one of the foremost suppliers of fresh produce to the major UK supermarkets. They provide a personal supervisor for all students.
Fruit Pickers/Packers. Wages national minimum wage or piecework rate. Accommodation available at £25 per week. Workers required from 6 June to 30 September. Overseas applicants are recruited through Concordia (see Work Permits and Special schemes section).
Applications from March to Mr Melvyn Newman at the above address.

R.H. NIGHTINGALE & PARTNER: Gibbet Oak Farm, Appledore Road, Tenterden, Kent TN30 7DH (☎01580-763492; fax 01580-763938). Ideally situated only 2 miles from town with all amenities, campsite and mobile homes with usual facilities.
Strawberry Pickers to work from May to July.
Apple Thinners to work from June to July.
Apple/Pear Pickers (up to 15) required to work from 25 August to 30 September.
Payment at piecework rates. To work 5 to 9 hours per day, depending on ripening of crops. Applicants should be fit, willing and able; age not important. Overseas applicants welcome, but those from outside the EU must hold a valid work permit.
Applications to P.J. Nightingale at the above address from April.

PERRYHILL ORCHARD: Bolebroke Lodge, Edenbridge Road, Hartfield, East Sussex TN7 4JJ (☎01892-770595).
Fruit Pickers (8-10). Wages £20 to £45 per day. To work 4 to 8 hours per day picking mainly apples and top fruit. Work available during August, September and October. Must be aged at least 18 and have plenty of common sense.
Please *apply* to Mr J. Smith at the above address.

REDSELL GROUP: Nash Court, Boughton, Faversham, Kent ME13 9SW (☎01227-751224; e-mail pat.goode@redsell.com).
Hop Pickers. Required to work on 200 acres of hops. Basic accommodation

provided free of charge. Wages on application.
For further *information*, contact Redsell Group using the above details.

SUNRISE FRUITS: The Street, Stourmouth, nr. Canterbury, Kent CT3 1HY (☎01227-721977; fax 01227-728633).
Strawberry/Raspberry Pickers to work from June to October. Also some general farm work. To work approximately 40 hours per week; good piecework rates paid. Accommodation is available at a small charge; a £5.00 booking fee is returnable after the first working week. Minimum period of work 4 weeks. No experience or qualifications needed but applicants should be self-motivated.
Early application is recommended to the above address.

VIBERT MARQUEES: Manor Farm, Rue du Manoir, St Ouen, Jersey JE3 2LF (☎01534-482970; fax 01534-482905; e-mail vibmarq@localdial.com; www. vibertmarquees.com). Long established, family run business with 6 full-time and 20 seasonal workers.
Marquee Erectors (10). Wages from £7.00 per hour. Required to work from 8am to finish, varied hours including overtime and weekends, approximately 50 hours per week. Period of work runs from April to September; minimum period of work from June to August. Applicants must be 17 or over and hard working. Foreign applicants who speak good English are welcome. No accommodation available, but there is a campsite within walking distance. Working shirts are provided free; shorts are recommended.
Applications should be made from January onwards to Gary Vibert at the above address.

L. WHEELER & SONS (EAST PECKHAM) LTD: Bullen Farm, East Peckham, Tonbridge, Kent TN12 5LX (☎01622-871225; fax 01622-872952; e-mail lwheelerandsons@yahoo.co.uk). A hop farm within an hour's journey of London. Local facilities such as shops and pubs are available.
Apple Pickers (20), Hop Pickers (20) required to work 8 to 9 hour days for 5½ days a week.
Wages approximately £5.35 per hour with the possibility of bonuses. Minimum period of work 5 weeks between 21 August and 30 September. Accommodation available with just a charge for electricity. Overseas applicants authorised to work in the UK welcome.
Applications from June to the Manager at the above address.

L. WHEELER & SONS (YALDING) LTD: Bockingfold, Marden, Tonbridge, Kent TN12 9PH (☎078-0820 0404; tel/fax 01892-722532). Farm is in mid Kent, near Paddock Wood railway station. Needs pickers for Gala and Bramley apples.
Fruit Pickers required for apple picking. Wages paid at piece-rate per bin filled, hours flexible with low cost accommodation available. Work available from 1 September for 3 weeks to a month (approximately). Applicants must be fit.
Applications to M.J. Wheeler, Director, at the above address.

WOLLETT HALL FARM: North Cray, Sidcup, Kent DA14 5ET (☎077-7568 4166; fax 020-8300 2103; e-mail bill.kelsey@fwi.co.uk).
Farm Shop/Farm Hand Assistant for duties including harvesting, delivering orders and working in a busy farm shop. Wages of £5 to £5.50 per hour, with accommodation provided in a caravan. To work 11 hours per day, 6 days per week. Period of work from mid-June.
Applicants must be aged in their mid 20s or older because of vehicle insurance

restrictions and be able to get on with the public and to work in a close hard-working family business. Must also be keen to help with setting up a new farm diversification business due to a family buy out of the business.

Applications to Bill Kelsey, Owner, at the above address.

WWW.WOWO.CO.UK: Wapsbourne Manor Farm, Sheffield Park, Uckfield, East Sussex TN22 3QT (☎01825-723414; fax 01285-722451; e-mail info@wowo.co.uk; www.wowo.co.uk). A specialist working holiday company offering a fully self-funding working holiday opportunity to young gap year students aged 18-30 years from all over Europe & British Commonwealth countries.

Industrial, Healthcare, Landscaping and Drivers. Wages range from minimum wage to sector standard. 35 hours and over per week. Intermediate English is required. Work requires flexibility, motivation and plenty of spirit. Applicants should be self-disciplined with good social skills, a valid working visa or European passport. Minimum stay 13 weeks. A refundable booking deposit is required.

The company provides accommodation for a reasonable weekly charge. Assistance with bank account set up, and National Insurance number.

Applications can be made to info@wowo.co.uk.

Sport

ALBOURNE EQUESTRIAN CENTRE: Henfield Road, Albourne, West Sussex BN6 9DE (☎01273-832989; fax 01273-833392;e-mail enquiries@albourneequestriancentre.co.uk; www.albourneequestriancentre.co.uk). An approved British riding school and livery yard, also Council approved. Regularly hold affiliated and unaffiliated shows and clinics.

Working Pupils (2-3) training for BHS exams. Work will consist of general yard work, riding tuition and the opportunity to compete at shows and events. Wages depending on experience; to work 5½ days a week from 8am to 6pm. Staff are required at any time for a minimum of 6 months. Applicants must be 16 and over. Accommodation is available at a charge of £30 per week. Students of all nationalities are considered; some experience with horses is preferred.

Applications should be sent to Megan Hughes at the above address. References required.

COOMBELANDS RACING STABLES: Coombelands Lane, Pulborough, West Sussex RH20 1BP (☎01798-873011; fax 01798-875163; e-mail aperrett@coombelands-stables.com). A successful, large thoroughbred racing yard.

Stable Hands (2). Wages £175 per week. To work 7½ hours a day, 6 days a week. Staff always required; B & L are included free of charge, living either on-site or nearby. Non-UK citizens are considered; fluent English is not essential. Those wishing to apply should be experienced work riders.

Applicants should apply to Amanda Perrett at the above address. An interview is not necessary.

DC LEISURE LTD: Aldershot Pools Complex, Guildford Road, Aldershot, Hampshire GU12 4BP (☎01252-323482; fax 01252-316499).

Lifeguards (15) needed from 28 May to 4 September. Wages are currently £5.35 per hour. Potential employees must have National Pool Lifeguard Qualification, and First Aid skills would be helpful. NPLQ training may be available.

Applications should be made in writing to the General Manager at the above address.

HILSEA LIDO: c/o Victoria Swimming Centre, Anglesea Road, Portsmouth PO1 3DL (☎023-667557; fax 023-9287 1781).
Casual Lifeguards (20) required for the open-air Hilsea Lido between 26 May and 14 September. Wages are at national minimum rate. To work from 11am to 7pm daily with overtime as required, although the work is dependent on the weather. Applicants must be over 16 and have a National Pool Lifeguard Qualification.
Applications in writing from May to Mr. A.D. Baker, Manager, at the Victoria Swimming Centre.

INGLESIDE RACING STABLES: Warren Road, Woodingdean, Brighton BN2 6DN (☎01273-620405; fax 01273-620106).
Stable Grooms (2), Work Riders (2) for duties including mucking out, grooming, attending race meetings with horses and exercising racehorses. Wages at national minimum wage rate plus bonuses. To work from 6am to 1pm and 3.30pm to 6pm. To have alternate weekends off and 1 afternoon off in the week. Period of work by arrangement. Applicants must have experience of working with horses; riders must be able to ride to a high standard.
Applications to Ms J. Moore, Partner, at the above address.

INSPIRE LEISURE: Phoenix House, Maltravers Road, Littlehampton, West Sussex BN17 5LF (☎01903-737924; fax 01903-725254; e-mail outdoor@inspireleisure. co.uk; www.inspireleisure.co.uk).
Seasonal staff required for putting greens, bowls greens and tennis courts in Bognor Regis and Littlehampton. Number of hours is negotiable to suit the applicant's needs, but must be available to work weekends and bank holidays. Staff needed between March and September. Applicants must be able to communicate well with the public and have good basic literacy and numeracy skills.
For an *application form* or to discuss this opportunity further, please contact the Outdoor Recreation team at the above address.

MEDINA VALLEY CENTRE: Dodnor Lane, Newport, Isle of Wight PO30 5TE (☎01983-522195; fax 01983-825962; e-mail info@medinavalleycentre.org.uk; www.medinavalleycentre.org,uk). An outdoor education and activity centre providing fieldwork courses for schools in Biology and Geography, Key Stage 2 to A-level. Also provides RYA dinghy sail training and open (Canadian) canoeing courses for adults and children.
Seasonal Temporary RYA Dinghy Sailing Instructors needed from the end of July to August. Must have RYA dinghy sailing instructor qualifications.
Applications to Peter Savory.

REGENT LANGUAGE HOLIDAYS: 40-42 Queens Road, Brighton BN1 3XB (☎01273-718620; fax 01273-718621; e-mail holidays@regent.org.uk; www.regent. org.uk). Regent operates four residential centres in Southern England. They specialise in summer language holidays combining English language tuition with a range of activities and excursions.
Programme Co-ordinators (4). £320-£350 per week. PGCE sports qualified preferred. Full board and accommodation provided.
Applications at any time to Recruitment at the above address.

ROGER INGRAM RACING LTD: Wendover Stables, Burgh Heath Road, Epsom, Surrey KT17 4LX (☎01372-748505).
Work/Rider Groom needed for riding work on racehorses, including mucking out

and yard duties and travelling with horses to races. Wages £220 per week. Period of work by arrangement. Must be an experienced rider.
Applications to Sharon Ingram at the above address as soon as possible.

TRAVEL CLASS LTD: 14 Queensway, New Milton, Hampshire BH25 5NN (☎0870-513 3773; fax 0870-513 3774; e-mail admin@travelclass.co.uk; www. travelclass.co.uk). A premier UK provider of adventure activity and environmental programmes for primary age children. Heroic and enthusiastic role models required.
Activity Instructors, Group Leaders, Watersports Instructors and Support Staff required for a summer job with a difference, to work with children in glorious coastal locations at Travel Class' 8 JCA Adventure and Environmental Activity Centres in Devon, Cornwall, the Isle of Wight and Somerset. Training and qualifications provided but applicants require enthusiasm, dedication and an affinity with children. Great lifestyle working as part of a multi-national, young and vibrant team. Positions available from March until September, excellent wages, superb food and quality accommodation.
Call or e-mail at any time for an application pack.

Voluntary Work

Archaeology

BUTSER ANCIENT FARM: Nexus House, Gravel Hill, Waterlooville, Hampshire PO8 0QE (tel/fax 023-9259 8838; e-mail rogerhedge@butserfriends.org.uk; www. butser.org.uk).
Butser Ancient Farm is a unique experimental archaeology site. A fully functioning replica of a British Iron Age farm, it has buildings, structures, animals and crops of the kind that would have existed at that time. Research programmes carried out at the site are in areas such as crops, constructs of prehistoric roundhouses, a Roman villa, ancient technologies and modern archaeological techniques.
Harvesting and General Site Maintenance Volunteers (10) are required to work on the farm for a minimum period of 1 week between July and September. Applicants should be over 18 and have an interest in archaeology, prehistory or Roman history. Foreign applicants with an interest in archaeology welcome. No accommodation available.
Applications should be sent to Christine Shaw, Principal, at the above address from January onwards.

Conservation and the Environment

CELIA HAMMOND ANIMAL TRUST: High Street, Wadhurst, East Sussex TN5 6AG (☎01892-783820; fax 01892-784882; e-mail info@celiahammond.org; www. celiahammond.org).
An animal rescue and re-homing service and sanctuary that also offers low cost neutering and vaccination clinics.
Volunteers required all year round. A love of animals and an interest in animal welfare are essential. Accommodation is available at a cost to be negotiated. An interview is required.
Applications to the above address.

MERRYWEATHER'S HERBS: Merryweather's Farm, Chilsham Lane, Herstmonceux, East Sussex BN27 4QH (☎01323-831726; e-mail info@ morethanjustagarden.co.uk; www.morethanjustagarden.co.uk).
Garden development and wildlife project extending to nearly six acres and incorporating a small nursery, situated in the beautiful Sussex High Weald. Whole project managed organically.
Volunteer Gardeners (4) to perform general garden maintenance and development, fruit and vegetable growing and wildlife habitat management, as well as some nursery propagation. To work 10am-5pm, 1-3 days per week (Thursday, Friday, Saturday). Minimum period of work 4 weeks between March and October. Training will be given but some experience preferred. Foreign applicants with good spoken English welcome. Non-smokers only. Accommodation not currently available.
Applications to Liz O'Halloran, Proprietor, at the above address from January. References required.

NORTH WEST KENT COUNTRYSIDE PARTNERSHIP: Mead Crescent, Mead Road, Dartford, Kent DA1 2SH (☎01322-294727; fax 01322-290787; e-mail richard. bayne@kent.gov.uk).
Based in Sevenoaks, Dartford, Gravesham and Bexley, the project promotes conservation through practical work and advice in both rural and urban areas. It works with schools, landowners, local authorities and other groups.
Volunteers to work in local conservation projects including woodland coppicing, pond creation and wild flower meadow management. To work most Wednesdays and Thursdays throughout the year. No accommodation available. Everybody welcome and no experience necessary, although applicants must be over 18 and speak English well enough to understand safety and working instructions.
Apply at any time to Mr Richard Bayne, Manager, at the above address.

Festivals and Special Events

BROADSTAIRS FOLK WEEK: Pierremont Hall, Broadstairs, Kent CT10 1JX (☎01843-604080; fax 01843-866422; e-mail jo@broadstairsfolkweek.org.uk; www. broadstairsfolkweek.org.uk).
The Broadstairs Folk Week Trust, a registered charity, organises events throughout the year and an annual festival. 2007 will be the festival's 42nd year. The whole town and its promenade, jetty, bandstand, taverns, halls, churches and streets become the venue for international music, song and dance.
Volunteers (150+) are needed as door stewards, information and shop staff, PA and sound technicians, drivers, campsite stewards and collectors. Volunteers are also needed to handle publicity and liaise with international personnel. Posts are unpaid, but staff receive a season ticket for access to all events. Free camping is available. Volunteers work 4 hours a day. Minimum period of work 5 days between 5 and 12 August. Overseas applicants with good English are considered.
Applications from March to Jo Tuffs. Interview is not necessary.

Heritage

BATEMANS: Burwash, East Sussex TN19 7DS (☎01435-882302; e-mail batemans@nationaltrust.org.uk; www.nationaltrust.org.uk).
Volunteers needed to help run and maintain a National Trust property open to the public. Batemans was the home of the writer Rudyard Kipling. The following volunteers are needed: **Room Stewards, Garden Stewards, Volunteer Gardeners,**

Mill Guides and **Millers** (training given), **Shop Volunteers**. Volunteers are needed from March to the end of October. Volunteer Gardeners are needed all year round.

Applications to Fiona Hancock or Sheona at the above address.

HAMMERWOOD PARK: Hammerwood, near East Grinstead, Sussex RH19 3QE (☎01342-850594; fax 01342-850864; e-mail latrobe@antibes.co.uk; www. hammerwood.mistral.co.uk).

A Grade I listed building built in 1792, open to the public and providing exclusive, limited accommodation. The restoration of the house and garden is a family project; the estate was derelict in 1982. Twenty-eight miles from central London and same distance from the south coast.

Voluntary Staff (2+) required to help in all aspects of running a historic house and garden. No wages are paid but full board and accommodation are provided. To work 3-4 days per week. Staff required from Easter to the end of September for a minimum period of 1 month. Applicants must have the ability to deal with the public and be able to carry out tasks as they arise, even the mundane. Help is also required with painting and carpentry – the house has 101 window frames, all falling apart! Suitable foreign applicants with a good level of English are welcome. An interview is desirable. Aims to give volunteers an interesting and enjoyable time as well as helping them to develop skills and introduce them to new ones.

Applications from January to David Pinnegar at the above address.

MID HANTS RAILWAY (WATERCRESS LINE): Railway Station, Alresford, Hampshire SO24 9JG (☎01962-733810; fax 01962-735448; e-mail info@ watercressline.co.uk; www.watercressline.co.uk).

A preserved steam railway running trains between Alresford and Alton.

Volunteers. Work available both full-time and part-time positions. Tourism students are particularly encouraged to apply, and there is the possibility of work for engineering students. Staff are required from May to September for a minimum of 2 months.

Applications should be sent to Volunteer Recruitment at the above address from the beginning of February.

Social and Community Schemes

THE SATURDAY VENTURE ASSOCIATION: (Disability Awareness UK), PO Box 9, Chichester, West Sussex PO20 7YD (☎01243-513464; fax 01243-513464; e-mail sva@talk21.com; www.satven.org).

A national registered charity promoting disability awareness in the community through talks in schools, demonstrations and drama workshops employing disabled speakers and occupational therapists.

Residential Worker. Working in fundraising, repairing jewellery, cultivating plants for re-sale and similar chores. Part-time hours. IT competence an advantage. Must be a non-smoker, preferably with a driving licence. Would suit gap year student. Wide range of activity. Small salary. No accommodation but the association might be able to help. Must hold current driving licence and be a non-smoker.

Applications to Jenny Bembridge on the above telephone or fax number.

Vacation Traineeships & Internships

Conservation and the Environment

HOWLETTS (CANTERBURY) & PORT LYMPNE (HYTHE): The John Aspinal Wild Animal Parks, Port Lympne, Hythe, Kent CT21 4PD (☎01303-264647; fax 01303-264944; e-mail info@howletts.net; www.totallywild.net).
Howletts and Port Lympne Animal Parks are part of the same charitable foundation for the breeding of rare and endangered animals with the aim of introducing them back into the wild.
Zoology students and other keen young people are welcomed on **Work Experience Schemes** in the animal parks. Applicants must be 18 years or over. There is no accommodation available.
For further *details*, contact the animal parks at the above address.

Travel and Tourism

HOTEL HOUGUE DU POMMIER: Castel, Guernsey, Channel Islands GU5 7FQ (☎01481-256531; fax 01481-256260; e-mail hotel@houguedupommier.guernsey. net; www.hotelhouguedupommier.com). An attractive farmhouse style hotel on the west coast of Guernsey. Busy in summer with visitors from the UK, France, Germany and Switzerland.Hotel Hougue du Pommier does not offer formal traineeships, but certain positions are open to **Students of Catering** hoping to develop their skills and gain valuable work experience. The positions are mainly in the restaurant.
B & L is provided at a cost of £50 per week. Applicants are not required to attend an interview.
Further details about jobs available and *applications* from Linda Letten, General Manager, at the above address.

East Anglia

Prospects for Work.

East Anglia is not one of the most promising of areas in which to look for temporary summer employment. However, Norfolk and Cambridgeshire are major agricultural areas and fruit picking, packing and processing work provide comparatively good prospects. King's Lynn, Wisbech and East Dereham (near Norwich) are the principal centres.

In and around King's Lynn the *Lynn News* carries general job advertisements. The *Eastern Daily Press*, which covers Norfolk and Suffolk, also carries lists of job vacancies. Local food factories employ temporary production operators between June and September, although this is dependent on the weather. Some local shops employ temporary staff. Staff at King's Lynn Jobcentre Plus can assist with a seasonal job search.

Temporary tourism and holiday-related jobs are most easily found in Hunstanton, Cromer, Lowestoft and above all Great Yarmouth which, after Blackpool, is Britain's major entertainment resort. Great Yarmouth Jobcentre Plus and Lowestoft Jobcentre Plus have seasonal vacancies for local holiday camps from around February each year, particularly in catering and retail. Telephone Jobseeker Direct on 0845-606 0234 or visit www.worktrain.gov.uk, or www.jobcentreplus.gov.uk. Hunstanton has a number of hotels, holiday parks and restaurants which consistently require staff, particularly in the summer season. Visit Hunstanton Jobcentre Plus for further details, or telephone Jobseeker Direct on the number above. While some live-in accommodation is provided by employers in Hunstanton, it is harder to come by in King's Lynn and Wisbech (where rented lodgings are also in short supply). In Wisbech general job adverts are posted in the *Fenland Citizen*, which comes out every Wednesday, and the *Wisbech Standard*, which comes out every Friday. Temporary factory work for local large employers and lots of seasonal picking/ packing work is available as well as many vacancies requiring skilled workers that cannot be filled.

In Ipswich it is worth visiting the Jobcentre Plus for details of local jobs, telephoning Jobseeker Direct on 0845-6060 234 or visiting www.jobcentreplus.gov. uk. The *East Anglian Daily Times* and the *Evening Star* have a jobs section every Wednesday, which services not only Ipswich, but also the surrounding areas.

As a major tourist attraction and language school centre, a number of associated jobs can be found in Cambridge. The city's Jobcentre Plus usually has summer opportunities in the catering and retail sector, and jobs teaching English as a foreign language. The burgeoning science and technology parks on the outskirts of the city can also be a lucrative source of vacation traineeships and internships. There is agricultural work available in the area picking soft fruits and later in the year, picking potatoes. The *Cambridge Evening News* (www.cambridge-news.co.uk) newspaper advertises job vacancies on Wednesdays and Fridays. There are also numerous employment agencies in Cambridge, details of which can be found in the Yellow Pages, or in a condensed list available from the Jobcentre Plus.

Felixstowe, on the Suffolk coast, is usually a good source of temporary work, particularly catering and retail together with a few jobs in leisure. Ipswich Borough Council and Suffolk County Council usually need to recruit temporary staff over the summer too.

Business and Industry

GRAND UK HOLIDAYS: The Old Bakery, Queens Road, Norwich, Norfolk NR1 3PL (☎01603-886700; fax 01603-616316; e-mail admin@grandukholidays.co.m; www. grandukholidays.com). Britain's largest coach tour operators catering exclusively for the over 55s in more than 140 resorts and destinations throughout the UK.

Couriers (25). £190 net per week plus optional excursion and tips. To work on eight-day coach tours. Applicants must be friendly and have an outgoing personality and the ability to relate to those aged over fifty-five. Accommodation and food provided. Staff needed from April to October.

Applications to the above address.

MONTHIND CLEAN: 91 London Road, Copford, Colchester, Essex CO6 1LG (☎01206-215300; fax 01206-212126; e-mail admin@monthindclean.co.uk; www.monthind-clean.co.uk). The company provides contract cleaners for various businesses.

Cleaners. Wages to be arranged. To work mainly during evenings and early mornings. Work available during any vacation. Minimum age 18. No experience necessary. Applicants must understand English and be able to comply with Health and Safety Rules. No accommodation available. Foreign applicants with work permits and acceptable spoken English welcome.

Applications can be made all year round to Penny Cander at the above address.

Children

IPSWICH BOROUGH COUNCIL: Grafton House, 15-17 Russell Road, Ipswich

IP1 2DE (☎01473-433514; fax 01473-433636; e-mail hr@ipswich.gov.uk).
Playworkers (12). Wages £6.41 per hour.
Supervisors (3). Wages £7.65 per hour.
Sportscheme Leaders (3) Daycamp Leaders (2). Wages £5.94 per hour; to work
Monday to Friday. Applicants must be aged 18 and over and have experience of
working with children.

Apply to the Leisure Services (☎01473-435000) at the above address from early
March. A standard disclosure is required for all positions.

THE KINGSWOOD GROUP: Group Operations, Kingswood House, Alkmaar
Way, Norwich, Norfolk NR6 6BF (☎01603-309350; fax 01603-404904; e-mail
jobs@kingswood.co.uk; www.kingswood.co.uk). Kingswood operates year round
educational activity centres for kids, including Camp Beaumont Summer Camps,
which have been running for 23 years at various locations across the UK.
Group Leaders (60-80) are responsible for round-the-clock welfare of a group of
children at our Camp Beaumont Summer Camps, including overnight dormitory
supervision. Also to instruct and initiate games and non-specialist activities, and to
monitor the welfare needs of individual children in their group. National minimum
wage applies according to age. Camps run for 8 weeks from the start of July to the end
of August. Accommodation provided at a cost of £24.50 per week and food at a cost
of £39.95 per week. Comprehensive training is provided. Applicants must be aged
between 19 and 25 and have some previous experience working with children and/or
a well developed interest in sports, music, drama, art and crafts or any recreational
pursuits. Foreign applicants with fluent English welcome.

Kingswood also recruits throughout the year for **Activity Instructors** to supervise
various high and low adventure activities such as caving, go-karting, rock-climbing
and archery. No experience is necessary, though as friendly and outgoing personality
and a love for working with children is a must. Activity Instructors are employed on
an initial 12 month Training and Development Package with food, accommodation,
nationally recognised qualifications and a training allowance provided throughout
the year.

Applications should be sent to the HR department at the above address in the
spring. Telephone interviews and an assessment weekend required.

SPORT AND EDUCATIONAL TRAVEL LIMITED: 3 Dukes Head Street,
Lowestoft, Suffolk NR32 1JY (☎01502-567914; fax 01502-500993; e-mail info@
set-uk.com). A company established since 1991 which organises group travel for
school parties, with students between 11 and 17 years old.
Couriers. £100 for a day trip; for longer stays £100 for the first day and £60 for
each subsequent day thereafter. One fluent language or more required. For overnight
visits or longer, accommodation and meals are provided on the same basis as the
group you are accompanying.

Applications should be sent to Mr G Bishop, Managing Director, at the above
address.

XUK: 48 Fitzalan Road, London N3 3PE (☎020-8922 9739; fax 020-8343 0625;
e-mail xuk@xkeys.co.uk; www.campsforkids.co.uk). Residential camps in East
Anglia for children aged 6 to 17 years.
Childrens Leaders, Cooks, Kitchen Assistants, Cleaners. Competitive wages plus
free board. Qualifications or experience in first aid, life saving, arts/crafts, sports, or
teaching are helpful. Applications from teachers or student teachers preferred.

More details and *application* forms available on the above website.

Holiday Centres and Amusements

ADVENTURE ISLAND: Western Esplanade, Southend-on-Sea, Essex SS1 1EE (☎01702-468023; fax 01702-601044; e-mail enquiries@stockvale.co.uk; www. adventureisland.co.uk).
Ride Operators, Catering Staff, Cashiers (50-60) required for the summer, wages and hours by arrangement, staff must be over 16.
Applications to the Personnel Department, at the above address.

COLCHESTER ZOO LTD: Maldon Road, Colchester, Essex CO3 0SL (☎01206-331292; fax 01206-331392; e-mail info@colchester-zoo.co.uk; www.colchester-zoo. co.uk). The zoo has gained a reputation as one of the most modern and forward-thinking zoos in the UK.
Retail Staff, Catering Staff, Site Cleaners, Play Area Staff, Groundsmen/ Gardeners, Administration Staff. No accommodation available.
To request an *application form* please apply online at the above website or write to the Directors at the above address. Note all applicants must be available for interview.

IMPERIAL WAR MUSEUM: Duxford, Cambridgeshire CB2 4QR (www.iwm.org. uk). Duxford was a former RAF fighter airfield during the Battle of Britain and is steeped in history. Today Duxford is Europe's premier aviation museum and visitor attraction.
Museum Assistants (6-9) to invigilate within the museum, assist visitors, monitor exhibitions and carry out cleaning duties. Wages £12,072 per annum, pro rata, to work 5 days out of 7 (2 weekends out of 3). Part-time working hours are also available. Must be 17 or over, hold a driving licence and be eligible to work in the UK. Period of work from March to October. Foreign applicants with good understanding of English welcome.
Application and details available from website in January.

LUCKY STRIKE AMUSEMENTS: Seafield Caravan Park, Newport near Hemsby, Great Yarmouth, Norfolk NR29 4NW (tel/fax 01493-732671). Family-run business established 21 years. Prize bingo and small amusement arcade on the east coast, just outside Great Yarmouth.
Cashier to work mainly in arcade. Must be over 18.
Bingo Callers (2), Change/Prize Attendants (2) to work in prize bingo. Minimum age 16.
Wages £120 to £300 per week, depending on hours worked. Shift work is on a 7 day rota basis with 1-2 days off a week. Minimum period of work 16 to 20 weeks. Work is available during Easter week and then from Whitsun to October. Accommodation is available at a nearby caravan site or in chalets. Applicants must have an outgoing personality and a smart and pleasant manner. Overseas applicants with fluent English welcome. Training can be given.
Apply in writing to Mrs Christine Gray, Partner at the above address from March.

MOLE HALL WILDLIFE PARK: Widdington, Saffron Walden, Essex CB11 3SS (☎01799-540400; fax 01799-542408; e-mail enquiries@molehall.co.uk; www. molehall.co.uk).
Animal Wardens (2/3) are employed during the summer. Pocket money and accommodation provided in return for 40 hours a week. Minimum age 16.

For further *details*, contact the Park at the above address.

POTTERS LEISURE RESORT: Coast Road, Hopton-on-Sea, Norfolk NR31 9BX (☎01502-734812; fax 01502-731971; e-mail recruitment@potters-leisure.co.uk; www.pottersholidays.com). The UK's only privately-owned 5-star holiday village. Operates all year, good facilities.
Housekeeping Staff. To work part-time, 18 to 20 hours over 6 days. Applicants must be 16 or older.
Food and Beverage Staff to work in bar, restaurant and catering positions. Full-time and part-time positions available up to 40 hours per week. Bar staff must be over 18.
Kitchen and Catering Staff must be over 16.
Lifeguard. Full- and part-time positions available up to 40 hours per week. Applicants must be over 16 and hold a PLG lifeguard qualification.
Wages are dependent on age. Positions available throughout the year. Accommodation may be provided, depending on availability, at a cost of 57p per hour worked, maximum of £22.75 per week. Foreign applicants with good spoken English welcome.
Applications at any time to Kim Wood, HR Officer, at the above address. Interview required.

PLEASURE AND LEISURE CORPORATION plc: Pleasure Beach, South Beach Parade, Great Yarmouth, Norfolk NR30 3EH (☎01493-844585; fax 01493-853483; e-mail gypbeach@aol.com or nigelthurs@aol.com). A family company operating a major leisure and amusement park with over 25 rides, two amusement arcades and a bar over 9 acres. More than 1 million visitors every year.
Ride Operators (50). At least national minimum wage, plus full uniform and staff concessions on rides and food outlets. Working hours are variable according to the time of the season. Minimum period of work of 8 weeks. Positions are available from March to September. Must be aged 18 or over, with good spoken English. No previous experience necessary as training provided. Accommodation not available.
Applications should be made from March onwards to Nigel Thurston, Personnel Manager. Interview and drug screening necessary.

Hotels and Catering

BANHAM ZOO: Kenninghall Road, Banham, Norfolk NR16 2HE (☎01953-715313; fax 01953-887445; e-mail lynn.mellish@banhamzoo.co.uk; www.banhamzoo.co.uk).
Catering Assistants (12+) for general catering duties, serving at tills, clearing tables, serving hot and cold food and working in snack shacks within the zoo. Wages at over the national minimum wage. Flexible working hours, including bank holidays and weekend work. Period of work from 1 July-31 October; vacancies also at Christmas and Easter. Minimum age 18; some positions will require a current health and hygiene certificate.
Applications to Lynn Mellish, HR Manager, at the above address.

GRAFHAM WATER CENTRE: Perry, Huntingdon, Cambridgeshire PE28 OBX (☎0845-634 6022; fax 01480-812739; e-mail info@grafham-water-centre.co.uk; www.grafham-water-centre.co.uk).
Catering Assistants (3) to work May to July, 8 hours per day. Wages of £214 per week plus food and accommodation. Applicants need a basic food hygiene certificate.

Domestic assistants also required.
Applications to Mr Ian Downing, Head of Centre, at the above address.

HAVEN PASSENGER CRUISES LTD: PO Box 401, Cambridge CB4 3WE
(☎01223-307694; fax 01223-307695; e-mail info@georgina.co.uk; www.georgina.
co.uk). The Georgina is a fully-appointed passenger craft on the river Cam, taking
mainly private bookings for weddings, birthdays, corporate events and the group
travel market.
Crew (5/6) for the Riverboat Georgina. Job involves bar work, serving food and
general crewing tasks (tying/untying ropes, opening/closing locks on river). Wages of
£5.35 per hour plus tips. To work between May and September. Full training given.
Applicants must be at least 18 and proficient in English.
Applications to Amy Burns, Operations Manager.

HOLIDAY INN NORWICH HOTEL: Cromer Road, Amsterdan Way, Norwich,
Norfolk NR6 6JA (☎01603-410544; fax 01603-487701). Close to Norwich
International Airport, the hotel has 121 rooms, a busy á la carte restaurant and carvery,
and large banqueting rooms.
Bar Hosts, Banqueting Hosts, Waiting Staff (20-30 in total). To work part-time or
full-time shifts - must be flexible. Positions are available all year; accommodation not
available Minimum age 16. Overseas applicants welcome.
Applications should be made to Karen Lawrence, H.R. Manager, as soon as
possible. Interview necessary.

KENTWELL HALL: Long Melford, Sudbury, Suffolk CO10 9BA (☎01787-310207;
fax 01787-379318; e-mail office@kentwell.co.uk; www.kentwell.co.uk). A privately-
owned moated Tudor Mansion, situated in its own park and farmland, approximately
1½ miles from the historic town of Long Melford, famous for its great annual re-
creations of Tudor life. The great annual re-creation takes place during June and July
and is visited by up to 1,500 children on weekdays and the public on weekends.
Retail and Catering Staff (10) needed for historical re-creations. In order to keep
the 16th and 21st centuries separate, the catering and shop are located outside of the
main gates. Staff on the 21st Century side ensure smooth running of the event for
the public and school parties. Duties consist of serving in a temporary souvenir shop
and restaurant in marquees and may also include marshalling school parties. Wages
by arrangement and employees must make their own accommodation arrangements.
Minimum age 16; applicants need a pleasant manner and to be physically fit as they
will be on their feet all day.
Applications should be sent to Estate Office at the above address.

THE LODGE HOTEL: Old Hunstanton Road, Hunstanton, Norfolk PE36 6HX
(☎01485-532896; fax 01485-535007). A Grade II listed Hotel close to a beach with
22 en suite bedrooms; popular with bird watchers and golfers.
Chefs, Waiting and Bar Person and Housekeeping Staff. Wages at national minimum
rate, depending on age and experience. Required for 20 to 40 hours per week from
early July to late September. Minimum period of work 6 weeks. Accommodation can
be provided. Must have some relevant experience. Overseas applicants welcome.
Applications should be made as soon as possible to Mr A.G. Best, Proprietor, at
the above address.

MARLBOROUGH HOTEL: Sea Road, Felixstowe, Suffolk IP11 2PJ (☎01394-
285621; fax 01394-670724).

Housekeeper/Waiting Staff (2) and Commis Chef (1). Wage national minimum plus tips, food and accommodation. To work a maximum of 40 hours per week.
Receptionist (1). Wage national minimum plus tips, food and accommodation. Shift work 7am to 3pm or 3pm to 11.30pm.
All staff needed to work 5 days in 7 from May to October inclusive. Minimum age 18. Applicants must be able to speak English.
Applications to Bob Fraser, General Manager at the above address.

MENZIES CAMBRIDGE HOTEL & GOLF CLUB: Bar Hill, Cambridge, CB3 8EU (☎01954-249988; fax 01954-249981; e-mail Cambridge@menzies-hotels. co.uk; www.menzies-hotels.co.uk).
Room and Food and Beverage Assistants: to work as and when required. Wages £5.35-£5.50 per hour. Minimum age 16 (18 for liquor service). No accommodation.
Applications to A Hartley, Human Resources Manager, at the above address.

STOKE BY NAYLAND CLUB: Keepers Lane, Leavenheath, Colchester, Essex CO6 4PZ (☎01206-262836; fax 01206-263356; www.stokebynaylandclub.co.uk). A 30-bedroom hotel with two 18-hole golf courses and a leisure centre.
Bar/Waiting Staff and Cleaners needed. Hours and wages to be discussed at interview. Accommodation possibly available, at an approximate charge of £30 per week. Foreign applicants with fluent English welcome; applicants must be 17 or over (18 for bar staff).
Applications to Ricardo Santa-Rita at the above address. Interview required but may be done by telephone.

TOPSAIL CHARTERS LTD: Cooks Yard, The Hythe, Maldon, Essex CM9 5HN (☎01621-857567; fax 01621-840567; e-mail info@top-sail.co.uk; www.top-sail. co.uk). Based in Maldon but also working in London and Ipswich. Private functions and public trips on historic sailing barges. A small company, very customer-orientated, with a great team of staff on board.
Bar Worker, Host/ess, Catering Assistants (3) for work on Thames sailing barges. Wages approximately £7.00 per hour. Must be flexible about hours, up to 50 per week. Positions are available from April to September. Some bar/catering experience preferable; must be flexible and combine galley and bar work. No accommodation provided, but can be arranged.
Applications to Stephanie Valentine from Easter onwards. Interview necessary.

Language Schools

ALEXANDERS INTERNATIONAL SCHOOL: Bawdsey Manor, Bawdsey, Woodbridge, Suffolk IP12 3AZ (☎01394-411633; fax 01394-411357; e-mail office@ alexandersschool.com; www.skola.co.uk/alexanders.index.htm). An international summer school for 11-18 year olds from all over the world. English language tuition plus specialist sports and activities courses.
Residential Sports Assistants. Wages £185-£250 per week; to work 48 hours per week over 6 days, including weekends. Applicants must be undergraduate sports teachers or qualified professional coaches and 21 years or older.
EFL Teachers. Wages £330-£350 per week; to work 6 days a week including a Saturday or Sunday. Must be RSA certified TEFL or better and 23 years or over.
Free accommodation is available. Period of work June to August inclusive. Minimum period of work is 4 weeks.
Applications to the Administration Office, from March to the above address.

BRIAR SCHOOL OF ENGLISH: 3 Dukes Head Street, Lowestoft, Suffolk NR32 1JY (☎01502-580203; fax 01502-500993; e-mail briar.school@set-uk.com). Established since 1958. Offers English courses to international students aged 12-25. Busy seasons are over the Easter period and from the beginning of June till the end of August. Also entertain out of season school parties at different times of the year.
EFL Teachers. From £9.00 per hour. TEFL qualifications or experience essential. Applicants must possess either a degree or a teacher's certificate.
Sports Instructors. From £5.50 per hour, required to work up to 6 hours per day. Minimum period of work 3 weeks (June-August). Ideal post for Physical Education students.
Successful applicants for both jobs can earn extra pay by leading half/full day excursions to Norwich, Cambridge, London and other local places of interest. Accommodation is not available.
Applications should be sent to Miss Lucy Oram, Director of Studies, at the above address.

CAMBRIDGE ACADEMY OF ENGLISH: 65 High Street, Girton, Cambridge CB3 0QD (☎01223-277230; fax 01223-277606; e-mail cae@cambridgeacademy. co.uk; www.cambridgeacademy.co.uk). Situated in the leafy suburb of Girton, the Academy runs non-residential courses for teenagers and young adults, and residential courses for 9 to 13 year olds and 14 to 16 year olds.
EFL Teachers to teach teenagers and young adults. Required for 3 week courses between June 20 and August 19; wages of approximately £900 per course. The job involves 21 to 24 hours teaching a week. Must have RSA TEFL/Trinity College certificate or equivalent and experience.
Applications to S. Levy at the above address.

THE CAMBRIDGE CENTRE FOR LANGUAGES: 70 Queensway, Trumpington Road, Cambridge CB2 2AY (☎01223-470535; fax 01223-722169; e-mail info@ camlang.co.uk; www.camlang.co.uk).
EFL Teachers (8), Activities Organisers (4), Social and Welfare Officers (1-2). Wages £260 per week with free full-board accommodation. Required July-August to staff residential summer camps for children aged 10-18.
For details and *applications* contact Mrs. R. Muir at the above address.

EFL INTERNATIONAL LANGUAGE SCHOOLS: 221 Hills Road, Cambridge CB2 2RW (☎01223-240020; fax 01223-412474; e-mail pippa.cusimano@ef.com).
Leaders required to work with adults and/or juniors during the summer. Responsibilities include organising events, entertainment and excursions. You will be expected to attend the events and to act as courier/guide on excursions. The hours of work are varied and will include evenings and weekends. Minimum age of 18 with good communication skills; experience of working with young people an advantage.
Applications to Pippa Cusimano, School Director.

FRIDAYBRIDGE INTERNATIONAL FARM CAMP LTD: 173 March Road, Wisbech, Cambridgeshire PE14 OLR (☎01945-860255; fax 01945-861088; e-mail fbifc@hotmail.com).
English Language Teachers (3) required to provide English conversation classes, mainly to East European students; mostly evening classes with no formal lesson plans. Also to provide more structured lessons to language school students on two week courses for approximately 8 hours per day. Wages of £240 per week/£960 per complete month plus attendance bonus; full board and accommodation provided free

of charge. Period of work from 29 June to 30 August. TEFL qualifications would be an advantage but are not essential. Most students are aged 16 to 25 so the camp has a youthful feel, but age is no barrier.

Applications or requests for further information to Jessica McDonald, Director, at the above address.

STUDIO CAMBRIDGE: 6 Salisbury Villas, Station Road, Cambridge CB1 2JF (☎01223-369701; fax 01223-324605; e-mail personnel@studiocambridge.co.uk; www.studiocambridge.co.uk). The oldest of the permanently-established Cambridge language schools, and a founder member of English UK.
EFL Teachers for young learners courses (age 10-14, 14-16 and 16-20). Applicants should have CELTA, TESOL and/or EFL experience.
Activity Organisers for young learners courses (ages as above). Applicants should have interests/abilities in sport, art, music or drama, and need stamina, initiative and enthusiasm.
Course Directors and Assistant Course Directors (ages as above). Applicants should have good organisational and managerial skills. Some EFL or summer camp experience preferred.

Residential and non-residential posts available, mainly between July and August but also at other times of the year; only those who speak English as if it were their first language need apply.

Applications to the above address.

YES EDUCATION CENTRE: 12 Eversfield Road, Eastbourne, East Sussex BN21 2AS (☎01323-644830; fax 01323-726260; e-mail dos@yeseducation.co.uk; www. yeseducation.co.uk). A friendly, independent school committed to high academic and professional standards.
EFL Teachers. Wages £175-£400 per week for adult and junior schools in Eastbourne. Staff required in July and August. No accommodation provided. Relevant teaching qualifications required.

Applications to the Director of Studies for Eastbourne.

Medical

CAREWATCH (PETERBOROUGH): Unit 2, Lady Lodge Art Centre, Orton Goldhay, Peterborough PE2 5JQ (☎01733-394649; fax 01733-371854; e-mail peterborough@carewatch-fps.co.uk;www.carewatch-care-services.co.uk).Carewatch is the largest UK provider of domiciliary care.
Homecare Assistant (10). Wages £6.36-£7.41 per hour. To work shifts between 7am and 10pm; minimum period of work 6 weeks. Must be over 18. No experience is necessary as all training provided. Fluent English essential, however non-UK citizens are considered as long as they have the proper work permits or a National Insurance number. Must drive a car since work involves travelling from one patient's house to the next.

Apply as soon as possible to Melanie or Susanna at the above address. An interview will be necessary.

ESSEX NURSING SERVICES: 3rd Floor, 7 St Botolphs Street, Colchester, Essex CO2 7DU (☎01206-578600; fax 01206-577899; e-mail aabel@ensrg.co.uk; www. essexnursingservices.co.uk). A busy employment agency covering homecare, nursing homes and hospitals.

Care Staff. Unlimited positions available for those with at least 6 months experience in a care environment. Wages from £5.00 to £10 per hour, full or part time and at any time of the year. Suitably qualified foreign applicants welcome, but fluent English is essential. Accommodation is not available.

Applications should be made at any time to the above address. Interview required.

HIGHFIELD HOMECARE: 17 Clarence Road, Southend-on-Sea, Essex SS1 1AN (☎0845-602 1757; fax 01702-433113; e-mail anthony.greenwood@bna.co.uk; www. bna.co.uk).

Care Workers (30) required to help the vulnerable to live in their own homes; shopping /errands and pension collecting, housework, bathing, washing and dressing and undressing, shaving, making snacks and feeding etc.

Pay weekdays up to 7pm (£5.52) per hour. After 7pm £5.77 per hour. Weekends £6.17 per hour plus £10 bonus per multiple of 8 hours worked in same weekend (to maximum of £30). Any period from June to October. Must be 18 years old with enhanced CRB clearance. Must have own car.

Applications to the above address.

Outdoor

1ST CHOICE PERSONNEL: Fenberry Farm, Peters Point, Sutton Bridge, Spalding PE12 9UX (tel/fax 01406-351044). Small family-run employment agency.

Factory and Farm Workers to carry out various tasks including factory tasks with fruit or flowers, picking, potato grading and fruit preparation. Wages approximately £200 per week. To work approximately 9 to 10 hours, 5½ days a week. Minimum period of work of 2 weeks. Positions are available all year. Foreign applicants with some knowledge of English welcome. No previous experience necessary. Accommodation available for £50 per week.

Applications should be made at any time to Keith Hargreaves at the above address.

BOXFORD (SUFFOLK) FARMS LTD: Hill Farm, Boxford, Sudbury, Suffolk CO10 5NY (☎01787-210348; fax 01787-211106). A family-owned company supplying fruit to major supermarkets. Situated in beautiful countryside within an hour's train journey from London.

Fruit Pickers and Fruit Packers required to work on farms and packhouse situated on the Suffolk/Essex border. The work involves the picking and packing of soft and top fruit (strawberries, raspberries, apples etc.). Hours of work and wages are variable subject to the crop and weather. The season is from June to July for soft fruit and the middle of August to the end of October for apples. Self-catering caravan accommodation is available and the camp has toilets, showers, laundry facilities and TV. Workers must be over 18 years old with a liking for outside work and with valid working visas and work permits. It is essential that the farm is contacted 24 hours before arrival.

Applications to the Personnel Manager at the above address.

CHELMER MARQUEES LTD: Waltham Road, Boreham, Chelmsford CM3 3AY (☎01245-450033; fax 01245-451133; e-mail hire@chelmermarquees.co.uk).

Marquee Erectors (5). Wages from £5.00-£5.50 per hour; time and a half paid on Sundays and Bank Holidays. To work 7.30am to 6.30pm or longer from Monday to Friday; 8am to 6pm on Sundays. Staff required from April to end of September. Work involves erecting and taking down marquees and equipment, cleaning and driving.

Minimum age 18. Must have a clean driving licence.
Applications should be made to Mr D. Potts at the above address.

CYGNET MARQUEES: 28 Hardys Way, Canvey Island, Essex SS8 9PT (☎0500-412999; fax 01268-525254; www.cygnetmarquees.com).
Marquee Erectors (3) needed from June to the end of September. Duties include loading vehicles and working away from the warehouse on customers' sites erecting marquees as part of a supervised team. Wages of £225 per week and basic hours 8am to 5pm; plenty of overtime available paid at time and a half.

Applicants should be fit; being reasonably tall would be an advantage. Someone aged over 25 with a clean driving licence could be paid extra.
Applications to the above address.

FIVEWAYS FRUIT FARM: Fiveways, Stanway, Colchester, Essex CO3 5LR (☎01206-330244; fax 01206-330828; e-mail fiveways.fruit.farm@farming.me.uk). A medium-sized farm run by two brothers growing mainly strawberries, cherries and apples. Situated in a rural oasis on the outskirts of Colchester with shops close by.
Fruit Pickers (4). Wages at piecework rates, approx. £150-£300+ per 5-7 day week. Hours flexible, start at 6am with hourly work also available. No overtime. Strawberry and raspberry picking from May-September; apple picking from August but principally from September to October; orchard work and other semi-skilled jobs in propagation tunnels and French tunnels; packing fruit for supermarkets.

Minimum period of work 12 weeks. Meadow next to farm available for camping. Caravans on site with all facilities, including showers, cooking facilities and television. Charge £27.30 per week. Supermarket, post office, off-licence and launderette within a 5 minute walk from the farm. Overseas students aged over 21 welcome.
Applications from the beginning of the year to Alistair Mead, c/o Fiveways Fruit Farm.

FRIDAYBRIDGE INTERNATIONAL FARM CAMP: March Road, Fridaybridge, Wisbech, Cambridgeshire PE14 0LR (☎01945-860255; fax 01945-861088). A very friendly, family run company offering the chance to meet people from all over the world.
General Agricultural Workers to harvest strawberries, apples, broccoli, potatoes and salads and to help with many other jobs. To work on average 5 to 6 days per week, although this cannot be guaranteed. Vacancies available April to November. Minimum period of work 3 weeks. Basic accommodation, breakfast and dinner provided at a reasonable weekly charge, payable in advance.

Club, disco, swimming pool, tennis courts, basketball, volleyball, day trips, free English lessons (conversational) and many other facilities provided. Staff vacancies also available for drivers, bar work, shop staff, kitchen assistants, administrative staff and English teachers. EU students aged 16- to 30 welcome.
Send an s.a.e. /IRC for brochure (applications on official forms only) to Bookings, Fridaybridge International Camp.

G'S MARKETING LTD: Hostel, Barway, Ely, Cambridgeshire CB7 5TZ (☎01353-727245; fax 01353-727353; e-mail recruitment@gs-marketing.com; www.gs-marketing.com).
Production Operatives. Wages at piecework rates (average £180 per week). Required from October to the end of April to trim, pack and label salad and vegetable crops plus some farming positions. Must be fit and willing to work. Evening meal and accommodation provided on site. Minimum age 18.
Applications to Sharon Gudgeon, Hostel Recruitment Officer, at the above address.

G.E. ELSWORTH & SON: Park Fruit Farm, Pork Lane, Great Holland, Frinton-on-Sea, Essex CO13 OES (☎01255-674621; e-mail s.elsworth@farmline.com).
Fruit Pickers (6) to pick apples in September.
Crop Thinners (6) required during June.
Wages as set by the Agricultural Wage Board. To work flexible hours between 9am and 5pm. Accommodation available. Please ensure job availability before arriving unannounced. Possibility of pruning work from January to March also.
Applications to S. Elsworth, Partner, at the above address.

GL EVENTS SNOWDEN'S: Second Drove Eastern Industry, Fengate, Peterborough PE1 5XA (☎01733-294614; fax 01733-345672; e-mail adrian@snowdens.co.uk). Snowden's is a subsidiary of GL Events, a leading marquee hirer in the show and hospitality market.
Marquee Erectors required. Wages, dependent on hours worked, average £300 per week. Applicants must be physically fit and able to work an average of 10 hours a day six days a week (extra hours are available) from 1 April – 30 September. Successful applicants may visit some prestigious sporting locations, e.g. Ascot, Newmarket and Silverstone.
Applicants must be over the age of 18. Foreign applicants with all relevant work permits and acceptable level of spoken English are welcome. Please note however that accommodation is only provided when working away on site.
Applications should be made from 1 March to Adrian West at the above address.

THE GRANTA BOAT AND PUNT COMPANY: Newnham Hill Pond, Newnham Road, Cambridge CB3 9EX (tel/fax 01223-301845; e-mail granta.boats@lineone.net; www.puntingincambridge.com). Boat and punt hire company situated on the River Cam.
Punt Chauffeurs (10). Wages at competitive hourly rates. Minimum age 18. Applicants must be outgoing, confident and physically fit. Previous experience of working in a customer service environment, as well as the ability to speak in a foreign language are preferable, but not essential. Applicants must also be able to provide informative verbal tours to guests, which will include memorising historical facts.
Ice Cream Servers (2). Wages at competitive hourly rates. Minimum age 16.
Various hours are available for both positions. Applicants must be flexible as the hours will include weekend and evening work. Staff required for a minimum period of 3 months from March to October. No accommodation is available. Overseas applicants are welcome to apply but must be able to speak English to the same standard as a native speaker.
Applications should be made from the end of February to Sarah Austen, Director, at the above address.

HIGHFIELD TIFFANY MARQUEES: Klondyke Farm, Broads Road, Burwell, Cambridge CB5 OBQ (☎01638-743860; fax 01638-743878; e-mail info@thehighfieldgroup.co.uk; www.thehighfieldgroup.co.uk).
Marquee Hire Labourers (up to 4) to assist with marquee hire from June to August. Long hours available subject to workload. Wages from national minimum wage. Accommodation can be arranged at a cost to be advised. Must be physically fit.
Contact Garry Chapman, Proprietor.

INTERNATIONAL FARM CAMP: Hall Road, Tiptree, Essex CO5 0QS (☎01621-815496; e-mail ifc@tiptree.com).

Fruit Pickers. Pay at piecework rates. Hours 6am-3pm Monday to Friday; some weekend work. Accommodation available at £30 per week for overseas workers only. Caravan site available for British applicants. Must be aged 20-25 years. Minimum work period 4 weeks between early June and mid-July.

Overseas applicants welcome, but places for non-EEA nationals are open only to full-time students who have not completed their studies.

Applications to be sent as early as possible to the above address.

M.R. LYNES MARQUEES: 20 Sir Williams Lane, Aylsham, Norwich, Norfolk NR11 6AW (☎01263-733134; e-mail mail@lynesmarquees.co.uk; www.marqueehire-norfolk.co.uk).
Assistants (1-2). Wages £5.35 per hour. To work 40 hours and over per week, from May to October. Must be 25 and over. Experience is an advantage. Fluent English is essential.

Apply from April to Paul Matthews at the above address.

D.A. NEWLING & SON: Turnover Farm, Decoy Road, Gorefield, Wisbech, Cambridgeshire PE13 4PD (☎01945-870749; e-mail p9ear@aol.com). A family fruit farm with a small and friendly workforce.
Apple and Pear Pickers (10). Piecework rates, average £40 to £50 per day depending on how hard you work. To work 8 hours per day with some overtime. Minimum period of work of 4 weeks. Positions are available from 30 August to 30 September. Accommodation in shared caravans. Showers and laundry facilities on site (£18 per week). Applicants must be 17 or over, clean, healthy and able; foreign applicants with sufficient English to understand instructions welcome. No previous experience necessary.

Applications should be made from April onwards to Edward Newling at the above address.

JARK RECRUITMENT LTD: 22/28 Blackfriars Street, Kings Lynn, Norfolk PE30 1NN (☎01553-660888/01553-774888; fax 01553-660880; e-mail klind@jark.co.uk; www.jark.co.uk). Recruitment agency that require staff all year round for production work in and around the Norfolk and Suffolk area.
Production Staff to pick, pack, cut, sort, label and box fruits, vegetables, meats, poultry, toys, dairy products, flowers and much more. Wages from £6.00 per hour plus overtime and holiday pay. Self-catering accommodation is available for £57.50 per week. Catered accommodation is available for approximately £82.50 per week, including 3 meals, laundry, wake-ups and tel/fax. B & B available for around £65 per week. Transport to and from work available at a cost of £2.50 per day.

Minimum period of work 12 weeks at any time of year. Applicants must be 18 to 35 years old. Overseas applicants with EU/EEA passport or work authorisation, and good English are considered. Interview not necessary.

Applications with I.D. at least 2 to 3 weeks before arrival date.

R. & J.M. PLACE LTD: Church Farm, Tunstead, Norwich NR12 8RQ (☎01692-536225; fax 01692-536928; e-mail info@ifctunstead.co.uk; www.ifctunstead.co.uk). Large soft fruit growers in the centre of the Broadland National Park.
Fruit Picking. Weather permitting, details on application. Accommodation available for £57.75 per week, including breakfast, in purpose-built dormitory blocks. Tents and caravans are not permitted. Must be in good health. No previous experience necessary. Social activities in camp include tennis, volleyball, badminton, basketball, football, pool and many more. Open all year round.

Overseas applicants welcome.

Applications with s.a.e. to the Administrator, R. & J.M. Place Ltd.

H.R. PHILPOT & SON LTD: Barleylands Farm, Barleylands Road, Billericay, Essex CM11 2UD (☎01268-290215; 01268-290222; e-mail robert@barleylands. co.uk; www.barleylands.co.uk). Highly mechanised progressive large arable farming company based in Essex and Suffolk.

Experienced Machine Operators, General Farm Workers required to work the harvesting season from the end of June until October. Working on a farm with modern equipment, CAT 85, Fastrac, Vaderstat Cultivators, Drills/FC, Pea Harvesters, Combine Harvesters, modern Potato Harvesting and grading equipment. Must be adaptable to take on any job when asked. Must have full UK driving licence, valid work permit and be able to understand and speak English. Accommodation will be provided for single persons.

Applications should be sent to Robert Willy at the above address from February onwards.

REMFRESH: Harts Lane, Ardleigh, Colchester, Essex CO7 7QH (☎01206-230144; fax 01206-233482; e-mail info@remfresh.com; www.remfresh.com).

Horticultural Workers (2) required to work in the glasshouse and outside on the production of baby vegetables and exotic lettuces. For general duties including all aspects of production from planting to packing. Wages at agricultural wages rates. To work from approximately 7am to 4pm Monday to Friday. No accommodation available. Period of work May to September. No special experience or qualifications needed but must be quite fit and able to work fast when necessary and to cope with work in the glasshouse, which can get hot at times.

Applications to Elaine Smith, Partner, at the above address.

RICHARDSONS (STAINHAM) LTD: The Staithe, Stalham, Norwich, Norfolk NR12 9BX (☎01692-581081; fax 01692-584002; e-mail info@horizonboating.co.uk; www. horizonboating.co.uk).

Boat Cleaners (4) to clean the interiors and exteriors of boats varying in size from 2 to 12 berth on their return from letting. Wages £4.64 per hour; accommodation available in a caravan with cooking facilities for £22.75 per week. Period of work by arrangement between June and September. Applicants must be aged at least 18; no special qualifications required other than the ability to enjoy housework and cleaning in a confined space to a high standard.

Applications to Ken Scott-Greenard, Group General Manager, at the above address.

STOKE FARM: Battisford, Stowmarket, Suffolk IP14 2NA (☎01449-774944; fax 01449-616045; e-mail rebeccaupson@btinternet.com). A family run fruit farm.

Fruit Pickers (5). To pick apples and pears. Wages as set by the Agricultural Wage Board; to work 6 or more hours a day. Applicants must be over 18 and should state whether they have had previous experience. Staff are required from September until the end of picking for a minimum period of 1 week. Please note that no accommodation is available.

Applications should be sent to David Upson at the above address from July onwards.

WALLINGS NURSERY LTD: 38 Harwich Road, Lawford, Manningtree, Essex CO11 2LS (☎01206-230163; fax 01206-230863; e-mail dtdunn@talk21.com). Three hectares of glasshouses and two hectares of polytunnels, growing strawberries off the ground.

Strawberry Pickers (10). Wages £250 per week, for 8 hours per day, 6 days per week. Minimum period of work 10 weeks. Positions available from 20 March to 1 May. Board and accommodation available in communal converted barns for £20 per week. EU and Commonwealth citizens with permission to work in the UK welcome; fluent English not essential. Work also available in the packhouse.
Applications should be made from February/March onwards to Christopher Batchelor at the above address.

PAUL WILLIAMSON LTD: Church Farm, Bradfield Combust, Bury St Edmunds, Suffolk IP30 0LW (☎01284-386333; fax 01284-386155; e-mail paul@ williamsongrowers.co.uk; www.thepoly.co.uk/paulw).
Horticultural Staff (10) wanted from mid-May to mid-October mainly for work picking strawberries, raspberries, apples and pears. Wages at Agricultural Wages Board rates. To work mainly from 8am to 4pm, Monday to Friday with some Saturday work. Applicants should be aged over 18. Plenty of space available for tents (own equipment required) with showers, toilets and kitchen and washing facilities available.
Applications to Mr P.R. Williamson, Director, at the above address.

Sport

BRADWELL OUTDOORS: Bradwell Waterside, nr Southminster, Essex CM0 7QY (☎01621-776256; fax 01621-776378; e-mail info.bradwelloutdoors@essex. gov.uk; www.bradwelloutdoors.com). A local authority-run high quality multi-activity residential centre for young people and adults. Based on the edge of the River Blackwater in Essex, it is an excellent site for all water and land based activities.
Sailing (3), Canoeing (1) and Archery Instructors. Wages negotiable. To include B & L. To work approximately 8 hours per day. Minimum work period 4 months between April and October inclusive. RYA Instructors Certificate essential or BCU/ GNAS.
Applications in January/March to the Manager, Bradwell Outdoors.

MICHAEL WIGHAM: Hamilton Stables, Hamilton Road, Newmarket, Suffolk CB8 7JQ (☎01638-668806 or 078-3145 6426; fax 01638-668806).
Stable Assistants (2) to work for a racehorse trainer from June to September. Wages approximately £4.00 per hour plus accommodation. To work from 6.30am to 11.30am and 4.30pm to 6pm. Should have previous experience with horses or ponies.
Applications to Michael Wigham at the above address.

Voluntary Work

Archaeology

SEDGEFORD HISTORICAL AND ARCHAEOLOGICAL RESEARCH PROJECT: 67 Victoria Avenue, Hunstanton, Norfolk PE36 8BY (☎01485-532343; e-mail tanzee@supanet.com; www.sharp.org.uk).
A long-term investigation of an English parish concentrating at present on Roman and Anglo Saxon periods.
Voluntary Archaeological & Historical Fieldworkers (50) wanted from early July to mid-August. Subsistence charge of £150 per week. Hours 8.30am to 5pm, 6 days a week with Saturdays off. If applicants have no prior digging experience, they must

enrol on a one-week Basic Excavation and Recording Techniques course with the project.

Visit the website above to download an application form or contact Brenda Huggins, Enrolment Secretary, at the above address.

Conservation and the Environment

BRITISH TRUST FOR ORNITHOLOGY: The National Centre for Ornithology, The Nunnery, Thetford, Norfolk, IP24 2PU (☎01842-750050; fax 01842-750030; e-mail info@bto.org; www.bto.org).
An organisation set up to promote the appreciation and conservation of birds.
Volunteers needed to participate in surveys run by the BTO. Surveys run by the BTO range from extremely long-term to short-term schemes.
Apply to the above address at any time.

EPPING FOREST CENTENARY TRUST: The Warren Lodge, Loughton, Essex IG10 4RN (☎020-8508 9061; fax 020-8508 2176; e-mail enquiry@efct.info; www. efct.info).
The Trust was set up to celebrate the centenary of the protection of the forest in 1978. It is involved in promoting the forest and its unique character.
Volunteers required to help with conservation work within the forest. Volunteers must be able to travel to Epping on their own.
Enquiries to the Conservation Project Manager at the above address.

SUFFOLK WILDLIFE TRUST: Carlton Marshes, Burnt Hill Lane, Carlton Colville NR33 8HU (☎01502-564250; e-mail carlton@suffolkwildlife.cix.co.uk).
Promotes and protects Suffolk Wildlife through education, including outdoor lessons and activities, games, crafts, events, family and adult talks and walks.
Volunteer Education Assistants (5) to help children in lessons, games, crafts, events, helping prepare and tidy resources. Hours vary but may include weekdays and weekends. Minimum age 18.
Volunteer Midweek Team Members (12) for practical conservation work on various nature reserves. Work includes building paths, cutting trees and maintaining reserve habitats. Volunteers needed all year round. Foreign applicants with some English welcome. No accommodation available.
Applications to the Education Officer at the above address. An informal "trial" day is required.

Festivals and Special Events

HESSE STUDENT SCHEME: Hesse Student Scheme, Aldeburgh Productions, Snape Maltings Concert Hall, Snape, Saxmundham, Suffolk IP17 1SP (☎01728 687100; fax 01728 687120; e-mail cbidder@aldeburgh.co.uk).
Aldeburgh Music has grown out of the Aldeburgh Festival founded in 1948 by Benjamin Britten, Peter Pears and Eric Crozier. Inspired by this legacy, Aldeburgh Music today ensures that the Suffolk Coast remains a world-renowned meeting place for artists, students, academics and audiences.
The Hesse Student Scheme enables **Volunteers** to assist in the varied duties involved in the day-to-day running of the Aldeburgh Festival of Music and the Arts running from 8-24 June 2007. Duties can include programme selling, page turning, invigilating exhibitions, assisting with stage moves and bus conducting on the coaches that run from Aldeburgh to all concert venues. In addition, students are also expected to devise,

rehearse and perform in a concert of their own – one of the free events publicised in the Aldeburgh Festival booking brochure. In exchange, two groups of 12 students are awarded a grant which covers tickets to all Festival events together with bed and breakfast accommodation in Aldeburgh for each half of the Festival.

Applications are welcomed from anyone between the ages of 18 and 25 (on 1 June) irrespective of current course or occupation. A willingness to help and a cheerful disposition, together with a passion for music are essential.

For further details and an *application* form contact Carole Bidder. The closing date for applications is 21 April.

Heritage

KENTWELL HALL: Long Melford, Sudbury, Suffolk CO10 9BA (☎01787-310207; fax 01787-379318; e-mail office@kentwell.co.uk; www.kentwell.co.uk).
A privately owned Tudor mansion, situated in park and farmland, approximately 1.5 miles from the historic town of Long Melford, famous for its annual recreation of Tudor life which takes place for 3 weeks during June and July. Up to 1,500 schoolchildren visit on weekdays and the public at weekends.

Volunteer Tudors (700) needed for historical re-creations and for other smaller events throughout the year. Duties consist of demonstrating 16th century life and activities to visiting schoolchildren and the public. The re-creations run for 7 days a week for 3 weeks; most volunteers stay one or two weeks during June/July. Take 16th century skills or learn them there. All ages and nationalities welcome.

All meals, evening entertainment and space on campsite provided for volunteers only. Applicants can be of any age; an interest in the 16th century would be helpful.

Applications should be sent to 'Live as a Tudor' in January/February at the above address.

RIVER STOUR TRUST: The Granary, Quay Lane, Sudbury, Suffolk CO10 2AN (☎01787-313199; fax 01787-313100; www.riverstourtrust.org).
The River Stour Trust is a charity dedicated to restoring and conserving the Essex/Suffolk River Stour navigation, by raising funds to rebuild locks, provide other navigation enhancements and encourage leisure boating.

Volunteer Tea Room Helpers (6) to work Sundays and bank holidays. Minimum age 18.

Volunteer Event Helpers (20) to work mainly Sundays and bank holidays. Full training given for each situation.

Working Party Volunteers (20) to work weekdays and weekends as required. Skilled and unskilled applicants required. Full training given for each situation.

Volunteer Marketing/Fund Raising Advisors (2) to work when required. Must have successful track record in these areas.

Boat Crew Volunteers (10) to work weekdays and weekends. Will be trained by charity and must meet appropriate standards.

Volunteer Boat Maintenance and Engineers (2) to help with electric launches. Volunteers needed all year round. Must have knowledge of electric boat engines and design.

Voluntary positions available mainly in the summer season although there may be some in the winter and autumn. All volunteers welcome but fluent English is essential for dealing with the public.

Applications should be sent to The Trust Administrator at the above address. Interview required.

Vacation Traineeships & Internships

Law

MILLS AND REEVE: 112 Hills Road, Cambridge CB2 1PH (☎01223-222336; fax 01223-355848; e-mail graduate.recruitment@mills-reeve.com; www.mills-reeve.com).

Mills and Reeve is a leading law firm based in Norwich, Cambridge and Birmingham who offer a full range of corporate, commercial, property, litigation, and private client services to a mix of regional businesses and national household names.

Mills and Reeve offer a **Formal 2 Week Placement Scheme** at each of their offices. Students gain experience in four main departments, attend seminars and take part in extra curricular events. Wages are £200 per week. There are 25-30 placements throughout June or July; preference is given to penultimate year law students, final year non-law students and all those who have already graduated and are interested in a legal career. Overseas applicants are welcome but must have a valid work permit.

Applications should be made online via the firm's website and should be submitted before 1 March 2007.

Media and Marketing

BRITTEN-PEARS YOUNG ARTIST PROGRAMME: Snape Maltings Concert Hall, Snape, Saxmundham, Suffolk IP17 1SP (☎01728-688671; fax 01728-688171; e-mail britten-pears@aldeburgh.co.uk; www.aldeburgh.co.uk).

Under the management of Aldeburgh Music, the Britten-Pears Programme, set in the inspirational surroundings of Snape, Suffolk, has a distinguished tradition of training emerging professional musicians.

Internship. An opportunity for one or two students/recent graduates to work on a voluntary basis in the Britten-Pears Young Artist Programme to support a small permanent team during the height of the season. Looking for someone to be appointed for the period June to September. Payment will be made at the rate of the current minimum wage for a 35-hour week. This is an invaluable opportunity to gain an insight into the workings of an internationally renowned arts organisation and to gain a grounding in arts administration which will be useful in furthering a career in this field. This position would suit an enthusiastic, energetic, level headed individual who would like to learn more about the running of a busy, unusual arts organisation.

Previous office experience is not as essential as the willingness and ability to learn and to adapt. Duties will include driving the company car, assisting with keeping files and databases in good order and providing clerical support to the school staff. Excellent secretarial and organisational skills together with a sound knowledge of English and its written and spoken use is essential; knowledge of classical music desirable.

Applications to the above address.

WORKPLACE LAW GROUP LTD: 2nd Floor, Daedalus House, Station Road, Cambridge CB1 2RE (☎0870-777 8881; fax 0870-777 8882; e-mail info@workplacelaw.net; www.workplacelaw.net).

A legal support network, based in central Cambridge, providing regular legislative updates, with a client base of 45,000. The company's specialist areas are health and safety, employment, environmental and premises law and practice.

Workplace Law Group offers **1 Internship** every year to work in electronic publishing, training administration or consulting, on a key project identified by the company's senior management team. The internship is only open to university students, though they need not be studying law. The internship lasts for 4-8 weeks over the summer vacation and is unpaid. The scheme is designed for students resident or studying within 20 miles of Cambridge, so no accommodation is available. Applications are subject to a rigorous selection process.

Applications should be sent to Jan Bond, Head of HR to jayn.bond@workplacelaw. net by 31 May.

Science, Construction and Engineering

GARDLINE GEOSURVEYS: Endeavour House, Admiralty Road, Great Yarmouth, Norfolk NR30 3NG (☎01493-850723; fax 01493-852106; e-mail hr@gardline.com; www.gardline.com).

The largest independent survey company which operates 9 fully equipped vessels covering Europe, the Far East and West Africa.

Gardline Geosurveys is involved in hydrographic and marine geophysical surveys. The company offers a variable number of **Placements** in several different fields, including Seismic/Hydrographic survey work for surveyors, geophysicists and electronic engineers; there will also be some office work.

Vacancies are open to students on relevant degree courses, with a preference for those in their second or third year of study. Overseas applicants are welcome. Trainees are based in Great Yarmouth from where they will be sent to work on survey. Shared accommodation is sometimes available.

Applicants should *contact* Andrew Daniels, Human Resources Manager, at the above address.

SYNTHOMER LTD: Central Road, Templefields, Harlow, Essex CM20 2BH (☎01279-436211; fax 01279-444025; e-mail humanresources@synthomer.com; www.synthomer.com).

Synthomer, part of the Yule Catto polymers division, is a world-class supplier of synthetic polymers to industries ranging from paints and adhesives to textiles, speciality papers and plastics. They are the only manufacturer of polyvinyl alcohol in the UK and the market leader in suspending agents for the PVC industry.

Synthomer Ltd offers **Vacation Traineeships** to two students each summer. These are to work within Research & Development or Technical Service Laboratories. The placements last for 6 to 8 weeks and are open to university undergraduates reading for a degree in Chemistry or related subject. Accommodation is not provided.

Applications should be made in April or May to the Human Resources Manager, at the above address.

The Midlands

Prospects for Work

The Midlands region includes a number of large industrial towns, the most notable being Birmingham. The West Midlands has a population of 5 million of which approximately a third reside in the central conurbation of Birmingham, Coventry, Wolverhampton, Walsall and a number of other small towns.

The majority of student opportunities will be found here as most of the rest of the area is rural and sparsely populated. The catering trade is a traditional employer of students in bars and in many of the fast food outlets. Registering with an agency for secretarial work during student holidays is also a popular choice. Most supermarkets welcome student applicants with the possibility of a long-term career in retailing.

In the absence of a coastline in the region, the peak periods for general seasonal recruitment are in February/March for the tourist parks and August/September for Christmas work. Among the large tourist recruiters are Alton Towers (around 600 per year) and Drayton Manor Park near Tamworth. Ideally, the attractions prefer staff who can work through the entire summer period but there is inevitably some staff turnover. To check on recruitment needs, visit www.jobcentreplus.gov.uk, contact Jobseeker Direct on 0845-606 0234, or the individual company websites.

Numerous other attractions such as the Black Country Museum and Dudley Zoo also recruit smaller numbers and undoubtedly there are opportunities for short-term work in tourist areas such as Stratford-upon-Avon, Ludlow, and Warwick. Be advised that accommodation in these towns will be the most expensive in the region. Each year, Wolverhampton Jobcentre handles vacancies for the three-day-long V Festival.

In the more rural areas, particularly, Herefordshire, there are still some opportunities for fruit picking although many employers prefer to bulk recruit from abroad. Jobcentres such as Hereford, Leominster, and Ross on Wye are worth visiting if you are nearby, otherwise try the Jobcentre Plus website. The *Hereford Times* (Thursday) and the *Hereford Admag* (Wednesday) both display local job vacancies.

Call Centres are prominent in Birmingham, North Staffordshire, and the Black Country with a number of organisations advertising weekly for additional staff. Generally openings are for permanent rather than temporary positions. However, shift work and limited hours are sometimes available while staff turnover is notoriously high. One other possibility is the region's major football clubs who often seek students in summer for ticket office work. Students are well received because of their abilities to understand complex procedures quickly. A direct approach is probably best.

Fruit and hop picking jobs are available in Lincolnshire, but in general the Midlands is an area where 'pick your own' farms are popular. Spalding and Boston in Lincolnshire are centres for agricultural packing. In Lincoln itself, most temporary jobs are in the retail or hotel trade. There is a very strong retail trade in Lincoln with the Tritton Road area attracting several large employers, such as Debenhams. There are good opportunities for employment at the Lincolnshire Show, a two-day event that is held yearly in mid June; job vacancies are advertised from April, and can be found in Lincoln Jobcentre Plus. The *Lincolnshire Echo* is the best local newspaper for job vacancies.

The two theme parks, American Adventure in Ilkeston and Gulliver's Kingdom in Matlock, Derbyshire, normally recruit for summer staff and are popular with students. Local supermarkets, such as Asda and Sainsbury's, tend to take on seasonal staff for the spring and summer period. There are also a high number of catering vacancies in Matlock and Buxton at this time of the year. In the north of Derbyshire, Federick Ice-Cream and Chesterfield Hotel are always looking for temporary workers, as are McDonalds, to cope with the school holidays.

Oxford is a popular centre for language schools and there are opportunities not only for EFL teachers but also for sports instructors and social organisers. Another source of casual employment may be the university's colleges, which have a high turnover of cleaning and catering staff and often host conferences and courses during the summer. These and other jobs may be advertised in the *Oxford Times* (out on Friday) and the *Oxford Mail* (daily). Alternatively, for up-to-the-minute information on both jobs and accommodation look out for the coloured spreadsheet *Daily Information* (daily in term time, weekly during vacations) on noticeboards, in shop windows, or visit www.dailyinfo.co.uk. There is, of course, competition for any summer jobs from those students at the city's two universities who choose to stay in Oxford for the summer.

The industrial heartlands of the Midlands provide plentiful opportunities for Vacation Traineeships and Internships, particularly in the fields of science and engineering.

THE WEST MIDLANDS

This section covers work in the following counties: Staffordshire, Shropshire, West Midlands, Warwickshire, Herefordshire and Worcestershire. See map at the start of the chapter for these counties' locations.

Business and Industry

DISCOVER TRAVEL & TOURS: International House, Pierpoint Street, Worcester WR1 1YD (☎0870-225 8000; fax 0870-225 8001; e-mail admin@discovertravelandtours.com; www.discovertravelandtours.com). Discover Travel & Tours is the UK's largest supplier of accommodation and services to the international travel trade in Europe.

Temporary Reservation Assistants required to take reservations, make bookings and input details on to the computer. Wages from £5.35 per hour. To work 37½ hours per five day week with possible overtime. Minimum period of work of three months. Positions are available between March and September. Applicants must be computer literate. Knowledge of German, French, Italian or Spanish useful. No accommodation available.

Applications from January/February to the above address.

HAY FESTIVAL: The Drill Hall, 25 Lion Street, Hay on Wye, Herefordshire HR3 5AD (☎0870-787 2848; fax 01497-821066; www.hayfestival.com). An international festival production company celebrating great writing in every medium in Britain and around the world. Hay is a tiny market town in the Brecon Beacons National Park. It has 1,500 people and 41 bookshops. Celebrating its 20th year in 2007, the Festival is a spectacular holiday party for people to enjoy their tastes for literature, food, drink, comedy, music, art and argument.

Box Office Staff (10) required for the build up to and during the Festival, which runs from 24 May to 3 June. Fair hourly rates of pay. Staff are required for up to 39 hours per week. Applicants need to be calm, good on the phone, familiar with computers and enjoy working with the public. Retail experience, a sense of humour and rhino-hide are also useful. Overseas applicants are welcome to apply but must have a very high standard of spoken and written English.

Applications should be made via the website from April.

PALETHORPES: Maer Lane, Market Drayton, Shropshire TF9 3AW (☎01630-692394; fax 01630-658785; e-mail amy.harrison@northernfoods.com; www.northernfoods.com).

Operatives to work on a factory line producing savoury products. Wages from national minimum rate (plus bonus) per hour plus a shift allowance where applicable (based on rates for an 18-year old). A 24-hour operation, all shifts available. Temporary or permanent positions are available. Placements also available for periods of 3 weeks over Christmas. A range of benefits typical of a large organisation is offered. No qualifications required, although food hygiene or first aid would be an advantage. Minimum age 16. No accommodation available.

Applications should be made to Amy Harrison at the above address.

Children

ACORN ADVENTURE: Acorn House, Prospect Road, Halesowen, West Midlands B62

8DU (☎0121-504 2066; fax 0121-504 2059; e-mail chris.lloyd@acornadventure.co.uk; www.acorn-jobs.co.uk). Acorn Adventure is the leading provider of outdoor adventure camps for schools, youth groups and families. They operate 9 activity centres in France, Italy, and the UK. Seasonal work available from April until September.

Instructors. Should hold at least Instructor/Trainee Instructor status with a National Governing Body e.g. BCU, RYA, SPA RLSS, GNAS, BOF or MLTB. Other nationally recognised coaching awards may be considered.

Assistant Instructors. Should be working towards the above qualifications/awards. Acorn runs an extensive pre-season training programme helping staff achieve these goals.

Support Staff. Maintenance and/or catering. No experience necessary. Full training given pre-season.

Village Managers. On-site representatives who welcome new groups, work closely with the children and organise evening events. No experience necessary. Full training given pre-season.

For further *information/applications* go to www.jobs-acorn.co.uk or contact the Recruitment Department for a full information pack at the above address.

ACTIVE TRAINING AND EDUCATION: Kildare, Manby Road, Malvern, Worcestershire WR14 3BD (☎01684-562400; fax 01684-562716; e-mail info@ ate.org.uk; www.ate.org.uk). An educational trust which runs residential holidays in various rented premises, including boarding schools, field study centres and conference centres, in various parts of the UK.

Matrons (10-15). Wages £200 per week, plus free board. For full-time residential work. Must be a trained nurse or have experience in looking after children residentially.

Caterer (10-15). Wages £300 per week, plus free board. For full-time residential work. Must have experience and qualifications in catering/cooking for 50-100 people.

General Assistants (6-10). Wages £100 per week, under 18, £135 per week, over 18, plus board. For full-time residential work. Must have a willingness to work hard and efficiently; duties include washing up, cleaning.

Staff are required from July 20 until August 30; minimum period of work is one week. Non-UK citizens are considered if they are suitably qualified/experienced; fluent English is useful. Reasonable travel costs are paid within the UK.

Apply, from January, to Chris Green, Director, at the above address. An interview is not necessary.

PGL TRAVEL LTD: Alton Court, Penyard Lane, Ross-on-Wye, Herefordshire HR9 5GL (☎0870-401 4411; e-mail recruitment@pgl.co.uk; www.pgl.co.uk/recruitment). PGL recruit around 2,000 staff each year to assist with the running of their children's activity centres throughout the UK, including Devon, the Isle of Wight, Lincolnshire, the south coast, Surrey, Shropshire, Perthshire and Wales. Europe's largest provider of adventure holidays for children has offered outstanding training and work opportunities to seasonal staff for almost 50 years. PGL jobs provide a break from the 9-5 routine. If you are enthusiastic, energetic and looking for real experience and responsibility in a stimulating environment, PGL could have the job for you.

Activity Instructors in canoeing, sailing, windsurfing, fencing, archery, motorsports, pony trekking, and more. Qualifications not essential for all positions as full training will be provided. Minimum age 18.

Group Leaders also needed to take responsibility for groups of children, helping them to get the most out of their holiday. Previous experience of working with children is an advantage. Minimum age 18.

Support Staff to assist the catering, domestic and maintenance teams.

From £70-£100 per week plus free B & L. Positions available from February-November, for the full season, as little as eight weeks, or any period in between, although there are very few summer-only vacancies.

Applications can be made online, downloaded from the website, or call for an information pack.

Holiday Centres and Amusements

THE ABBEY COLLEGE: Wells Road, Malvern Wells, Worcestershire WR14 4JF (☎01684-892300; fax 01684-892757; e-mail jobs@abbeycollege.co.uk; www.abbeycollege.co.uk). A beautiful residential campus with students from more than 30 nations.

Activities Staff/Sports Staff (15). £150-£160 per week for 6 days' work. Minimum age 18.

Welfare And Admin. Staff (3). £150 per week for 6 days' work.

Sports qualifications and experience of summer schools preferred. Accommodation and meals provided for all staff, plus free use of all sports and leisure activities and excursions. Work available from beginning of June to end of August. Overseas applicants welcome to work 3 weeks, they would not be paid, but will receive 1 week's free English classes (or work 6 weeks and get 2 weeks' free classes) and accommodation free of charge, worth £520 per week.

Applications from March to the Personnel Department at the above address.

ALTHORP: Althorp House, Northampton, Northamptonshire NN7 4HQ (☎01604-770107; e-mail jobs@althorp.com; www.althorp.com). The home of the Spencer family for over 500 years, Althorp House now welcomes visitors every summer to explore the house, gardens and their awarding-winning *Diana: A Celebration* exhibition.

Seasonal Staff (approx. 40) required for both outdoor and indoor work including positions in the house, stable block, café, gift shop and grounds. All staff are paid £5.50 per hour. Various shifts are available. Staff are required from 1 July to 31 August. No qualifications are necessary, but staff need to be friendly and enthusiastic. Overseas applicants are welcome to apply, as long as they have the relevant documents and can speak a high standard of English.

Applications should be made from February, to the Visitor Manager, at the above address. An informal interview will be necessary.

ALTON TOWERS: Alton, Staffordshire ST10 4DB (☎0870-444 6998; fax 01538-703007; www.altontowers.com). Part of the Tussauds Group, Alton Towers is a large and nationally known theme park. Two themed hotels, a Caribbean waterpark, spa and conference centre all offer excellent career opportunities for customer service focused people who want to work as a team. Up to 1,200 seasonal positions are available.

Rides and Shows: Operators, Ride Assistants, Hosts.

Retail: Food and Beverage, Games, Shops, Ride Photos.

Front of House: Admissions and Guest Services, Car Parks and Monorail Operators.

Security, Medical and Traffic: Security Officers, Nurses, Traffic assistants.

Finance: Strongroom team members.

Hotel: Housekeeping, Restaurant and Bar, Conference and Events, Chefs and Kitchen Teams, Reception, Leisure.

Lifeguards: To work within the Waterpark development at £6.25 per hour.

Alton Towers PCV Drivers at £7.10 per hour.

Other wages are £5.50 per hour and above depending on position. Staff also receive free tickets to The Tussauds Group attractions (Alton Towers, Madame Tussaud's, Thorpe Park, Chessington World of Adventures, the London Eye and Warwick Castle) and use of an active social club. To work full time, 5 days per week, or part time, including weekends and bank holidays. Positions are available from February to November. No specific qualifications or experience are required as training is given. Minimum age 16. Overseas applicants with work permits welcome. Help with finding accommodation can be given.

Applications should be made from December onwards at www.altontowersjobs. com or the Employment Service at the above address. Interviews and assessment centres form the recruitment process.

DRAYTON MANOR PARK LTD: near Tamworth, Staffordshire B78 3TW (☎01827-287979; fax 01827-288916; info@draytonmanor.co.uk; www. draytonmanor.co.uk). A family owned and run theme park of 54 years standing, one of the top 5 theme parks in the UK. Owns a catering company and three hotels. **Seasonal Caterers (150), Seasonal Ride Operators (150), Ticketing Staff (30), Retail Staff (30).** Wages by arrangement, but paid at an hourly rate; hours negotiable. Period of work from the end of March to the end of October. No accommodation is available. No experience necessary as full training is given. Applicants must be 16 or over. Foreign applicants with a work permit and able to arrange their own accommodation are welcome. Fluent English is not essential.

Applications from 1 January to Tim Sadler at the above address. Interview is generally necessary, but they do not expect applicants to travel long distances.

HATTON COUNTRY WORLD: Hatton Country World, Hatton House, Warwick CV35 7LD (☎01926-843411; fax 01926-842023; e-mail hatton@hattonworld.com; www.hattonworld.com). Two unique attractions: Hatton Shopping Village, comprising 25 craft and gift shops, antiques centre and farm shop; and Hatton Farm Village with farm animals and adventure playground. **Assistants for Retail Outlet, Farm Village, and Restaurant.** Required between March and October. Wages on application. Variable hours. Some accommodation available. Applicants must be prepared to take on a variety of roles. Clean driving licence an advantage/own transport essential to rural location.

Applications/CV to the Personnel Administrator, at the above address.

Hotels and Catering

THE ABBEY COLLEGE: Wells Road, Malvern Wells, Worcestershire WR14 4JF (☎01684-892300; fax 01684-892757; e-mail jobs@abbeycollege.co.uk; www. abbeycollege.co.uk). **Catering and Cleaning Staff (5).** Salary £120 per week. Accommodation and meals provided for all staff, and free use of all sports and leisure activities and excursions. To work minimum 40 hours per week. Work available from mid-June to the end of August. Relevant experience an advantage. Overseas students are welcome, although they will not be paid, but will work 3 weeks and get 1 week's free English classes and accommodation (or work 6 weeks and get 2 weeks' free classes), worth £520 per week.

Applications from March to the Personnel Department at the above address.

ATTINGHAM PARK (NATIONAL TRUST): Attingham Park, Atcham, Shrewsbury, Shropshire SY4 4TP (☎01743-708196; fax 01743-708155; e-mail

elaine.deakinbothun@nationaltrust.org.uk).
Part Time Kitchen and Tearoom Assistants (2) to work 6-8 hours per week, mainly at weekends, from Easter until mid-September.
Full Time Kitchen and Tearoom Assistant to work over the school summer holiday period. Accommodation may be available free of charge for these 5 weeks.
Wages depend on age, but are above national minimum. Training will be given but knowledge of food hygiene would be helpful, and customer care experience very useful. Foreign applicants with fluent English are welcome to apply for the full time position. Telephone interview required.
Applications from early March to Mrs Elaine de Akinbothun, catering manager, at the above address.

GROVE HOUSE: Bromesberrow Heath, near Ledbury, Herefordshire HR8 1PE (☎01531-650584; e-mail ross@the-grovehouse.co.uk). This large country house is set only 3 miles outside Ledbury and has a tennis court and next door swimming pool for use of guests and students. Students are treated as part of the family. The Malvern Hills are within walking or biking distance.
General Assistants (1/2) to work in the guest house, providing general maintenance both in and out of doors and gardening. Wages £50 per week including free B & L and outings on days off. Work available all summer for any length of time.
Applications with CV and photo, to Mrs E. M. Ross at the above address.

HOW CAPLE GRANGE HOTEL: How Caple, Herefordshire HR1 4TF (☎01989-740208; fax 01989-740301). Set in a rural location approx. 3 miles from the M50 motorway. Business is mainly party bookings and function trade.
Chef/Cook(1-2). Approximately £240 per week plus free B & L. To work approximately 40 hours per week. Staff needed between Easter to October and Christmas period. No experience necessary but must be willing to work within other aspects of hotel work. Own transport absolutely essential. Minimum age 18.
Applications to the Proprietor, How Caple Grange Hotel. Please telephone to check for vacancy availability.

MARRIOTT FOREST OF ARDEN HOTEL & COUNTRY CLUB: Maxstoke Lane, Meriden, Warwickshire CV7 7HR (☎01676-526101; fax 01676-521176; www.marriott.co.uk).
Bar Staff to provide bar and table service, minimum age 18.
Waiting Staff for food and beverage service, minimum age 16.
Room Attendants needed to clean and service guest rooms. Minimum age 16.
Wages at £5.00 for all posts. Hours of work can vary between 20 to 40 per week, with overtime possible; staff get 2 days off in every 7. All positions available from May-to September.
Applications should be made to the HR Officer, at the above address.

NOW 'n ZEN: (e-mail jobs@nowandzen.co.uk; www.nowandzen.co.uk.)
Now 'n Zen is one of the most popular festival caterers at music festivals for the past 19 years, specialising in vegetarian world foods (including Japanese noodles, French crepes, and Italian pastas). This is a lively, friendly, happy, and efficient organisation.
Catering Assistants needed to help in busy vegetarian world food stalls, working around Britain at summer music festivals. Duties include food preparation, light cooking, cleaning, serving, packing, and so on. You will become an important part of a mainly student team. Living expenses provided as well as an opportunity for home-stay with accommodation and food provided.

Applicants must be able to work happily in a team and must have lots of energy and stamina, be lively and adaptable, conscientious, and good humoured. Will not suit a person who likes a 9-5 job.

Applications to Ron Zahl, Proprietor.

PEN-Y-DYFFRYN COUNTRY HOTEL: Rhydycroesau, Nr Oswestry, Shropshire SY10 7JD (☎01691-653700; fax 01691 650066; e-mail stay@peny.co.uk; www. peny.co.uk). A small family-run hotel located 5 minutes from Oswestry.
General Hotel Worker (1), General Kitchen Assistant (1). Wages at national minimum rate with accommodation provided. To work 4/5 days a week. Minimum period of work 8 weeks between May and October. Overseas applicants considered.
Applications at any time to Miles Hunter. Interview necessary.

QUALITY HOTEL WARWICK: Chesford Bridge, Kenilworth, Warwickshire CV8 2LN (☎01926-858331; fax 01926-858153).
Housekeeping/Restaurant Staff (2-3). Wages at national minimum rate; to work 5 days out of 7. Staff are required all year round. Minimum period of work 10 weeks. Accommodation is available at £22 per week. No experience necessary. Minimum period of work 10 weeks.
Applications to the Manager at the above address at any time.

SEASONAL STAFF UK: Old Mining College, Queen Street, Chasetown, Staffordshire WS7 8QH (☎01543-675707; fax 01543-672046; e-mail admin@ seasonalstaff.co.uk; www.seasonalstaff.co.uk). Agency placing students, graduates, working travellers in seasonal jobs.
Country Inn and Pub Work. Wages at least national minimum rate. All positions live-in with on-duty meals provided. Staff required all year round. Applicants must be aged 18-28 and be motivated and well presented. Experience not always necessary as training will be given. All nationalities welcome.
Application forms can be downloaded from the company website.

THE WATERMAN PUB, CANALSIDE PUB AND RESTAURANT: Birmingham Road, Hatton, Warwick CV35 7JJ (☎01926-492427; fax 01926-409922; e-mail info@thewatermanpub.co.uk; www.thewatermanpub.co.uk). Previously a unique historical Coaching house. Recently refurbished to a very high standard.
Full- and Part-time Car/Waiting/Kitchen Staff. Wages on application. Variable hours. Some accommodation available otherwise own transport essential to rural location. Clean driving licence an advantage.
Application/CV to the General Manager, Mr Doug Johnson, at the above address.

WESTON PARK ENTERPRISES LTD: Weston Park, Weston-under-Lizard, Shifnal, Shropshire TF11 8LE (☎01952-852100; fax 01952-850430; e-mail elizabeth@western-park.com; www.weston-park.com). A magnificent Stately Home set in 1,000 acres, offering a very high standard of cuisine and service. Operates on an exclusive basis year round.
Housekeeping, Cleaning, General Catering, Waiting, Event Assistance, Ticket Selling and Gate Staff required for casual positions all year round Hours variable, dependent on position. Staff are required all year round. Minimum age 16. No accommodation available. Overseas applicants with appropriate work permits welcome. Full time positions are also available, some with accommodation.
Applications should be sent to the Personnel Officer at the above address as soon as possible. Interview required.

WORCESTER RIVER CRUISES CO: 37 Tything, Worcester WR1 1JL (☎01905-611060; fax 01905-611060; e-mail events@worcesterrivercruises.co.uk; www. worcesterriversruises.co.uk).
Bar Staff/Crew Members (10) to perform mostly general bar duties. Wages from £4.50 per hour plus bonus scheme. To work mostly evenings and weekends. Positions are available from Easter to October. Good English essential. Minimum age 18. No accommodation available.
Applications should be made as soon as possible to Kristen Leith at the above address. Interview required.

Language Schools

THE ABBEY COLLEGE: Wells Road, Malvern Wells, Worcestershire WR14 4JF (☎01684-892300; fax 01684-892757; e-mail jobs@abbeycollege.co.uk; www. abbeycollege.co.uk). A beautiful 70-acre residential campus with students from more than 30 nations. Has developed, over the last 30 years, an English course to meet every requirement alongside the main academic school. Wide range of on-site facilities.
EFL Teachers (20). £240-£310 per week. Accommodation and meals provided. Work available from the beginning of June to the end of August. Minimum period of employment 3 weeks. All year positions also available. Must hold at least an RSA/ Trinity Prep. Certificate. Previous summer school experience preferred. Free use of all sports and leisure activities and excursions open to all employees.
Applications from March to Personnel Department at the above address. Interview necessary.

CONCORD COLLEGE: Acton Burnell Hall, Acton Burnell, Shrewsbury, Shropshire SY5 7PF (☎01694-731631; fax 01694-731389; e-mail the principal@ concordcollegeuk.com; www.concordcollegeuk.com). An independent international school. Fully residential with excellent facilities on campus.
Residential Summer Course EFL Tutors (10-15). Applicants must hold as a minimum the RSA Certificate in TEFL.
Summer Course Sports Tutor (2-4). Applicants must have the appropriate coaching qualifications.
For both positions working hours are variable and the salary is dependent on qualifications and experience. Accommodation is provided at no charge. Staff are required from the beginning of the month for July course (4 week) and/or August course (3 weeks).
Applications and enquiries should be sent to John Leighton, Director of Summer Courses at the above address as soon as possible.

SEVERNVALE ACADEMY: 25 Claremont Hill, Shrewsbury, Shropshire SY1 1RD (☎01743-232505; fax 01743-272637; e-mail enquiry@severnvale.co.uk; www. severvale.co.uk). A small school running English courses for foreign students, both adults and juniors.
EFL Teachers (5-10). From £290 a week. To teach Monday to Friday daytime. Minimum period of work of 4 weeks. Period of work 1 July to 20 August. Degree and TEFL qualification (e.g. RSA/UCLES/TESOL certificate) and experience necessary. Spoken English to the standard of a native required. Board and accommodation available for £95 per week.
Applications from Easter onwards to Mr J.W.T. Rogers, Principal, Severnvale Academy. Interview required.

SUL LANGUAGE SCHOOLS: 31 Southpark Road, Tywardreath, Par, Cornwall PL24 2PU (☎01726-814227; fax 01726-813135; e-mail efl@sul-schools.com; www. sul-schools.com). A well-established business that provides language holiday courses in Cornwall, Devon, Somerset, Midlands, Scotland and Ireland for foreign teenagers. Courses run for 2-4 weeks from April to September.

EFL Teachers. Wages dependent on experience and qualifications but are usually from £26 per morning of 2½ hours. To work mornings and possibly afternoons, supervising activities. Teachers required from April-August for a minimum period of 2 weeks. Applicants should be TEFL qualified or hold a languages degree or teaching qualification. Preferred CRB checked applicants. Accommodation is available at some centers.

Applications from January to Director of Studies at the above address. Interview usually required.

Medical

BNA: The Reform Club, 5 Warwick Row, Coventry CB1 1EX (☎01926-883653; fax 02476-522134; e-mail coventry@bna.uk.com; www.bna.co.uk). A nursing agency supplying regular staff to various sectors including private patients, nursing homes, residential homes and NHS hospitals.

Auxiliary Nurses And Care Assistants to work with private patients and in nursing and residential homes. Wages approx. £5.13-£11.63 per hour. Job may involve working at night and weekends. Applicants must be aged 18+; no experience is necessary as training will be given. Vacancies are ongoing and there is no minimum period of work. Overseas applicants are welcome.

Applications should be sent to Linda Robinson, Team Leader at the above address. Two references are needed.

CARING HANDS: Suite 1, Georgian Mews, 24a Bird Street, Lichfield, Staffordshire WS13 6PR (☎01543-417874; fax 01543-418546).

Community Care Workers to assist elderly clients with day-to-day activities in their own homes. Duties include assisting with personal hygiene and some practical assistance around the home. Wages from £6.60 per hour. Enhanced pay at bank holidays and weekends. Hours to suit between 7am and 10pm, Mon to Sun. Staff needed around the year. Own car and telephone essential.

Applications to A. Heathcote.

GUARDIAN HOMECARE:5 Elmdon Lane, Marston Green, Solihull B37 7DL (☎01217-707 755; fax 01217-706 766; e-mail jillywhe@aol.com).

Care Workers (2) to care for both young and old people with various problems in their own homes, thus promoting their independence. Wages of £6.60 per hour on weekdays and £8.00 per hour at weekends. Staff needed around the year, period of work and hours by arrangement. A CRB enhanced check will be made of applicants prior to appointment. Applicants should have experience of care work; car owners preferred.

Applications to Jill Whetstone at the above address.

Outdoor

A1 MARQUEES: 25 Castlecroft Road, Finchfield, Wolverhampton, West Midlands WV3 8BS (☎01902-765353; fax 01902-765353; e-mail enquiries@a1marquees. co.uk; www.a1marquees.co.uk).

Marquee Erectors (3+). Wages at national minimum rate. Hours flexible, sometimes long. Needed from May to September to erect marquees, load and unload, set up furniture, carpet interiors, clean etc. Must be fit and willing to work hard.
Applications to the Proprietor at the above address.

BADSEY FIELDS NRS LTD: Badsey Fields Lane, Badsey, Evesham, Worcestershire WR11 7EX (☎01386-830944; fax 01386-833668).
General Horticultural Workers (10+). Wages at Agricultural Wages Board rates. To work a 40 hour week or as arranged. To work from June onwards.
Applications to P. Campagna, Director, at the above address.

S.H.M. BROOMFIELD & SON: Elmbridge Fruit Farm, Addis Lane, Cutnall Green, Droitwich, Worcestershire WR9 0ND (☎01299-851592; fax 01905-621633; colin@broomfieldsfarmshop.co.uk). Award-winning family farm growing apples, pears, plums, cherries and raspberries. Established for over 90 years.
Fruit Pickers (10). Wages £5.35-£8.00 per hour. To work 6 days per week, Monday to Saturday. Minimum period of work 2 weeks between June and October. No experience or qualifications are necessary as full training is given on site. Minimum age is 16. Foreign applicants with work permits welcome; ability to speak basic English would be helpful. Room/mobile home accommodation available for £3 per night; camping places available for £1.50 per night.
Applications from 25 May to Colin Broomfield, Partner, at the above address.

CELEBRATIONS MARQUEE & FURNITURE HIRE: The Hall Buildings, Childs Ereall, Market Drayton, Shropshire TF9 2DB (☎01952-840302; fax 01952-840385; e-mail john@celebrationsmarquees.co.uk). Marquee and furniture hire organisation specialising in up-market equipment and work.
Marquee Erectors (3). £5.00 to £5.50 per hour. To work 40 hours per week. Fitness is essential; applicants should be between 20 to 24 years of age and robust, both by nature and physically. Staff are required between the end of May and October; accommodation will be given to foreign students. Non-UK applicants are considered and expected to send a full CV. Those from the UK will be interviewed.
Applications should be sent to J.T. Thornicroft, at the above address, from March.

CW GARDEN MARQUEES: Unit 4, Southern Avenue, Leominster, Herefordshire HR6 0QF (tel/fax 01568-613011; e-mail gardenmarquees1@btconnect.com).
Marquee Erectors to work from June to September. Wages £5.00 per hour. To work 40 hours per five day week plus some overtime.
Applications by CV to the above address.

FEWS MARQUEES: Orchardside, Ditchford Bank Road, Hanbury, Bromsgrove, Worcestershire B60 4HS (☎01527-821789; fax 01527-821032; e-mail info@fewsmarquees.co.uk; www.fewsmarquees.co.uk).
Marquee Erectors (2). Competitive rates of pay. Accommodation is provided. Applicants will sometimes have to work long hours. Required between May and October. All applicants must be 18 or over with a clean driving licence.
Applications should be made to Ian Few, at the above address.

HERITAGE MOTOR CENTRE: Banbury Road, Gaydon, Warwickshire CV35 OBJ (☎01926-645033; ; e-mail enquiries@heritage-motor-centre.co.uk; www.heritage-motor-centre.co.uk).

Car Parkers to cover the 2007 events programme; must be able to attend at least 12 of the 15 planned events days. Duties include maximising the safety of visitors and staff, controlling and directing visitors entering and parking in the site, directing pedestrians towards pay points, and being alert to any unsafe movement, including speeding vehicles. To report for duty at 7.30 am and work until approximately 1.30pm; wages of £6 per hour plus a completion bonus.

Applicants must possess good communication skills and be fit enough to perform their duties; full training will be given.

Applications to Ralph Buckland at the above address.

HAYGROVE FRUIT: Redbank, Ledbury, Herefordshire HR8 2JL (☎01531-633659; fax01531-635969; e-mail evelinat@haygrove.co.uk; www.haygrove.co.uk). Large soft fruit farm with long season.
Field Assistants, Supervisors, Irrigation/Plastic Tunnel Construction Team, Drivers. Wages £200 to £300 per week. To work 6 days per week. Mobile home accommodation available from £4.00 per day.

E-mail the above address for more information. Non EEA nationals must arrange work permits before applying. Cannot arrange work permits for you.

S & P HODSON-WALKER: Coulter Lane Farm, Coulter Lane, Burntwood, Staffordshire WS7 9EU (tel/fax 01543-674871; e-mail phodsonwalker@farming. me.uk). Fruit farm supplying top quality restaurants, supermarkets and farmers' markets.
Farm Shop Staff (2/3). Minimum wage. To work 5-6 days per week.
Fruit pickers (10) to pick strawberries, raspberries. Piecework rates. To work 5-6 days per week.
Minimum period of work for all positions 1 month. Positions available beginning of June to September. Accommodation available for pickers, for approximately £25 per week. Foreign applicants welcome; fluent English not necessary, though some is helpful. Minimum age 18.

Applications should be made from May to Shirley Walker at the above address. Interview required.

MR & MRS JOHN LEWIS: Yearsett Court Farm, Linley Green, Whitbourne, Worcestershire WR6 5RQ (☎01886-884782; fax 01886-884351). Located 25 miles south of Birmingham, the farm provides fruit for major supermarket and wholesalers.
Strawberry Pickers. Paid by weight picked. To work approximately 8 hours per day, 6 days a week.
Packhouse Staff . To work approximately 8 hours per day, 6 days a week.
People must travel to farm daily. Workers required from 1 June to 15 July for periods from one day or up to 6 weeks as desired. No experience necessary as training is given. Must be over 18 and fit. Students must produce student cards and university documents.
Applications from February to Mrs J. Lewis at the above address.

LITTLE PETERSTOW ORCHARDS: Peterstow, Near Ross on Wye, Herefordshire HR9 6LG (tel/fax 01989-730270). Small, family-run fruit farm growing apples, pears and strawberries for Asda.
Fruit Pickers needed from 1 June to 6 July and 10 September to 5 October. Payment at hourly rates of at least £5.00 per hour or at piecework rates with which an average picker will earn £5.00 per hour but £8.00 per hour is possible. To work approximately 7 hours per day, 6 days per week weather permitting. Showers, cooking, TV, clothes

washing, table tennis etc. provided in a separate block on a caravan/camp site. Minimum age 18.
Applications to Richard J. Wheeler, Owner/Partner, at the above address.

MAN OF ROSS LTD: Glewstone, Ross-on-Wye, Herefordshire HR9 6AU (☎01989-562853; fax 01989-563877; e-mail fruitpick@yahoo.co.uk). Situated in the Wye Valley, Man of Ross Ltd is a family-run, 250 hectare farm, which supplies mainly to supermarkets.
Fruit Harvesters (30) to work in cherry, plum, apple and pear orchards. Hourly and/or piecework rates. Hours according to crop needs, approximately 6 to 8 hours a day, 5 to 6 days a week. Minimum period of work 2 months between July and September (July is a quiet month). Minimum age 18 years. Overseas applicants welcome, provided they have the necessary work permits.
Applications from January to William Jackson at the above address.

PENNOXSTONE COURT: Kings Caple, Hereford HR1 4TX (☎01432-840289). A busy fruit farm with a multi-national atmosphere situated in a beautiful part of England.
Strawberry Pickers (35) from mid-May to end September.
Raspberry Pickers (10) for month of July.
Wages on average £30 to £60 per day, based on piecework rates. To work 6 days per week. Accommodation is limited. Some caravan accommodation may be available, though plenty of camping accommodation is available with full facilities. Trips arranged to places of interest on days off. Applicants should be able to fit in with cheerful, friendly atmosphere. Minimum age 18. Overseas applicants welcome.
Applications for all pickers to be submitted, between April and first week in July and enclosing s.a.e. or IRC, to Mr N. J. Cockburn at the above address.

S & A PRODUCE (UK) LTD: Brook Farm, Marden, Hereford, Herefordshire HR1 3ET (☎01432-880235; fax 01432-880644; e-mail workers@sagroup.co.uk; www. sagroup.co.uk). S & A Produce is an independent strawberry grower supplying UK supermarkets. The company is managed and operated by a young dynamic team with a wealth of experience in growing and other related industries, who are able to cope with a fast moving and profitable business.
Strawberry Pickers (1000). Wages at national minimum rate. Overtime paid according to the Agricultural Wages Order. Pickers are expected to work 39 hours per week. Workers are required for a minimum period of 12 weeks from 15 May. Accommodation is available at a charge of £34.50 per week (2006 figure). Workers must be aged between 18 and 45. No experience is necessary, but applicants must be in good physical health. Overseas applicants are welcome. Fluent English is not essential as they have a number of interpreters on site.
Applications should be sent to Elena Tustin or Ewelina Kurcaba via e-mail to the above address. All applicants are registered on an internal system and receive a reply to their application within 1 to 3 working days.

SIDDINGTON FARM: Leadington, Ledbury, Herefordshire HR8 2LN (☎01531-632262; fax 01531-632262).
Strawberry Pickers. Piece work rates. Workers required 25 May to the end of October. Campsite provided for those bringing their own camping and cooking equipment. Kitchen, TV room, toilets and showers are provided. No fruit picking experience necessary. Friendly working atmosphere. Overseas applicants eligible to work in the UK welcome.
Applications to Mrs Houlbrooke at the above address.

STOCKS FARM: Suckley, Worcestershire WR6 5EH (☎01886-884202; fax 01886-884110). The farm is set in an area of outstanding natural beauty within reach of Worcester, Hereford and Malvern. It supplies supermarkets with fruit and breweries with hops.
Harvest Workers for harvesting hops by machine and fruit picking. Wages at usual agricultural rates. Work available August, September, and October. Self-catering accommodation available. Applicants should like working in the countryside.
Applications to Mr R. M. Capper, Stocks Farm, at the above address.

WITHERS FRUIT FARM: Wellington Heath, Ledbury, Herefordshire HR8 1NF (tel/fax 01531-635504; e-mail withersfruitfarm@farmline.co.uk; www.members. farmline.com/withers). A large soft fruit farm and apple grower in a beautiful setting with a large accommodation block.
Casual Farm Workers (10) for various jobs including driving, supervising and picking. Wages either per hour or piecework; to work 6 days per week. Accommodation available. Minimum period of work 4 weeks between 1 March and 31 October.
Strawberry Pickers (10). Wages per hour or piecework rates; to work 6 days per week. Picking in the mornings and weeding, planting and irrigation in the afternoons.
Supervisors (4). Wages by arrangement; to work 6 days per week. Must be strong and be able to use own initiative.
   Accommodation is available in shared caravans. Minimum period of work 1 month between June and September. Overseas applicants with work permits welcome.
Applications from January onwards to the above address.

Sport

PEAK DISTRICT HANG GLIDING CENTRE: York House, Ladderedge, Leek, North Staffordshire ST13 7AQ (☎07000-426445; e-mail mike@peakhanggliding. co.uk; www.peakhanggliding.co.uk). The longest established hang gliding school in the UK; based in the Peak District National Park.
Hang Gliding Instructor(s) (1/2). Wages £80 per day. Hours by arrangement. To work from July to September. Must be experienced.
Telesales Assistant/Secretary. Wages and period of work by arrangement. Must have a good telephone manner.
Applications to Mike Orr at the above address.

RACING FOR YOU: Basford Grange Racing Stables, Basford, Leek, Staffordshire ST13 7ET (☎01538- 360324; fax 01538-361643; candlishracing@aol.com). Racehorse trainer, training both flat and national hunt horses.
Yard Persons (2). Wages at national minimum rate. To work 9 hours per day full time or 4 hours per day part time. Minimum period of work 6 months from August. Knowledge of horses an advantage. Minimum age 16. Accommodation may be available.
Applications from mid-July to Mr. J.R. Candlish.

STEVE & CAROLINE WALKER: The Brick House, Bearwood, Pembridge, Herefordshire HR6 9EF (tel/fax 01544-388988). Smallholding of 20 acres. Grow apples, for apple juice production, and Christmas trees, which are dug up from 1 December. Also a small livery yard of up to 10 horses for breaking, schooling and racing.
Fruit Pickers required to pick apples carefully from trees and store them in bins. Also involves tractor driving to move bins. Wages upon application. To work 6 hours per day, 5 days a week. No experience necessary but applicants must be over 17.
General Yard/Horses Helpers (2) required to clean stables, exercise horses, drive

tractors and perform yard duties and field maintenance. Wages to be negotiated. To work 4 hours per day, 5 days a week. Applicants must be over 16. Some experience preferred.

Period of work August to November. No accommodation available but camping could be arranged. Foreign applicants with fluent English welcome.

Apply from 21 July to Steve or Caroline Walker at the above address. Interview required.

WATERWORLD: Festival Way, Festival Park, Etruria, Stoke-on-Trent ST1 5PU (☎01782-205747; fax 01782-201815; www.waterworld.co.uk; info@waterworld. co.uk).

Lifeguards required for holiday periods. Wages dependant on age. Applicants must be over 16 and hold RLSS National Pool Lifeguard qualification.

For details please *contact* the Personnel Manager at the above address.

Voluntary Work

Children

BIRMINGHAM PHAB CAMPS: c/o M.S. Wallis, 2 Lenchs Green, Edgbaston, Birmingham B5 7PX (☎0121-440 5727; www.bhamphabcamps.org.uk).

Established in 1967, PHAB Camps is a charity run by volunteers, so administrative costs consume less than 1% of funds. 100 children from Birmingham, most of whom come from disadvantaged backgrounds, take part each summer.

Volunteers (17+) to take groups of disabled children, or mixed groups of disabled and able-bodied children, aged 8-17 for one-week holidays. No pocket money, but board and lodging provided; volunteers will need to get to Birmingham to meet the coach. Period of work between the end of July and end of August. Must be able to work, play with, care for, and entertain the children; many children need feeding and changing, but the holidays are fun. (Volunteers who are male, qualified nurses or able to drive mini-buses especially welcome). More information available at the above website.

Applications to Maxine Wallis, Chairman, at the above address.

B.Y.V. ASSOCIATION LTD: 4th Floor, Smithfield House, Digbeth, Birmingham B5 6BS (☎0121-622 2888; fax 0121-622 1114; e-mail byvvols@yahoo.co.uk; www. byvadventurecamps.co.uk).

Volunteers act as key-workers with 2 or 3 children during the week. Children are from disadvantaged backgrounds and greatly benefit from the positive contact.

Volunteers (120 per year) needed to accompany children on week-long summer breaks, either residential or camping, in Wales and the Midlands. No qualifications are necessary as training is available, but an interest and experience of work with children and young people is advantageous. All volunteers are CRB checked, which is carried out free of charge. No wages are given, but all expenses on the camp are met. Camps take place in the school summer holidays; approx. 21 July to 31 August. Commitment is required 24 hours a day for the length of the camp. Birmingham and Midlands based volunteers are particularly encouraged to apply, but applications are accepted from any area of the country.

Applications to the BYV Volunteer Co-ordinator at the above address.

Conservation and the Environment

COMMUNITY CONSERVATION LTD: Unit 61, Shelton Enterprise Centre, Bedford Street, Shelton, Stoke-on-Trent, Staffordshire ST1 4PZ (☎01782-284004; e-mail community_conservation@hotmail.com).
A not-for-profit volunteer-based organisation providing the means and opportunities for people in Stoke-on-Trent to improve and enhance their local environment and quality of life.
Volunteer Officers (up to 2). To work 25 to 40 hours per week. Expenses paid. No qualifications required, although experience preferable.
Conservation Volunteers (up to10) are needed for conservation work including woodland management. To work 9.30am to 4.00pm, 3 to 4 days per week, to be based around Stoke-on-Trent and North Staffordshire. No experience required.
  Positions available all year round. Foreign applicants welcome but no accommodation available. Minimum age 16.
  Applications at any time to Richard Harrison or Stephen Walters at the above address.

MARINE CONSERVATION SOCIETY (MCS): Unit 3 Wolf Business Park, Alton Road, Ross-on-Wye, Hereford HR9 5NB (☎01989-566017; fax 01989-567815; e-mail info@mcsuk.org; www.mcsuk.org).
The MCS is the only charity in the UK devoted solely to protecting the marine environment.
Volunteers are sometimes needed in the Society's offices and for participation in campaigns and surveys. At certain periods of the year, large amounts of data need to be entered into databases; volunteers with computer skills are particularly welcome at these times. Unfortunately, the Society is unable to provide any financial payment, accommodation or transport. There are also several campaigns in which volunteers can participate; check the website (www.mcsuk.org) for further details.
  For further *information*, contact the Society at the above address.

Festivals and Special Events

HAY FESTIVAL: The Drill Hall, 25 Lion Street, Hay on Wye, Herefordshire HR3 5AD (☎0870-787 2848; fax 01497-821066; www.hayfestival.com). An international festival production company celebrating great writing in every medium in Britain and around the world. Hay is a tiny market town in the Brecon Beacons National Park. It has 1,500 people and 41 bookshops. Celebrating its 20th year in 2007, the Festival is a spectacular holiday party for people to enjoy their tastes for literature, food, drink, comedy, music, art and argument.
Volunteer Festival Stewards (approx. 150) required to make sure both the authors and the audience are safe and happy, before, during and after each event. Stewards work in teams of 4 to 10 people. Shifts last for 3 to 4 hours per day. Volunteers must commit to a minimum of 2 shifts during the festival which runs from 24 May to 3 June. Stewards receive free entry to any talk, although the work must come first. Accommodation is provided at a local campsite, for a small charge. Overseas applicants are welcome to apply but must have a very high standard of spoken English.
  Applications should be made via the website from April.

Heritage

BERRINGTON HALL: Near Leominster, Herefordshire HR6 0DW (☎01568-615721; e-mail tina.salter@nationaltrust.org.uk; www.nationaltrust.org.uk).

A National Trust Property. Provides the opportunity to mix with people from all walks of life with a common interest in conservation.
Car Park Attendant. To work Bank Holidays.
Garden Help, Guides and Education Help.
Volunteer Room Stewards required every day from April to October.
These are volunteer posts which are available all year round. Minimum age 18 years. No accommodation is available but travel costs are provided (up to 40 miles round trip). Volunteers who offer 50 hours of work receive a volunteer card entitling them to free entry to National Trust Properties in the UK and 20% discount in the shops. Overseas applicants welcome.
Anyone interested should *apply* to the House Steward at the above address.

IRONBRIDGE GORGE MUSEUM TRUST: Coach Road, Coalbrookdale, Telford, Shropshire TF8 7DQ (☎01952-435900; www.ironbridge.org.uk).
A World Heritage site.
Volunteers required for demonstrations of exhibits, site maintenance, street animation and wardrobe. The Trust is open Monday to Sunday, 9.45am to 5.15pm. Minimum period of work 6 weeks, maximum 34. Volunteers required from April to October. Minimum age 18. Must have good communication skills, be reliable and self-motivated, and have excellent spoken English.
Some historical background is a plus, although training, costume, equipment and supervision are provided. Workers are given a luncheon voucher for a full day's volunteering, plus free entry to other I.G.M.T. sites. Museum insurance covers all volunteers. No accommodation available. Overseas applicants welcome providing their English is of a good standard.
An interview is not essential although it would help both parties to visit prior to placement. Other opportunities to volunteer are available at the Museum's other sites in the valley.
Applications year round to the Volunteer Office, at the above address.

LUDLOW MUSEUM: Ludlow Museum Resource Centre, Parkway, Ludlow, Shropshire SY8 2PG (☎01584-813666; fax 01584-813601; e-mail ludlow.museum@ shropshire-cc.gov.uk).
The museum covers the geology and history of the area around the town of Ludlow. It is a small place attracting mainly tourists visiting this beautiful region of Britain.
Voluntary Museum Workers (2-3) needed from June to August. To work either 9am-5pm Monday-Friday or part-time at least three days a week. Applicants should be interested in museums and need good spoken and written English as well as basic computer skills.
Those interested in making *applications* should contact the County Curator of Natural Science, at Ludlow Museum Office.

Vacation Traineeships & Internships

The Law
WRAGGE & CO: 55 Colmore Row, Birmingham B3 2AS (☎freephone 0870-903 1000; fax 0870-904 1099; e-mail gradmail@wragge.com; www.wragge.com/ graduate).
Wragge & Co is a top 20 UK law firm providing a full service to some of the world's

largest and most successful organisations, listing 33 of the FTSE 100 as clients. Main base in Birmingham and offices in London and Brussels, with 70% of work generated outside the Midlands and over 25% international.

Easter and Summer Vacation Placements are run at Wragge & Co. As part of our scheme, you will get the opportunity to experience different areas of the firm, attend client meetings and get involved in real files. There are also organised social events with our current trainees.

Apply on-line (paper application available on request) by 31 January 2007.

THE EAST MIDLANDS

This section covers work in the following counties: Derbyshire, Nottinghamshire, Lincolnshire, Leicestershire, Northamptonshire, Oxfordshire and Bedfordshire. See map at the start of the chapter for these counties' locations.

Business and Industry

ADVANCED ALCHEMY LTD: St Edburg's Hall, Priory Road, Bicester OX26 6BL (☎01869-363700; fax 01869-363710; e-mail enquiries@advanced-alchemy.com; www.advanced-alchemy.com).

Inside Sales Executives wanted to work for at least 20 hours per week. Callers with all European languages required to conduct interviews by telephone. Wages start at £7.75 an hour. To work for a minimum of 20 hours a week; flexible hours between 8am and 5.30pm. Cosmopolitan working environment.

For details call Anna Gillam on ☎01869-363719 or e-mail recruitment@ advanced-alchemy.com.

BELL BROTHERS NURSERIES LTD: West End, Bennington, Boston, Lincolnshire PE22 0EE (☎01205-760319; fax 01205-760422; e-mail info@bellsplants.co.uk; www.bellsplants.co.uk). Family-run nursery with nine acres in production at three sites near Boston.

Temporary Glasshouse Operatives (5-10) to work alongside permanent staff in large modern nursery. Duties include pricking out plants, labelling products and collating orders. Much of the work is mechanised. Wages are variable depending on job undertaken. Period of work three months, though may be extended subject to performance. 10 to 25 hours of overtime generally available. Shared accommodation provided in a house in the village. Rent is payable and deducted from wages each week. No previous experience necessary, however, an interest in horticulture and/or relevant qualifications would be an advantage. All successful applicants will be required to sign an employment contract detailing their terms and conditions of employment.

Applications at any time to Sally Hooper, Personnel Manager. Only e-mail applications will be considered.

CATHEDRAL SECRETARIAL AGENCY: 2nd Floor, Akrill House, 25 Clasketgate, Lincoln LN2 1JJ (☎01522-530955; fax 01522-530721; e-mail mail@ cathedralsecretarial.co.uk; www.cathedralsecretarial.co.uk). Suppliers of reliable, experienced office staff to local businesses for over 35 years.

Temporary Secretaries, Temporary Office Staff. Pay above national minimum wage, applicants should have keyboard skills and experience is an advantage.

Legal Secretaries required at good rates of pay.
Applications to Mrs G. Brown, Proprietor, at the above address.

THE CERTIFICATE FRAMING COMPANY LTD: End Cottage Studios, 32 Station Road, Denby, Derbyshire DE5 8ND (☎01332-780232; e-mail scott@ certificateframing.co.uk; www.certificateframing.co.uk). A certificate and photo-framing company who provide 'while you wait' framing at university graduation ceremonies.
Staff (13-15) required to sell merchandise at graduation ceremonies around the country. Wages £50 per day, with B & L included. Required to work from approximately 8am to 6pm, Monday to Friday. Minimum period of work 1 week. Staff required during July only. Foreign applicants are welcome to apply, provided they speak fluent English. Full training given.
Applications at any time to Scott Straughan via e-mail. An interview may be necessary depending on where you live.

PORTABLE FLOORMAKER LTD: Redhill Marina, Ratcliffe on Soar, Nottingham NG11 0EB (☎01509-673753; fax 01509-674749; e-mail enquiries@ portablefloormaker.co.uk; www.portablefloormakers.co.uk).
Labourers (4) needed from May to September to work on a production line packing, loading and assembling floor panels. Wages at minimum of £5.35 per hour possibly rising to £6.25 per hour, plus piecework.
Applications to the above address.

RUTLAND WATER CYCLING LTD: Whitwell Cycle Centre, Rutland Water, Nr Oakham, Rutland LE15 8BL (☎01780-460705; fax 01780-460792; e-mail sales@ rutlandcycling.co.uk; www.rutlandcycling.co.uk). Most successful commercial cycle hire operator in the UK, housing an extensive range of bikes to hire and buy.
Retail Staff (4). Wages at national minimum rate. To work 3 to 5 days a week. Positions are available from Easter to September. Fluent English essential. Minimum age 17. Must be fit, healthy and able to use a computerised till. Foreign applicants with work permits and very good spoken English welcome. No accommodation available.
Applications should be made by March to Tim Harris at the above address. Interview required.

K.H. TAYLOR LTD: The Freezing Station, Sheffield Road, Blyth, Worksop, Nottinghamshire (☎01909-590000; fax 01909-590001). Frozen vegetable processors and packers situated 2 miles off the A1, 10 miles south of Doncaster.
Inspection and Quality Control Personnel, Packers, Stackers (approx. 50). Wages £5.00 per hour. To work 8 hours per day in shifts 6am-2pm, 2pm-10pm or 10pm-6am, Monday to Friday, with some weekend work available. No experience or qualifications needed. Must have own transport.
Applications (quoting telephone number) from the beginning of June to K.H. Taylor Ltd at the above address.

PREMIER TRAVEL INN: Oakley House, Oakley Road, Luton, Bedforshire LU4 9QH (☎01582-567972; fax 0870-241 9000; www.premiertravelinn.com). The largest hotel chain in the UK.
Call Centre Team Members. Wages from £5.35 per hour plus bonuses. To work within the hours of operation, 8am to 8pm. Positions are available from May. Prior experience helpful but not essential but communication and keyboard skills

are necessary. Minimum age 16. Foreign applicants welcome. No accommodation available.
Applications should be e-mailed to linda.thomasson@whitbread.com. Interview necessary.

Children

ALLESTREE SCHOOL'S OUT HOLIDAY CLUB: 1 Wyaston Close, Allestree, Derby DE22 2TS (☎01332-737947; e-mail allestreeschoolsoutclub@hotmail.com; www.allestreeschoolsoutclub.com).
Playworkers (4), Sports Coaches (2). Approx £5.50 per hour. Staff are required during every school holiday, to work between 16 and 45 hours a week. Playworkers must have an NVQ 2 (or equivalent) in playwork/childcare; the sports coaches must have previous sports experience and possibly be studying towards becoming a PE Teacher. Accommodation is not provided. Non UK applicants with suitable qualifications and fluent English are considered.
Apply to Amanda Hudson at the above address as soon as possible.

LEICESTER CHILDREN'S HOLIDAY CENTRE: Mablethorpe, Quebec Road, Mablethorpe, Lincolnshire LN12 1QX (tel/fax 01507-472444; e-mail helen@lanzetta.freeserve.co.uk; www.childrensholidaycentre.co.uk). A charity that provides free holidays for children from the inner city of Leicester, based on the East Coast of England. For anyone interested in working with children this is a fairly unique opportunity offering practical experience and an excellent grounding for a future career.
Activity Leaders (14), Kitchen/Dining Room Staff (5). Wages paid at national minimum wage, based on a 48 hour week.
Cook/Chef. National minimum wage is paid, based on a 48 hour week. To work a 6-day week. Deduction made for B & L.
Activity Leaders required to organise, instruct and supervise an outdoor activities programme for children aged 7 to 12 years. Energy, enthusiasm and a good sense of humour essential.
Staff needed from beginning of May to end of August. Minimum age 18. No experience needed as full training is given.
Write or e-mail for an *application* form (enclosing s.a.e.) from December to H. Eagle-Lanzetta at the above address.

PGL TRAVEL LTD: Alton Court, Penyard Lane, Ross-on-Wye, Herefordshire HR9 5GL (☎0870-401 4411; e-mail recruitment@pgl.co.uk; www.pgl.co.uk/recruitment). PGL recruit around 2,000 staff each year to assist with the running of their children's activity centres throughout the UK, including Devon, the Isle of Wight, Lincolnshire, the south coast, Surrey, Shropshire, Perthshire and Wales. Europe's largest provider of adventure holidays for children has offered outstanding training and work opportunities to seasonal staff for almost 50 years. PGL jobs provide a break from the 9-5 routine. If you are enthusiastic, energetic and looking for real experience and responsibility in a stimulating environment, PGL could have the job for you.
Activity Instructors in canoeing, sailing, windsurfing, fencing, archery, motorsports, pony trekking, and more. Qualifications not essential for all positions as full training will be provided. Minimum age 18.
Group Leaders also needed to take responsibility for groups of children, helping then to get the most out of their holiday. Previous experience of working with children is an advantage. Minimum age 18.

Support Staff to assist the catering, domestic and maintenance teams. From £70-£100 per week plus free B & L. Positions available from February-November, for the full season, as little as eight weeks, or any period in between, although there are very few summer-only vacancies.

Applications can be made online, downloaded from the website, or call for an information pack.

Holiday Centres and Amusements

BILLING AQUADROME LTD: Crow Lane, Great Billing, Northampton NN3 9DA (☎01604-408181; fax 01604-784412; www.aquadrome.co.uk). Inland holiday park open 10 months a year for static holiday homes and tourers. 235 acres of park, jet-ski lake, bars, swimming pool and clubs.

Lifeguards (3). Wages £5.25 per hour. To work 5 or 6 days per week. Applicants must hold lifeguard qualifications.

Bar Staff (3). Wages £5.35 per hour. To work shifts by arrangement up to full time. Applicants must be over 18 with good presentation and communication skills.

Groundskeeper/General Maintenance (3). Wages £5.35 per hour. To work 7.30am to 5pm, Monday to Friday. Applicants must be able to undertake physically demanding work.

Positions available for a minimum of 8 weeks from mid-June to early September. No accommodation available. Foreign applicants with good spoken English welcome.

Applications from 1 April to the Personnel Consultant, at the above address. Interview required.

BJ's LEISURE LTD: Sea Lane, Ingoldmells, Skegness, Lincolnshire PE25 1NU (☎01754-874212; fax 01754-871805; e-mail bjsingoldmells@hotmail.com). Amusement arcades, combining ten pin bowling, go-karts, family showbar and diners.

Bar Staff, Catering Staff, Play Area Staff, Floor Walkers, Cleaners, Bowling Receptionist. Wages and hours on application. Minimum period of work of 26 weeks. Positions available from March to October. No accommodation available.

Applications should be made from February onwards to Patricia Harrison at the above address. Interview required.

FANTASY ISLAND: Blue Anchor Leisure Ltd, Sea Lane, Ingoldmells, Skegness, Lincolnshire PE25 1RH (☎01754-874668; fax 01754-874146; www.fantasyisland. co.uk). Fantasy Island is the largest indoor theme park in Britain, with a large funfair.

Maintenance Staff (15). Wage negotiable. To work 6 days a week.

Ride Operators (100+), Cleaners (20+), Arcade Floorwalkers (20+), Cashiers (12+) required for seasonal work. Wages at national minimum rate. Staff required to work a six day week. No accommodation is available. Period of work from 1 March to 31 October. Full training is provided and foreign applicants who speak English are welcome.

Applications, including 2 named photos, should be made from January to the Human Resources Department at the above address.

Hotels and Catering

THE BANBURY HOUSE HOTEL: Oxford Road, Banbury, Oxon OX16 9AH

(☎01295-259361; fax 01295-270954; e-mail jobs@banburyhouse.co.uk; www. banbury-house.co.uk). A three-star 80-bedroom hotel in the heart of Oxfordshire. An extensive menu is offered and the hotel caters for company dinners, weddings and conferences.

Waiting Staff (4) to serve food and beverages to customers and be responsible for hygiene and general preparation. Areas of work include bar (must be over 18), restaurant, and function rooms.

Room Attendants/Cleaners (2-3) to service the guest bedrooms and public areas to a high standard; daytime hours.

Commis Chefs (2) to assist in the preparation of food for all outlets and maintain a clean, safe and hygienic environment.

Minimum rate of pay £5.35 per hour. Can offer live-in accommodation at £45 per week. Meals provided. Various shifts and hours available.

Applications to Debbie Churchman at the above address.

THE BRANT INN: The Brantings, Groby, Leicester LE6 0DU (☎0116-287 2703; fax 0116-232 1255). A traditional country inn set in a rural position, yet only minutes away from the city centre. Comprises a comprehensive bar and restaurant which is open 7 days a week.

Bar Staff (3), Restaurant Staff (3) for full or part-time work between June and September. Wages by arrangement. Minimum age 18. Foreign applicants with work permits and acceptable spoken English welcome.

Applications to Karen Pollard at the above address.

DONINGTON PARK FARMHOUSE HOTEL: Melbourne Road, Isley Walton, Nr Derby DE74 2RN (☎01332-862409; fax 01332-862364; e-mail info@parkfarmhouse. co.uk; www.parkfarmhouse.co.uk). A small family-run hotel with friendly young staff (mostly in their mid 20s). The hotel has 19 bedrooms, a function barn and a caravan park. Located next to Donington Park Motor Racing Circuit.

General Assistant (1-2). Wages £5.50 per hour. To work 35 to 45 hours over 5 days a week; mainly split shifts in all areas (bar, breakfast serving, evening waiting, washing up, room cleaning etc.). Minimum period of work 4 months between March and October. Accommodation is provided at £28.50 per week.

Previous relevant experience preferred but not essential. Overseas applicants with good spoken English will be considered. Interview preferred, unless distance makes this difficult.

Applications from February to Linda Shields or Emma Zwozny.

THE JERSEY ARMS HOTEL: Middleton Stoney, Bicester, Oxfordshire OX25 4AD (☎01869-343234; fax 01869-343565; e-mail jerseyarms@bestwestern.co.uk; www.jerseyarms.co.uk). A privately-owned and managed high-class country inn with 20 bedrooms.

Housekeeping Assistant (1). Wages £5.35 per hour. To work 45 hours over 5 days a week. Minimum period of work 1 month at any time of year. Accommodation and meals provided for £32 per week. Uniform is provided. Minimum age 18.

Applications to Mrs Livingston at the above address.

MICHAEL WISHER AND ASSOCIATES: Griffin House, Nottingham Trent University, Clifton Campus, Nottingham NG11 8NS (☎0115-984 6000; fax 0115-984 6001; e-mail caroline@michaelwisher.co.uk; www.michaelwisher.co.uk). Specialises in providing temporary hospitality staff to major corporate and sporting events across the UK.

Bar and Waiting Staff. Wages from £5.35 to £6.50 per hour. Hours of work are variable depending on the event and venue. The work is flexible so staff can choose hours to suit. Work is available throughout the year, however the summer months are the busiest period with many sporting events taking place over this time. Transport is always provided, free of charge, to and from the venues. No experience necessary. Applicants should be 18 and over. Overseas applicants with fluent English, relevant work permits and documentation are welcome to apply.

Application forms should be downloaded from the above website and returned to Caroline McBriar at the above address. Successful applicants must attend an informal induction session.

THE NATIONAL TRUST: Belton House, Grantham, Lincolnshire NG32 2LS (☎01476-566116; fax 01476-579071). The National Trust was founded in 1895 to preserve places of historic interest or natural beauty for the nation to enjoy.
Catering Assistants to work in a busy assisted service restaurant. To work Wednesday to Sunday, including Bank Holiday Mondays. Staff needed from end of July-end of September. Experience of working with the public desirable. No accommodation available.

Applications from February/March to Becky Fawcett, Visitor Services and Administration Manager, at the above address.

THE RANDOLPH HOTEL: Beaumont Street, Oxford OX1 2LN (☎0870-400 8200; fax 01865-203047; www.macdonaldhotels.co.uk/randolph). Oxford's premier hotel.
Housekeeping/Catering Assistants needed to work at The Randolph in Oxford, The Eastgate Hotel in Oxford and The Bear Hotel in Woodstock. Wages on application. To work 40 hours over five days per week. No accommodation available. To work from June to September; minimum period of work is eight weeks. Overseas applicants with good English welcome. Minimum age is 18.

Apply from April to the Human Resources Manager at the above address.

SHERWOOD PINES VISITOR CENTRE: Sherwood Pines Forest Park, Old Clipstone, Mansfield, Nottinghamshire NG21 9JL (☎01623-822500; e-mail nigel@ redmile.freeserve.co.uk).
Cooking Staff (2) to work over the summer season until the end of August. Wages by arrangement. Must be aged over 18. Basic Food Hygiene Certificate preferable.

Applications to Jean Watts at the above address.

SHILLINGFORD BRIDGE HOTEL: Shillingford Hill, Wallingford, Oxfordshire OX10 8LZ (☎01865-858567; fax 01865-858636; e-mail shillingford.bridge@ forestdale.com; www.shillingfordbridgehotel.co.uk). The Shillingford Bridge Hotel nestles on the banks of the River Thames in Oxfordshire. It has an award winning restaurant, forty bedrooms, three function suites, an open-air swimming pool, squash courts and a public bar.
Housekeeping and Laundry Staff, Restaurant and Functions Staff, Kitchen Porters, Commis Chefs, Reception, Night Staff and General Assistants. Full-time, seasonal and permanent positions available. Varying rates of pay. Limited staff accommodation. Live in and live-out positions offered for a minimum period of 3 months. Longer term applications preferred.

Applications to the Duty Manager at the above address.

WESTWOOD COUNTRY HOTEL: Hinksey Hill Top, Oxford OX1 5BG (☎01865-735408; fax 01865-736536; e-mail reservations@westwoodhotel.co.uk; www.westwoodhotel.co.uk). Situated in lovely woodland gardens just 2½ miles from Oxford city centre, the hotel is recently refurbished and offers high quality food and accommodation.

General Assistants (2). Minimum £150 (net) per week plus B & L. To work approximately 48 hours per 5½ day week. Hours by arrangement with flexible day off. Minimum period of work 3 months between May and October. Minimum age 20. Tidy appearance required. Overseas applicants welcome.

Applications to Mr Tony Healy, Proprietor, at the above address.

Language Schools

ASPECT ILA OXFORD: 108 Banbury Road, Oxford OX2 6JU (☎01865-515808; fax 01865-310068; www.aspectworld.com). A language school in North Oxford with a young and lively atmosphere.

EFL Teachers (10-15). Teaching general English to mixed nationality groups aged 16+. CELTA or equivalent required plus degree. Minimum age 21.

Social Assistants (1-2). To assist the social organiser with arranging and promoting social events and sporting activities. Minimum age 18.

Accommodation Assistant. To assist the accommodation officer, mainly by recruiting and inspecting new host families. Minimum age 18; must have access to a car.

Administration Assistant. To undertake general administrative duties; computer literacy an advantage. Minimum age 18.

Jobs are on a full-time or part-time basis with wages to be arranged. Some accommodation may be available in student residences; this is free if 'warden' responsibilities are undertaken. Staff are required from May/June until the end of August, and an interview is necessary. Suitably qualified overseas students with valid working visas are welcome.

Applications from March/April to the Principal or Director of Studies at the above address.

BRITISH STUDY CENTRES OXFORD: 5 Cambridge Terrace, St. Aldates, Oxford OX1 1UP (☎01865-246620; fax 01865-246857; e-mail oxford@british-study.com; www.british-study.com). English Language school in the centre of Oxford, providing general and business English, IELTS, Cambridge examinations and Business Foundation Year.

EFL Teachers (4-6). English Language teaching to adults and social activities. Wages £13-£15 per hour. To work up to 25 hours per week teaching plus extra hours available for social activities, 9.15am-4.30pm, Monday to Friday. Minimum period of work 3 to 8 weeks between June and September. Accommodation is available from £90 per week. Applicants must have a university degree and a CELTA qualification and they must speak English to the standard of a native speaker.

Apply to Nicky Seth at the above address from April onwards. Interview necessary.

EF LANGUAGE TRAVEL: Cherwell House, 3rd Floor, 1 London Place, Oxford OX4 1AL (☎01865-200720; fax 01865-243196; e-mail lt.oxford@ef.com; www. ef.com).

EFL Teachers, Leaders, Activity Coordinators needed to teach teenage overseas students and organise leisure activities between June and the end of August. Teachers are paid £26+ per half day session (or £31+ if with a TEFL qualification); leaders are

paid £270+ per week. Applicants should be university students aged at least 19. Good knowledge of Oxford and London required.
Applications to the Manager at the above address.

GLENFIELD ENGLISH COURSES: Glenfield, Boars Hill, Oxford OX1 5DL (☎01865-735370; fax 01865-730246). An extremely friendly residential school offering intensive EFL together with a range of sports, excursions and social activities to overseas students aged 10-18.
EFL Teachers (2) live-in, to teach students on residential courses. Salary subject to contract but roughly £300 per week with all meals and own study bedroom provided. Periods of work: usually July only or July/August. Minimum age 21, maximum age 25. Sporting ability, particularly in tennis, and some TEFL experience useful but applicants must speak English perfectly, that is, as well as a native speaker.
General Domestic Assistant to help with cooking, housework etc. Salary subject to contract but roughly £90 per week. Live-in, with meals and own study bedroom provided. To work from 20 June for either 5 or 9 weeks. Minimum age 20. Overseas applicants especially welcome. Knowledge of English is not essential. Applicants must be legally entitled to work in the UK.
Applications for all posts to Mr or Mrs Horwood at the above address. Applicants must be available for interview in May or early June. In exceptional cases interviews may be arranged in Paris or Madrid.

OISE YOUTH LANGUAGE SCHOOLS: OISE House, Binsey Lane, Oxford OX2 0EY (☎01865-258300; fax 01865-244696; e-mail younglearners@oise.com; www. oise.com). Part of the OISE education group. Offers summer language courses to foreign teenagers. Courses are intensive and fully structured.
EFL Teachers (100). Wages £9.00 to £11 per hour, with free accommodation on residential courses. Flexible hours. Minimum period of work 2 weeks. Positions are available in June, July and August. Applicants must have a degree and a CELTA or Trinity TESOL qualification. Fluent English essential.
Applications should be made from May onwards to the above address. Interview required.

OXFORD ENGLISH CENTRE: 66 Banbury Road, Oxford OX2 6PR (☎01865-516162; fax 01865-310910; e-mail info@oxfordenglish.co.uk; www.oxfordenglish. co.uk). A year-round school of English recruiting staff in July and August for summer courses.
EFL Teachers (5-10). Salary by arrangement based on qualifications. To work 15-30 hours per week in July and August. Applicants should have at least a first degree and RSA Prep. certificate.
Activities Helpers (4) to work full- or part-time between June and September. Applicants should be at least 19, job suits students on vacation.
Cafe Staff (2). Competitive wages in international cafe. To work from 8am-3pm in July and August. Training given but applicants should be clean, quick and have good presentation skills.
Applications to Graham Simpson, Principal.

OXFORD HOUSE SCHOOL OF ENGLISH: 67 High Street, Wheatley, Oxford OX33 1XT (☎01865-874786; fax 01865-873351; e-mail study@oxfordhouseschool. co.uk; www.oxfordhouseschool.co.uk). Small, personal school near Oxford, catering for mixed nationality students (individuals and small groups only). A friendly working environment.

EFL Teachers (1-2). Wages approx. £290 per week. 23 hours of class contact per week plus occasional supervisory/social duties. Required from July to the end of August or September. Minimum RSA CELTA or equivalent plus relevant experience.

Applications a.s.a.p. to Mr R.I.C. Vernede, Principal, Oxford House School of English.

ST CLARE'S OXFORD: 139 Banbury Road, Oxford OX2 7AL (☎01865-552031; fax 01865-310002; e-mail shortcourses@stclares.ac.uk; www.stclare.ac.uk). An international college and educational charity operating a range of courses for students from around the world throughout the year, with residential premises in North Oxford.

EFL Teachers (30). To teach 15-26 hours per week. From £15 per hour. Dip. TEFLA preferred; CTEFLA plus 1 to 2 years of experience.

Activity Staff (20). Wages £245 to £285 per 48 hour week, plus free meals. Minimum age 20 years. Experience of organising activities and sport essential. Drivers also required.

Accommodation available free to those who also undertake pastoral duties. Minimum period of work 3 weeks between June and September. All applicants must be available for interview and be prepared to complete an enhanced Criminal Records Bureau check.

Applications from March to the Short Courses Division at the above address.

SUL LANGUAGE SCHOOLS: 31 Southpark Road, Tywardreath, Par, Cornwall PL24 2PU (☎01726-814227; fax 01726-813135; e-mail efl@sul-schools.com; www. sul-schools.com). A well-established business that provides language holiday courses in Cornwall, Devon, Somerset, Midlands, Scotland and Ireland for foreign teenagers. Courses run for 2-4 weeks from April to September.

EFL Teachers. Wages dependent on experience and qualifications but are usually from £26 per morning of 2½ hours. To work mornings and possibly afternoons, supervising activities. Teachers required from April-August for a minimum period of 2 weeks. Applicants should be TEFL qualified or hold a languages degree or teaching qualification. Preferred CRB checked applicants. Accommodation is available at some centres.

Applications from January to the Director of Studies at the above address. Interview usually required.

Medical

ABACUS CARE (DERBY) LTD: 84-86 Glass House Hill, Codnor, Derbyshire DE5 9QT (☎01773-512226; fax 01773-745522; e-mail application@abacuscare.biz).

Healthcare Assistants needed for work in nursing homes; duties mainly consist of general care for the elderly including washing, dressing and reading. Minimum wage £6.20 per hour. Part-time and full-time work available; flexible hours. Applicants must be at least 18 years old and have a minimum of 6 months' previous experience and a current moving and handling certificate.

Registered Nurses to work in nursing homes, EMI Units and with people with learning disabilities. General nursing duties including applying dressings conducting medicine rounds. Wages from £11.00 (EN) and £12.75 (RN) per hour. Working hours by arrangement. Applicants must be on the NMC register; no age restrictions. Accommodation is not available. Staff needed around the year; dates of work by arrangement.

Applications should be sent to the above address.

ABACUS CARE NURSING AGENCY: 137b London Road, Headington, Oxford OX3 9HZ (☎01865-744174; fax 01865-744547; e-mail oxford.swe@abacuscare. com). Part of a national nursing agency with 25 other branches in the UK. Also offer TOPPS training and NVQ in care.
Nurses (5-20) of all grades for temporary positions in Oxford, Oxfordshire and the Cotswolds. A variety of positions available in nursing homes, private and community hospitals, the prison service and with private patients. Minimum wage £19 per hour. Includes shift work. Must possess current UK nursing qualifications and be able to provide proof of permanent National Insurance number.
Care Assistants (5-30) required for temporary positions in residential and nursing homes and with private patients. Minimum wage £7.50 per hour. Must have had previous experience and be able to prove permanent National Insurance number.
Support Workers (1-5) required to work in learning disability units. Minimum wage £7.50 per hour. Must have previous experience.
Live-in Carers (10) to provide everyday care and help with cooking and shopping. Wages to be arranged, but include free board and accommodation. To work full time, with 10 hours off a week and a weekend off every month. Applicants must be over 18 years of age. Basic common sense essential.
All the above positions are temporary and are available at all times of year. Clear spoken English essential.
Applications to the above address.

EXPRESS CARE SERVICES LTD: Hazel House, Churchthorpe, Louth, Lincolnshire LN11 0XL (☎01507-363238; fax 01507-610700; e-mail expresscare@ expresscareservices.com; www.expresscareservices.com).
Carers (5), Cooks (2), Support Workers (3) for work providing home care, cooking and supporting adults. To work various hours. Wages of £5.35 per hour, £5.75 at weekends. Period of work by arrangement over the summer. Applicants must be aged at least 18 and will be required to take a CRB check.
Applications to B. Richards, MD, at the above address.

OXFORD AUNTS CARE: 3 Cornmarket Street, Oxford OX1 3EX (☎01865-791017; fax 01865-242606; e-mail enquiries@oxfordaunts.co.uk; www.oxfordaunts. co.uk). Providing live-in services to older people who need general care and support and those with more complex health care requirements.
Temporary Positions to live-in the homes of the elderly and frail. Care experience and good standards of oral and written English essential, as well as an up-to-date police check from country of origin. Driving licence preferred. Availability of 12 weeks required.
All *applicants* must be able to attend an interview and attend 3½ days (unpaid) training.

Outdoor

C. FRANCIS: Paddock House, Bear lane, Pinchbeck, Spalding, Lincolnshire PE11 3XA (☎01775-723953; e-mail cecilfrancis@aol.com). A small family company in the fens close to Peterborough. All strawberries are grown in large polytunnels and on a table top system, so pickers stay dry and do not need to bend down.
Soft Fruit Pickers (20). To work approximately 8 hours a day, 5 days per week. Staff needed from 1 June to 1 October. Minimum period of work 4 weeks. Accommodation provided for weekly charge of £30 (hostel). Showers, cooking and sporting facilities included. Minimum age 18. Overseas applicants with work

permits welcome.
Applications from 1 April to the Office Manager at the above address.

C.M. & G.W. GOACHER LTD: Green Acres, Wood Lane, N. Whatley, Retford, Nottinghamshire DN22 9NG (☎01427-880341; fax 01427-880341).
Fruit Pickers/Packers. Wages at Agricultural Wages Board stipulated rate. To work from 8am to 3pm, with some extra work available; some weekend work possible. Period of work from mid-June to mid-July. Limited accommodation may be possible with sufficient notice. Applicants must be fit and have common sense.
Applications to Mrs Judith Goacher, Company Secretary, at the above address, giving background info and reference contacts.

THE EVENTS AND TENTS COMPANY: Hilltop Farm, Caythorpe Heath, Grantham, Lincolnshire NG32 3EU (☎0800 027 4492; fax 01400 275044; e-mail info@eventsandtents.co.uk; www.eventsandtents.co.uk).
Marquee Erectors (5-10). Pay from £5.50 per hour. Required to work for up to 60 hours per week erecting tents (5/6 days per week) from May to September. Driving licence required.
Applications to Andy Beamish at the above address.

HARGREAVES PLANTS LTD: Cowpers Gate, Long Sutton, Lincolnshire PE12 9BS (☎01406-366300; fax 01406-366321; e-mail sales@hargreavesplants.co.uk; www.hargreavesplants.co.uk).
Plant Nursery Workers. A wide range of work is available from April-September, at both good piecework rates and hourly pay. Mobile home accommodation is available on a campsite which is noted for its friendly atmosphere. Student and foreign applicants are particularly welcome.
Applications by both post and e-mail are welcomed.

FIELD AND KAWN MARQUEES: 1 Eldon Way, Crick Motorway Industrial Estate, Crick, Northamptonshire NN6 7SL (☎01788-822922; fax 01788-823333; www.fieldandlawn.com).
Marquee Erectors for a well-established and fast growing company supplying modern aluminium frame structures. Work involves installing marquees and associated equipment at stately homes, sports grounds, corporate venues, race tracks in the Midlands and throughout the UK from May to October inclusive. Overseas applicants from Australia, New Zealand and South Africa especially welcome.
Pay at least national minimum wage. Usually 50 hours and over per week, with most work at weekends. Must be prepared to find own accommodation near Northampton, Rugby or Leicester. Applicants have to be physically fit and able to work long hours with enthusiasm and able to learn quickly.
Contact the Recruitment Manager, at the above address.

JUST RIGHT MARQUEES: 46 Haydon Road, Didcot, Oxfordshire OX11 7JR (☎01235-211596; e-mail simon.maugham@ntlworld.com; www.justrightmarquees. co.uk).
Marquee Erectors (3). Pay rate is £6 per hour. Required to work through the summer.
Applications to Simon Maughan, Managing Director, at the above address.

OWEN BROWN LTD: Station Road, Castle Donington, Derbyshire DE74 2NL (☎01332-850005; fax 01332-819343; e-mail info@owen-brown.co.uk; www.owen-

brown.co.uk).
Marquee Erectors for general labouring work building temporary structures all over the UK. Wages £300 per week plus night out allowance. Staff required from May to September. Must be aged over 18.
Applications to Tim Hall, Operations Director, at the above address.

OXFORD MARQUEES: Langford Lane, Kidlington, Oxford, Oxon OX5 1HT (☎01865-373173; fax 01865-842020; e-mail mail@oxfordmarquees; www.oxfordmarquees.co.uk).
Marquee Erectors (5). Wages from £6 per hour. Required to work 42.5-hour week, from Monday to Friday. Need to be flexible with start and finish times as some early starts. End of May to end of September. Need to be available for weekend work, which is paid as overtime. Loading, unloading, erecting and dismantling marquee equipment. A lot of outdoor work, based in/around Oxfordshire.
Applications, to the above address.

PRESTIGE MARQUEES: South Lawn Farm, Swinbrook, Oxfordshire OX18 4EN (tel 01993-823817; 01993-823818; e-mail info@prestigemarquees.com; www.prestigemarquees.com).
Marquee Erectors (2). £7-£8 per hour. Required to work as required from 1 June to 30 September as needed. Preferably over 25 years old.
Applications to Anna Horn at the above address.

SENTANCE MARQUEES: Castle View Road, Easthorpe, Bottesford, Nottinghamshire NG13 0DX (☎0800-027 4492; fax 01949-842130; e-mail info@sentancemarquees.co.uk; www.eventsandtents.co.uk). A total event hire company.
Marquee Erectors (2-6). Wages start at £5.50 per hour. To work 5 to 6 days per week for 8 to 10 hours a day between April and the end of September. Minimum period of work is 2 to 3 months. Must be 18 or over, strong and fit with a driver's licence. Non-UK citizens will be considered; fluent English is useful.
Applications to Andrew Beamish at the above address at any time.

STANLEY & PICKFORD: Rectory Farm, Stanton St John, Oxford OX33 1HF (☎01865-351214; mobile 079-7630 2404; fax 01865-351679; e-mail s.and.p@farmline.com; www.rectoryfarmpyo.co.uk). Runs a pick-your-own, and are suppliers of potatoes, strawberries, raspberries and other fruits.
Fruit Pickers (30) to pick mainly strawberries and raspberries. Wages at piece-work rates. Period of work approximately 5 June to 5 August. If the weather is suitable there is picking every day; hours of work are informal, but pickers can expect to work in the mornings and part of the afternoon. Accommodation is available on the farm in mobile homes and caravans with cooking facilities, communal room, showers etc. Previous experience would be an advantage.
Contact Mr R.O. Stanley, Partner, at the above address for a full information pack giving information on the work available, rates of pay, accommodation, training etc.

Sport

JAMES GIVEN RACING LTD: Mount House Stables, Long Lane, Willoughton, Gainsborough DN21 5SQ (☎01427-667618; fax 01427-667734, e-mail jobs@jamesgivenracing.com; www.jamesgivenracing.com).
Stable Staff for duties including riding out, mucking out and all yard duties; will

be able to take horses racing. Wages depend upon experience, with accommodation provided; approximately £70 per week. To work from 7.30am to 1.30pm and from 4.30pm-6pm, with overtime available. To work from March until November or by arrangement. Applicants must have previous experience of riding racehorses.

Applications to Lucy Coney, Secretary, at the above address. An interview will be necessary.

NORTHFIELD FARM: Flash, nr Buxton, Derbyshire SK17 0SW (☎01298-22543; e-mail northfield@btinternet.com; www.northfieldfarm.co.uk). BHS approved riding centre and working farm, situated in a small village. There is a post office and a pub 100 yards away. 30 horses are used, an Andalusian stallion at stud, a few breeding mares and young stock.

Trek Leaders (2). Approx. minimum pay £150 per week plus free accommodation. To work 8am-5pm, 5½ days per week. Work available from April to September; minimum work period June-August. Applicants must be competent riders, good with people and preferably car drivers. Riding and Road Safety Test and First Aid qualification also preferred. Must also be prepared to help out on the farm when needed. Applicants must speak the same standard of English as a native speaker.

Applications between March and May only (no applications before March) to Mrs E. Andrews, Northfield Farm, at the above address. Interview required.

NORTH KESTEVEN SPORTS CENTRE: Moor Lane, North Hykeham, Lincoln LN6 9AX (☎01522-883311; fax 01522-883366; www.nkleisure.org.uk).

Part-Time Lifeguards required during all vacations. Must have RLSS Pool Lifeguard (NPLQ), with spinal qualifications preferred. Previous experience preferred. Wages from £5.00 per hour, with uniform provided. To work variable hours between 7.15am and 10.30pm including bank holidays.

Application forms available from Paul Watkins at the above address.

WOODLANDS STABLES: Woodlands Lane, Market Rasen, Lincolnshire LN8 5RE (☎079-7194 0087). Stables with 25 horses in training for flat and jump races.

Work Riders/Grooms (1-20) to ride and take care of horses and for general stable work. Wages approximately £200 per week depending on experience. To work 7am to 4pm with 3 hours for lunch. Minimum period of work of 3 months. Positions are available all year. Applicants should preferably weigh under 10 stone, not smoke, ride well and live in. Accommodation cost is £25 per week. Foreign applicants welcome.

Applications should be made as soon as possible to Mr M. Chapman at the above address. Interview necessary.

Voluntary Work

Archaeology

PIDDINGTON: Upper Nene Archaeological Society (UNAS), Toad Hall, 86 Main Road, Hackleton, Northampton NN7 2AD (☎01604-870312; e-mail unas@ friendship-taylor.freeserve.co.uk; www.unas.org.uk).

UNAS was formed in 1962 as a group of active local fieldworkers interested in the area's early history. Now it comprises nearly 200 members and aims to promote study and interest in archaeology, the discovery and investigation of sites and the preservation of items of archaeological interest. In 2007, UNAS is excavating a late Iron Age settlement and Roman villa at Piddington (27th year). Site Museum opened in Piddington August 2004; please telephone for details.

Volunteers are required for 3 weeks in August for excavation work, site recording, planning and finds processing. No experience necessary. Minimum age usually 18, though some special consideration may be given to very keen 16 to 17 year olds. Accommodation and meals can be arranged and there is camping next to the site with basic facilities. Two weeks at the site costs approximately £50, less for UNAS members, although costs are subject to change.

To apply, send a s.a.e or 2 IRCs for details to Roy or Liz Friendship-Taylor, or download forms and information from the website.

Fundraising and Office Work

OXFAM: Oxfam House, John Smith Drive, Oxford OX4 2JY (☎01865-473259; e-mail givetime@oxfam.org.uk; www.oxfam.org.uk/what_you_can_do/volunteer/index.htm). Oxfam runs a number of different **Volunteering Programmes**, including volunteering opportunities through its shops. Oxfam advertises more specialised volunteer vacancies on its website at www.oxfam.org.uk/what_you_can_do/volunteer/latest.htm, all of which are UK based, and many of which are at its head office in Oxford. Speculative applications are also welcome. Please e-mail CVs to givetime@oxfam.org.uk, along with ideas of what you would like to do and when. Oxfam reimburses reasonable local travel and lunch expenses. For those interested in a career with Oxfam, volunteering is an excellent way to gain relevant experience and to get to know the organisation.

Further *information* is available from givetime@oxfam.org.uk, or call into your local Oxfam shop.

Heritage

WIRKSWORTH HERITAGE CENTRE: Crown Yard, Wirksworth, Derbyshire DE4 4ET (☎01629-825225; e-mail enquiries@storyofwirksworth.co.uk; www.storyofwirksworth.co.uk). The Centre is a small registered museum telling the story of a small, formerly very important town in Derbyshire.The 'Wirksworth Story' in a former silk mill offers information about local customs and social history. Some 'hands-on' exhibits and family friendly. A small gallery exhibits and sells the work of local artists, ceramicists, sculptors and photographers.

Voluntary General Museum Assistant. Ideal post for a museum studies student, working hours to be arranged. Minimum period of work of 1 month. Positions are available all year. Must be able to communicate confidently with the public, be pro-active and enthusiastic and able to help with all aspects of running a small museum. Knowledge of museum documentation systems useful. No accommodation available.

Applications should be made to Mrs M. Vaughan at the above address. Interview necessary.

Vacation Traineeships & Internships

Accountancy and Insurance

NEWBY CASTLEMAN: West Walk Building, 110 Regent Road, Leicester LE1 7LT (☎0116-254 9262; fax 0116-247 0021; e-mail info@newbyc.co.uk; www.newbycastleman.co.uk).
Chartered accountancy practice with 10 partners and 130 employees providing total financial service to small and medium-sized enterprises.
The company offers **Vacancies for 2 Students** to experience working in a chartered accountant's practice. The work will involve assisting in accounts preparation and audit. Students at any level are invited to apply. Salary of £100 per week minimum. Placements last for 8 weeks in the summer and are located in Leicester. No accommodation is provided.
Applications by 3 March to M.D. Castleman, Partner.

Conservation and the Environment

CHESTNUT CENTRE CONSERVATION PARK: Castleton Road, Chapel-en-le-Frith, Derbyshire SK23 0QS (☎01298-814099; fax 01298-816213; e-mail enquiries@ottersandowls.co.uk; www.ottersandowls.co.uk).
An owl and otter haven covering several acres in the Peak District.
Occasionally takes on **Work Experience Trainees**. Trainees must stay a minimum of two weeks and be enrolled on an animal-related course at college or university. No accommodation is available.
For further *details*, contact the Park at the above address.

LINCOLNSHIRE WILDLIFE TRUST: Banovallum House, Manor House Street, Horncastle, Lincolnshire LN9 5HF (☎01507-526667; fax 01507-525732; e-mail info@lincstrust.co.uk; www.lincstrust.org.uk).
Lincolnshire Wildlife Trust is a nature reserve with visitor centre.
Residential Placement. Training and involvement opportunity available only to applicants seeking a career in nature conservation and with a keen interest in wildlife. The varied placement includes habitat and species management, surveying and monitoring and environmental education and interpretation. Minimum period 3 months. Accommodation provided.
Applications should be made to Mr Kevin Wilson, Site Manager, at the above address.

Media

VACATION WORK PUBLICATIONS: 9 Park End Street, Oxford OX1 1HH (☎01865-241978; fax 01865-790885; e-mail info@vacationwork.co.uk; www.vacationwork.co.uk).
Since its establishment in 1967, Vacation Work has become widely recognised as a leading publisher of employment directories and travel guides for young people. It currently features over forty titles in its catalogue including *Summer Jobs in Britain*, *Work Your Way Around the World* and *Taking a Gap Year*.
In 2007 the company will be looking for one or two people to work in an **Editorial Capacity** during the summer vacation. The work will involve assisting the editorial staff in the process of revising and up-dating the company's books. Duties are likely to include general secretarial and clerical work, organising mailings to featured

organisations and editorial research and re-writing. All candidates should be proficient at operating a word processor, and should be able to demonstrate an interest in or knowledge of the publishing business. Some writing or editorial experience is preferred. Applicants must be capable of working on their own initiative without direct supervision, although help and guidance will be given where necessary. They must be entitled to work in the UK and speak English as well as if it were their first language. The pay will be around £222 per week. Please note that no direct assistance can be given with finding accommodation.

Applications should be sent to Mr David Woodworth at the above address around Easter in order to arrange an interview.

Science, Construction and Engineering

BOMBARDIER TRANSPORTATION: Litchurch Lane, Derby DE24 8AD (☎01332-344666; www.bombardier.com).
Bombardier is a complete provider of railway systems, with sites in Derby, Crewe, Ilford, Ashford, East Ham, Reading, Burton-on-Trent and Plymouth.
Vacation Placements available throughout the company. Successful applicants will most likely be placed in Derby or Crewe since these are the largest operations. Wages and minimum qualifications vary depending on the work. Engineering and Production students are particularly sought, though requirements vary according to the business area. Further information can be obtained from the above address.

Applications should take the form of a covering letter and CV to Sarah Saxon, UK HR Managerat the above address; potential candidates will be invited to interview.

CONOCOPHILLIPS LTD: Humber Refinery, South Killingholme, Immingham, North Lincolnshire DN40 3DW (☎01469-571571; fax 01469-555141; e-mail engrecruit@conocophillips.com; www.conocophillips.com/careers).
ConocoPhillips Ltd. has positions for **Summer and Industrial Placements** to work in its Chemical and Mechanical Engineering Department during the summer. Applicants should be university students in their penultimate year. The work involves trouble-shooting, de-bottlenecking, assisting with the day-to-day running of the plant to optimise throughput. Students receive £14,000 (pro rata). Help in finding accommodation is given and lunches are provided.

Applications for the following year should be e-mailed to engrecruit@ conocophillips.com no later than 14 November.

POWERGEN UK PLC: Waterfront House, Osier Drive, Sherwood Park, Annesley, Nottingham NG15 0DS (☎01623-788500; fax 01623-788502 e-mail undergradplacements@pgen.com; www.powergenplc.com/jobs).
One of the largest private sector electricity generating companies in the world. They also offer telecom and internet services.
Summer Vacation Placements available in areas including **Business, IT, Engineering** and others to be confirmed. Wages to be arranged. Placements begin during June and run until the end of August. Applicants must be first or second year undergraduate students. The majority of placements are located in Coventry, although engineering placements tend to be in the company's various power stations.
Powergen also offers undergraduate **Placements for sandwich-year students**, lasting 48 weeks and commencing in the summer. More information for all vacancies can be found on the website above.

Applications, comprising CV and covering letter, should be sent to the above e-mail address. Before sending, applicants are advised to look at the company website, as they may begin to list a new address specifically for summer placements. Interview required.

SIEMENS COMMUNICATIONS: Technology Drive, Beeston, Nottingham NG9 1LA (☎0115-943 3371; fax 0115-943 3078; www.siemenscomms.co.uk/grad). Siemens Communications is a world class solutions provider, employing 1,800 people and improving the business of their 40,000 customers. They currently have opportunities for **Undergraduate Software Engineers** seeking placement experience at the site in Nottingham, within their Engineering Development Centre. Placements are 12 months duration commencing summer 2007.

Applications online only, at the above website.

The North

Prospects for Work.

While job vacancies in the tourist trade are scattered throughout the northern region, they are most abundant in the larger coastal resorts, the Yorkshire Dales and the Lake District.

The main resorts along the east coast are Bridlington, Filey, Whitby and Scarborough, one of Britain's most popular seaside destinations. Scarborough and Filey have a large number of seasonal vacancies, including plenty of care and hospitality work, comparatively few of which have live-in accommodation. Further north lie South Shields, Whitley Bay and Berwick. Berwick has two large holiday centres run by British Holidays employing seasonal staff from April-October with some live-in work available. As well as hotels and restaurants, amusement arcades are another source of employment, particularly in Bridlington. Live-in jobs are comparatively rare. South of Scarborough along the coast are three major holiday centres run by Haven Holidays; Primrose Valley, Blue Dolphin, and Reighton Sands. Jobcentre Plus throughout the area advertise vacancies; seasonal vacancies appear in the *Scarborough Evening News* six days a week (Thursday is the main day). Anyone interested in a seasonal position should contact Scarborough Jobcentre Plus on 0845-6060 234, or visit the Jobcentre Plus website www.jobcentreplus.gov. uk. It is best to apply in February.

The principal tourist centre of the west coast is Blackpool, which has several vacancies for its many hotels, amusement arcades and fun parks. In addition Blackpool has an especially long season; the end of the summer season is given a boost when the illuminations are turned on at the end of August; these remain an attraction until late November. The *Blackpool Evening Gazette* offers a mailing service on request and has a special 'Jobs Night' edition every Thursday. Few jobs offer live-in accommodation and accommodation can be difficult to find during the summer months.

Morecambe, Fleetwood, Southport, Thornton, Cleveleys and Lytham St Anne's, also in Lancashire, are popular tourist haunts too. Hexham in Northumberland has a new golf course. It is worth contacting the local Golf Clubs directly.

There are lots of seasonal jobs in Northumberland, for example at Haggerston Castle Holiday Park in Berwick and in hotel and catering all around the county; Alnwick Jobcentre Plus has a student register that matches people to seasonal vacancies.

In the main tourist centres in the Lake District – Windermere, Bowness-on-Windermere, Ambleside, Keswick and Grasmere – hundreds of seasonal and permanent jobs are available in hotels, restaurants, caravan parks, pubs and youth hostels. The holiday season in the lakes is now largely all year round, with an influx of visitors in the summer season. Unfortunately, unless you are lucky, renting a room in the Lake District is likely to cost more than your weekly wage. However, many hotels do now offer live-in accommodation or offer assistance with finding lodgings. Camping is also a possibility. The Jobcentre Plus website (www.jobcentreplus.gov.uk) includes details of whether a position offers accommodation. Hotels in the Lake District start advertising for staff about three weeks before Easter; wherever possible they will take on the same staff for the summer season too.

York and Harrogate are both on the tourist trail, and there is therefore a demand for extra hotel staff and shop staff. Your best chance of getting a job is to apply well in advance of the end of the student term. Attractions like the York Dungeons and Jorvik Viking Centre and events such as the York Races may offer opportunities for two or three days' work. Similarly, a wide range of short-term work is usually available in early July during the Great Yorkshire Show in Harrogate: jobs are advertised in the Jobcentre Plus about a month beforehand. There are a number of Call Centres in York; CPP, an insurance company for credit cards, is always looking for staff, particularly during peak times, holidays, and Christmas. The holiday company, Superbreak, also looks for staff at these times. Three miles north of Ripon, the Lightwater Valley Theme Park takes on large numbers of seasonal staff; these are also advertised in the Harrogate Jobcentre Plus. In this area consult the *Yorkshire Evening Post, York Evening Press*, or *The Harrogate Advertiser* for job advertisements.

Factory work provides a source of seasonal work in the North, with large factories recruiting extra people to work over the summer, mainly from June until September. They include Nestlé Rowntree and Terry Suchard in York and KP foods in Cleveland. Other factories to approach, either directly or through the local Jobcentre Plus, are: Ben Shaws in Pontefract; Crystal Drinks Ltd in Featherstone; Unique Images in Bradford; and Glaxo Operations, Kerry Foods Ltd and Autobar Packaging in Durham. In the Durham area agencies such as Manpower usually recruit for this type of work.

The North has experienced rapid growth in call centre operations, notably at Doxford Park in Sunderland. Companies such as EDF, T-Mobil, Acxiom, Littlewoods Home Shopping, Barclays and the Post Office have relocated to this site. Other call centre operations throughout the region include Transco and BT call centre at North Tyneside, Abbey at Stockton and Orange Telecommunications at Darlington. These operations are known to employ students on a temporary basis, since their overall staff turnover is generally high. There is usually a training period and most applicants need good keyboard and customer service skills. Local Jobcentre Plus offices should be contacted for details.

Various local authorities, such as Gateshead, Greater Manchester, South Tyneside and Sunderland, may have work on playschemes or may need holiday cover in their many clerical departments. Large towns such as Leeds and Newcastle are the best places to try for retail jobs. The tourist trade in the Manchester area grew immensely following the Commonwealth Games and was also aided with attractions such as the Imperial War Museum North, Urbis and the Lowry Arts Centre. Other places recommended for general summer work are Alnwick, Bamburgh, Corbridge, Haydon Bridge, Hexham, Seahouses, Barnet Castle, Durham and Redcar.

City Councils and Local Authorities are worth contacting to find out about significant forthcoming events that may need extra staffing. Most local newspaper websites now have local job search facilities using *Fish4Jobs* – for example, try www.thisislancashire.co.uk; substitute the name of the county or town where you are hoping to find a job.

THE NORTH WEST

This section covers work in the following counties: Cumbria, Lancashire, Greater Manchester, Merseyside, Cheshire and the Isle of Man. See map at the start of the chapter for these counties' locations.

Business and Industry

ABC RECRUITMENT: 3-5 Anderson Chambers, 34 Great King Street, Dumfries DG1 1BD (☎01387-270718; fax 01387-266383; e-mail enquiries@abcrecruitment. net; www.abcrecruitment.net). Specialists in temporary and contract recruitment in hospitality and catering, administration/clerical, customer services/retail, sales etc.
Vacancies year round in the UK, mainly in South West Scotland and Cumbria. Most clients look for candidates with some previous experience.
Contact Clive Rumbold, Owner, for further information.

FIELD STUDIES COUNCIL: Blencathra Centre, Threlkeld, Keswick, Cumbria CA12 4SG (☎01768-779601; fax 01768-779264; e-mail enquiries.bl@field-studies-council.org; www.field-studies-council.org). An educational centre offering courses in geography, geology and ecology, providing accommodation for up to 105.
Centre Assistants (6) for general duties in the busy centre. National minimum wage plus accommodation. To work 37½ hours, 5 days per week. Minimum period of work 3 months. Positions available throughout the year. Suitably qualified foreign applicants authorised to work in the UK welcome. Fluent English essential.
Applications should be made from late January/ early February to the centre director at the above address. Interview and Criminal Record Bureau check required.

SUNNYHURST NURSERIES LTD: Blackgate Lane, Tarleton, Preston, Lancashire PR4 6UT (☎01772-812266; fax 01772-816420). Salad and vegetable plant suppliers to commercial growers.

Pallet Stackers (2). Wages from £5.50 per hour. To work up to 40 hours per five day week. Minimum period of work one month. Positions are available from April to July. Applicants should have fork-lift truck driver's certificate. Fork-lift driving is necessary to assist the manual aspects of the work. Minimum age 21. No accommodation available. Foreign applicants with work permits and acceptable spoken English welcome.

Applications should be made from February to K. Marshall at the above address. Interview required.

Children

LAKESIDE YMCA NATIONAL CENTRE: Ulverston, Cumbria LA12 8BD (☎0870-727 3927; fax 01539-530015; email personnel@lakesideymca.co.uk; www. lakesideymca.co.uk). The camp is set in 400 acres of woodland on the shores of Lake Windermere in the Lake District National Park, and is one of the largest camps in Europe.

Day Camp Leaders (40). The work involves leading groups of children aged 8-15 years in a wide range of activities, from environmental awareness to rock climbing. Wages £50 per week and free B & L. To work 5 days a week. Minimum period of work 8 weeks between early July and the end of August. Minimum age 18 years. Some experience of outdoor activities is advantageous and experience of working with children necessary.

Application forms are available from January to May from Personnel, YMCA National Centre, Lakeside, by email or via the website.

NST TRAVEL GROUP PLC: Discovery House, Whitehills Business Park, Brooklands Way, Off Preston New Road, Blackpool FY4 5LW (☎0845-6711357; fax 01253-833844; e-mail info@nstjobs.co.uk; www.nstjobs.co.uk). An Outdoor Activity and ICT residential centre for children aged 9-13. NST Travel Group is Europe's leading educational tour operator.

Activity/ICT Instructors (38). To instruct a range of outdoor activities and ICT and to assist with the evening entertainment programme. While qualifications are valued they are not essential as full training will be given prior to working with guests.

Catering Assistants (6) to assist the Catering Manager and be involved in all aspects of kitchen work. No previous experience required.

Maintenance/Cleaning Assistants (2) to assist the Maintenance Manager. No previous experience required, but an interest in DIY useful.

Wages in line with the national minimum wage. Average working week 42 hours over 6 days. Minimum period of work 2 months. Staff required from January through to November. All positions are residential.

For more information and an *application form* please contact the above address.

Holiday Centres and Amusements

ALLEN (PARKFOOT) LTD: Howtown Road, Pooley Bridge, Penrith, Cumbria CA10 2NA (☎01768-486309; fax 01768-486041; e-mail jobs@parkfootullswater. co.uk; www.parkfootullswater.co.uk). Family-run caravan and camping park by Lake Ullswater. Set in magnificent scenery only 6 miles from Penrith and perfect for outdoor activities.

Bar and Catering Staff to work various shifts from 8am to midnight. Minimum age 18 years.

Cook/Chef to prepare cooked breakfasts, lunches and evening meals. Hours 8am to

2pm and 6pm to 11pm.

Adventure Supervisor (1) to run a children's action club from the park. Activities include archery, tennis, baseball, volleyball, football, arts (crafts) and pool tournaments. Hours 9am to 5pm Monday to Friday during school holidays.

Secretary/Receptionist (2). To work alternative early/evening shifts and shared weekends. Required from May-September. Must enjoy meeting people and have a pleasant telephone manner.

Wages negotiable according to experience. Accommodation can be arranged in shared staff caravans. Period of work Easter, May Bank Holidays and from June to mid-September.

Applications from Easter, enclosing colour photo, details of work experience and dates of availability, to Mrs B. Allen or Mrs F. Bell, Parkfoot Caravan Park.

NEWLANDS ADVENTURE CENTRE LTD: Stair, Keswick, Cumbria CA12 5UF (tel/fax 01768-778463; e-mail info@activity-centre.com; www.activity-centre.com). An outdoor centre located 3½ miles outside Keswick offering multi activity holidays in the heart of the Newlands Valley. Activities include climbing, abseiling, mountain biking, kayaking, archery and orienteering among others.

Domestic Assistants (4) to maintain a clean and hygienic environment and to assist with the preparation of meals for guests and staff. To work a 44-hour week. Minimum age 16.

Kitchen Assistant to help prepare meals and to maintain a clean environment in all food preparation areas. To work a 44-hour week. Minimum age 16.

All positions run from March to October; applicants must be able to start in April or May at the very latest. Staff have their own single room with shared bathrooms and TV lounge. All meals are provided. There is also an opportunity to take part in the activities free of charge. Further details of hours, salary and accommodation costs available on application. Foreign applicants with a reasonable level of English and current visas and work permits welcome.

Applications should be sent to the Manager at the above address from January to May only.

OASIS WHINFELL FOREST HOLIDAY VILLAGE: Temple Sowerby, Penrith, Cumbria CA10 2DW (☎01768-893004; fax 01768-893001; e-mail workopportunities@centerparcs.co.uk; www.centerparcs.co.uk). Set in the beautiful Lake District, Oasis Whinfell is part of the CenterParcs group.

Bar and Waiting staff, Kitchen Staff, Sports Attendants. Wages a minimum of £5.00 per hour, to work 40 hours per week. Staff receive large discounts and free use of facilities. Previous experience not essential. Permanent positions are available.

Application forms can be obtained by phoning the above number.

PLEASURELAND LTD: Pleasureland Amusement Park, Marine Drive, Southport PR8 1RX (☎01704-532717; fax 01704-537936; e-mail mail@pleasurelandltd. freeserve.co.uk; www.pleasureland.uk.com). An approved Investor in People and Positive Against Disability employer.

Ride Operators (60), Car Park Attendants (6), Arcade Cashiers (6), Arcade Attendants (12). Minimum age 18 years.

Cleaners For Grounds (4), Toilet Cleaners (5), Catering Assistants (40). Minimum age 17 years.

Supervisors and Team Leaders.

Wages start at the national minimum wage and go up according to age and experience. Minimum period of work one day between March and April. No experience necessary unless otherwise stated as full training will be provided. No accommodation available but local B & Bs cost approximately £15 per night. National Vocational Qualification (level II) offered in Mechanical Ride Operations and Customer Service, with others pending. All staff to work 5 or 6 days per week. Overseas applicants with a good standard of English considered. Applicants should be able to attend an interview.

Applications to Stuart Cragg, Personnel Manager at the above address or contact Southport Jobcentre (☎0845-606 0234; www.jobcentreplus.gov.uk).

Hotels and Catering

BRACKENRIGG INN: Watermillock, Penrith, CA11 0LP (☎01768-486206; e-mail enquiries@brackenrigginn.co.uk; www.brackenrigginn.co.uk). Rural lakeside hotel 5 miles from the nearest town.
General Assistants. Wages and hours by arrangement with 2 days off per week. Period of work from June to September. Minimum age 18 years. Applicants must enjoy the countryside and be prepared to work hard. Training is provided so experience is not necessary. Overseas applicants welcome.
Applications to the Manager at the above address.

BRATHAY HALL TRUST: Ambleside, Cumbria LA22 0HP (☎015394-33041; fax 015394-32531; e-mail personnel@brathay.org.uk; www.brathay.org.uk). A management training centre situated in a secluded area on the north west shore of Lake Windermere.
General Assistants needed for general duties such as washing-up, cleaning rooms, assisting chefs, bar work. Good pay and conditions, single room accommodation available if necessary. To work 43 hours a week with 2 days off per week. Staff needed all year round, minimum period of work 3 months. Minimum age 18 Applicants must be prepared to attend an informal interview if possible.
Applications should be written or e-mailed to Wendy Harris, Venue Manager, at the above address.

CHADWICK HOTEL: South Promenade, Lytham St. Annes, Lancashire FY8 1NP (☎01253-720061; fax 01253-714455; e-mail sales@thechadwickhotel.com; www.thechadwickhotel.com).
Restaurant Personnel (2). Wages £159.60 to £201.60 per week depending on age and experience. To work 42 hours per week. Minimum period of work 8 weeks at any time of year. No accommodation is available. Overseas applicants are considered. Interview preferable but not necessary.
Applications to Mr. Davison at any time.

CROWNE PLAZA MANCHESTER AIRPORT: Ringway Road, Manchester M90 3NS (☎0161-498 4065; fax 0161-498 6503; e-mail diane.prince@ichotelsgroup.com; www.ichotelsgroup.com).
Housekeeping Team Members (3) required to clean and prepare guest rooms, replenish guests' supplies, clean public areas, work in the linen room. Wages £4.85 per hour with meals provided and the possibility of tips. Period of work from May until October (must be available for a minimum of 5 months). Applicants should be aged over 18 and physically fit.
Applications to Diane Prince, HR Administrator, at the above address.

GRAND ISLAND HOTEL: Bride Road, Ramsey, Isle of Man IM8 3UN (☎01624-

812455; fax 01624-815291; e-mail reservations@grandislandhotel.com; www. grandislandhotel.com). A beautiful Georgian hotel overlooking the Ramsey Bay, offering a restaurant, bars and leisure facilities.

Day/Night Porters, Chef De Partie/Commis Chefs, Chamber Staff, Food/Beverage Staff. To work 40 hours per week. Details of wages, accommodation, on application. Live-in staff accommodation as part of the package at £20 a week. To work from April onwards. All applicants must be college trained.

Applications should be sent to The Deputy Manager, at the above address.

HOLMHEAD FARM GUESTHOUSE: Hadrian's Wall, Greenhead via Brampton, nr Carlisle CA8 7HY (☎01697-747402; www.holmhead.com). A bed and breakfast offering evening dinner parties situated on the Hadrian's Wall path with beautiful rural surroundings; positions therefore not suitable for socialites. Only 4 bedrooms to service and a clientele from all over the world, especially America.

General Assistant (1) required to help run a guest house. Duties include helping prepare meals, washing up and cleaning rooms. Wages £100 a week including B & L within a friendly home environment. Own mobile home with all facilities.

To work up to 9 hours per day, 5 days a week with extra days off wherever possible. Period of work Easter to 1 November. Minimum period of work June to end of August. Minimum age 18. No experience required. Overseas applicants with spoken English and the correct documentation welcome (owner speaks Norwegian). Candidates should be available for interview, though if this is difficult references may suffice.

Applications from January to P. Staff, Proprietor, at the above address.

LEEMING HOUSE HOTEL: Watermillock, Ullswater, nr Penrith, Cumbria CA11 0JJ (☎01768-486622; fax 01768-486443; e-mail leeminghouse@macdonald-hotels. co.uk; www.macdonaldhotels.co.uk/leeminghouse). Beautiful country house hotel set in own grounds with access onto the lake. Very good staff accommodation available within grounds.

Waiting Staff (4). Experience needed.
Bar Staff/Porters (2). Previous bar work experience required.
Chamber Staff (4).

Salary for all staff from £194 a week. To work 5 days a week with consecutive days off. Minimum period of work 6 months. Individual accommodation available for £40 per week plus all meals. Shared accommodation available at £25 per week plus all meals. Ages 18 to 35 years. Overseas applicants eligible to work in the UK and with good English welcome.

Applications to the Personnel Manager, Leeming House Hotel.

MICHAEL WISHER AND ASSOCIATES: Technology House, University of Salford, Lissadel Street, Manchester M6 6AP (☎0161-278 2419; fax 0161-278 2581; neil@michaelwisher.co.uk; www.michaelwisher.co.uk). Michael Wisher and Associates specialise in providing temporary hospitality staff to major corporate and sporting events across the UK.

Bar and Waiting Staff. Wages from £5.35 to £6.50 per hour. Hours of work are variable depending on the event and venue. The work is flexible so staff can choose hours to suit. Work is available throughout the year, however the summer months are the busiest period with many sporting events taking place over this time. Transport is always provided, free of charge, to and from the venues. No experience necessary. Applicants should be 18 and over. Overseas applicants with fluent English, relevant work permits and documentation are welcome to apply.

Application forms should be downloaded from the above website and returned to

Neil at the above address. Successful applicants must attend an informal induction session.

THE NEW PRESIDENT HOTEL: 320-324 North Promenade, Blackpool FY1 2JG (☎01253-624460; fax 01253-291269; e-mail goldenthistle@aol.com).
Reception, Restaurant (2), Bar (2) Staff to work a 40-hour, 5-day week. Wages at national minimum rate. Applicants for the reception post must be computer literate.
Housekeeping Staff (2) to work 30 hours per week. Payment at the national minimum wage rate.
Chefs (2) to work 40 hours per week. Wage at £15,000 per year pro rata. Possession of NVQ 2 and 3 and advantage.
   Period of work by arrangement. Assistance may be given with accommodation for all positions.
   Applications to Alan French, General Manager, at the above address.

PATTERDALE HOTEL: Patterdale, Lake Ullswater, near Penrith, Cumbria CA11 0NN (☎01768-482231; fax 01768-482440; e-mail jonathonhurst@choicehotels. co.uk; www.choicehotels.co.uk). A friendly family-run, busy 57-bedroom Lake District hotel in beautiful surroundings.
Housekeeping, Kitchen, Waiting Staff. Wages by arrangement.
   B & L provided at £10 per week. Meals provided on and off duty. Opportunities for walking and climbing. Minimum period of work 6 months. Positions available all year round. Minimum age 16. Overseas applicants with good English welcome.
   Applications from early 2007 to the above address.

QUEEN'S HOTEL: Main Street, Keswick, Cumbria CA12 5JF (☎01768-773333; e-mail info@queenshotel.co.uk; www.queenshotel.co.uk). A 35-bedroom hotel in the heart of the Lake District. Situated in the centre of the lively town of Keswick, which has plenty of shops, bars and night-clubs. Fishing, sailing and walking nearby.
Chamber Staff (1), Waiting Staff (1), Bar Staff (2). Wages £220 per week gross; B & L available only a minute's walk away. To work 40 hours a week. Period of work between June and September. No qualifications or experience necessary. Overseas applicants with good English welcome.
   Applications a.s.a.p. to Mr Peter Williams, Proprietor, The Queen's Hotel. Only successful applicants will receive a reply.

ROWTON HALL COUNTRY HOUSE HOTEL AND HEALTH CLUB: Whitchurch Road, Rowton, Chester CH3 6AD (☎01244-335262; fax 01244-335464). Set in eight acres of award winning grounds, Rowton Hall is renowned for fine food and wine and its wedding and conference facilities.
Waiting Staff. Wages depend on age. To work a five-day week. Staff are required from April to October.
   Applications including a CV at any time to the Hotel Manager at the above address.

SHARROW BAY HOTEL: Lake Ullswater, Penrith, Cumbria CA10 2LZ (☎01768-486301/86483; fax 01768-486349; e-mail sharrow@relaischateaux.com; www. sharrowbay.co.uk). Luxury hotel and Michelin starred restaurant set in a tranquil postion on the edge of Lake Ullswater.
Stillroom Assistants. Approximately £165 a week.
General Assistants. Minimum £165 a week. To work in bedrooms and restaurant.

Free B & L provided. All staff to work 50 hours over 5 days a week. Ages 17 to 30 years. Must have domestic interests and lots of common sense, and should enjoy living in the country and working as part of a team of perfectionists. References required.
Applications from January to the Manager, Sharrow Bay Hotel.

USL TRADING LTD: Botany Bay, Botany Brow, Coral Mill, Chorley, Lancashire PR6 9AF (☎01257-261220; fax 01257-230888; e-mail info@botanybay.co.uk; www. botanybay.co.uk). A 150,000sq ft retail shopping outlet with shops, catering outlets and a children's play area.
Catering Staff (15), Sales Staff (15). Wages vary depending on applicants age. Experience is preferred, but not essential. Hours vary, part-time work is possible. Accommodation is not included.
Applications should be sent to Jane Emanuel for sales, Simon Taylor for catering, at any time. Interview required.

THE VENTURE CENTRE: Maughold, Isle of Man IM7 1AW (☎01624-814240; fax 01624-815615; e-mail contact@adventure-centre.co.uk; www.adventure-centre. co.uk). Adventure training centre giving introductory instruction in outdoor activities to children aged 9 to 15 years.
Catering and Domestic Staff. Qualified or experienced cooks to cook, prepare and serve. Also to run the kitchen for groups of residential children (up to 60). Positions available from March to September.
Applications before March to Mr S. Read, Director, the Venture Centre.

WILD BOAR HOTEL: Crook, nr Windermere, Cumbria LA23 3NF (☎01539-445225; fax 01539-442498; e-mail wildboar@elhmail.co.uk; www.elh.co.uk/hotels/wildboar). A small, friendly hotel with a large proportion of live-in personnel, located in the National Park. A former coaching inn, the Wild Boar has traditional oak beams and log fires and is surrounded by beautiful countryside.
General Assistant to work in any area of the hotel, but mainly the restaurant, waiting, bar, portering or housekeeping (which involves serving teas/coffees, cleaning the lounges, setting and serving function rooms and other duties). Wages approximately £690 per month live-in (no deductions made from the figure for live-in).
Work is live-in in own bedroom with communal facilities, all food, with 5 days work out of 7. Period of work from May to the end of September/early October. The job involves dealing directly with guests, so pleasant and outgoing personalities are essential. Common sense is more desirable than previous experience. Staff are taken on all year, not only in the summer months.
Applications to Wayne Bartholomew at the above address.

Language Schools

INTERNATIONAL STUDENT CLUB LTD: 21 Park Road, Hale, Cheshire WA1J 9NW (☎0161-929 9002; fax 0161-929 4156; e-mail info@student-club.co.uk; www. student-club.co.uk). A small, family-run organisation offering English language and activity courses to foreign students aged 10-17.
Activity Monitors (10) required to supervise young people during sports sessions, excursions, discos and competitions. Wages £200 per week with board and accommodation available free of charge. To work 6 days per week. Minimum period of work 2 weeks. Positions available between 7 July and 19 August 2007.
Applicants must be over 19 years of age – preference will be given to those with sports qualifications or experience in dance and drama. Foreign applicants are

welcome to apply but fluency in English is essential. Interview required. *Applications* should be sent to Jill Cutting at the above address from January onwards.

MANCHESTER ACADEMY OF ENGLISH: St Margaret's Chambers, 5 Newton Street, Manchester M1 1HL (☎0161-237-5619; fax 0161-237-9016; e-mail info@ manacad.co.uk; www.manacad.co.uk). City Centre English language school for international students, a member of English UK, and British Council accredited.
EFL Teachers (6-7). Approx. £12 per hour for approximately 20 hours per week. Minimum period of work of one month. Positions are available between 1 July and 31 August. Applicants should have a degree and an RSA/Cambridge or Trinity Certificate or Diploma; two years experience also required. Must be 22 or over.
No accommodation for any position.
Applications should be made from February onwards to Sandra Kaufman, Principal, at the above address. Interview required.

Medical

APEX NURSING & CARE SERVICES: Emery House, 195 Fog Lane, Didsbury, Manchester M20 6FJ (☎0845-600 3041; fax 0161-447 6494; www.apex-nursing. co.uk).
Trained/Auxiliary Nurses, Support Workers, Care Assistants to work in hospitals, nursing homes, people's own homes, and social care involving working with clients with learning disabilities and challenging behaviour. Rates of pay will be discussed at interview. Required for all vacations and during term-time. No experience is necessary as full free training is given. Minimum age 18.
Requests for application forms can be made via recruitment@apex-nursing. co.uk.

APOLLO PERSONNEL SERVICES: St Austins Chambers, St Austins Lane, Warrington, Cheshire WA1 1HG (☎01925-444332; fax 01925-657651; e-mail apollops@hotmail.com). Provides staff to numerous areas of the healthcare industry and can provide training where necessary.
Care Workers (15). Wages £5.35 per hour, to work 30 hours per week caring for elderly or disabled people in nursing homes or private residences. Positions available all year round; no minimum period of work. Applicants must be 18 or over. Foreign applicants with fluent English welcome. Training given; no accommodation available.
Applications should be made at any time to Janet Kearns at the above address. Interview required.

Outdoor

BRIAR POOL FARM: Cledford Lane, Middlewich, Cheshire CW10 OJS (☎01606-737670; fax 01270-528241; e-mail millennium.marquees@dsl.pipex.co.uk).
Seasonal Marquee Erectors to put up and dismantle tents during season May to October; there is a possibility of starting work in June, July, August or September according to applicant's availability. Work also available during December. Pay at least national minimum wage, but is related to performance at erecting and dismantling. Must be able, fit and strong. Driving licence an advantage.
Apply to Andrew Willis or Rachel Williamson.

EVANS MARQUEE HIRE: Butler Works, Wyresdale Road, Lancaster, Lancashire

LA1 3JJ (☎01524-63090; fax 01524-69929; e-mail evans_marquee@hotmail. com; www.evansmarqueehire.co.uk). A small family-run marquee hire company specialising in weddings and special events.
Seasonal Marquee Erectors (20). Wages £220 per week (22 years and over); £189 per week (18-21 years).
Drivers (10). Wages £230 per week; must be over 25. Must have full, clean driving licence.
To work 40+ hours per week; required from May to September. Applicants should be fit and healthy; work can at times be physically demanding and uncomfortable if the weather is poor. No accommodation available. Suitably qualified foreign applicants with work permits will be considered; fluent English not essential.
Applications should be made from April onwards to the above address. Interview required.

PANAMA SPORTS HORSES: The Stables Cottage, Gisburn Park, Gisburn, Lancashire BB7 4HU (tel/fax 01200-445687; e-mail info@panamasporthorses.co.uk; www. panamasporthorses.co.uk).
Yard Staff (2) to work with 40 horses in a Treatment/Rehabilitation yard. Must be a competent, confident rider able to work on the flat and over fences. Will undertake general yard duties, including the general day to day care of the horses, riding out, and so on. Wages are negotiable depending on age and experience. Accommodation can be provided.
For further details and for *applications*, contact Ailsa Richardson at the above address.

Sport

ALSTON TRAINING & ADVENTURE CENTRE: Alston, Cumbria CA9 3DD (☎01434-381886; fax 01434-382725; e-mail alstontraining@btconnect.com; www. alstontraining.co.uk).
Assistant Outdoor Activity Instructors. Free B & L and training provided. Should have current driving licence. MLC or Canoe qualification useful.
Domestic staff also required.
For further details and *applications* contact Mr Dave Simpson, Head of Centre, at the above address.

RAMBLERS HOLIDAYS LTD: Hassness, Buttermere, Cockermouth, Cumbria, CA13 9XA(☎01768-770227; e-mail susangarethhassness@btinternet.com). Walking centre situated on shore of Buttermere lake. Offer week-long walking holidays with up to 21 guests, normally aged 40 and over.
General Assistants (2) required. To work 5½ days a week, split shifts. Wages to be negotiated. Applicants should have a pleasant personality and be able to work to a high standard in housekeeping. Period of work March to November. Non-smokers, please.
Contact Susan and Gareth Roberts for further information.

MRS G.S. REES: Cross Farm Racing, Sollom, Tartleton, Preston, Lancashire PR4 6HR (☎01772-812780; fax 01772-812799; e-mail info@geraldinerees.co.uk). A small, friendly yard situated in the Lancashire countryside, near to Southport and Preston.
Stable Staff needed for the racehorses. Wages of £202.80 per week plus overtime when going to meetings. To work 40 hours per week from Monday to Friday and

Saturdays until 1pm; one weekend in three must be worked. Must be an experienced and capable rider. Weight should be under 9st. 7lbs.
Apply to Mrs Rees at the above address.

ROOKIN HOUSE EQUESTRIAN & ACTIVITY CENTRE: Troutbeck, Penrith, Cumbria CA11 0SS (☎01768-483561; fax 01768-483276; e-mail deborah@ rookinhouse.co.uk; www.rookinhouse.co.uk). Situated on a hill farm, Rookin House is a multi-activity centre offering quad biking, go-karting, archery as well as an equestrian centre with 38 horses offering trekking, hacking and lessons.
Trek Leaders (2). Wages from £180 per week, to work 40 hours per week. Applicants must be 18 or over, hold Riding and Road Safety qualifications and be able to ride well.
Activity Instructor. Wages from £180 per week, to work 40 hours per week. Applicants must be 18 or over and preferably hold GNAS for Archery Leader Award, First Aid Certificate and ATV Qualification. In-house training can be provided if applicant does not hold the above.
For both positions work will involve taking clients on activities and the maintenance of equipment and surroundings. There is also a self-catering unit which will require cleaning. Accommodation is available at a charge of £20 per week. Overseas applicants are welcome but must have a work permit and speak good English. Staff are required from June to September and must work July and August.
Applications should be sent to Deborah Hogg at the above address from March.

THE VENTURE CENTRE: Maughold, Isle of Man IM7 1AW (☎01624-814240; fax 01624-815615; e-mail contact@adventure-centre.co.uk; www.adventure-centre. co.uk). Adventure training centre giving introductory instruction in outdoor activities to adults and children aged 9-90.
Instructors (3). Wage according to experience. Free B & L. Hours dependent on groups under instruction: 7-day week at times. Minimum period of work 1 month between March and August.
Minimum age 18 years. Essential training given to suitable candidates. At least one NGB Award helpful.
Applications before March to Mr S. Read, Director, The Venture Centre.

Voluntary Work

Archaeology

NORTH PENNINES ARCHAEOLOGY LTD: Nenthead Mines Visitor Centre, Nenthead, Alston, Cumbria CA9 3PD (☎01434-382037/382045; fax 01434-382294; e-mail info@nparchaeology.co.uk; www.nparchaeology.co.uk)
Organisation managing a variety of building conservation projects including one at Diston Castle. Ongoing research project on lead mining remains at Nenthead.
Volunteers are accepted to work in survey, excavation, restoration, post-excavation, archiving and research in Nenthead, Cumbria, from the end of October to the end of May. There is no minimum period of work. An archaeological field school will also be run between June and September working on a number of projects relating to the lead mining industry. Applicants to the field school will pay a fee towards tuition and accommodation and will be expected to stay for a minimum of 2 weeks. Accommodation is provided at a bunk house with a kitchen, bathroom, lounge area

and washroom. Volunteers must be over 17 but no previous experience is necessary. The cost varies between different projects, but usually volunteers pay only for their travel and a small contribution towards food and accommodation.

Applications should be sent to Frank Giecco, Principal Archaeologist or Matthew Town, Project Archaeologist at the above address.

POULTON RESEARCH PROJECT: 17 Canadian Avenue, Hoole, Chester CH2 3HG (tel/fax 01244-400858; e-mail chris@caroe.freeserve.co.uk; www.poultonproject. org).
A long-term research investigation based on a medieval chapel in Chester, associated with the lost Cistercian Abbey of Poulton and its cemetery. The project examines the evolution of the historic, environmental, social and economic landscape of Cheshire. There is also evidence of a Roman villa/farmstead/temple. Recent work has uncovered a bronze-age ring ditch, broadening the scope of research. The project is community based and welcomes special needs groups, volunteers and students.
Volunteers needed to help with excavation work for 1 week in July or August. Applicants must be over 16 and physically fit enough to endure hard labour. No experience required. No accommodation provided, but there is a nearby campsite and hostel, with transport provided to and from the site. The cost for all tuition is £100 per week.
Applications can be made online at the above website, or contact Chris Caroe at the above address.

Heritage

LAKELAND ARTS TRUST: Abbot Hall Art Gallery, Kendal, Cumbria LA9 5AL (☎01539-722464; fax 01539-722494; e-mail info@abbothall.org.uk; www. lakelandartstrust.org.uk).
An independent charity which runs a prize-winning and thriving art gallery, museum and prestigious Arts and Crafts House, Blackwell, overlooking Windemere.
Volunteer Curatorial Assistants, Reception Staff, Event Helpers and Coffee Shop Staff are required to work in Abbot Hall Art Gallery, Blackwell and the Museum of Lakeland Life. To work during July, August and September; there may be vacancies at other times. The work would suit both undergraduates and postgraduates hoping to gain museum and gallery experience.
The gallery also requires graduate or postgraduate students for **unpaid museum and gallery work experience**. To work 9.30am to 5.30pm or part-time hours if living out. Interview if possible. Overseas students welcome, but working English is required.
Applications at any time to Cherrie Trelogan at the above address.

WORDSWORTH TRUST: Town End, Grasmere, Cumbria LA22 9SH (☎015394-35544; fax 015394-35748; e-mail m.oskoui@wordsworth.org.uk; www.wordsworth. org.uk).
A registered charity (no. 1066184) in the heart of the Lake District. Responsible for maintaining Dove Cottage, the Wordsworth Museum and the Wordsworth Library. An internationally renowned literary centre with a unique collection, which offers accredited museum training.
Volunteer Museum Assistants needed around the year to guide visitors around Dove Cottage, the home of William Wordsworth, help in the shop and assist in the museum with tasks including providing reception and information services, cataloguing the collection and security. To work a 37½ hour, 5-day week on a 7-day rota; accommodation is available. Applicants must be aged 18 and over and have a

high standard of spoken English.
Applications to Michelle Oskoui, Assistant Curator at the above address.

Social and Community Schemes

GREAT GEORGES COMMUNITY CULTURAL PROJECT: The Blackie, Great George Street, Liverpool L1 5EW (☎0151-709 5109; fax 0151-709 4822; e-mail staff@theblackie.org.uk; www.theblackie.org.uk).
Volunteering Opportunities for anyone over 18 to try alternative education and the arts together with some sport, recreation and welfare in an inner-city context: usual programme of youth work, crafts and games; workshops with local youngsters; staging exhibitions and events; and projects from cookery to contemporary and African dance, from photography to fashion is reduced till April 2007 during major building programme, but volunteers are still welcome to join outreach youth projects until then and after to share in expanded programme in new building. Share cooking, cleaning, administration and some building work. Endless opportunities to learn and unlearn, to teach and to create. Wonderfully long hours. Stamina, a sense of humour and a sleeping bag required. Accommodation provided. Volunteers are expected to stay for at least four weeks and to provide their own food costs. Volunteers are welcome throughout the year and particularly over the summer, winter and spring holiday periods. The Blackie has recently passed its 38th anniversary.
   For further information write to the Duty Office at 40 Canning Street, Liverpool L8 7NP until April 07, after that at the above address.

MANJUSHRI KADAMPA MEDITATION CENTRE: Conishead Priory, Ulverston, Cumbria LA12 9QQ (☎01229-584029; fax 01229-580080; e-mail info@manjushri. org.uk; www.manjushri.org.uk).
A residential Buddhist community with around 100 residents, founded in 1977 to provide a peaceful and inspiring environment where people can learn about the Buddhist way of life and practice meditation.
Volunteers needed for various duties including building, kitchen/garden help, and general household work/cleaning. Working visitors are asked to cover the cost of their meals, the same as residents. Full board accommodation, including all meals and teachings is £50 for 7 nights and £40 for students. Volunteers work 29 hours per week, Monday to Friday. Weekends free to explore and relax. Minimum period of work 1 week. Positions available all year round. Minimum age 16. No smoking or drinking allowed on site. Volunteers are welcome to join in centre activities such as meditation classes and courses.
   Applications in advance are essential. Please complete an application form, which can be obtained at www.manjushri.org.

Vacation Traineeships & Internships

The Law

HALLIWELLS: St James Court, Brown Street, Manchester M2 2JF (☎0870-365 9492; fax 0870-365 9493; e-mail hlrecruitment@halliwells.com; www.halliwells.com).
Commercial law firm with offices in Manchester, London and Sheffield. The firm has grown in size fourfold over the last 5 years and embraces an internal culture of motivation, commitment, enthusiasm and reward.

Halliwells offers **Summer Vacation Placements (45)** for university students to gain experience in three different areas of the practice, assisting current trainee solicitors and other solicitors and partners. Students are supervised by trainee solicitors and assist the trainee in any aspect of their work which can include legal research, drafting letters, filing and attending court. The placements are open to second-year law undergraduates and third-year non-law undergraduates. There are four schemes, each lasting for two weeks, during July and August. The schemes take place in the Manchester office and placement students receive £133 per week.
Apply by 31 March to Ekaterina Clark, Graduate Recruitment Assistant, at the above address.

PANNONE LLP SOLICITORS: 123 Deansgate, Manchester M3 2BU (☎0161-909 3000; fax 0161-909 4444; e-mail julia.jessop@pannone.co.uk; www.pannone.com). A high-profile full service firm, the best law firm to work for in the UK, according to the Sunday Times 2005 survey.
Pannone & Partners offers **60 Vacation Traineeships** in Manchester for students planning a legal career, with approximately 20 taking place at Easter and 40 over the summer vacation. Students are given a real experience of the kind of work that trainee solicitors do, drafting correspondence or documents, researching, and spending time with trainees, fee-earners and partners. Placements last for one week and are aimed at those seeking a training contract in 2009, mainly second year law and third-year non-law undergraduates. Non UK applicants will be considered as long as they are planning a career as a solicitor in Manchester. No accommodation is available.
Applications online on above website. For enquiries e-mail Julia Jessop. The closing date is 26 January 2007 for Easter placements and 27 April 2007 for summer placements. Full graduate recruitment information is available at the above website.

THE NORTH EAST

This section covers work in the following counties: Northumberland, Tyne and Wear, Durham, Cleveland, and the North, West, South and East Ridings of Yorkshire. See map at the start of the chapter for these counties' locations.

Business and Industry

ANGEL HUMAN RESOURCES plc: (☎01325-481026, Darlington; ☎01423-531200, Harrogate; ☎0191-565 4466, Sunderland). Established in 1965. It adheres strictly to the statutory codes of practice and specialises in commercial, healthcare, hospitality, and industrial appointments.
Office Workers. Pay may vary from £6.00-£11 per hour dependant on experience and qualifications.
Apply by telephoning our offices on the above numbers.

GOLD CREST HOLIDAYS LTD: Holiday House, Valley Drive, Ilkley, West Yorkshire LS29 8PB (☎0870-700 0007; fax 01943-600006; e-mail malcolm@gold-crest.com; www.gold-crest.com).
Telesales/Reservations/Booking/Administration Clerks (1 or 2). Wages of £5.60 per hour; to work five 7½ hour days per week, with weekend working on a rota basis. Period of work by arrangement between June and October. Must be aged over 17 with a good telephone manner and keyboard skills.

Applications to Malcolm Grant, Operations Manager, at the above address.

Children

CHERUB NURSERIES & PRE-SCHOOLS LTD: Cherub Childcare Centre, Lindsey Place, Arcon Drive, Anlaby Road, Hull HU4 6AJ (☎01482-509598; fax 01482-576650). A well-established company of 3 children's day nurseries in the Hull Area that has been in practice for more than 25 years.

Nursery Nurses (2), Nursery Assistants (2). To care for children 6 weeks to 5 years old, providing a high standard of care; a clean and hygienic nursery with safety is always the main priority. Basic wages. To work a maximum of 40 hours per week. Minimum period of work of 4 weeks. Positions are available from June to September. Should be 18 and over and NNEB B-tec qualified. Foreign applicants welcome. No accommodation available.

Applications should be made to Paula Walton at the above address. Interview necessary.

Holiday Centres and Amusements

FARSYDE STUD & RIDING CENTRE: Robin Hood's Bay, Whitby, North Yorkshire YO22 4UG (☎01947-880249; fax 01947-880877; e-mail farsydestud@ talk21.com). A family-run stud farm with five holiday cottages. The centre is set in 70 acres of grassland in the North Yorkshire Moors National Park, and a short walk from the beach and village.

General Assistant for support duties. £4 per hour for minimum of 20 hours per week. Minimum period of work 6 weeks between May/June and September/October. Accommodation in house or cottage for £60 per week. Applicants must be competent riders, willing, self-motivated, cheerful, non-smokers, adaptable, able to relate well to children and adults, and also enjoy country life. Overseas applicants eligible to work in the UK and with basic English welcome.

Applications to Mrs A. Green, Owner/Manager, Farsyde Stud & Riding Centre.

RIPLEY CARAVAN PARK: Ripley, Harrogate, North Yorkshire HG3 3AU (☎01423-770050;e-mail info@ripleycaravanpark.com; www.ripleycaravanpark. com). Family-run, country caravan park.

Assistant Wardens (2) for general duties, including gardening, and cleaning shower block and swimming pool. Wages specified on application. Period of work Easter to end of October. Positions suitable for a mature couple. Accommodation not provided, but can bring own tent/caravan.

Applications from early in the year to Mr P. House, at the above address. Applicants must be able to attend an interview.

WENSLEYDALE CREAMERY VISITOR CENTRE: Gayle Lane, Hawes, North Yorkshire DL8 3RN (☎01969-667664; fax 01969-667638; e-mail creamery@ wensleydale.co.uk; www.wensleydale.co.uk/centre).

Visitor Centre Staff (up to 6) to work in the five departments of the Visitor Centre. **Dairy Staff** to work in the cheese production factory.

Wages from £5.00 per hour depending on age. To work 40 hours per week, five days a week. Staff needed from May to November. Minimum age 18. Accommodation is available.

Apply to Janet Mudd, Catering Manager.

Hotels and Catering

THE BLUE BELL HOTEL: Market Square, Belford, Northumberland NE70 7NE (☎01668-213543; fax 01668-213787; www.bluebellhotel.com). A privately-run hotel with a large number of young staff in its 3-star hotel in Northumberland.
Receptionists (2) for telephone/reception duties. Wages by arrangement with variable tips. To work from 7.30am to 7.30pm, 5 days per week. Should ideally be aged 21.
Waiting Staff (2). Wages by arrangement plus good tips. To work from 7.30am to 3pm or 6.30pm to 11pm. Minimum age 18.
Accommodation provided. Period of work from April to November. Applicants for either position need commitment and dedication.
Applications to Bill Dean, Manager, at the above address.

THE FAMOUS SCHOONER HOTEL: Northumberland Street, Alnmouth, Northumberland NE66 2RS (☎01665-830216; fax 01665-830287). The Famous Schooner Hotel, a listed 17th Century Coach Inn is 100 yards from the beach and a golf course.
General Assistants. Wages negotiable. There is a high tipping potential. To work 40 to 45 hours per week. Live-in accommodation available. Minimum work period 4 weeks between mid-June and mid-September. Overseas applicants with good English welcome.
Applications a.s.a.p. to the Manager, the Schooner Hotel.

GEORGE WASHINGTON HOTEL: Stone Cellar Road, High Usworth, Washington, Tyne and Wear NE37 1PH (☎0191-402 9988; fax 0191-415 1166). The hotel has 103 bedrooms, a restaurant and conference facilities for up to 200, a leisure club and an 18 hole golf course.
Restaurant Waiting Staff, Bar Staff. Wages at national minimum rate. To work hours as required. Staff needed from July to December. Minimum age 16 (restaurant) 18 (bar). Previous experience required. No accommodation available.
Applications from June to the above address. Applicants must be available for interview.

LADY ANNE MIDDLETON'S HOTEL: Skeldergate, York (☎01904-611570; fax 01904-613043; e-mail bookings@ladyannes.co.uk; www.ladyannes.co.uk). Independent 52-bedroom hotel located in the city centre, with own health and fitness club, conference and event rooms. Primarily catering for the leisure and conference trade.
Waiting Staff (2), Chamberpersons (2). Pay rate meets the national minimum wage and above depending on experience. To work 39 hours per week. Minimum period of work 3 months at any time of year. Accommodation is *not* available. Minimum age 21. Overseas applicants welcome.
Applications at any time to Andy Clark at the above address. All applicants should be able to supply a current CV.

LUCY LOCKETTS & VANESSA BANCROFT AGENCY: 400 Beacon Road, Wibsey, Bradford, West Yorkshire BD6 3DJ (tel/fax 01274-402822; e-mail lucylocketts@blueyonder.co.uk; www.lucylocketts.com). In business since 1984.
Hotel Staff placed throughout the UK. Wages from £140 per week. Live-in positions available from April to November. Shorter stays sometimes possible.
Applications to Lucy Holland, Owner, at the above address by May.

MACDONALD LINDEN HALL GOLF & COUNTRY CLUB: Longhorsley, Morpeth, Northumberland NE65 8XF (☎01670-500000; fax 01670-500001; www. macdonaldhotels.co.uk/lindenhall).
Restaurant and Bar Staff/Silver Service Staff required for summer or weekend work. Staff will carry out general food and beverage service in two restaurants, bars and banqueting suites. Wages at national minimum rate. Hours of work are flexible, up to 8 hours per shift, days and evenings. Candidates should be between 18-30 years old, have basic food and beverage experience and a smart, clean appearance. Must have own transport. Accommodation sometimes available at a cost of £40 per week.
Applications should be made to the HR department at the above address.

NEWCASTLE HOLIDAY INN: Great North Road, Seaton Burn, Newcastle-upon-Tyne NE13 6BP (☎0870-787 3291; fax 0191-236 8091; www.newcastle.holiday-inn. com). The hotel caters for families, leisure and conference/business clients. Situated in pleasant surroundings on the outskirts of Newcastle, just off the A1/A19.
Casual Room Attendants to work approximately 7 to 21 hours a week.
Casual Banqueting, Restaurant and Bar Staff to work approximately 5 to 15 hours a week.
Wages by arrangement. Staff must be flexible and prepared to work shifts and late nights. Minimum period of work 2 months between June and September. No accommodation is available. Applicants must be over 16 (over 18 for Bar Staff positions) and have a good general education. Overseas applicants considered.
Applications from May to Human Resources Manager. Interview required.

ST LEONARD'S FARM PARK: Chapel Lane, Esholt, Bradford BD17 7RB (tel/fax 01274-598795; e-mail farmerjames1@aol.com; www.stleonardsfarm.com). A family farm open to the public.
Tea Room Waitresses/Waiters (2). Food handling/preparation an advantage but training is given.
General Farm Workers (2). Experience of working with animals is essential.
Shop Assistants (2). Experience not required as training is given.
For all positions wages are dependent on age and experience; to work weekends and school holidays. Maximum of 6 hours work per day, 3 days per week. Staff required from April to September. Overseas applicants are welcome. No accommodation available.
Applications should be sent to Denise Wainhouse at the above address from March onwards.

YORK MARRIOT: Tadcaster Road, York YO24 1QQ (☎01904-701000; fax 01904-702308; e-mail timothy.frear@marriotthotels.com; www.marriott.co.uk). An IIP accredited hotel that has won awards for 5 Star employment practices. Set in idyllic surroundings, overlooking the racecourse with friendly and cheerful staff.
Seasonal Staff required for this high calibre York hotel. The culture at the hotel is people focused. The hotels believe that when they look after their employees, they will look after their customers. They demonstrate this through their extensive benefits package that is worth approximately £2000 per employee. Benefits include: complimentary B&B stays in other Marriott UK based hotels; International discount card for use in Marriott hotels overseas for both you and your friend and family; discounts on car and health insurance; car hire; holidays and an Associate incentive scheme.
Employees are offered 40 hours of training and development per annum to support their career aspirations, be it sponsorship for a college course or completion of an NVQ. Staff are also supplied with a free uniform and access to the staff canteen.

For more *information* about employment opportunities at the York Marriott, contact the Human Resources Department on 01904 770628.

Medical

SURECARE (WEST YORKSHIRE): Staincliffe House, Halifax Road, Staincliffe, Batley WF17 7RB (☎01924- 404570; fax 01924-410978; e-mail enquiries@ surecarewy.com; www.surecarewy.com). An equal opportunities employer with Investors in People status, specialising in homecare and healthcare services for all sectors of the community.
Community Support Workers (5), to support vulnerable clients of all ages and ethnic backgrounds in their own homes or in the community. Clients may have physical or learning disabilities. Good work experience opportunities for nursing, community services or social work students. Wages £6.00 to £10.00 an hour. Staff required from May until October; minimum period of work is 10 weeks. Work available weekdays and weekends including evenings and nights. Accommodation is not available.
   Applicants must be over 18, with own transport and relevant experience. A CRB check at enhanced level will be required.
   Apply to Teresa Mcmahon, the Personnel Officer for an application form at the above address or via email.

Outdoor

ALL OCCASIONS MARQUEE HIRE: Unit 20 Temple Street Industrial Estate, Beverley Road, Hull HU5 1AD (☎0871-250 2505; fax 01482-348970; e-mail sales@ marquees4alloccasions.co.uk; www.marquees4alloccasions.com). A family-run business in the event industry providing high quality surroundings for all occasions.
Assistants (4). Wages at national minimum rate. To work 7am to 7pm for a minimum of 40 hours a week from May until September or October. Must be physically fit; training will be provided. Fluent English is essential. No accommodation is provided.
   Apply by contacting Mr C. Harrison at the above address. An informal interview will be required.

BAMFORD BROS: Law Farm, Law Lane, Southowram, Halifax, West Yorkshire HX3 9UG (☎01422-362788; fax 01422-362871; e-mail magsbamford@hotmail. com).
Drivers Mates (2) to work 7am-5pm from Monday-Friday plus overtime at weekends. Possibility of driver's job if applicants hold a driving licence.
Farm Trail Maintenance Assistant to see to the welfare and care of animals and maintain and build up a farm trail attached to the farm shop. To work 4-6 hours daily, with hours to suit.
   Wages at national minimum wage rates. Periods of work by arrangement around the year.
   Applications to Margaret Bamford, Manager, at the above address.

COOPERS MARQUEES LTD: Bolton Lane, Wilberfoss, York YO41 5NX (☎01759-380190; fax 01759-380381; e-mail office@coopersmarquees.fsnet.co.uk; www.marqueesuk.co.uk).
Marquee Erectors (5) needed May-September. Wages and period of work by arrangement. Minimum age 16.
   Applications to Jonathan Cooper, Managing Director, at the above address.

JAMES DABBS & CO MARQUEE HIRE: Bretfield Court, Savile Town, Dewsbury WF12 9BB (☎01924-459550; fax 01924-453829; e-mail jim@james-dabbs-marquees.co.uk; www.james-dabbs-marquees.co.uk).
Marquee Erectors (4). Wages £6.00 per hour. To work 6 or 7 days, 60 hours a week. No experience is necessary; applicants need only to be hard-working.
Apply to Jim at the above address, at any time.

FLORIDA MARQUEES: The Old Forge, Bradbury Street, Sheffield, South Yorkshire S8 9QQ (☎01142-589626; e-mail admin@marqueehiresales.com; www.marqueehiresales.com). Private company erecting marquees around the UK.
Marquee Erectors (10). National minimum wage. To work 60 hours per week. Minimum period of work 1 month. Positions are available from May to September. Foreign applicants with work permits welcome to apply; fluent English is not essential. No previous experience necessary. No accommodation available.
Applications should be made from March onwards to the Senior Manager at the above address.

HOWARD CROSS MARQUEE HIRE: Quarryhouse Farm, Marwood, Barnard Castle, County Durham DL12 9QL (☎01833-650351; fax 01833-650127).
Driver to drive a 7½ ton lorry; duties include driving, loading and unloading the lorry and erecting/dismantling marquees. Wages of £8 per hour; at least 50 hours work a week guaranteed with Saturdays off. Space available for tent, caravan or motorhome or accommodation can be arranged. Period of work from June to September. Applicants must be physically fit and able to drive a 7½ ton lorry.
Applications to Howard Cross, Proprietor, at the above address.

LEITH UK LTD: Pier Road, Berwick upon Tweed, Northumberland TD15 1JB (☎01289-307264; fax 01289-330517; e-mail enquiries@leith-uk.co.uk; www.leith-uk.co.uk).
Marquee Erectors (10). Good rates of pay for unlimited hours. Applicants must be over 18; driving licence an advantage.
Applications to the above address.

MILL NURSERIES LTD: Ottringham Road, Keyingham, Hull, East Ridings of Yorkshire (☎01964-623664; fax 01964-622986).
Glasshouse Tomato Pickers (20). Agriculturally based work, picking glasshouse grown tomatoes. Agricultural Wages Order pay rates. To work 40 to 50 hours per week, Mondays to Saturdays. Minimum period of work is 4 months between March and November, and full-time permanent positions available to suitable candidates. Accommodation provided for £35 per week. No previous experience necessary.
Applications should be made from the beginning of February to Mr de Lang at the above address. No interview required. Foreign applicants with appropriate visa welcome.

NORTHERN MARQUEES: Unit 5, Steps Lane, Magdale, Honley, Holmfirth HD9 6RA (☎01484-664958; fax 01484-666307).
Marquee Erectors (3) needed from June to September. Wages on application. Minimum age 18.
Contact Andrew Tinker, Owner, at the above address.

E. OLDROYD AND SONS LTD: Hopefield Farm, Leadwell Lane, Rothwell, Leeds, Yorkshire LS26 0ST (☎0113-282 2245; fax 0113-282 8775; e-mail eoldroyd@

btconnect.com). Five generations of experience with fruit and vegetables: Britain's leading rhubarb producer – busy both in the winter and summer. Farms are close to Leeds city centre's excellent shopping and nightlife and only 5 minutes from the supermarket. E-mail access available.

Strawberry Harvesters (20). Piecework rates. Minimum period of work 1 month.
Rhubarb and Vegetable Harvesters (10). Piecework rates or hourly agricultural wage rates where applicable. To work full or part time, up to 8 hours a day for up to three months. Positions available from January to March and May to September. Minimum age 17. Full training given. Approved accommodation available. Foreign applicants welcome.

Early applications recommended to avoid disappointment. Write, enclosing a CV with references, to Mrs J. Oldroyd Hulme at the above address. Interview possibly required.

THE POD PEOPLE LTD: 2 Church Hall, Luddenden, Halifax, West Yorkshire HX2 6PZ (☎079-0308 1477; fax 01422-882800; e-mail info@thepodpeople.co.uk; www. thepodpeople.co.uk).
Marquee Labourers (2). Wages of £8 per hour; to work 10 hour days with no overtime. Required to work from June to September. Must be fit, healthy and strong.
Applications to D. Compston, Director, at the above address.

Sport

MICHAEL DODS: Denton Hall, Piercebridge, Darlington, County Durham DL2 3TY (☎01325-374270; fax 01325-374020; e-mail info@michaeldodsracing.co.uk; www.michaeldodsracing.co.uk). Racehorse trainer.
Grooms (2) for part-time general work with horses. Wages at national minimum rate, with the possibility of free board and accommodation. To work 6 days a week from August to October. Minimum period of work 1 month. Must have experience of horses. Overseas applicants welcome and fluent English is not essential. Interview necessary.
Applications to M. Dods from June.

KILNSEY PARK AND TROUT FARM: Kilnsey, Near Skipton, North Yorkshire BD23 5PS (☎01756-752150 (days) and 01756-752320 (evenings); fax 01756-752224; e-mail info@kilnseypark.co.uk; www.kilnseypark.co.uk).
General Assistant to work in the fish farm, with tourist visitors, in the children's fishery etc. To work a five day week from 9am to 5.30pm or later. Must like the public, including children, be able to handle fish, have a friendly attitude and be happy to muck in.
Pony Trekking Leader to work a 5 to 6 day week in July and August. Should be a good experienced rider able to cope with and organise school groups.
Wages for above positions depend on age and experience; no tips. Accommodation available free of charge.
Applications to the above address.

THE OUTDOOR TRUST: Windy Gyle, Belford, Northumberland NE70 7QE (tel/fax 01668-213289; e-mail trust@outdoor.demon.co.uk; www.outdoortrust. co.uk). Registered charity providing outdoor activities and development courses for a wide range of groups and individuals of all ages and abilities. Based in North Northumberland and Scotland.
Senior Training Instructors (5). Remuneration dependent on one or more of the

following NGB awards: BCU, RYA, MLTB. Must hold a full clean driving licence with DI entitlement and be willing to take responsibility for at least one area of the operation. **Trainee and Voluntary Instructors (10).** Proficiency in at least one of the traditional outdoor activities required and an enthusiasm for helping with a variety of additional duties associated with residential outdoor centres. Trainees/volunteers will receive full board and training with ample opportunities to develop skills and gain NGB awards. Long hours, 6 days per week. Work is demanding but very rewarding. Minimum period of work 2 months but longer term preferable. Discount on outdoor equipment possible.
Applications to recruiting at the above address.

Voluntary Work

Archaeology

ARBEIA ROMAN FORT: Tyne & Wear Museums Service, Baring Street, South Shields, Tyne & Wear NE33 2BB (☎0191-454 4093; fax 0191-427 6862; e-mail liz. elliott@twmuseums.org.uk).
Part of the Tyne and Wear Museums service and within easy reach of Newcastle by Metro. South Shields has good parks and beaches and is an ideal base from which to visit nearby cities or countryside.
Volunteers (5 per week) to excavate the site, record and process finds, draw the site and take photographs. To work from 8.45am-4.45pm, Monday-Friday. Needed from June to 30 September. Volunteers are responsible for their own travel, board and other costs. Min age 16; disabled people may find access to the site difficult.
Applications to Elizabeth Elliott, Office Manager, at the above address.

BAMBURGH RESEARCH PROJECT: Bamburgh Castle, Bamburgh, Northumberland (☎01904-330727; e-mail paulgething@bamburghresearchproject. co.uk; www.bamburghresearchproject.co.uk).
A project centred on Bamburgh Castle dedicated to using the most modern field techniques to provide training for both students and volunteers. The castle is located 50 miles north of Newcastle on the coast.
Volunteers (35 per week) are required from the end of June to the end of August for excavation, training, field walking, test pitting and media. There are many sites being excavated, including an early medieval cemetery within the castle and a medieval port. There is also a comprehensive survey programme and a media department dedicated to filming the archaeological process. The sites excavated range in period from medieval to modern.
Volunteers of all ages and levels of experience are welcome. Accommodation is provided at a fully equipped campsite but volunteers must bring their own camping equipment. The nearest railway station is Berwick on Tweed and there is a regular bus service to Bamburgh, or pick up can be provided. Youth or disabled volunteers may be picked up in Newcastle if arranged in advance. The cost of approx. £120 per week which includes tuition, travel to and from the site, food and space for camping.
Applications should be sent to the above address as soon as possible.

Heritage
THE CLEVELAND IRONSTONE MINING MUSEUM: Deepdale, Skinningrove, Saltburn, Cleveland TS13 4AP (☎01287-642877; fax 01287-642970; e-mail visits@

ironstonemuseum.co.uk; www.ironstonemuseum.co.uk).
The Cleveland Ironstone Mining Museum preserves and interprets the ironstone mining heritage of Cleveland and North Yorkshire. This is a unique, award-winning, small, independent museum run by volunteers on a day-to-day basis.
Museum Guides (6+), Visitor Receptionists (2+), Collection Care (2+). Expenses only are paid; no accommodation provided. Museum is open Mondays to Saturdays. Minimum period of work is four hours per week. Positions are available from May to October. Applicants should be interested in local history and heritage. Minimum age 16.
   Applications can be made all year round to the Museum Manager at the above address. Interview preferred.

LOSANG DRAGPA BUDDHIST CENTRE: Dobroyd Castle, Pexwood Road, Todmorden, West Yorkshire OL14 7JJ (☎01706-812247 ext.201; fax 01706-818901; e-mail info@losangdragpa.com; www.losangdragpa.com).
Losang Dragpa Centre is a Buddhist College and Meditation Centre based at Dobroyd Castle in the heart of the Pennines. The Centre is a registered charity dedicated to serving the community by providing a place of inner peace for everyone regardless of spiritual inclination.
Volunteers are welcome to join the resident community in various development projects, which include restoring Dobroyd Castle to its former glory. The working week consists of 35 hours from Monday to Friday and the cost is £40, which includes food, accommodation and the opportunity to attend Buddhist teachings and meditation sessions. Working visitors may stay for 1 week or 2 weeks (for international volunteers) during specific periods throughout the year.
Applicants must be at least 18 and able to speak a basic level of English. Interest in Buddhism is recommended. They particularly need help from those with specialised skills such as building, marketing, fundraising, decorating and landscaping. However, skills are not essential as work can be found for any willing hands.
   For more information or to *apply*, look at their website or contact reception at the above address.

Social and Community Schemes

MADHYAMAKA BUDDHIST CENTRE: Kilnwick Percy Hall, Kilnwick Percy, York YO42 1UF (☎01759-304832; fax 01759-305962; e-mail info@madhyamaka. org; www.madhyamaka.org).
A large residential Buddhist college situated in a beautiful 40-acre historic estate. The centre offers a range of meditation classes and retreats suitable for all.
Volunteers for a variety of jobs including gardening, cleaning, painting, building and making repairs. Three vegetarian meals a day and dormitory accommodation are provided in return for work; free access is granted to a range of Buddhist meditation classes for those who are interested.
   Volunteers may stay for periods of up to one week every three months; overseas applicants may stay for up to two weeks. Volunteers are expected to work for 35 hours a week, or 5 hours per day if staying for a shorter period. No particular qualifications or experience are required but applicants aged over 18 are preferred. Volunteers are asked to bring their own sleeping bag and work clothes.
   Application forms can be obtained from the above address.

Vacation Traineeships & Internships

Accountancy and Insurance

COULSONS: P.O. Box 17, 2 Belgrave Crescent, Scarborough, North Yorkshire YO11 1UD (☎01723-364141; fax 01723-376010; e-mail postmaster@coulsons. co.uk; www.coulsons.co.uk).

Coulsons, a firm of chartered accountants, occasionally takes on **Trainees** to work in its Scarborough office, mainly during the summer vacation. Candidates would normally be UK undergraduates intending to pursue chartered accountancy as a career. Vacation work would be offered only to students giving an undertaking to take up a training contract with Coulsons on the completion of their academic studies. Local candidates are at an advantage as accommodation is difficult to find.

For *further details* contact Mr P. B. Hodgson, Student Training Officer in April, at the above address. Please note that only those short-listed will be contacted.

Conservation and the Environment

HAREWOOD BIRD GARDEN: Harewood House, Harewood, Leeds LS17 9LQ (☎0113-2813723; fax 0113-2181034; e-mail birdgdn@harewood.org; www. harewood.org).

Harewood is a general collection of 400 birds from 105 species.

One or two **Trainees** are usually taken on by the bird garden for work experience programmes, as well as one to three university students working on projects related to zoology. Trainees must pay for their own expenses including accommodation.

For further *details*, contact Dan Stevens, Research Officer at the above address.

KIRKLEATHAM OWL CENTRE: Kirkleatham Village, Redcar TS10 5NW (☎01642-480512; fax 01642-480512; e-mail reallybigowls@hotmail.co.uk; www. jillsowls.co.uk).

The Centre is small and family-run with a varying owl population from around the world.

Volunteers are taken in all year round for work experience. There is no accommodation available.

For further *details*, contact the above address.

Science, Construction and Engineering

RELIANCE GEAR COMPANY LTD: Rowley Mills, Lepton, Huddersfield HD8 0LE (☎01484-601000; fax 01484-601001).

Reliance Gear is a design and manufacturing company which specialises in the production of precision electro-mechanical assemblies for use in servo-mechanisms and control applications. The company serves clients in the defence, aerospace, robotic and medical engineering industries.

The company usually offers **Work Experience** over the summer to two or three students who are about to enter their final year of study. Candidates should be motivated and keen to explore the engineering sector as a potential career field. Training is offered through general experience gained in a number of the company's departments, including business sales, marketing, engineering, design, production control and quality control.

Wages are commensurate with the candidate's age, experience, qualifications and the job offered. Overseas applicants will be considered. *Applications*, in early January and February, to A.D. Durie, Design Manager, at the above address.

TEXTRON POWER TRANSMISSION: Park Gear Works, Lockwood, Huddersfield, West Yorkshire HD4 5DD (☎01484-465500; fax 01484-465512; e-mail sbuczek@davidbrown.textron.com; www.textronPT.com). As a worldwide resource for high quality technology solutions, Textron serves a comprehensive range of industries including utility, nuclear, oil, gas, water, petrochemical, mining, marine, defence, construction, paper, metals and food processing applications.

Textron Fluid and Power specialises in the design and manufacture of industrial pumps, gears and gearboxes. They have built their business into what it is today by combining the collective strengths and expertise of some of the most highly respected gear and pump manufacturing specialists in the world. Familiar brand names include: Bell Helicopter; Cessna Aircraft, E-Z-Go and Greenlee, among others. It has occasional **Summer Vacancies** for students, who will be employed in such areas as Manufacturing Engineering, Production Control, Manufacturing and General Site Services. Applicants should be studying Mechanical Engineering and have an interest in engineering manufacturing processes and/or gearing. Suitably qualified overseas applicants will be considered. The salary is discussed at interview and no assistance with accommodation is given.

Applications should be made to Steve Buczek, HR Manager UK at the above address.

Scotland

Prospects for Work.
The tourist industry in Scotland remains buoyant, particularly in the Highlands, Perthshire and the Islands, and has received huge boosts during the hot spells of recent summers. Since many hotels are in isolated areas, a considerable number of staff have to be recruited from outside. However, you will almost certainly be expected to work for the entire season, and should have the temperament to suit living in a remote place. The Jobcentre Plus in Fort William is a good source for this type of work, as are the Jobcentre Plus offices in Perth and Blairgowrie. The majority of hotels in rural Perthshire offer live-in accommodation, and frequently employ students over the summer. Due to the high level of local unemployment in less remote parts the only vacancies that remain are usually for skilled or experienced staff. While in many areas employers routinely offer accommodation, Inverness is an exception and few live-in jobs are available there.

Fruit picking jobs are particularly abundant in Perth and Tayside. The season usually lasts from the end of June until mid-September. In addition to the vacancies listed in this chapter, fruit-picking jobs are also advertised in the Jobcentre Plus in Blairgowrie, but not in the Jobcentre Plus in Perth; however, this Jobcentre Plus does list other vacancies.

Edinburgh attracts over a million tourists each year, particularly during the Festival in August. As a result there is a wide range of jobs available, especially in hotels. The success and income of the festival is growing year on year and so the jobs it generates look set to increase. With the introduction of the Scottish Parliament the need for hotel and catering staff in Edinburgh has increased even further. If you speak a foreign language you could land yourself a job as a guide, and the District Council employs extra assistants and experienced gardeners to maintain the city gardens and flowers. There are always plenty of vacancies displayed in the Edinburgh Jobcentre Plus. Note that accommodation is rarely provided with a job in Edinburgh, and can be difficult to find.

In the winter season, those seeking employment could try the skiing resorts of Aviemore, Aonach Mor, Glenshee and Glencoe Ski Centre. All Jobcentre vacancies can be accessed from both www.jobcentreplus.gov.uk and from any local Jobcentre. A self-service vacancy system is also now available in the Jobcentres; computers and phones are available in every office for this purpose. Therefore, it is no longer necessary to go to certain Jobcentres for certain vacancies depending on the geographical area. It's important to note that since the new Eastern European countries joined the EU in May 2004, competition for jobs in the tourism industry is high, particularly those offering live-in accommodation.

Business and Industry

ABC RECRUITMENT: 3-5 Anderson Chambers, 34 Great King Street, Dumfries DG1 1BD (☎01387-270718; fax 01387-266383; e-mail enquiries@abcrecruitment. net; www.abcrecruitment.net). Specialists in temporary and contract recruitment in hospitality and catering, administration/clerical, customer service/retail, sales.
Vacancies year round in the UK, mainly in South West Scotland and Cumbria. Most clients look for candidates with some previous experience.
Contact Clive Rumbold, the Owner, for further information.

THE EDINBURGH SMOKED SALMON CO. LTD: 1 Strathview, Dingwall Business Park, Dingwall, Ross-shire IV15 9XD (☎01349-860632; fax 01349-860626). Situated in the picturesque town of Dingwall, 12 miles from Inverness, Edinburgh Smoked Salmon processes salmon and rainbow trout for distribution throughout the UK and for export to America, Europe and Japan.
Process Workers (80) required throughout the summer. Attractive rates of pay, plus attendance and production bonuses. Flexible hours to suit. No qualifications or experience necessary as training will be given.
Applications to the Personnel Officer at the above address.

Children

EAC ACTIVITY CAMPS LTD: 59 George Street, Edinburgh EH2 2LQ (☎0131-477 7570; fax 0131-477 7571; e-mail sdonnelly@eac4english.com; www.activitycamps. com).
Activity Staff (100). Salaries dependant on position and experience. Hours of work from 42 per week according to each centre. Positions available from the end of June to the end of August. All staff should have experience of working with children in some capacity and have experience in and/or enthusiasm for a sporting or artistic field. RLSS and/or sports coaching qualifications a distinct advantage. RLSS very useful.
Applications from February to Susan Donnelly, HR and Recruitment Manager at the above address.

PGL TRAVEL LTD: Alton Court, Penyard Lane, Ross-on-Wye, Herefordshire HR9 5GL (☎0870-401 4411; e-mail recruitment@pgl.co.uk; www.pgl.co.uk/recruitment). PGL recruit around 2,000 staff each year to assist with the running of their children's activity centres throughout the UK, including Devon, the Isle of Wight, Lincolnshire, the south coast, Surrey, Shropshire, Perthshire, and Wales. Europe's largest provider of adventure holidays for children has offered outstanding training and work opportunities to seasonal staff for almost 50 years. PGL jobs provide a break from the 9-5 routine. If you are enthusiastic, energetic and looking for real experience and responsibility in a stimulating environment, PGL could have the job for you.

Activity Instructors in canoeing, sailing, windsurfing, fencing, archery, motorsports, pony trekking, and more. Qualifications not essential for all positions as full training will be provided. Minimum age 18.

Group Leaders also needed to take responsibility for groups of children, helping then to get the most out of their holiday. Previous experience of working with children is an advantage. Minimum age 18.

Support Staff to assist the catering, domestic and maintenance teams.

From £70-£100 per week plus free B & L. Positions available from February-November, for the full season, as little as 8 weeks, or any period in between, although there are very few summer-only vacancies.

Applications can be made online, downloaded from the website, or call for an information pack.

Holiday Centres and Amusements

ARCHAEOLINK PREHISTORY PARK: Oyne, Insch, Aberdeenshire AB52 6QP (☎01464-851500; fax 01464-851544; e-mail info@archaeolink.co.uk; www. archaeolink.co.uk). Archaeolink was started in 1997 to introduce the public to Aberdeenshire's rich archaeological heritage. It operates reconstructions including stone-age camps, a Roman Marching camp and an iron age farm based on archaeological evidence from northeast Scotland.

Guides to interpret reconstructions to the public. Wages to be negotiated. To work approximately 20 hours per week all year. Applicants should be good communicators and be able to demonstrate an interest in history. Some experience of archaeology would be useful. Accommodation available in local B & B.

Applications to the above address as soon as possible.

ARDMAIR POINT HOLIDAY CENTRE: Ardmair Point, Ullapool, Ross-shire (☎01854-612054; fax 01854-612757; e-mail pete@ardmair.com; www.ardmair. com). Situated in a scenic area 3 miles north of the fishing village of Ullapool on a beach headland facing the Summer Isles.

Caravan Site Assistants (1). Duties include reception/shop work, cleaning and grass-cutting. A large proportion of the work is outside and involves some driving. Wages £5.50+ per hour.

To work 40 hours/6 days per week, with shifts covering 8am-8pm. Accommodation available. Minimum age 18 years. All jobs best suited to people interested in water sports and/or outdoor pursuits. Overseas applicants with fluent English welcome.

For further details and an *application* form send s.a.e. to the above address.

WILLIAM GRANT & SONS: The Glenfiddich Distillery, Dufftown, Banffshire AB55 4DH (☎01340-820373; fax 01340-822083; e-mail david.mair@wgrant.com). Staff conduct tours of Glenfiddich Distillery in an educational but informal way. The

distillery is fully operational. The work may particularly suit people interested in Scottish culture or keen on improving their foreign language skills.
Tour Guides to conduct members of the public on tours of the distillery. £200 for 32½ hours per five-day week. Limited accommodation available on site but local B & B costs approximately £60-£70 per week including evening meal. Self-catering accommodation can usually be found at £50-£60 per week. Minimum age 18 years. Minimum period of work end of June to end of August. Must be fluent in at least one foreign European language.

Experience with the general public very desirable but not essential. Job requires a bright, cheery and very outgoing personality. Only applicants with fluent English considered. All applicants must be able to attend an interview at the distillery. Interviews are held before or during the Easter Vacation period.

Applications between January and March to Mr D.C. Mair at the above address in writing or by e-mail.

LADY MACPHERSON: 27 Archery Close, London W2 2BE (tel/fax 020-7262 8487). Scottish Highland home at 1,000 ft altitude, on the river Spey. Swimming, tennis, riding and fishing possible.
Holiday Helpers required for some housework and general help outside. Pay by agreement: some travel costs reimbursed. Ample time for touring, e.g. Loch Ness, BalmoraL, the Isle of Skye etc. Weather rarely warm. Two character references required.

Applications to the above address.

Hotels and Catering

ATHOLL ARMS HOTEL: Bridgehead, Dunkeld, Perthshire PH8 0AQ (☎01350-727219; fax 01350-727991; e-mail enquiries@athollarmshotel.com; www.athollarmshotel.fsnet.co.uk). A 17-bedroom hotel catering mainly for fishing parties and tourists, overlooking the River Tay in a conservation village.
Kitchen Porter. No experience required.
Staff (3). Waiting, bar and reception.

Wages £5.35 per hour. Accommodation available at a price to be arranged. Required to work 5 days per week. Period of work April to October. Minimum period of work 6 months. Minimum age 21. Applications from foreign nationals permitted to work in the UK who speak English to a conversational level welcomed.

Applications from January to Mr Cameron at the above address. Interview necessary.

AVIEMORE HIGHLAND RESORT: Aviemore, Inverness-shire PH22 1PN (☎01479-810771; fax 01479-811576; e-mail jobs@aviemorehighlandresort.com; www.aviemorehighlandresort.com). The Macdonald Aviemore Highland Resort is located in the heart of the Cairngorms National Park. The resort consists of 4 hotels plus luxury self-contained woodland lodges, leisure and beauty arena and a large conference facility, which encompasses both retail and food court thus offering boundless opportunities to enjoy the best of Highland hospitality.

If you are motivated and focused, have a desire to succeed, are committed to excellence, and wish to become part of a team, the resort would like to hear from you.

To *apply* visit the website, download and complete the application form and e-mail to jobs@aviemorehighlandresort.com or post to Aviemore Highland Resort, Central Admin Building, Aviemore PH22 1PN, or call the recruitment hotline on ☎01479-815256.

THE BALMORAL HOTEL: 1 Princes Street, Edinburgh EH2 2EQ (☎0131-622 8891; fax 0131-558 1766; e-mail hr@thebalmoralhotel.com; www.thebalmoralhotel. com). An elegant, 5-star hotel in the centre of Edinburgh. Part of the Rocco Forte Hotel group, with 188 bedrooms, Michelin star restaurant, brasserie, Palm Court Bar and Nb's Bar, as well as extensive Conference and Banqueting facilities.
Food, Beverage and Housekeeping staff required for various casual and full-time positions. National minimum wage will be paid. Working 5 days out of 7. Candidates must be flexible and motivated and enjoy delivering the best.
Applications or CVs can be submitted from April to the HR Department at the above address.

THE BRIDGE INN: 27 Baird Road, Ratho, Edinburgh EH28 8RA (☎0131-333 1320; fax 0131-333 3480; e-mail info@bridgeinn.com; www.thebridgeinn.com).
Waiting Staff (3) required to work in restaurant and on boats.
Kitchen Assistants (4) required to help prepare food and with general cleaning.
Wages of £5.35 per hour plus tips. No accommodation provided. Needed from May. Own transport necessary (Inn is 10 miles from Edinburgh) and must be 18 or over.
Applications to Jim Slavin, General Manager, at the above address.

CALEDONIAN THISTLE HOTEL: 10-14 Union Terrace, Aberdeen AB10 1WE (☎01224-640233; fax 01224-641627; e-mail reservations.aberdeencaledonian@ thistle.co.uk; www.thistlehotels.com). Part of the Thistle Hotel chain, the 77-bedroom Caledonian is situated in the heart of Aberdeen city centre.
Food Service Staff for the cafe/bar or dining room. Wages at national minimum (B & L included). To work split shifts for a 39 hour week. Minimum period of work 3 months from April to October.
Staff should be at least 18 years old, and experience is preferred. Suitably qualified overseas applicants are welcome.
Applications to the above address from January onwards.

CARLTON HOTEL: North Bridge, Edinburgh EH1 1SD (☎0131-472 3000; fax 0131-556 2691; e-mail carlton@paramount-hotels.co.uk; www.paramount-hotels. co.uk). Hotel with 200 bedrooms, a restaurant, banqueting facilities and a leisure club.
Housekeeping Staff (15), Food and Beverage Staff (15). Wages at national minimun rate. Hours can be either full-time or part-time; must be 18 or over. Minimum period of work is 3 months. Non-UK citizens are considered as long as they have a valid work permit and fluent English.
To *apply*, contact the Personnel Office at the above address. An interview is necessary.

THE CEILIDH PLACE: West Argyle Street, Ullapool, Ross-shire IV26 2TY (☎01854-612103; e-mail effie@theceilidhplace.com; www.theceilidhplace.com). A complex of buildings including a small hotel with 13 rooms, a bunk house, bar, café/ bistro, restaurant, bookshop, gallery and venue for music and drama.
Cooks (3) with natural skill and enthusiasm.
Housestaff (2). Must be fit.
Waiting Staff (6). Serving food and drink and clearing tables.
Bar Staff (2). Serving/stocking drinks and assisting with food service.
Wages paid monthly (less board and lodging allowance). Work available between April and October, minimum period 3 months: no shorter period considered. Overseas

applicants eligible to work in the UK and with necessary documentation welcome. *E-mail* or *write* to the General Manager at the above address for further information and an application form.

CLACHAIG INN: Glencoe, Argyll PH49 4HX (☎01855-811252; fax 01855-812030; e-mail inn@clachaig.com; www.clachaig.com). A busy, vibrant country inn set in the heart of Glencoe. Popular year-round with hillwalkers, climbers, mountain bikers, skiers and travellers. Specialists in real ale (award winning) with a significant food trade. A unique experience for customers and staff alike.

General Assistants (15) required throughout the year to help in all aspects of the business; bar work (serving both drinks and food), waiting on tables and helping out in the kitchen, housekeeping and various odd jobs.

The minimum period of work is at least 3 months. Positions are available year round; those able to work over the New Year and Easter have priority when it comes to the summer months. Accommodation and all meals may be provided. Previous experience is helpful, but a friendly outgoing personality and enthusiasm are more important. You must be clean and presentable, able to communicate well, and be able to work well as part of a team.

Applications (with a covering letter and detailed CV) should be sent to Guy Daynes at the above address approximately one month before you are available for work.

CRAW'S NEST HOTEL: Bankwell Road, Anstruther, Fife KY10 3DA (☎01333-310691; fax 01333-312216; e-mail enquiries@crawsnesthotel.co.uk; www.crawsnesthotel.co.uk). Sandy and Eleanor own and manage this family hotel situated to the East of Fife, 9 miles south of St Andrews. It has 50 guest bedrooms, a large function suite, dining room and 2 bars.

Kitchen Hands (2). £200 per week plus end of season bonus. No experience necessary.

Waiting Staff (3). £200 per week. Some silver service experience would be useful, though is not essential.

All staff to work 5 days per week. Accommodation available and meals provided on duty. Good knowledge of English essential. Minimum period of work 3-4 months between May and October.

Applications with photograph and s.a.e. to Mr A. Bowman at the above address.

CRIEFF HYDRO LTD: Ferntower Road, Crieff, Perthshire PH7 3LQ (☎01764-651612; fax 01764-651649; e-mail sarah.glen@crieffhydro.com or hr.administrator@crieffhydro.com; www.crieffhydro.com). Crieff Hydro is a family run hotel and leisure resort set in 900 acres of central Perthshire countryside, approximately 20 miles north of Stirling. The hotel has 213 bedrooms and 42 self-catering units and over 55 activities on site including quad biking, horseriding and golf.

Food and Beverage Service Assistants. To work approximately 39 hours per week with overtime available. Minimum period of work is 6 months. Positions are available all year. Applicants should have a good level of spoken English. Previous hospitality experience preferred. Overseas applicants welcome subject to valid work permits/visas and other travel documents. Accommodation and meals available for approx. £27.30 per week; this does not include insurance or supplies (towels).

Applications should be made to Sarah Glen at the above address, or through the website. A phone interview is required.

CRINAN HOTEL: Crinan, Lochgilphead, Argyll PA31 8SR (☎01546-830261; fax 01546-830292; e-mail enquiry@crinanhotel.com; www.crinanhotel.com). The hotel

is in a beautiful location in a small sailing village which is 15 minutes from the centre of the nearest town (Lochgilphead).
General Assistants wanted for all departments; team working environment. Wages by arrangement plus food and live-in accommodation.

Send or e-mail *applications* with passport photo to Mr N.A. Ryan, Managing Director.

DALMUNZIE HOUSE HOTEL: Glenshee, Perthshire PH10 7QG (☎01250-885 224; fax 01250-885225; e-mail reservations@dalmunzie.com; www.dalmunzie.com). Country house hotel on 6,000-acre estate in a remote mountain situation.
General Hotel Staff (6). Wages and hours by arrangement according to type of job. B & L provided. To work 5 days a week. Period of work January to late October. Must be able to work the whole of September and for a minimum period of 6 months in total. Minimum age 18 years. Overseas applicants with good English welcome.

Applications to Scot and Brianna Poole, Proprietors, Dalmunzie House Hotel. Only an application enclosing s.a.e. will receive a reply.

DOUNAN'S OUTDOOR CENTRE: Aberfoyle, Stirling FK8 3UT (☎01877-382291; fax 01877-382812; www.scottish-centres.org.uk). Provides environmental outdoor education and activities to both schools and business groups.
Domestic Assistants (4) to work in the dining room and in outside accommodation blocks. National minimum wage paid, to work up to 40 hours per week, any 5 days out of 7. Work available from March to October. Minimum period of work 2 months. Board and accommodation available. No experience necessary as full training given. Overseas applicants welcome. Relevant work permits must be held prior to commencement. Disclosure Scotland enhanced level check will be undertaken.

Apply to Centre Manager at the above address from February/March. Interview necessary.

DUISDALE HOTEL: Sleat, Isle of Skye IV43 8QW (☎01471-833202; e-mail info@ duisdale.com; www.duisdale.com). A country house hotel set in superb location, with 35 acres of gardens and woodland. 500 metres from sea.
Kitchen Assistant. Some cooking experience preferred.
General Assistants (2). Mainly room servicing and waiting; some barwork and reception work.

Wages by arrangement. Free B & L provided. Staff have each afternoon free as the hotel does not open for lunch. Minimum period of work 2 months between April and October. Minimum age 20. Previous experience preferred. Overseas applicants with fluent English accepted. Work permits are essential.

Applications to Mr J Cook, Duisdale Hotel.

EDINBURGH CITY CENTRE PREMIER TRAVEL INN: 1 Morrison Link, Edinburgh EH3 8DN (☎0870-238 3319; fax 0131-228 9836; www.premiertravelinn. com). Premier Travel Inn is the biggest and best budget hotel brand in the UK. City centre location, very busy during the summer months.
Room Attendants (10). To work for 5 days and approximately 40 hours per week.
Food and Beverage Waiting Staff (10). Full and part-time work available. Some experience is necessary.

Wages above national minimum rate. Minimum period of work of 3 months. Positions are available from July to September. Foreign applicants are welcome but good English must be spoken and bank account and a National Insurance number required.

No accommodation available.
Applications should be made from June onwards to the above address. Interview necessary.

FREEDOM OF THE GLEN FAMILY OF HOTELS: Kinlochleven PH50 4SH (☎01855-831800; e-mail jobs@freedomglen.co.uk; www.freedomglen.co.uk). Three distinctive hotels all in superb Lochside locations offering quality Highland hospitality. Staff can enjoy leisure facilities as well as living and working in the Scottish Highlands.
Service Staff (45), Porters (5), Housekeeper (25), General Assistants (14), Receptionists (11). Wages at national minimum plus. To work approximately 45 hours per week with a mixture of straight and split shifts. Minimum period of work of 3 months. Positions are available all year round. Live-in accommodation is available from £28.50 per week. Previous experience useful, but not essential. Foreign applicants with work permits and acceptable spoken English welcome.
Applications should be made from mid-February onwards to Ruth Sime at the above address or completed online using www.freedomglen.co.uk 'Vacancies' section.

THE GROG AND GRUEL: 66 High Street, Fort William PH33 6AE (☎01397-705078; fax 01855-812030; e-mail greatbeer@grogandgruel.co.uk; www. grogandgruel.co.uk). A traditional alehouse situated in the town centre serving a selection of real ales and malt whiskies, with a family restaurant on the upper level, offering home-cooked dishes. Run by brothers Guy and Edward Daynes whose approach to business is informal and friendly – a blend of fun and hard work.
General Assistants (5) to help in bar and restaurant, and possibly in the kitchen. To work a 5 day week (occasionally 6 days) of typically 40 hours. Minimum period of work 3 months.
Accommodation cannot be provided, but is available locally. Staff should be at least 18 years old, but enthusiasm and a friendly, outgoing personality are more important than experience.
For further details, or an *application form,* contact the General Manager at the above address, or visit the website.

HILTON PLC: Coylumbridge Hotel, Coylumbridge, Aviemore, Inverness-shire PH22 1QN (☎01479-813076; fax 01479-811706; e-mail hr.coylumbridge@hilton.com; www. hilton.co.uk). Hilton Colyumbridge is a family-orientated hotel situated in the heart of the Scottish Highlands. Local attractions include golf, watersports and horse riding.
Kitchen, Restaurant Waiting, Bar, & Housekeeping Staff required. Salary £5.00 per hour. To work 39 hours over a 5-day week. Staff required from June to October. Minimum period of work 12 weeks. Minimum age 18. Experience preferred. Overseas applicants with basic English (communication level) welcome. Accommodation with basic facilities available.
Applications from April/May to the Personnel Department at the above address.

HOLIDAY INN EDINBURGH: Corstorphine Road, Edinburgh EH12 6UA (☎0870-400 9026; fax 0131-334 9237). Edinburgh's largest hotel with 303 bedrooms, various restaurants, bar and leisure facilities.
Waiting Staff, Housekeeping Assistants, Kitchen Porters. Wages at national minimum rate for a 39 hour week completed over shifts; uniforms and meals when on duty also provided. Min. period of work of 3 months. Positions are available all year round. Full training provided. Minimum age 16. No previous experience necessary. Foreign applicants with work permits and acceptable spoken English welcome. No

accommodation available.
Applications should be made to the Operations Manager at the above address. Interview required by phone if necessary.

HUNTINGTOWER HOTEL: Crieff Road, Perth PH1 3JT (☎01738-583771; fax 01738-583777; e-mail manager@huntingtowerhotel.co.uk; www.huntingtowerhotel. co.uk).
Restaurant and Bar Staff for the service of food and beverages including breakfasts, lunches, dinners as well as private parties, weddings and functions. Wages depend on experience plus tips. Staff accommodation is available. The job will involve shift work, 5 days out of 7 including weekends. Term of employment by arrangement. Applicants with experience of working in a four star environment preferred.
Applications to Sacha Cauwels, General Manager at the above address.

IGGS RESTAURANT: 15 Jeffrey Street, Edinburgh EH1 1DR (☎0131-557 8184; fax 0131-652 3774; e-mail iggsbarioja@aol.com). A Spanish fine dining restaurant with a tapas bar attached.
Waiting Staff (3-4), Kitchen Help (1-2). Wahes at national minimum rate; to work hours as required. Waiting experience is preferred. Staff are required throughout the summer, especially in the festival period. Spanish applicants are particularly welcomed; some English is necessary.
Apply in person at the restaurant.

INTERCONTINENTAL THE GEORGE EDINBURGH: 19-21 George Street, Edinburgh EH2 2PB (☎0131-225-1251; fax 0131-226-5644; www.interconti.com). This 195-bedroom hotel is a 4-star de luxe establishment in the city centre. There is a fine dining room, a carvery restaurant, bar and banqueting facilities.
Hall Porter. Applicants must possess a driving licence.
Customer Service Agents (3) for the restaurant.
Customer Service Agents (5) for banqueting operations.
Room Attendants.
For all positions: wages from £10,258 p.a. pro rata plus shift allowances and weekend premiums, working 39 hours per 5 day week (less considered for banquet work). Minimum age 18; minimum period of work is six months; positions are available between March/April and November/December. Applicants should enjoy working in a busy and friendly environment, and be able to provide a highly professional service. Foreign applicants with work permits and the ability to understand and speak English are welcome.
Applications should be made from February/March onwards to Catherine MacFarlane at the above address. Interview required.

INVERORAN HOTEL: Bridge of Orchy, Argyll PA36 4AQ (☎01838-400220; e-mail booking@inveroran.com; www.inveroran.com). A small family run hotel in a rural setting, catering for those who enjoy walking the West Highland Way.
Housework/Waiting Assistant, Bar/Waiting Assistant, Kitchen/General Assistant required to work in a busy hotel. Wages approximately £150 to work 5 or 6 days per week. Work available from April to October, with a minimum work period of 3 months. Board and lodging provided at a minimal charge. Applicants must be over 20 years of age, physically fit, cheerful, and not daunted by the rural setting (it is three miles to the nearest bus stop). Overseas applicants with a reasonable standard of English are welcome.
Apply to Anne Marshall at the above address from January.

INVERSNAID PHOTOGRAPHY CENTRE: Inversnaid Lodge, by Aberfoyle, Stirling FK8 3TU (☎01877-386254; e-mail linda@inversnaidphoto.com; www. inversnaidphoto.com). A residential photography workshop centre which hosts tutors of international repute in areas such as landscape, wildlife,documentary and digital. Situated on the shores of Loch Lomond, in an area of outstanding natural beauty, 1½ hours from Glasgow.
Domestic Helper (1) for general cleaning duties and helping in the centre. Wages £180 per week. To work 40 hours a week. Minimum period of work 6 months between April and October. Accommodation provided at a charge of £25 per week. Minimum age 20 and non-smoker. Cleaning and waiting experience preferable. Overseas applicants with good English will be considered.
Applications from February to Ms Linda Middleton at the above address. Interview preferred.

LOCH NESS LODGE HOTEL: Drumnadrochit, Inverness-shire IV63 6TU (☎01456-450342; fax 01456-450429; e-mail info@Lochness-hotel.com; www.lochness-hotel. com). Highland lodge which dates back to 1740, near Loch Ness.
Staff (50) for all positions in a hotel. Wages by arrangement with accommodation provided. Period of work from May to October. Applicants should be aged between 17 and 50; previous experience not necessary.
Applications to Mr Gregor MacKinnon, Manager, at the above address.

LOCHS & GLENS HOLIDAYS: School Road, Gartocharn, Dumbartonshire G83 8RW (☎01389-713713; fax 01389-713725; e-mail jobs@lochsandglens.com; www. lochsandglens.com). A family run hotel and tour group with 5 hotels located in beautiful and remote areas of Scotland with its own fleet of coaches.
Kitchen, Dining Room, Housekeeping & Reception/Bar team members required to work 40 hours a week. Wages in accordance with national minimum wage, accommodation available. Minimum period of work 12 weeks at any time of year; dates of work negotiable. Both temporary and permanent positions available, as well as opportunity for career development.
Applications at any time to the above address.

McTAVISH'S KITCHENS (OBAN) LTD: McTavish's Kitchens, 34 George Street, Oban PA34 4BA (☎01631-563064; e-mail oban@mctavishs.com; www.mctavishs. com). Restaurant in the beautiful West Highland town of Oban.
Food Service, Self-Service Assistants, Kitchen Assistants, Cooks, Drinks Service And Cleaners. There are a number of vacancies, particularly for students, between April and October and also late availability from mid-August to end of September. Wages at national minimum rate. Accommodation available. EU Nationals or evidence of permission to work in the UK.
Applications in writing with photograph and s.a.e., to the above address.

THE MILLERSTON HOTEL: 29 West Bay Road, Millport, Isle of Cumbrae, Ayrshire KA28 OHA (☎01475-530480; fax 01475-530125; e-mail themillerston@ fsmail.net; www.millerstonhotel.org).
Waiting Staff (2) to serve in the bar, beer garden and dining room; duties also include helping kitchen staff to keep kitchen free of clutter and some dishwashing duties. Accommodation in a caravan may be available. To work various shifts 5 days per week; shifts are 8.30am-10am, 11.30am-4.30pm and 4.30pm-9pm. Must be aged over 16.
Chamber Staff (2) to service bedrooms and en-suite shower rooms and clean public areas. To work from 9.30am-noon. 5 days a week. Must be aged over 16.

Bar Assistant to serve drinks and take food orders in the bar, clean tables and assist waiting staff when required. To work 5 days per week, hours by arrangement. Must be aged over 18.
Wages at the national minimum rate plus tips as earned. Period of work from mid-June to end-August. No special qualifications are necessary but previous experience preferred.
Applications should be sent to Jennifer Hamilton, Proprietor at the above address.

NEWTON LODGE: Kylesku, Sutherland IV27 4HW (☎01971-502070; e-mail info@newtonlodge.co.uk; www.smoothhound.co.uk/hotels/newtonlo). A small hotel in the remote North West Highlands. Ideal place to save money for the summer.
General Assistant required for duties as required including dining room, kitchen help, bedroom work and general cleaning. Wage £160 per 6 day week, including room with shower and meals. Period of work mid-May to mid-September. Must have previous hotel experience. Non-smoker only.
Applications with photo and reference to Mrs Brauer.

OLOROSO: 33 Castle Street, Edinburgh EH2 3DN (☎0131-2267614; fax 0131-2267608; e-mail info@oloroso.co.uk; www.oloroso.co.uk). An award-winning restaurant. cocktail bar and roof top terrace in the heart of Edinburgh. A modern and contemporary company with an emphasis on quality.
Barstaff, Waiting Staff, Commis Chefs, Chef de Parties (10-15 in total). Wages dependant upon experience and position. To work shift patterns, from June until September; minimum period of work 8 weeks. Must be between 18 and 35. Limited B & L available. Suitably qualified non-UK citizens will be considered, although fluent English is necessary, along with good communication skills.
Apply to David Mackenzie, General Manager, from May. An interview will be necessary.

PRIORY HOTELS LTD: The Square, Beauly, Inverness-shire IV4 7BX (☎01463-782309; fax 01463-782531; e-mail reservations@priory-hotel.com; www.priory-hotel.com). Small company operating hotels and restaurants in Inverness-shire.
Kitchen Assistants (4), Front Of House Staff/General Assistants (6) required to work in busy hotels in Beauly and Dalwhinnie. From £160, plus free B & L. 40 hours per week. Minimum period of work 3 months but six month contract preferred. Smart appearance, good interpersonal skills and bags of common sense essential. Good fun with a bustling team of people. Overseas applicants with valid work permit welcome.
Applications any time to Blair Sinclair, General Manager, at the above address.

QUALITY HOTEL CENTRAL: 99 Gordon Street, Glasgow G1 3SF (☎0141-221 9680; fax 0141-226 3948; e-mail HR@quality-hotels-glasgow.com; www.quality-hotels-glasgow.com). A 222-bedroom Victorian railway hotel.
Waiting Staff (1) to work in hotel restaurant.
Housekeeper/Room Attendant (1).
All staff receive national minimum wage. Hours for waiting staff are 7am-10.30am, 11am-2.30pm and 5.30pm-10.30pm. Hours for housekeeping staff are 8am-3pm and 5pm-8pm. Period of work June to December. Accommodation available for £27.30 per week.
Applications to Paul Catford, Regional Personnel Manager, at the above address.

RAASAY OUTDOOR CENTRE: Isle of Raasay, By Kyle, Ross-shire, Scotland IV40 8PB (☎01478-660266; fax 01478-660200; e-mail info@raasay-house.co.uk; www.raasay-house.co.uk). An outdoor centre located on a remote and peaceful Hebridean

Island. Sailing, windsurfing, kayaking and climbing offered to clients.
Kitchen Manager (1). Wages negotiable depending on experience. Must have at least 6 years cooking and organisational experience.
Preparation Cooks (2). Wages negotiable depending on experience. Must have general cooking experience.
Kitchen Assistants (2). Wages negotiable depending on experience. To perform kitchen preparation and washing up duties. Must be motivated.
Cafe/Bar/Shop Assistants (3). Wages negotiable depending on experience. Must have experience and be organised and motivated.
Housekeeper (1). Wages negotiable depending on experience. Must have organisational and cleaning experience.
Office Person (1). Must have worked in an office and have good computer skills, enjoy working with people and be organised.
    All positions are for 44 hours work per week between March and October. Minimum period of work 1 month. Board, accommodation and activities provided. Overseas applicants must speak good English. Interview is necessary.
    Applications from March to Freya Rowe at the above address.

THE RADISSON SAS HOTEL EDINBURGH: 80 High Street, The Royal Mile, Edinburgh EH1 1TH (☎0131-473 6514; fax 0131-557 9798; e-mail yvonne.magnier@ raddisonsas.com; edinburgh.radissonsas.com). A busy 4-star deluxe city centre hotel situated halfway between a castle and a palace, aiming to provide first class service for an international clientele.
Waiting Staff (10). Applicants must be over 18.
Chamber Staff (15). Applicants must be over 16.
Wages for all positions at national minimum rate, paid fortnightly. Minimum period of work is 4 months. No experience necessary; full training is provided. Uniform and meals on duty as well as access to range of discounts/benefits from day one. Assistance offered in finding accommodation. Interview necessary (but could be conducted by telephone).
    Applications from March to Human Resources Department.

ROSEDALE HOTEL: Beaumont Crescent, Portree, Isle of Skye IV51 9DB (☎01478-613131; fax 01478-612531; e-mail rosedalehotelsky@aol.com; www. rosedaleskye.co.uk). A family-run hotel located on the harbourside in Portree, the administrative and commercial capital of the island and the adjoining mainland.
Receptionist/Duty Manager (1). Minimum age 24. Must be educated to at least A Level standard and be well presented, articulate, friendly and mature. Training will be given.
Second Chef (1). City and Guilds 706/1 and 706/2 required, plus two years' post-qualification experience. To assist AA rosette chef and be able to take charge in his absence preparing quality food with imagination and style.
General Assistants (6). To work a mixed rota in many departments but mainly restaurant and bar, with some housekeeping. Aged 21 and over. Should be well presented, articulate and interested in working with people.
    Wages specified on application. All staff work approximately 40 to 45 hours per week. Minimum period of work early April to mid-October. Priority given to those able to work the full or greater part of the season. An end of season bonus is paid upon completion of contract period. Non-smoking applicants only.
    Write for an *application form* from mid-February to Mrs Rouse, Manager, at the above address.

THE ROYAL HOUSEHOLD: Buckingham Palace, London SW1A 1AA (☎020-7930 4832; fax 020-7360 7125; www.royal.gov.uk).
Housekeeping Assistants to work at Balmoral Castle to carry out a range of cleaning and housekeeping duties. No previous experience is necessary as full training will be given. Accommodation and meals are provided and applicants must be available for the whole period. Non EU nationals must have a valid work permit prior to application.
Application forms are available from the website, www.royal.gov.uk/recruitment. Completed applications should be returned to: The Chief Housekeeper, Buckingham Palace, London SW1A 1AA. Closing date is the end of January 2007.

RUFFLETS COUNTRY HOUSE HOTEL: Strathkinness Low Road, St Andrews KY16 9TX (☎01334-472594; fax 01334-478703; e-mail reservations@rufflets. co.uk; www.rufflets.co.uk). A privately owned 24-bedroom upmarket hotel which holds two AA rosettes for food quality; young and friendly staff.
Housekeeping Assistant, Restaurant Assistant, Lounge Service Assistant. Wages at national minimum rate. All staff to work hours as required, 5 days out of 7. Accommodation is available at £3.75 per day. Minimum period of work 6 months between 1 April and 30 November.
Experience is not essential, but all applicants must be over 18 years old. Foreign applicants fluent in English considered. Interview not always necessary.
Applications from January to the Manager.

SCOTLAND'S HOTEL: 40 Bonnethill Road, Pitlochry, Perthshire PH16 5BT (☎0870-950 6276; fax 01796-473284; e-mail stay@scotlandshotel.co.uk; www. scotlandshotel.co.uk). A 71-bedroom hotel with conference facilities, a leisure club, and an Italian restaurant, situated in an excellent location, just two hours away from Edinburgh, Glasgow, Aberdeen and Inverness.
Bar Assistant. Minimum age 18 years. Split and straight shifts.
Waiting Staff. Silver service training or experience preferred. Split shifts.
House Staff. Cleaning or housekeeping experience preferred. Split and straight shifts.
Wages approximately £160 per week. All staff to work 8 hours per day, 5 days per week with no overtime. Accommodation available. Free meals on and off duty. Health and Leisure club restricted membership for all staff. Uniform provided and training will be given. Minimum period of work 2 months between April and October. Overseas applicants with a good knowledge of English welcome. Where possible it is preferred that applicants are available for interview.
Applications from March to the Personnel Manager at the above address.

STONEFIELD CASTLE GROUP: Stonefield Castle Group, Castlehill, Howwood, Renfrewshire PA9 1LA (☎0150-570 4000; fax 0150-570 3000; e-mail enquiries@ innscotland.com; www.stonefieldhotels.com). Stonefield Castle Group is a collection of hotels and other leisure businesses all located in the West of Scotland.
Waiting Staff. Full-time and part-time positions are available. To work at least 16 hours per week. Applicants should be at least 16 years old.
Leisure Club Staff. To work 40 hours per week. Applicants must be 18 or over, those who have pool lifeguard and first aid certificate are preferred.
Housekeeping Staff. To work at least 16 hours a week. Applicants must be at least 16.
Wages at national minimum rate. Period of work from May to September. Minimum period of work 2 months.
Applications from April to the Personnel and Training Manager at the above address.

SUMMER ISLES HOTEL: Achiltibuie by Ullapool, Ross-shire IV26 2YG (☎01854-622282; e-mail summerisleshotel@aol.com; www.summerisleshotel. co.uk). Wonderful Highland location of hills, lochs and islands. A 4-star, family-run hotel – a great opportunity to learn the business and save money.
General Assistants for waiting, bar, housekeeping and kitchen.
Wages minimum £200 for 48 hours/6 days per week. End of season bonus. Free B & L provided. Experience preferred but training given. Applicants should be available for whole season, starting April/May. The jobs are suited to professional motivated people prepared to work hard and make the most of their free time by enjoying outdoor activities.
Applications, with s.a.e. and photograph, to Mr Mark Irvine, Summer Isles Hotel.

THAINSTONE HOUSE HOTEL: Inverurie, Aberdeenshire AB51 5NT (☎01467-621643; fax 01467-625084; e-mail swallow.thainstone@swallowhotels.com; www. swallow-hotels.com). A 4-star country house hotel and leisure club, committed to training employees to a high level.
Waiting Staff, Bartenders, Housemaids. Wages by arrangement. All positions to work a 39 hour week. Minimum period of work 3 months between May and the end of September.
Live-in accommodation is available at £20 per week sharing a twin/double, and £40 for a single. There are no deductions for meal breaks, and staff may use the hotel leisure facilities. Experience is preferable, but training will be given. References are required.
Applications from April onwards to the Personnel Manager.

THE WESTIN TURNBERRY RESORT: Turnberry Hotel, Maidens Road, Turnberry, Ayrshire KA26 9LT (☎01655-334164; fax 01655-334165; www.westin. com/turnberry). A 5-star luxury golf resort with 221 guest bedrooms set in 800 acres on the South West Coast of Scotland. The Resort is part of Starwood Hotels & Resorts Inc, the world's leading upscale hotel company spanning more than 80 countries.
Commis Chef, Food and Beverage Waiting Assistant, Guest Service Agent – Front Desk & Concierge. Wages approx £10,850 per annum, pro rata.
Spa/Beauty Therapists. Wages approx £11,835 per annum, pro rata.
Accommodation can be provided if required. This will be at a charge of approximately £130 per month and includes free transport from the resort to accommodation and all meals. Staff are required to work from the beginning of March until the end of October. Applicants must be eligible to work in the European Union. The resort offers excellent training and development facilities plus great career opportunities.
Applications should be made in writing to Jennifer Paton, Human Resources Administrator at the above address or via e-mail to jennifer.paton@westin.com.

Language Schools

EDINBURGH SCHOOL OF ENGLISH: 271 Canongate, The Royal Mile, Edinburgh EH8 8BQ (☎0131-557 9200; fax 0131-557 9192; www.edinburghschoolofenglish. com). Founded in 1969, Edinburgh School of English is a year round school and one of the premier providers of English Language training in the UK. Courses are directed by permanent staff, and have the back up of a permanent organisation. Arranges English language summer courses for school children (10-17 years) in Edinburgh and Strathallan. Accredited by the British Council.
Activity Leaders to be responsible for the smooth running of the afternoon, evening and

weekend leisure programme. The job involves taking students on various cultural visits and organising and supervising sports. One leader is employed for every 15 students. Some leaders are required to live and supervise in halls of residence in addition to the above. Courses are run between mid-June and early September, and also during April.

Applicants should be aged over 21, with a sound knowledge of one of the above locations. They should be enthusiastic and energetic, have good organisational abilities, get on well with teenagers and be interested in sports and cultural visits. Fluent English speakers only.

Applications to the Vice Principal at the above address.

Medical

INVALID SERVICES LTD: 4 Alfred Place, St Andrews, Fife KY16 9XG (☎01334-472834; e-mail joan.reid@virgin.net; www.invalid-services.co.uk).
Carers (many). To provide care in clients' own homes. Age 21+ and own transport helpful.
Nurses (many). May to September for nursing home shifts and in clients' own homes. Must have care and/or nursing qualifications.
Domestics (many) for Easter and Christmas vacations. Experience essential. Accommodation not provided but arrangements can be made. Flexible hours. Pay from £5.35 per hour.

Applications to Joan Reid, Manager, at the above address.

MEDICO: Top Floor, 8 Atholl Crescent, Perth PH1 5NG (☎01738-632311; fax 01738-621105; e-mail perth@bna.co.uk). National Nursing Agency with more than 170 branches throughout the UK.
Care Workers (10). Applicants must have worked previously as a care worker or care assistant in a recognised institution.
Trained Nurses (5). Applicants must be registered with the Nursing and Midwifery Council.

Wages to be discussed at interview. On-going positions all year round: minimum period of work can be just a few days. To work between 6 and 40+ hours per week. No accommodation available. Foreign applicants must have experience, references and confirmation from the Home Office that they can work.

Applications to Karen Hamilton, Branch Manager, at least 1 month prior to work period. Interview required.

Outdoor

ALLANHILL FARM: St Andrews, Fife KY16 8LJ (☎01334-473224; fax 01334-479969; e-mail abissett@ukonline.co.uk; www.allanhill.co.uk).
Strawberry Pickers (100+). More than 100 strawberry pickers needed over the summer. Farm located on the east coast of Scotland. Accommodation is in self-catering mobile caravans.

Contact the Fruit Manager, Alan Bissett, at the above email address for further information.

BLOOMSBERRIES MARKET GARDEN: Fairburn Gardens, Marybank, By Muir-of-Ord, Ross-shire IV6 7UT (☎01997-433238; e-mail bloomsberries.garden@virgin.net).
Gardener needed to work over the summer. Pocket money of £50 per week with three meals per day and accommodation in a 2-berth caravan provided. Working hours

10am-5pm. Applicants should have some previous experience of gardening. Applications to the above address.

MR S. CAMPBELL: Cairntradlin, Kinellar, Aberdeenshire AB21 0SA (☎01224-790056; fax 01224-791581). A farm growing strawberries and raspberries for supermarkets and a local pick-your-own, situated 7 miles from Aberdeen. **Strawberry/Raspberry Pickers (15).** Piecework rates paid daily. Picking guaranteed – crops grown in tunnels; days off as arranged. Social evenings,. barbecues and Scottish nights, arranged for student workers. Self-catering accommodation (7) provided in portacabins, with male and female dormitories, kitchen, toilets and showers. Camping area also available for those with equipment. Applicants must bring eating utensils, warm sleeping bags and warm clothing. There are 2 work periods. Five workers are needed from 15 March until 31 May; and ten from 31 May until 31 August. Overseas applicants welcome.

Applications to Mrs E. Campbell at the above address. Enclose a stamped addressed envelope to ensure a reply.

HAROLD CORRIGALL: Leadketty Farm, Dunning, Perthshire PH2 0QP (☎01764-684532; fax 01764-684146; e-mail haroldcorrigall@btconnect.com). A small farm growing 40 acres under tunnels and 5 acres of raspberries.
Fruit Pickers (10). Wages approximately £35-£55 per day. Required to work 6am-3pm per day, 6 days a week. Accommodation is available at a charge of £4 per day. Staff required for a minimum of 4 weeks between June and late August. Applicants must be 18 or over. The farm takes many European students with appropriate permits or authorisation. Good English speaking personnel required for **managerial posts** for approximately 3 months (June-August).

Applications from February to Harold Corrigall at the above address.

D & B GRANT: Wester Essendy, Blairgowrie, Perthshire PH10 6RA (☎01250-884389; e-mail cmgrant99@yahoo.com).
Fruit Pickers (50) to pick strawberries and raspberries. Help also required to process fruit for freezing. Rates and shifts to be negotiated. To work 6 days a week. Period of work from July 10 to August 31. Caravan accommodation available.

Applications to Colin M. Grant via e-mail or telephone only.

FIELD AND LAWN (MARQUEES) LTD: Barnhill Farm, Houston Road, Inchinnan, Renfrew, Renfrewshire PA4 9LU (☎0141-8127787; fax 0141-8127797; e-mail glasgow@fieldandlawn.com; www.fieldandlawn.com). Company requiring staff to erect and dismantle marquees throughout the UK.
Marquee Riggers (10). £5.50 per hour; must be over 21.
7T Drivers (2). £6.00 per hour; must be over 25.
To work from 7am until the job is finished. Minimum period of work 2 weeks between May and September. No accommodation provided. No experience required as full training given. Non-UK citizens will be considered as long as they have the relevant work documents.

Apply from April to Iain Whitaker at the above address. An interview and induction will be necessary.

W. HENDERSON: Seggat, Auchterless, Turriff, Aberdeenshire AB53 8DL (☎01888-511223; fax 01888-511434). Situated in the heart of the castle and distillery county of Aberdeenshire.
Strawberry Pickers/Packers. Piece work rates: around £30 per day but dependent

on size of crop and weather. Minimum period of work 4 weeks between early July and mid August.
Potato Pickers/Packers. Wages at national minimum wage rate. Period of work September and October, but dependent on weather.
To work 7 hours per day, 6 days per week, but must be prepared to work variable hours. Self-catering accommodation available, for which there is a charge of £10 per week, but must bring own sleeping bag and eating utensils. Situated 1 mile from main road, with regular bus service between Aberdeen and Inverness.
Applications from 30 January onwards to Mr W. Henderson, at the above address.

J & C McDIARMID: Mains of Murthly, Aberfeldy, Perthshire PH15 2EA (tel/fax 01887-829899).
Soft Fruit Pickers (about 20) required from 1 July to 30 August for picking and packing. Wages £40 per day. Shower and toilet block available at campsite. Applicants should be 18 or over.
Applications to Calum McDiarmid at the above address.

PETER MARSHALL & CO: Muirton, Alyth, Blairgowrie, Perthshire PH11 8JF (☎01828-632227; fax 01828-6333070; e-mail meg@petermarshallfarms.com; donna@petermarshallfarms.com). Farm growing 100 acres of raspberries over extended season.
Fruit Pickers (200). Wages £40, piecework rates. New pickers often earn below average in their first week, whilst more experienced pickers earn far more.
Farm Assistants, Raspberry Field Supervisors to work on raspberry machines and tunnel building. Hourly wage to be arranged.
To work 7 hours a day. Minimum period of work 1 month between June and August. Accommodation is available at a cost of £3 per night. Minimum age 18. Foreign applicants welcome. Fluent English not essential. No experience necessary.
Applications from January to Meg Marshall, Partner, at the above address.

PURVIS MARQUEES: 4 East Mains, Ingliston Road, Edinburgh EH28 2NB (☎0131-335 3685; fax 0131-335 0294; e-mail sales@purvis-marquees.co.uk; www. purvis-marquees.co.uk).
Marquee Erectors wanted to work over the summer for around £5.00 per hour dependent on skills. The work involves erecting and dismantling marquees throughout the UK often working a 7-day week. Applicants should be quick to learn, impervious to the weather and have a sense of humour.
Applications to the above address.

L.M. PORTER: East Seaton, Arbroath, Angus DD11 5SD (☎01241-870290; fax 01241-871220; e-mail susan@lmporter.co.uk). East Seaton is situated on the clifftops by Arbroath where conditions are ideal for growing fruit for Tescos, Sainsburys and Asda.
Strawberry/Raspberry Pack House Staff/Pickers (20) for soft fruit picking, in July and August. Wages at piecework rate. Hours can vary with the weather conditions but otherwise average 8 hours a day. Youth hostel type accommodation and camp site facilities available. Applicants must be fit as work is hard but well rewarded.
Applications to Susan Fairweather at the above address.

Sport

CAIRNWELL MOUNTAIN SPORTS: Gulabin Lodge, Spittal of Glenshee, Blairgowrie, Perthshire PH10 7QE (☎01250-885255; fax 01250-885255; e-mail admin@cairnwellmountainsports.co.uk; www.cairnwellmountainsports.co.uk). A multi- activity centre and hostel for 30 persons. Winter activities include ski school, snow board school and nordic skiing; in summer climbing, walking, hang gliding and adventures activities.

Ski Instructors(2). Wages £220 per week; to work 6 days per week. Required from 5 January to 10 March for a minimum of 5 to 10 weeks. Must have a national qualification.

Activity Instructors (2). Wages £240 per week; to work 6 days per week. Required from 16 April to 16 June for a minimum of 4 weeks. Applicants must have a national qualification.

Lodge Worker (1). Wages £200 per week. Required from December to 30 May. No experience necessary.

Overseas applicants are welcome for the posts of lodge worker and ski instructor. Accommodation is available at a cost of £50 per week.

Applications should be sent to Gustav Fischnaller at the above address as soon as possible. Interview and references are necessary.

CALEDONIAN DISCOVERY LTD: The Slipway, Corpach, Fort William PH33 7NB (☎01397-772167; fax 01397-772765; e-mail info@fingal-cruising.co.uk; www.fingal-cruising.co.uk). Organises activity holidays based on a barge cruising the Caledonian Canal/Loch Ness. The 12 guests take part in various outdoor activities at numerous stops along the way. Activities include sailing, canoeing, windsurfing, walking, and biking, with other specialist weeks available. The work is hard, but varied and great fun.

Mate/Instructor. Wages £190 to £250 per week net depending on experience. Experience and preferably qualifications in open canoeing and mountain walking required (windsurfing and sailing an advantage).

Bosun. Wages £100 per week. Main duties: maintenance of boat, driving of safety boat, helping on deck. Training provided. Personal experience of outdoor sports an advantage. Must be keen to learn, with practical nature.

Cook to prepare food for 18 people. £190 to £230 per week net. Must have experience in good cooking.

Assistant Cook (1 each week, part-time). To work their passage: no wage paid.

All full-time staff to work 6½ days a week and all crew live on board the barge. To work from mid April to mid October. Staff must be available for the whole season to qualify for a bonus with the exception of the assistant cook whose minimum period is one week. A two day recruitment event will be held in February or March.

Applications from December to Martin Balcombe at the above address.

GALLOWAY SAILING CENTRE: Shirmers Bridge, Loch Ken, Castle Douglas DG7 3NQ (☎01644-420626; e-mail gsc@lochken.co.uk). A family owned centre in a picturesque setting, which aims to give its visitors an enjoyable yet educational time in a safe and friendly atmosphere.

Instructors: Dinghy (15), Windsurfers (5), Canoes (5), Climbers (3), Archery Leaders (2). Courses start at 10am and finish 5pm. Must be NGB qualified. Overseas applicants with equivalent qualifications welcome.

Kitchen Assistant (2). No special qualifications needed but experience an advantage.

Chalet Girl (1). Must enjoy working with children. Wages negotiable, hours variable. Applicants should be versatile, good with people and prepared to accept responsibility. Knowledge of DIY an advantage. Free B & L provided. Period of work from May to September, or peak season only.
Applications to Mr R. Hermon, Principal, at the above address.

GLENCOE OUTDOOR CENTRE: Glencoe, Argyll PH49 4HS (☎01855-811350; e-mail gocdebbie@aol.com; www.glencoeoutdoorcentre.org.uk). A residential holiday and outdoor activity training centre situated in the north west Highlands amongst the spectacular scenery of Glencoe.
Domestic Assistants/Assistant Instructor (4). Wages from £50 per week plus board and accommodation. To work 7 ½ hours per day for 5 days per week: 3 out of 4 weeks domestic work (split shifts, afternoons free) and 1 out of 4 weeks assisting the team of instructors.
Group Instructors (4). Wages from £50 per week plus board and accommodation. To work 7 ½ per day for 5 days per week. Work involves leading a group of young people working as both instructor (where qualified) and assistant instructor. Minimum period of work 6 months between January and the end of June. Minimum age of 18. Applicants should be committed Christians willing to work hard as part of a Christian team.
Applications a.s.a.p. to Debbie Williams, Director, at the above address.

HILTON PLC: Hilton Coylumbridge Hotel, Coylumbridge, Aviemore, Inverness-shire PH22 1QN (☎01479-813076; fax 01479-811706; e-mail hr.coylumbridge@ hilton.com). Hilton Coylumbridge is a family oriented hotel situated in the heart of the Scottish Highlands. Local attractions include golf, watersports and horse riding.
Kitchen, Waiting, Bar and Housekeeping Staff. Wages comply with national minimum rate. Required for 39 hours over a 5 day week. Staff required from June to October. Minimum period of work 12 weeks. Experience preferred. Minimum age 18. Overseas applicants with basic English (communication level) welcome. Live in accommodation with basic facilities available.
Applications from April/May to the HR Department at the above address.

LOCH INSH WATERSPORTS & SKIING CENTRE: Insh Hall, Kincraig, Inverness-shire PH21 1NU (☎01540-651272; fax 01540-651208; e-mail office@ lochinsh.com; www.lochinsh.com). Loch Insh Watersports and skiing centre nestled in the foothills of the Cairngorm Mountains in the scenic Spey Valley. Lochside Restaurant and Watersports Centre. Skiing December to April. Bed and Breakfast ensuite accommodation and self catering log chalets on site.
Watersports Instructors. RYA and BCU qualified, or trainee instructor standard. To work 5 days a week.
Skiing Instructors. BASI-qualified, or trainee instructor standard. To work 5 days a week.
Restaurant Staff. To work a 5 or 6 day week. Experience preferred.
Wages variable. B & L provided at a charge of £50 a week. Free watersports and skiing for staff. Minimum period of work 4 months, with work available all year round. Non-smokers preferred. Overseas applicants with good spoken English welcome.
Applications to Mr Clive Freshwater, at the above address.

PERTH AND KINROSS LEISURE: Company Head Office, Caledonia House, Hay Street, Perth PH1 5HS (☎01738-450750; fax 01738-450740; e-mail dmgaffney@pkc. gov.uk). Provide leisure and community facilities throughout the Perth and Kinross

area to promote development, health, fitness and wider leisure services.
Relief Leisure Assistant (Wet Facilities). Wages £5.75 per hour. RLSS pool lifeguard qualification needed.
Relief Leisure Assistant (Dry Facilities). Wages £5.75 per hour. First aid at work qualification needed.
Sports Coaches. Wages from £5.35-£10 per hour. Appropriate coaching certificates needed.
Relief Catering Assistants. Wages from £5.37.
Hours are variable. Positions are available at variable times throughout the year, especially holiday periods, weekends and evenings. No accommodation available. Foreign applicants welcome with appropriate work permit.

Applications should be made to Diane Gaffney, Administration and Staffing Manager, by letter. Interview necessary.

RAASAY OUTDOOR CENTRE: Isle of Raasay, By Kyle, Ross-shire IV40 8PB (☎01478-660266; fax 01478-660200; e-mail info@raasay-house.co.uk; www.raasay-house.co.uk). An outdoor centre located on a remote and peaceful Hebridean island. Sailing, windsurfing, kayaking and climbing offered to clients.
Outdoor Activity Instructors (8). Wages depend on responsibility and experience. To work 44 hours per week between March and October. Minimum period of work 1 month. Must have first aid qualifications plus one of the following: Windsurfing RYA, Sailing RYA, Kayak BCU, Abseil and Climb, Walking S.P.S.A. Board, accommodation and activities provided.

Applications to Freya Rowe from March at the above address. All applicants must speak good English. An interview is required.

Voluntary Work

Archaeology

ARCHAEOLINK PREHISTORY PARK: Oyne, Insch, Aberdeenshire AB52 6QP (☎01464-851500; fax 01464-851544; e-mail info@archaeolink.co.uk; www. archaeolink.co.uk).
Archaeolink was started in 1997 to introduce the public to Aberdeenshire's rich archaeological heritage. It operates reconstructions including stone-age camps, a Roman Marching camp, a bronze-age metal-smith workshop and an iron age farm based on archaeological evidence from northeast Scotland.
Volunteers are needed to work in reconstruction and living history all year. No experience is necessary and volunteers may be as young as 14 if they are accompanied by a guardian. Minimum period of work 1 day. Accommodation is available at a local B & B, and volunteers must pay for travel, food and accommodation. Lunch is provided by the company on days of volunteering.

Contact the park, at the above address, for further information.

Conservation and the Environment

BTCV SCOTLAND: Balallan House, 24 Allan Park, Stirling FK8 2QG (☎01786-479697; fax 01786-465359; e-mail scotland@btcv.org.uk; www.btcv.org.uk).
BTCV Scotland is one of the UK's largest environmental conservation charities. It operates a network of local centres in, or close to, Scotland's 5 major cities.

Volunteer Officers required to assist in a varied range of projects, such as community groups, recycling, environmental projects, administration and residential projects. Hours of work vary, expenses are paid to volunteers. Volunteer officers are required all year round for a minimum of 3 to 6 months. Training is provided in skills needed such as Health and Safety or First Aid. Those over 21 with a clean driving licence held for 2 years are particularly desirable.

Applications to Gemma Johnson at the above address.

HESSILHEAD WILDLIFE RESCUE TRUST: Gateside, Beith, Ayrshire KA15 1HT (☎01505-502415; email info@hessilhead.org.uk; www.hessilhead.org.uk). A wildlife rescue and rehabilitation centre in Scotland.

Volunteers (40 annually) help with a range of jobs involving rescue, daily care and cleaning of wild birds and animals, as well as treatment and hand-rearing, assessment for release and post-release monitoring. Minimum period of work two weeks, maximum 6 months in the period between April and October. Accommodation with heating and cooking facilities. Experience with animals is advantageous, but not necessary, as full training is given. Cost £10 per week.

For further *details*, contact Gay Christie at the above address.

MORAY FIRTH WILDLIFE CENTRE: Spey Bay, Moray IV32 7PJ (e-mail volunteering@wdcs.org; www.wdcs.org).

The Whale and Dolphin Conservation Society takes on seasonal **Volunteers** to work at the Moray Firth Wildlife Centre. Accommodation is provided and a contribution is made towards expenses. The work is varied and includes research, interpretation, and awareness-raising events around Scotland.

For more *information*, e-mail the above address.

JOHN MUIR TRUST: 41 Commercial Street, Edinburgh EH6 6JD (☎0131-554 0114; fax 0131-555 2112; e-mail admin@jmt.org; www.jmt.org).

This Trust believes that the only way to protect wild land is to own and then manage it carefully. It currently owns more than 49,000 acres of land in the Highlands.

Volunteers needed to participate in a number of ways, such as organising local meetings, raising funds and helping with general administration, as well as carrying out most of the practical conservation on the Trust's land.

A programme of work parties is organised throughout the year. Volunteers need to bring their own tent, food and transport.

For *details*, contact Conservation Activities, 69 Hyndland Street, Glasgow G11 5PS.

OPERATION OSPREY: RSPB, Loch Garten Nature Reserve. (☎01767-680551; fax 01767-692365; e-mail volunteers@rspb.org.uk; www.rspb.org.uk/volunteering). Operation Osprey, one of the RSPB's special projects, involves protection and conservation work for ospreys, one of Scotland's rarest species of bird.

Volunteers are needed for one-week stints from March through to early September for Osprey nest site protection and surveillance, and to provide information to the public. Chalet accommodation is provided.

For further *information*, write to The Volunteering Development Department (Residential), The RSPB UK Headquarters, The Lodge, Sandy, Bedfordshire SG19 2DL.

THISTLE CAMPS: The National Trust for Scotland, 28 Charlotte Square, Edinburgh EH2 4ET (☎0131-243 9470; fax 0131-243 9593; e-mail conservationvolunteers@

nts.org.uk; www.nts.org.uk).
The Charity protects and promotes Scotland's natural and cultural heritage. Thistle Camps are voluntary work projects organised by The National Trust for Scotland to help in the care and practical management of its countryside properties. Each year there are approximately 40 camps, running from March to October and lasting from one to three weeks. They are always of a practical nature, undertaking such tasks as mountain footpath improvement, habitat management, archaeology or working with crofting communities on Fair Isle (Britain's most remote inhabited island). Volunteers must be aged over 18.

Volunteers are usually accommodated in a Trust basecamp or in similar hostel-type lodgings. All food is provided but volunteers are expected to help with the preparation of meals as well as general domestic tasks during the week. Participation in a camp costs from £50 (£35 for students), and volunteers must pay their own travel expenses to a central pick-up point. All volunteers must bring good waterproofs and sturdy footwear.

The programme for 2007 is available from January and *applications* should be made to the above address.

SEALIFE SURVEYS: Ledaig, Tobermory, Isle of Mull, Argyll PA75 6NU (☎01688-302916; e-mail enquiries@sealifesurveys.com; www.sealifesurveys.com).
An award-winning business involved in cetacean research.
Volunteers are taken on for eight-week periods between March and November. At sea volunteers are involved in crewing the research vessel, collecting data and looking after the fare-paying passengers; on land they process data, perform office duties and look after visitors.

Volunteers must have stamina, good eyesight, a driving licence, a sense of humour and the ability to work as part of a team. Useful skills for volunteers include boat maintenance, computing and DIY. In return for their work volunteers receive B & L.

To *apply*, send a CV and covering letter to the above address, stating the dates that you are available.

TREES FOR LIFE: The Park, Findhorn Bay, Forres IV36 3TZ (☎01309-691292; fax 01309-691155; e-mail trees@findhorn.org; www.treesforlife.org.uk).
Scottish charity dedicated to the restoration of the Caledonian Forest to a large, significant area of the Highlands of Scotland.
Volunteers (10 a week, around 300 annually) needed for a week at a time. To carry out practical restoration work including tree planting, fence removal, tree-felling, wetland restoration, tree nursery work, stock-fencing and seed collecting.

Weeks run from midday Saturday to midday Saturday, including 5 working days. Volunteers may participate in more than one week. Required mid-March to beginning of June and beginning of September to end of October. All food, accommodation and transport from Inverness provided. Cost is £90 per week/£55 concessions. Minimum age 18. Applicants must understand English and be reasonably fit, as work is physical. Foreign applicants welcome.

Applications should be sent to 'Trees For Life Work Week Booking' at the above address, or book on-line.

Heritage

HOUSE OF DUN: House of Dun by Montrose, Angus DD10 9LQ (☎01674-810264; fax 01674-810722; e-mail mbrownlow@nts.org.uk; www.nts.org.uk).
Guides (2) required to work 11.30am to 5.30pm daily.
Gardeners (2) required to work 8am to 4pm daily.

Events Assistants (4) required to work 11am to 5pm or evenings 6pm to 11pm and weddings as required.

Opportunity for both paid and voluntary work at a beautiful Georgian mansion dating from 1730 and designed by William Adam. Free accommodation may be available. Period of work is from June to September.

Applications to Mary Brownlow, Area manager at the above address.

STRATHSPEY RAILWAY CO. LTD: Aviemore Station, Dalfaber Road, Aviemore PH22 1PY (☎01479-810725; e-mail information@strathspeyrailway.co.uk; www.strathspeyrailway.co.uk).

Highland steam railway (not-for-profit organisation) which runs for 10 miles between Aviemore, Boat of Garten and Broomhill; tourist attraction with limited public services. Work is being done to extend the line to Grantown-on-Spey. The railway has a small, permanent staff but is highly dependent on volunteer input.

Volunteer Guards, Ticket Inspectors And Booking Clerks. Volunteers are also needed to help maintain the railway and its rolling stock and locomotives. Hostel for members who work at Aviemore £5.00 per night. Minimum age 16. Age range of volunteers is wide. Fitness needed for some jobs. Willingness to be a team player essential. Vacancies all year.

Applications to the above address.

Physically/Mentally Disabled

BEANNACHAR: Banchory-Devenick, Aberdeen AB12 5YL (☎01224-869138; e-mail elisabeth@beannachar.org; www.beannachar.co.uk).

Beannachar is one of the Camphill communities in which vulnerable children and adults can live, learn and work with others in healthy social relationships based on mutual care and respect.

Beannachar is a training community for teenagers and young adults with learning disabilities. **Volunteers** are needed for household, workshop, garden and farm duties during the summer, and also long-term volunteers at any time of year. Free B & L plus pocket money provided. To work long hours, 6 days a week. Minimum age 19. Must have lots of enthusiasm and a positive attitude. Overseas applicants must speak fluent English. Minimum work period 2 months between June and September, 1 year for long-term volunteers.

Applications at any time to Ms E.A. Phethean at the above address.

SPEYSIDE TRUST: Badaguish Outdoor Centre, Aviemore, Inverness-shire PH22 1QU (☎01479-861285; fax 01479-861258; e-mail info@badaguish.org; www.badaguish.org).

The Centre specialises in outdoor recreation holidays for children and adults with learning or multiple disabilities. Clients enjoy various adventure activities and 24-hour respite care in a spectacular setting. Badaguish is 7 miles out of Aviemore in the Greenmore Forest Park; nearest shops are 2 miles away in Glenmore. Volunteers must enjoy the outdoors and take part in all activities offered.

Volunteer Care Assistants (2 per week) to work with people with Special Needs for 2 or more weeks. £30 pocket money per week plus B & L. Volunteers are expected to work 10 hours a day with 2 days off a week. No qualifications necessary but applicants must want to work outdoors with people with special needs.

Seasonal Care Assistant/Instructor. Wages £15,000 to £17,000 pro rata. To work 40 hours over 5 days per week, with two evenings off a week. Applicants must have experience of working with people and experience of special needs. They must also

be over 18 and enjoy the outdoors.
Period of work April to October. Accommodation available at the Centre in a chalet or caravan at no charge. Food is provided while on duty. Foreign applicants with related qualifications in care, nursing, social work or physiotherapy welcome.
For more information and *applications* write to Silvie Mackenzie at the above address from January onwards.

YOUNG DISABLED ON HOLIDAY: 37/11 Orchard Brae Avenue, Edinburgh EH4 2UP (☎0131-332 1944; e-mail aliwalker1@aol.com).
Voluntary Workers (as many as possible) required for holidays for disabled people in the U.K. and abroad for one week throughout the summer. Each volunteer needs to help a disabled person on a one-to-one basis. Workers are expected to make a minimum contribution towards accommodation, food and trips. Preferred age group 18-35, though anyone up to the age of 40 will be considered. No previous experience required, just patience. Overseas applicants welcome.
Applications to Alison Walker at the above address.

Social and Community Schemes

BRAENDAM FAMILY HOUSE: Thornhill, Stirling FK8 3QH (☎01786-850259; fax 01786-850738; e-mail info@braendam.org.uk; www.braendam.org.uk).
Volunteers required throughout the year to work for a minimum of 6 months at a short stay family house for families experiencing disadvantage and poverty. £32 pocket money and full board provided in return for a 40-hour week within a 2 week rota (5 days off in 14 days); most accommodation is in a single room although it may be necessary to share. Tasks include direct support to families, participating in trips and outings, domestic chores, driving, organising children's activities and play and generally responding to the needs of families.
Volunteers are entitled to holidays, use of house car and bicycles for a small charge, and access to internet/e-mail, again for a small charge. Volunteers will also have the opportunity to explore Scotland on days off. Applicants must be over 18, be willing to work long days and to carry out domestic chores and maintain enthusiasm and energy for supporting families in need. A clean driving licence would be an advantage.
Applications to Brian Guidery, Manager, at the above postal or e-mail address.

EDINBURGH CYRENIANS: Norton Park, 57 Albion Road, Edinburgh EH7 5QY (☎0131-475 2354; e-mail admin@cyrenians.org.uk; www.cyrenians.org.uk).
A professional and respected local charity, providing all kinds of practical help for homeless people since 1968. It is not a religious group and the only mission is to help homeless people.
The Cyrenian Trust runs two community houses (one in the city centre and another on an organic farm in West Lothian) that are primarily for young adults who are otherwise homeless, and who have experienced a variety of difficulties which they are seeking to overcome. **Residential volunteers**, of a similar age to residents, live alongside residents sharing the life and work of the community. Support and regular training is provided by non-residential staff. No experience needed.
Volunteers receive full B & L, weekly pocket money, holiday, leaving grants, and access to a time-off flat. Minimum commitment of 6 months. Vacancies all year round. Overseas applicants with good working use of the English language welcome.
For further information and an *application* form contact Volunteer Recruitment at the above address. Online applications are possible via website.

IONA COMMUNITY: Iona Abbey, Isle of Iona, Argyll PA76 6SN (☎01681-700404; fax 01681-700460; e-mail ionacomm@iona.org.uk; www.iona.org.uk).
An ecumenical Christian Community sharing work, worship, meals and programme with guests visiting the Macleod and Abbey centres on Iona, and Camas, the more basic outdoors centre on nearby Mull. Guests come and stay for a week to take part in the common life of work, worship and programme.
Volunteers work in the kitchen, shop and office, help with driving, maintenance, housekeeping and with the children's and craft work activities programme.
Volunteers are needed for between 6 and 12 weeks between March and November. They receive full B & L, travelling expenses within the U.K. and pocket money of around £30 per week. They work 5½ days per week. Volunteers should be in sympathy with the Christian faith and the ideals of the Iona Community. Volunteers of 18+ are required. Overseas applicants with a working knowledge of English are welcome. Recruitment begins in the autumn.
For details and *applications* write to the Staff Co-ordinator at the above address, enclosing a stamped addressed envelope if applying by post.

Vacation Traineeships & Internships

Science, Construction and Engineering

CELTIC WELCOMES LTD: Eglington Chambers, 21 Wellington Square, Ayr, Ayrshire KA7 1HD (☎01292-885656; fax 01292-885757; e-mail info@celticwelcomes.com; www.celticwelcomes.co.uk).
A tour wholesaler organising tours for group operators throughout the UK and Europe, specialising in Scotland, Ireland and Northern Europe.
Administration & Marketing Support Assistants (2) to assist with admin. and any marketing in the company. Accommodation and living expenses covered. Hours by arrangement. Good spoken and written English essential. Other European languages (especially French and German) an advantage. Admin., business, marketing or computer skills also an advantage.
Applications should be sent with CV at any time to the above address. Interview required.

HALCROW: 16 Abercromby Place, Edinburgh EH3 6LB (☎0131-272 3300; fax 0131-272 3302; e-mail fincr@halcrow.com; www.halcrow.com).
Transport, Development and Environmental Consultants..
Trainee Placements (2-3). Wages by arrangement. Variable hours; duration and timing of placement by arrangement. Applicants must be at least 18, though graduates are preferred. Good numeracy, computer skills and English essential. Applicants should have studied, or be studying towards, a qualification in development planning, traffic engineering, economics, geography or similar. Suitably qualified foreign applicants with appropriate permits and fluent English welcome.
Applications should be made at any time to the above address to Rick Finc. Interview required.

Wales

Prospects for Work.
Most of the seasonal jobs in Wales are to be found in hotels, restaurants and holiday centres. The towns offering the largest number of vacancies are Aberystwyth, Brecon, Cardiff, Llangollen, Llandudno, Newport, Porthcawl, Rhyl, Rogerstone, Swansea and Tenby. If you have some knowledge of riding, or are a good group leader, there are numerous riding schools and trekking centres in more remote locations; for those not local to Wales the advantage with this work is that accommodation will normally be provided. In the resort towns rented accommodation is limited and expensive.

Most Jobcentre Plus branches, including those in Llandudno and Llangollen, advise jobhunters to contact them early. Local job ads appear in the *Brecon and Radnor Express*. The best paper for jobs around Llandudno is the *North Wales Weekly News* or the *Liverpool Daily Post*. Llandudno Jobcentre Plus usually has a high number of vacancies for staff between April and September. In and around Llangollen, try the *Evening Leader* or the *Shropshire Star*. It is worth noting that there is very little chance of finding work with accommodation provided in the

Llandudno area. In Tenby *The Tenby Observer* and *The Western Telegraph* are worth looking at while Swansea Jobcentre Plus recommends the Thursday edition of *Western Mail* and the *South Wales Evening Post* on Wednesdays for jobs in that area.

Aberystwyth can offer a comparatively good supply of jobs – not only in pubs, hotels and restaurants, but at nearby holiday parks and caravan sites too. Rented accommodation in the town is limited since students from the local university take up most vacancies; this may be an advantage, however, since it means that short term lets are more available in summer. The local *Cambrian News* carries job advertisements.

In South Wales, Newport Leisure Services usually advertises vacancies for its playscheme in March or April each year. While Newport may not have the appeal of Llangollen or Brecon, it is one of the few cities in Wales to have plenty of rentable accommodation.

Call centres often recruit temporary staff, the main centres being in Cardiff and Swansea. Local Jobcentres have details of recruitment. Large manufacturing firms which may require temporary staff include Tetra Pak (who make cardboard milk and juice cartons) in Wrexham, the Driver and Vehicle Licensing Agency in Morriston, and R.F. Brookes in Rogerstone. Apply early to these firms and contact the necessary Jobcentre Plus, or telephone Jobseeker Direct on 0845-606 0234 to establish whether or not application forms will be available.

The Royal Welsh Show in Builth Wells in mid-July provides a number of jobs for a few weeks.

Business and Industry

THE PEMBROKESHIRE ICE CREAM COMPANY: Pwll Cottage, Marros, Pendine, Carmarthenshire SA33 4PW (☎01834-814594; e-mail danny@icecream. uk.com). A company with retail sites all over south Pembrokeshire.

Kiosk Assistant (10-14). Wages at national minimum rate. Applicants must be at least 16 years old.

Drivers (4-6). Wages £6.00 per hour. Applicants must be at least 24 years old.

Staff needed from April until September, working either part- or full-time. Applicants must not have any prior plans between mid-July and the end of August. There is no accommodation available; the work is weather-dependent.

Applications should be sent to Danny Voaden or Charlotte Kinder, at the above address, from April. Interview required.

Children

GRANGE TREKKING CENTRE: The Grange, Capel-y-Ffin, Abergavenny NP7 7NP (☎01873-890215; fax 01873-890157; www.grangetrekking.co.uk). Family-run guest house and trekking centre situated high in the Black Mountains, Wales. Remote area with breathtaking scenery; 8 miles to the nearest shops and no public transport.

Nanny and Mother's Help required between April and November, wages by arrangement. Applicants should be aged 18 or over, duties include looking after 2 children aged six and seven plus some cleaning, food preparation, waiting on tables, and going riding.

Applications to Jessica Griffiths at the above address.

TRACEY LEES: Riverside Manor, 77 Castle Street, Lower Swansea SA4 6TS (☎01792-893392).

General Help needed by young and busy family of self-employed children's entertainers. Required to help renovate the house and garden. £60 per week for a single person or £100 per week for a couple, plus B & L. Any time period considered. No qualifications are necessary; non-UK applicants will be considered. Driving licence and references needed.
Apply to Tracey Lees on the above number.

Holiday Centres and Amusements

ANGLESEY MUSEUMS SERVICE: c/o Oriel Ynys Mon, Rhos-meirch, Llangefri, Anglesey LL77 7TQ (☎01248-724444; www.angleseyheritage.org).
Seasonal Museums Attendants to work in the museum shop, in ticketing and admissions, cleaning, security, guiding, customer care and stock control. Wages £5.35 per hour. To work from Easter until the end of September. All applicants must be available for the entire season. Minimum age 18. Must speak Welsh fluently, be organised and a good communicator and have an interest in museums and heritage.
Applications to the Museums Officer at the above address before the end of February.

BEAUMARIS GAOL AND COURT MUSEUM: c/o Oriel Mon, Leisure Heritage Department, Llangefri, Anglesey LL77 7TW (☎01248-811691; www.angleseyheritage.org). The gaol and court at Beaumaris is a specialist crime and punishment museum with a strong educational role.
Seasonal Museum Attendants (5). Duties include front of house work, reception, sales and customer care as well as operational maintenance and cleaning, care of the museum and guiding tourists around the museum. Wages £5.32 per hour; to work 30 hours per week from 10.00am to 5.30pm on a 7-day rota. Welsh-speaking applicants preferred. Preferably available to work full-time from Easter to September 30th.
Applications from early February to the above address. Interview necessary.

HAFAN Y MOR HOLIDAY PARK: Pwllheli, Gwynedd, North Wales LL53 6HX (☎01758-612112; fax 01766-810379; e-mail tony.thomas@bourne-leisure.co.uk). Part of the Bourne Leisure Group. An all-action family holiday park on the picturesque Llyn Peninsula in the shadow of Snowdon.
Bar Staff, Catering Staff, Chefs, Lifeguards, Sport & Leisure Staff, Retail Staff, Receptionists, Security Staff, Cleaners (400 in all). Needed from late March to late October. Wages in line with national minimum wage legislation, with increments according to age and experience. Uniform provided and attractive staff package.
With the exception of Lifeguards and Chefs no qualifications are required, as full training will be given. Recognised qualifications can be gained in most positions. Live-in accommodation available to successful applicants aged over 18.
Applications to be sent to Personnel at the above address.

PEMBROKESHIRE COAST NATIONAL PARK AUTHORITY: Llanion Park, Pembroke Dock, Pembrokeshire SA72 6DY (☎0845-3457275; fax 01646-689076; e-mail pcnp@pembrokeshirecoast.org.uk; www.pembrokeshirecoast.org.uk). A national park authority, responsible for building planning control, conservation and education regarding the environment within the national park.
Visitor Centre Assistants, Site Guide Assistants to work from 2-5 days per week including weekends. Applicants should have good communication skills and enjoy working with the

public. It may be an advantage to have knowledge of the area.

Coast Path Warden to work Monday to Friday. Applicants should have countryside skills. Main duty is maintenance of footpaths.

Car Park Attendants working hours vary but will include weekends and holidays. Applicants should have good communication skills, experience of cash handling and practical skills for machine maintenance.

For all positions the wage is £5.68-£6.36 per hour. Staff are required from April/ May to September. No accommodation available. Ability to speak Welsh is desirable, but not necessary for all jobs. Information, when recruiting, will be available on the website.

Applications should be sent to June Skilton at the above address during February and March.

PRESTHAVEN SANDS HOLIDAY PARK: Shore Road, Gronant, Prestatyn, Flintshire LL19 9TT (☎01745-856471; fax 01745-855635; www.havenholidays.com). Part of the Bourne Leisure Group; an attractive all-action family holiday park near Prestatyn and Rhyl.

Lifeguards, Pool Attendants, Bar Staff, Chefs, Receptionists, Retail Staff, Store Persons, Waiting Staff (200 in all). Wages in line with national minimum rate, with increments according to age and experience. 39 hours of work a week including Public Holidays, from April until late October.

Except for lifeguards no qualifications are necessary, as training will be given. No live in accommodation is available, therefore applicants must secure accommodation within the local area before applying.

Applications should be sent to the Administrator, Haven Leisure Ltd, at the above address.

TRANS-WALES-TRAILS: Pengenfford, Talgarth, Brecon, Powys LD3 0EU (☎01874-711398; fax 01874-711122; e-mail riding@transwales.com; www. transwales.com). Based at a remote farm guesthouse in the Black Mountains of S.E. Wales. Specialists in horse riding holidays for international adult visitors in the Brecon Beacons National Park. Ambient atmosphere, glorious countryside.

General Domestic Assistants (2). Wages £120 per week. To work approximately 40 hours a week, with 1 day off which may be carried forward. Free horse riding, and free B & L. Age 18-30 years. Duties include helping in the kitchen, bedmaking and cleaning. Assistants must be smart, responsible, of high moral standard and prepared to speak English clearly to foreign guests. Minimum period of work 3 months between 1 April and 30 September. Overseas applicants with college-level English welcome.

Applications to Mr Paul Turner, Trans-Wales-Trails. Note: Only affirmative responses will be made.

Hotels and Catering

AMBASSADOR HOTEL: Grand Promenade, Llandudno, North Wales LL30 2NR (☎01492-876886; fax 01492-876347). A family-run, seafront hotel in the largest resort in Wales, near to the main shopping area. Known for its unspoilt Victorian image, the hotel has 57 bedrooms, coffee shop and bar. It is also close to Snowdonia National Park.

Waiting Staff (2), Bedroom Staff (2). Wages by arrangement. Good conditions and hours. B & L. Must be over 17 years of age. Minimum work period 2 months at any time of year.

Applications to Mr D.T. Williams, Proprietor, Ambassador Hotel.

CLARENCE HOTEL: Gloddaeth Street, Llandudno LL30 2DD (☎01492-860193; fax 01492-860308; e-mail clarencehotel1@aol.com; www.theclarence-hotel.co.uk). **Waiting Staff (4)** to work from 7.30am to 10.30am and from 6pm to 9.30pm. Some knowledge of food service and customer care preferred but not essential. **Domestic staff (2)** to work 9.30am to 2.30pm. **Café Assistant (2)** to work 9am to 5pm. Duties include food service, till and customer care. Wages at national minimum rate. All required from June to October. Minimum age 18.

Applications to the owner at the above address.

COBDENS HOTEL: Capel Curig, Snowdonia National Park, North Wales LL24 0EE (☎01690-720243; fax 01690-720354; e-mail info@cobdens.co.uk; www.cobdens.co.uk). Situated in the heart of Snowdonia, Cobdens is family-owned and popular with climbers and walkers.
Housekeeping/Bar/Waiting Staff and Trained Kitchen Staff (3). Live-in positions including food and linen available at a small weekly fee. The hotel will try to provide an average of 40 hours work over five days per week. Experience and good personality important. Minimum period of work 6 months preferred. Staff required all year round. Work is hard and to a high standard, but good fun. Overseas applicants with a high standard of English welcome.

Applications any time to the General Manager at the above address.

THE FEATHERS ROYAL HOTEL: Alban Square, Aberaeron, Cardiganshire, West Wales SA46 0AQ (☎01545-571516; fax 01545-571516; e-mail hotelfeathers@aol.com). Originally an 18th century coaching inn, the Feathers Royal Hotel is now a modern well-equipped hotel with a restaurant and conference facilities.
General Assistants (4). Minimum period of work the summer vacation. Live-in. Flexible hours and adequate free time. Must be energetic and adaptable. Minimum age 18. Overseas applicants with good working knowledge of English welcome.

Applications (with photograph) to Kathy Hunter, Feathers Royal Hotel.

GRANGE GUEST HOUSE: The Grange, Capel-y-ffin, Abergavenny NP7 7NP (☎01873-890215; fax 01873-890157; www.grangeguesthouse.co.uk). A small, informal family-run centre situated in a very rural area, high in the beautiful Black Mountains, Wales. Remote area with breathtaking scenery; eight miles to the nearest shops and no public transport.
Accommodation Worker/Assistant to perform cleaning, waiting, taking two little girls aged six and seven for a walk, and customer care duties. Wages and hours negotiable, with free accommodation in a caravan with shower block. Minimum period of work one month between Easter and October. Overseas applicants with good English welcome; preferable that candidates can visit for an interview, but not essential.

Applications should be directed to Jessica Griffiths from February onwards at the above address.

GWYNDY HOTEL: Llanystmdwy, Cricieth, Gwynedd LL52 0SP (tel/fax 01766-522720; e-mail gwyndy@lineone.net). 10-bedroom hotel with 30-seat restaurant serving breakfast and evening meals.
Kitchen Porter. Wages at national minimum rate. To work 5 days per week. Must be over 16 years of age.
Assistant Chef. Wages at national minimum rate. To work 5 days per week. Experience required.

Housekeeper. Wages at national minimum rate. To work a 6-day week. Must be over 16 years of age.
Waiting Staff (5). Wages at national minimum rate. To work variable shifts. Previous experience preferred.
Staff needed between Easter and October and must speak fluent English. Accommodation not available.
Applications should be sent to Carol Jones from February. Interview required.

LAMPHEY COURT HOTEL: Lamphey, Pembroke, Pembrokeshire SA71 5NT (☎01646-672273; fax 01646-672480; e-mail info@lampheycourt.co.uk; www. lampheycourt.co.uk). A 4-star country hotel and leisure spa set in a pleasant village near the coast. Under present owner for 20 years with a friendly team of 25 staff.
General Assistants/Waiting Staff/Chamber Staff. Wages £160-£180 a week.
Breakfast Cook (1). Wages £160-£180 a week.
All staff work 5 days a week. Minimum work period 10 weeks, between Easter and the end of September. Some full-time positions are also available. B & L is available. Hotel experience helpful. Overseas applicants welcome.
Applications from February onwards to the Hotel General Manager, at the above address.

LION HOTEL: Y Maes, Criccieth, Gwynned LL52 0AA (☎01766-522460; fax 01766-523075; e-mail info@lionhotelcriccieth.co.uk; www.lionhotelcriccieth.co.uk). A busy 3-star hotel centrally situated in a seaside resort.
General Assistants (2). Wages at national minimum rate and over depending on age. To work 39 hours a week over 6 days.
Cook/Kitchen Assistant (1). Wages at national minimum rate depending on age and experience. Single accommodation and food is available, at a price to be negotiated. Minimum period of work 4 months.
Applications from 1 March to Mrs S.A. Burnett, Manageress, at the above address.

METROPOLE HOTEL: Temple Street, Llandrindod Wells, Powys LD1 5DY (☎01597-823700; fax 01579-824828; e-mail info@metropole.co.uk; www.metropole. co.uk). Family-owned and a member of the Best Western group, The Metropole is a 3-star Victorian style hotel with 120 bedrooms and extensive conference and banqueting facilities.
Waiting Staff (6), Commis Chefs (4). Wages at national minimum rate. All staff to work 5 days per week plus overtime if necessary. Minimum period of work 8 months; staff required all year round. Accommodation available at a cost of £22.75 per week. Minimum age 18 years. Overseas applicants welcome. All applicants must be available for interview.
Applications at any time to Mr Robert Wyn Hughes, General Manager, at the above address.

MIN-Y-DON HOTEL: North Parade, Llandudno LL30 2LP (☎01492-876511; fax 01492-878169; www.llandudno.com/minydon). Located on the north shore seafront, opposite the famous Victorian pier.
Room Assistants (2), Hotel Assistants (2), Dining Room Assistants (2) to work from June to October. Wages and hours by arrangement. Accommodation is available. Applicants should be under 21. Overseas applicants welcome.
Applications to the Manager at the above address.

PORTH TOCYN HOTEL: Abersoch, Gwynedd LL53 7BU (☎01758-713303; fax 01758-713538; e-mail bookings@porthtocyn.fsnet.co.uk; www.porth-tocyn-hotel.co.uk). A country house hotel by the sea, filled with antiques. The house has been in the family for 56 years, and has been in the Good Food Guide for more than 40 years.

General Assistants (10), Assistant Cooks (4). Wages guaranteed above the national minimum wage. Free B & L and use of tennis court and swimming pool. Intelligence and sense of humour required. Cooking experience useful but not essential. Minimum period of work 6 weeks between March and November.

Applications from those who are able to work over Easter and/or outside the summer university vacation period especially welcome. Travel expenses will be paid for those able to work for short stints over Easter and the spring bank holidays.

Applications with s.a.e. to Mrs Fletcher-Brewer, Porth Tocyn Hotel.

THE ST DAVID'S HOTEL AND SPA: Havannah Street, Cardiff CF10 5SD (☎02920-313043; fax 02920-313044; e-mail thestdavidshotel@roccofortehotels.com; www.thestdavidshotel.com). The St David's Hotel and Spa, Wales's premier 5-star hotel, is located at the waterfront of the Cardiff Bay development. One of Rocco Forte's Hotels, it offers excellent opportunities for staff development.

Waiting Staff, Housekeeping Staff and Kitchen Staff. Wages around £5.35 per hour. All to work five days per week. Fluent English essential.

Applications should be sent to the above address. Interview required for UK residents.

TYN-Y-COED HOTEL: Capel Curig, Betws-y-Coed LL24 0EE (☎01690-720331; e-mail res@tyn-y-coed.co.uk; www.tyn-y-coed.co.uk). A small, friendly 4-star inn in the centre of Snowdonia, which caters mainly for mountain users and tourists.

General Assistants (4). Wages from national minimum wage for approximately 40 hours a week. To work 5 days per week on split shifts. Full board accommodation available. Minimum age 18.

Applications to G.F. Wainwright, Tyn-y-Coed Hotel.

Language Schools

ENGLISH STUDY CENTRE: 19-21 Uplands Crescent, Swansea, West Glamorgan SA2 0NX (☎01792-464103; fax 01792-472303; e-mail info@escwales.co.uk; www.escwales.co.uk).

EFL Teachers (3-4) to teach adults or junior groups. £11.50 to £12.50 per hour, 15 to 30 hours per week. Minimum period of work three weeks between the beginning of June and the end of August. No accommodation provided. Must be graduates with TEFL qualifications and/or experience and able to speak English to the level of a native speaker.

Applications from March to Esther Richards, Principal, at the above address. Interview if possible.

UNIVERSITY OF WALES ABERYSTWYTH: Language and Learning Centre, Llandinam Building, Penglais Campus, Aberystwyth SY23 3DB (☎01970-622545; fax 01970-622546; e-mail tesol@aber.ac.uk; www.aber.ac.uk/tesol). Attractive working environment in a secure seaside location between the coast of Cardigan Bay and the Cambrian Mountains. The centre offers courses to language learners and language teachers in a warm and welcoming academic environment.

EFL Teachers (6-10). £385 per week. Work involves 20 hours of teaching per week, plus 16 hours of social duties per month and 12 hours of administration per month. Minimum period of work one month between mid-July and early September. B & L available. Applicants must have native-speaker competence in English. First degree, TEFL qualifications and 3 years experience required. Interview necessary.
Applications from 1 January to Rex Berridge, Director, at the above address.

Medical

A & D NURSING AGENCY: 1-2 Moorcroft Mews, High Street, Saltney, Flintshire CH4 8SH (☎01244-679111; fax 01244-677913; e-mail adcareplus@axis-connect.com). Family-run agency. Winner of the Investors in People Award.
Qualified RGN, RMN and SEN Nurses needed to cover for the sickness, holiday and maternity leave of permanent staff in various establishments including nursing homes, hospitals, industry and community. Wages £13-£19 per hour.
Health Care Assistants for care duties. Wages £6.20-£8.00 per hour.
Staff required at any time of year. Applicants should be aged between 18 and 65. For employees with no experience in the field of care, the agency runs a 3 week 'introduction to care' course.
Applications to Debra Lee Mahon, Proprietor, at the above address.

Outdoor

ROUSTABOUT LTD: Frongouch Boatyard, Smugglers Cove, Nr. Aberdovey, Gwynedd, LL35 ORG (☎01654-767177; fax 01654767842; e-mail info@roustabout. info).
Tent Crew (5): for setting up and dismantling tents at events all over the UK and expanding to mainland Europe. Long, unsocial hours, masses of travel. Stay in own tents at events. May to September. Driving licence useful, but not essential. Must be physically fit.
Applications to Geoffrey Hill, Managing Director, at the above address.

Sport

ARTHOG OUTDOOR EDUCATION CENTRE: Arthog, Gwynned LL39 1BX (☎01341-250455; info@arthog.co.uk; www.arthog.co.uk). A Local Education Authority run centre situated below mountains, about 1km from the sea. Fully staffed by 7 professional instructors, it takes up to 90 clients.
Outdoor Instructors. Activities include mountaineering, canoeing, sailing, walking. Wages according to qualifications. RYA, ML, or BCU qualifications useful, teaching certificate a bonus. Interested applicants without qualifications may be taken on, but on a voluntary basis. Work equivalent to 5 days a week, but long hours. Free board and accommodation provided. Overseas applicants considered.
Applications to Head Office at the above address.

CANTREF TREKKING CENTRE: Brecon, Powys LD3 8LR (☎01874-665223; e-mail info@cantref.com; www.cantref.com). Situated in the Brecon Beacon mountain range. Lots of riding involved and contact with a variety of people of all ages and from many countries.
Pony Trekking Guides (2). Wages on application. B & L available. Hours according to length of treks, with possibility of overtime. To work 5 days a week. Period of work July to 1 September. Applicants must be prepared to work the specified length of time. Minimum age 18. Must be experienced rider and able to get along well with people.

Applications, enclosing s.a.e., from March to M. Evans, Cantref Pony Trekking Centre.

CLYNE FARM ACTIVITY CENTRE: Westport Avenue, Mayals, Swansea SA3 5AR (☎01792-403333; fax 01792-403339; e-mail info@clynefarm.com; www. clynefarm.com). Multi-activity centre in converted stone buildings with a wide range of client groups from school and youth groups to adults and families. Activities include everything from archery to windsurfing.
Activity Instructor, Riding Instructor. Wages from £180 per week depending on qualifications and experience. To work 40 hours per week. Minimum period of work one month between May and September. No accommodation available. Foreign applicants with recognised qualifications and good English welcome.
Applications to Geoff Haden at the above address from January. Interview required.

GRANGE TREKKING CENTRE: The Grange, Capel-y-ffin, Abergavenny NP7 7NP (☎01873-890215; fax 01843-890157; www.grangetrekking.co.uk). A small, informal family-run centre situated in a very rural area, high in the beautiful Black Mountains, Wales. Remote area with breathtaking scenery; eight miles to the nearest shops and no public transport.
Trek Leader and Assistant Leader for a variety of work including mucking out, trek leading, cleaning, maintenance and dealing with customers. Some training available. Salary and hours negotiable. Free accommodation in caravan with shower block. Must be over 18 years old; first aid qualifications preferable. Also the possibility of looking after two little girls, aged six and seven, for a few hours a day.
Minimum period of work 1 month between Easter and October. Overseas applicants with good English welcome. Preferable that candidates can attend an interview but not essential.
Applications from February onwards to Jessica Griffiths at the above address.

PGL TRAVEL LTD: Alton Court, Penyard Lane, Ross-on-Wye, Herefordshire HR9 5GL (☎0870-401 4411; e-mail recruitment@pgl.co.uk; www.pgl.co.uk/recruitment). PGL recruit around 2,000 staff each year to assist with the running of their children's activity centres throughout the UK, including Devon, the Isle of Wight, Lincolnshire, the south coast, Surrey, Shropshire, Perthshire, and Wales. PGL jobs provide a break from the 9-5 routine. If you are enthusiastic, energetic and looking for real experience and responsibility in a stimulating environment, PGL could have the job for you.
Activity Instructors in canoeing, sailing, windsurfing, fencing, archery, motorsports, pony trekking, and more. Qualifications not essential for all positions as full training will be provided. Minimum age 18.
Group Leaders also needed to take responsibility for groups of children, helping then to get the most out of their holiday. Previous experience of working with children is an advantage. Minimum age 18.
Support Staff to assist the catering, domestic, and maintenance teams.
From £70-£100 per week plus free B & L. Positions available from February-November, for the full season, as little as eight weeks, or any period in between, although there are very few summer-only vacancies.
Applications can be made online, downloaded from the website, or call for an information pack.

SNOWDONIA RIDING STABLES: Waunfawr, Caernarfon, Gwynedd LL55 4PQ (☎01286-650342; e-mail riding@snowdonia2000.fsnet.co.uk; www.snowdonia2000.

fsnet.co.uk). A trekking centre/riding school with approximately 50 horses including dressage/event horses, young stock and liveries.
Trek Leaders (2). Work includes care of horses, yard work, trek leading and light maintenance work. Accommodation is available in self-catering caravans free of charge.
Wages on application; to work approximately 40 hours per week. Staff are required from mid-July to mid-September. Applicants must be over 18 with good riding ability. Overseas applications are welcome.
Applications should be sent to Mrs R. Thomas at the above address from Spring onwards.

SOUTH WALES CARRIAGE DRIVING CENTRE: Llwyn Mawr Farm, Gowerton, Swansea SA4 3RB (☎01792-874299; e-mail info@rowena-moyse.com; www.rowena-moyse.com). Small company teaching people how to drive a horse and carriage for commercial work and just for fun.
Volunteer Stable Staff, Carriage Driving Horse Assistants (max. 2 at any one time). Hours to suit, must be over 16. Accommodation could be provided. Fluent English is essential.
Apply to Rowena Moyse at the above address at anytime.

TAL-Y-FOEL RIDING CENTRE: Dwyran, Anglesey LL61 6LQ (☎01248-430377; e-mail riding@tal-y-foel.co.uk; www.tal-y-foel.co.uk). A friendly BHS approved centre on the shores of the Menai Straits. Facilities include indoor and outdoor menage, cross country training course, four miles of grass tracks, liveries, lessons and treks.
Yard Staff/Ride Leaders (4). £75 per week plus free accommodation in a caravan. To work from June to August; minimum period of work 8 weeks. Must be qualified in riding and stable management. Overseas applicants who are available to attend an interview welcome.
Applications from January to Kayte Lloyd-Hughes at the above address.

Voluntary Work

Conservation and the Environment

BARDSEY ISLAND BIRD AND FIELD OBSERVATORY: Cristin, Bardsey off Aberdaron, via Pwllheli, Gwynedd LL53 8DE (e-mail warden@bbfo.org.uk; www.bbfo.org.uk).
Volunteer programme for assistant wardens on a bird island 2 miles off the tip of the Lleyn Peninsula. On account of the location, postal mail can often be delayed due to bad weather, as can normal ferry service. Only Orange and Vodafone mobiles work.
For further *details* contact the warden..

THE CENTRE FOR ALTERNATIVE TECHNOLOGY: Machynlleth, Powys SY20 9AZ (01654-705950; fax 01654-702782; e-mail info@cat.org.uk; www.cat.org.uk).
Established in 1974, the Centre for Alternative Technology is an internationally renowned display and education centre promoting practical ideas and information on technologies, which sustain rather than damage the environment.
The Centre runs a short term volunteer programme, from March to September inclusive,

for stays of one or two weeks. There is also a long-term volunteer programme for individuals to help in specific work departments for 6 months. Short-term volunteers help with gardening, landscaping, site maintenance and preparation for courses. Long-term jobs for volunteers include the following departments: biology, engineering, gardening, information, media and site maintenance.

Applicants for the long-term programme should have relevant experience. Applicants for either programme can be of any nationality; long-term volunteers must be eligible for British state benefit payments, or be able to fund themselves. Accommodation for short-term is basic, youth hostel style, shared with other volunteers and with food and drinks provided. Other arrangements for long-term volunteers.

Applicants for the 60 short-term places and the 16 long-term places available annually should contact Rick Dance at the above address.

THE WILDLIFE TRUST OF SOUTH AND WEST WALES: The Welsh Wildlife Centre, Cilgerran, Pembrokeshire SA43 2TB (☎01239-621212/621600; fax 01239-613211; e-mail islands@welshwildlife.org for Skomer Island or wwc@welshwildlife. org for other enquiries; www.welshwildlife.org).
The fourth largest wildlife trust in the UK, covering more than 100 nature reserves. Concerned with educating people about the Welsh environment, and its protection and potential.
Voluntary Assistant Wardens required for Skomer Island, a national nature reserve off the Welsh coast. Work involves greeting visitors, census work, general reserve maintenance and wildlife recording, etc. Island volunteers will work for a full week (Saturday to Saturday) or a maximum of 2 weeks between Easter and October. Self-catering accommodation is available free of charge but food is not included. Minimum age 16 with an interest in natural history. Overseas applicants welcome.
Application forms available from Island Bookings or apply via e-mail if overseas.

Heritage

FFESTINIOG RAILWAY COMPANY: Harbour Station, Porthmadog, Gwynedd, North Wales LL49 9NF (☎01766-516035; e-mail tricia.doyle@festrail.co.uk; www. festrail.co.uk).
Hundreds of volunteers are needed throughout the year to help in the operation and maintenance of a 150-year old narrow gauge railway between Porthmadog and Blaenau Ffestiniog. The work done by individual volunteers depends on their skills, many of which are built up over a period of regular commitment to the railway which provides on-the-job training. The railway is divided into various diverse departments, and so jobs range from selling tickets and souvenirs to the 'elite' task of driving the engines.
Railway enthusiasts and non-enthusiasts of any nationality may apply provided they speak a good standard of English. Minimum age of 16 years. Limited self-catering accommodation is provided for regular volunteers, for which a small charge is made; food is extra. Camping space and a list of local accommodation is also available.
Further information may be obtained from the Volunteers Resource Manager, Ffestiniog Railway Company.

WELSHPOOL AND LLANFAIR RAILWAY: The Station, Pool Road, Llanfair, Caereinon, Welshpool, Powys SY21 OSF (☎01938-810441; fax 01938-810861; e-mail info@wllr.org.uk; www.wllr.org.uk).
Volunteer operated steam railway in mid-Wales offering working holidays in a

leisurely atmosphere. Travels through the beautiful mid-Wales countryside in the delightful Banwy Valley.
Volunteer Maintenance Staff (up to 10 at any time) for varied duties including the clearing of vegetation at any time of year. No pocket money paid, but accommodation available at cheap rates. Should be over 16, fit, healthy and enthusiastic.
Applications to the above address.

Social and Community Schemes

CHRISTIAN MOUNTAIN CENTRE: Pensarn Harbour, Llanbedr, Gwynedd LL45 2HS (tel/fax 01341-241646; e-mail office@cmcpensarn.org.uk; www.cmcpensarn. org.uk).
Support Staff (4). To volunteer 40 hours per week year round. Food, accommodation and a small allowance provided. No qualifications necessary.
Apply all year round to Mr M. Downey at the above address.

Workcamps

UNA EXCHANGE: Temple of Peace, Cathays Park, Cardiff, South Glamorgan CF10 3AP (☎029-2022 3088; fax 029-2022 2540; e-mail info@unaexchange.org; www. unaexchange.org).
Registered charity number 700760 that has been organising international volunteer projects since 1973, exchanging people between the UK and more than 60 countries worldwide.
Volunteers can take part in international voluntary action throughout all continents through a wide range of social, construction, cultural and environmental projects. Usually 6-8 hours work per day, 5 days per week. Must pay own travel costs but administration fee covers B & L. Administration fee is £110-£140, some projects require a further supplement. Minimum age for most projects is 18 but there is also a teenage project within Europe. No qualifications required. Period of work varies according to project; many projects are 2-4 weeks and longer term opportunities range from 1-12 months. Camps arranged virtually all year round. The UNA Exchange projects in Wales are primarily for overseas volunteers, though there are places for UK workers on some camps. Volunteers resident outside the UK must apply through the workcamp organisation in their own country.
Project Leaders are also required for Wales projects. They are trained every year over the Easter bank holiday weekend, pay no fee and have travel expenses reimbursed. This can lead to further opportunities including leading projects abroad.
Applications preferably by e-mail to outgoing@unaexchange.org or by post to the above address.

Northern Ireland

Prospects for Work.
Over the last decade the economy of Northern Ireland has been the fastest growing of all the UK regions with unemployment rates now lower than some regions on the mainland, and strong economic growth. In and around Belfast most vacancies are in the retail, hotel and restaurant trade. Further afield, hotel work is more plentiful in the lakeland areas of Co. Fermanagh and in seaside towns such as Portrush and Newcastle. Short-term relief rangers are needed at the various country parks in Northern Ireland from April-May onwards; recruitment is through the local Jobs and Benefits offices and JobCentres. Students may register for seasonal work with private employment agencies or Jobs and Benefits and JobCentre offices, which are located throughout Northern Ireland. Holiday job vacancies for specific areas are usually advertised in local newspapers, job clubs and libraries.

Business and Industry

JOHN BROWNLEE: Knockmakagan, Newtownbutler, County Fermanagh (☎028-6773 8277/028-6773 8275 (home) or 0798-432 131; e-mailsales@ fermanaghspringwater.com; www.fermanaghspringwater.com).
Bottlers of Spring Water (2). Wages at national minimum rate. Free accommodation at farm. Work available all year round. Overseas applicants welcome.
Applications to Mr John Brownlee at the above address.

Holiday Centres and Amusements

GREENHILL YMCA NATIONAL CENTRE: Donard Park, Newcastle, County Down BT33 0GR (☎028-4372 3172; fax 028-4372 6009; e-mail doreen.mcneilly@ greenhill-ymca.org; www.greenhill-ymca.org). Situated at the foot of the Mourne Mountains, overlooking the seaside town of Newcastle.
Instructors (20). To work up to 3 sessions per day. Experience or qualifications in one of the following is required: mountaineering, canoeing, orienteering, archery, environmental studies or working with young people on day camps. Minimum age 18 but persons over age 20 preferred. Staff will be responsible for children and young people, so vetting references as to suitability in this area will be required.
Drivers. Must be over 25 years old, reliable, safe and experienced in driving minibuses and towing trailers. An up to date clean driving licence will be required.
Domestic Hosts (5). Must be hard-working, sociable and responsible.
Summer Camp Staff.
   All staff are given expenses of £60 plus free B & L. Hours variable, 5 days a week in most cases. Minimum period of work is 6 weeks. Instructors and day camp staff must attend a staff training programme from 1 July to 28 August. Greenhill is a Christian Centre; applicants should therefore be supportive of its Christian ethos and promotion of the same. Applicants must speak fluent English and supply photocopies of relevant qualifications. One year Instructor posts (September-August) are also available for mature people who are active in the Christian faith.
   Applications should be sent a.s.a.p. to the Volunteer Co-ordinator at the above address.

OASIS RETAIL SERVICES: 4 Trench Road, Mallusk, Newtonabbey, County Antrim BT36 4TY (☎028-9084 5845; fax 028-9084 5840; e-mail sjomalley@oasisrs.com). A network of amusement centres in Northern Ireland, with about 100 employees in total.

Arcade Operatives (10-15). Wages at national minimum rate. To work either full-time or part-time between Easter and October; minimum period of work is 2 months. Must be 18 or over. Fluent English is required; any non-UK citizen with fluency in the language will be considered.

Apply, from January, to Mrs S.J. O'Malley at the above address. An interview will be required, but this can be conducted by telephone.

Hotels and Catering

CHIMNEY CORNER HOTEL: 630 Antrim Road, Newtonabbey, County Antrim BT36 4RH (☎028-9084 4925; fax 028-9084 4352; e-mail info@chimneycorner.co.uk; www.chimneycorner.co.uk).

Waiting Staff (2), Commis Chef, Receptionist. Wages from national minimum wage (waiting staff may also get tips) plus meals. All posts work 40 hours per 5-day week. Staff required from 1 July. The work is mainly restaurant work and overtime may be available at the hotel's nightclub. Training will be given for all posts; waiting staff should have a pleasant disposition, and applicants for receptionist should have good telephone skills and a basic knowledge of computers.

To apply contact the Manager at the hotel.

Outdoor

LADY P BLACKWOOD: 141 Crawfordsburn Road, Newtownwards, County Down, N Ireland BT23 4UJ (☎028-9181 2603).

Horse Carer to clean stables and care for horses. Agricultural wage rates paid and accommodation in shared bungalow. Required from May to October. Previous jobs with horses and experience of caring for them is essential.

Applications to P Blackwood at the above address.

JOHN BROWNLEE: Knockmakagan, Newtownbutler, County Fermanagh (☎028-6773 8277/028-6773 8275 (home) or 079-8943 2131; e-mail sales@fermanaghspringwater.com; www.fermanaghspringwater.com). 5 apple orchards situated half an hour from Enniskillen, on the border with the Republic of Ireland. Many tourist attractions in the area.

Fruit Pickers (4-6) required for apple orchard work, either hand-picking or shaking. Wages at piece work rates. Period of work September and October. No accommodation, but workers can camp at farm. Overseas applicants, preferably from EU countries, welcome. Applicants must be in good physical condition as work is heavy manual labour.

Applications and enquiries to Mr John Brownlee at the above address, in July.

DAVISON CANNERS LTD: 107 Summerisland Road, Portadown, County Armagh BT62 1SJ (☎028-3885 1661; fax 028-3885 2288; info@davisoncanners.com). Harvests and processes fruit for retail, catering and bakery markets, mainly in the UK and Ireland.

Fruit Pickers. Wages at piece work rates. To work five to six days a week for approximately six weeks from September until the end of October. Accommodation is available.

Applications to Mr Alan Davison at the above address.

NORTH DOWN MARQUEES LTD: 39 Ballynahinch Road, Carryduff, County Down BT8 8DL (☎028-9081 5535; fax 028-9081 2344; e-mail enquiries@ northdownmarquees.co.uk; www.northdownmarquees.co.uk). One of the largest marquee companies in Ireland, established 20 years ago, always busy.
Marquee Erectors (10). Wages negotiable. Physically demanding work and hours can be long; applicants must be able to work under pressure and take responsibility. Positions are available from June to October. Foreign applicants welcome. No accommodation available.
Applications should be made from April onwards to the above address. Interview necessary, may be by telephone.

Sport

SHARE HOLIDAY VILLAGE: Smiths Strand, Lisnaskea, County Fermanagh BT92 OEQ (☎028-6772 2122; fax 028-6772 1893; e-mail katie@sharevillage.org; www. sharevillage.org). The largest activity centre in Northern Ireland. A charity dedicated to providing opportunities for able bodied and disabled people to take part in a wide range of activities together. A team of 25 to 30 paid staff and volunteers works with families, individuals and groups of all ages.
Outdoor Activity Instructors (6) to work 5 days plus one night a week. Applicants must be aged over 18 and have one of the following qualifications; RYA dinghy sailing instruction; BCU canoe or kayak instructor plus current first aid certificate; or RYA powerboat handling level II. Wages £50 to £120 per week depending on qualifications plus meals and accommodation. To work from early May to the end of September/ early October.
Applications to Katie Furfey, Volunteer Co-ordinator, at the above address.

Voluntary Work

Conservation and the Environment

CONSERVATION VOLUNTEERS NORTHERN IRELAND: 159 Ravenhill Road, Belfast BT6 0BP (☎028-9064 5169; fax 028-9064 4409; e-mail CVNI@btcv. org.uk; www.btcv.org.uk).
Conservation Volunteers Northern Ireland is part of BTCV, which involves more than 70,000 volunteers each year in environmental projects throughout Northern Ireland, England, Wales and Scotland, making it the largest practical conservation charity in the country.
Volunteers to participate in projects to inspire people to improve the places they live in throughout Northern Ireland. These include community development work, biodiversity projects, health initiatives and use of practical skills etc. There are opportunities to suit all levels of commitment. For those who wish to take on extra responsibility, a commitment of at least six months is requested.
All training, protective clothing and tools are provided according to the role the volunteer takes on. No experience is necessary. Minimum age is 18. Limited amount of free accommodation for volunteer officers.
Applications for volunteers and volunteer officers to Kate Holohan, at the above address, at any time of the year.

Physically/Mentally Disabled

SHARE HOLIDAY VILLAGE: Smith's Strand, Linaskea, County Fermanagh BT9 0EQ (☎028-6772 2122; fax 028-6772 1893; e-mail katie@sharevillage.org; www. sharevillage.org).

A residential outdoor activity centre for the disabled and the able bodied, located on the shores of Upper Lough Erne. Activities include day trips, barge trips, evening social events and a wide range of outdoor and art activities.

Share Holiday Village is looking for volunteers to work as **Carer Companions** to elderly and disabled guests who come on respite care holidays in the summer months. There are also limited places for volunteer outdoor pursuit instructors with relevant recognised qualifications e.g. RYA, BCU and First Aid.

Approximately 60 volunteers are required for a minimum stay of 7 days from May until September. Shared accommodation and all meals are provided as are necessary travel expenses within Northern Ireland. Minimum age 18.

Applications to the Volunteer Co-ordinator at the above address.

Au Pair, Home Help & Paying Guest Agencies

Prospects for Work.
Finding a job as a mother's help or au pair in Britain is reasonably easy and is ideally suited to overseas visitors eager to improve their English. Families taking home helps are most common in London and the South-East, but mothers returning to work have brought a steady increase in demand nationwide. The majority prefer a commitment of six months to a year, but others require help for just two or three months over the summer.

The work may involve little more than light housework, playing with the children and some simple cooking. The pay, hours and training of au pairs in Britain can vary since the job is seen more as an opportunity to learn English and experience another culture than actual employment. So, while a few work longer hours, others are given great freedom, the use of the car and *Cordon Bleu* meals. Most enjoy something between the two and find working with a family to be a positive experience.

Hours vary according to the position: au pairs work 25 to 30 hours per week, *au pair plus* more than that, and the now rare *demi pairs* should expect to work about 3 hours per day. Mother's helps tend to work longer hours still, and are therefore usually UK nationals (see below) although nationals of the new EU countries are increasingly taking on this work. While the earning potential of qualified nannies has seen a dramatic rise recently, with the weekly salary of some as high as £380 per week with lucrative perks, au pairs should still expect to receive pocket money of at least £55 or so per week. Mother's helps and au pairs plus can expect in the region of £65-£70. Free board and lodging are included. Qualifications are rarely required (except for nannies), but babysitting experience is always useful.

Males can also find employment in what has been a traditionally female trade. Undeniably, au pairs remain predominately female, however, the growing number of progressive agencies taking male au pairs increasingly find that more and more families are willing to try one and are, in general, pleased with their decision. Kingston College in Surrey accepts male students on their National Nursery Examination Board nanny training course. Some agencies estimate that male au pairs account for up to 30% of the placements they make, but around 3% is nearer the norm.

Many agencies specialise in the recruitment of home helps, and it is important to contact several in order to compare terms. They should not charge for this service. You will be asked to fill out a questionnaire and should then receive a contract laying down working conditions, hours, pay etc. Insist on being given more choice if you are not satisfied with the family allotted to you.

Immigration: nationals of the EU and of European Economic Area Countries are free to take employment in the United Kingdom including taking up 'au pair' placements – including, of course, the countries that entered the EEA in May 2004 (Estonia, Latvia, Lithuania, Poland, the Czech Republic, Slovakia, Hungary, Slovenia, Malta and Cyprus).

Nationals of any of the following countries are also permitted to work as au pairs in the UK: Andorra, Bosnia-Herzegovina, Bulgaria, Croatia, The Faroes, Greenland, Macedonia, Monaco, Romania, San Marino and Turkey. Nationals of Bosnia-Herzegovina, Bulgaria, Croatia, Macedonia, Romania and Turkey must obtain a visa before travelling to the United Kingdom. The au pair scheme now falls under Tier 5 of the new Points Based System of Migration. Visa application forms (form VAF1 non-settlement) can be obtained from the applicant's nearest UK Overseas Mission with a visa section, or at www.ukvisas.gov.uk/forms. Some au pair agencies only deal with EEA nationals. Further information and guidance can be found at the UKVisas website: www.ukvisas.gov.uk/aupairs.

The Home Office lays down certain regulations regarding au pairs; they must be single and without dependants; aged 17-27; should help in the home for a maximum of 5 hours per day, with 2 free days per week; receive full board and their own room, a reasonable allowance (normally at least £55 per week) and sufficient time to attend language classes. Foreign nationals from outside the EU must not intend to stay in the UK as an au pair for longer than two years, and must be able to maintain and accommodate themselves without recourse to public funds.

The au pair should produce, on arrival, a valid passport and a letter of invitation from the host family giving full details of the family and household, the duties they will be expected to undertake, the allowance they will receive and the amount of free time they will have for study and recreation.

AA AU PAIRS UK LTD: 11 Roy Road, Northwood, Middlesex HA6 1EQ (☎01923-450714; fax 01923-833555; e-mail aaaupairs@aol.com). Agency offering UK-wide placements and a reliable friendly service.
Au Pairs, Mother's Helps, Nannies and Housekeepers Minimum stay 3 months for summer placements. Applicants must be able to provide references that can be checked – those already in the UK can sometimes be placed within one or two days. The agency tries to match applicants to families with similar interests.
Applications and enquiries to Mrs Savi Cockeram, Director, at the above address.

A-ONE AU-PAIRS & NANNIES: Court Lodge House, 9 Rookes Lane, Lymington, Hampshire SO41 8FP (☎01590-689496; fax by arrangement; e-mail info@aupairsetc.co.uk; www.aupairsetc.co.uk).
Au Pairs, Au Pairs Plus and Temporary And Permanent Nannies placed in the United Kingdom. Wages/pocket money are £55-£65 for up to 25 hours work per week. Higher pocket money for Au Pairs plus. £3 per hour for extra hours worked over 25 hours per week. Minimum stay is 6 months during the year. Summer placements can be made.
Applicants should be aged 18-27 and have some childcare experience and be able to hold at least a basic conversation in English. Nationalities placed according to Home Office Guidelines for the UK. Au pairs plus must be from EU countries in accordance with British law. About 20% of applicants placed are male. Placement time varies; longer waiting time for males than females. Language classes are available in every town.
Applications to Mrs. Karen Hopwood, Proprietor.

ABBEY AU PAIRS: 8 Boulnois Avenue, Parkstone, Poole, Dorset BH14 9NX (☎01202-732922; fax 01202-466098; e-mail ursula.foyle@ntlworld.com). Established in 1988, the agency places girls with families mainly around Bournemouth and Poole. Regular coffee mornings are held and advice is given on language classes and activities.

Au Pair Placements. Normal housework and childcare duties. 2/3 evenings per week babysitting. Wages £55 per week for a 25-hour week with full board and lodging. Minimum period of work 2 months. Positions are available all year round.
Applications should be made at any time to Mrs Ursula Foyle at the above address.

ACADEMY AU PAIR & NANNY AGENCY: 42 Milsted Road, Gillingham, Kent ME8 6SU (tel/fax 01634-310808; e-mail enquiries@aupair-select.com; www.aupair-select.com). Established for 15 years and full members of REC. Staff are friendly, knowledgeable, and always available to assist in enquiries.
Au Pairs. Wages £45 for 25 hours work per week. Must be aged between 18 and 27 with some babysitting experience. Non smokers and drivers preferred.
Au Pairs Plus. Wages £50-£60 for a minimum of 30 hours work per week. Conditions as above.
Mothers Helps. Starting at £150 per week for a 40/45 hour week, must be experienced in sole charge childcare. Must be able to produce a current CV and references.
Nannies. Minimum of £200 for 40/45 hours work per week. Qualifications required, such as BTECH, NNEB, NAMCW. CV and references required.
Placements are throughout the UK from Edinburgh to the south coast of England. Work is available from mid-June/early July to the beginning/mid-September; minimum period of work 2 months. Accommodation available at no extra charge. Overseas applicants welcome. An interview is not necessary for the au pair positions, but may be necessary for those wishing to work as nannies.
Applications should be made before 1 March to J Bosworth at the above address.

ACE AU PAIRS: 27 Chickerell Road, Park North, Swindon, Wiltshire SN3 2RQ (tel/fax 01793 430091; e-mail info@aceaupairs.co.uk; www.aceaupairs.co.uk). Friendly family agency offering free of charge service to au pairs.
Au pairs (800). Wages minimum of £55 per week. Some 6-week placements available, otherwise minimum stay is 2 to 3 months in the summer. Applicants must have proven childcare experience, and be aged 17 to 27. All nationalities eligible to work in the UK welcome. Male applicants must provide police check.
Applications with a minimum of 2 childcare references to V. Huntley, Proprietor. Telephone interviews required with both agency and interested family.

ACROBAT AUPAIRS AGENCY: 435 Chorley Road, Horwich, Bolton BL6 6EJ (☎01204-694422; e-mail info@aupairsnannies.co.uk; www.acrobataupairs.com). Specialist au pairs agency with opportunities to work with families in Britain and learn languages at a local college or university.
Demi Pairs (20) for a maximum of 2-3 hours per day plus babysitting usually 2 evenings a week. Two days will be completely free for own leisure time. Own room and meals provided plus £15 pocket money a week.
Au Pairs (70) for up to 5 hours per day with 2 days off per week. Own room and meals provided plus £55 per week. Also opportunity to have English classes.
Au Pair Plus (40) for 35 hours per week plus babysitting 2-3 evenings a week. Two days free each week. Room and meals provided free of charge plus £70 a week salary. Can sometimes attend English classes.
Nannies (20) for 8-9 hours a day. Must have NNEB qualification or similar. Salary £120-£250 per week.
All positions open for girls and boys aged 17/18-27 years old. Vacancies range from 1 month to 2 years. Au Pair Plus for EC Nationals only and Nannies minimum age 18 years old.
Applications welcome from all EC Nationals and Andorra, Bosnia-Herzegovina,

Croatia, Cyprus, Faroe Islands, Greenland, Liechtenstein, Macedonia, Malta, Monaco, San Marino, Slovenia, Switzerland and Turkey.

ANGELS INTERNATIONAL AU PAIR AGENCY: 3 The Hollies, Brunswick Close, Twickenham, Middlesex TW2 5JZ (☎020-8893 4400; e-mail admin@ angelsint.demon.co.uk; www.aupair1.com). An au pair agency specialising in placements within the UK as well as Spain, Italy, France and Switzerland.
Au Pairs (350). Pocket money between £55 and£120 per week. To work 25 to 40 hours per week. Childcare experience necessary. Placements can be anywhere in length from 3 months to 2 years. Applicants applying from abroad pay no fees; applicants wishing to go abroad pay £100 in fees. Angels International offers full support for both families and au pairs, offering help with language classes, trouble shooting and accommodation if necessary.
To *apply*, e-mail the above address.

THE AU-PAIR AGENCY: 231 Hale Lane, Edgware, Middlesex HA8 9QF (☎020 8958 1750. Fax: 020 8958 5261. E-mail: elaine@aupairagency.com. Website: www. aupairagency.com).
Au Pairs, Au Pair Plus And Mother's Help positions throughout Britain. Minimum stay 9 to 12 months or longer, or summer holidays stays of 10 weeks minimum. Wages/pocket money of £55 per week for au pairs, £75 for au-pair plus, £150 net for mother's helps. Reasonable conversational ability in English language plus proven childcare ability required.
Contact the agency for an application or apply on-line by visiting the website www.aupairagency.com.

AU PAIR CONNECTIONS: 39 Tamarisk Road, Hedge End, Hampshire SO30 4TN (☎01489-780438; fax 01489-692656; e-mail info@aupair-connections.co.uk; www. aupair-connections.co.uk). An Au Pair agency operating in Southern England; some of the loveliest locations in the UK.
Au Pairs/Mothers Helps (300). Wages £45 per week for Au Pairs and a minimum of £60 for Au Pairs Plus. To work 25 hours per week or more. Period of work mid-June to mid-September; minimum period of work six weeks. Must have a minimum of two years childcare experience and be at least 18. Accommodation available free of charge.
Applications from January to mid-June to Denise Blighe at the above address. Note that all applicants must enclose either an IRC or a s.a.e.

A2Z AUPAIRS: Catwell House, Catwell, Williton, Taunton TA4 4PF (☎01984-632422; e-mail enquiries@a2zaupairs.com; wwwa2zaupairs.com).
Au Pairs (20) required in May/June, to work 25 hours per week looking after children and carrying out light housework. Pocket money of £60 per week plus accommodation. Applicants should be aged between 17 and 27.
Summer Jobs in the tourist industry also available.
Applications should be made to Rebecca Haworth-Wood at the above address.

AU-PAIR INTERNATIONAL: Cherry Gardens, Nouds Lane, Lynsted, Kent ME9 0ES (☎ 01795-522544; fax 01795 522878; e-mail info@aupairinternational.co.uk; www.countyaupairs.co.uk).
Au Pairs placed in the UK for a minimum stay 6 to 12 months, but summer stays of 2 to 3 months also available. Pocket money is £55 per week for Au-Pairs, £70 per week for Au-Pair Plus. Applicants should be 17 to 27yrs old, with some childcare

experience and childcare references. All nationalities that are within the British au-pair scheme can be accepted. Male applicants can also be placed. 2 to 3 childcare references and 2 character references needed with application; personal interview held wherever possible.

Applications to Benedicte Speed, Managing Director.

AU PAIRS/NANNIES GALORE (THE SAPPHIRE AU PAIR/NANNY AGENCY): 4 Brookmans Avenue, Brookmans Park, Hatfield, Hertfordshire AL9 7QJ (tel/fax 01707-652187; e-mail sapphireaupairs@aol.com). Specialist agency for placing au pairs/nannies/mothers helps/housekeepers throughout the UK and Europe. Located near to north London/Hertfordshire. Free service to applicants.
Au Pairs, Mother's Helps, Nannies and Housekeepers. Excellent conditions. Good locations with colleges and essential amenities closeby. Minimum age 20. Must have a fair or reasonable conversational standard of English. Car drivers preferred but not essential. Non smokers essential.

Applications via e-mail or in writing to above address with current CV, 3 written references, current medical certificate, smiling photos and 'dear family' letter.

BELAF STUDY HOLIDAYS: Banner Lodge, Cherhill, Calne, Wiltshire SN11 8XR (☎01249-812551; fax 01249-821533; e-mail enquiries@belaf.com; www.belaf.com). Since 1975 Belaf has been organising holiday placements for European students in carefully selected families in Southern England, London and the surrounding regions, Wiltshire, Dorset, Hampshire, Gloucestershire and Somerset.
Au Pairs (200). Wages £40 to £60 per week plus accommodation. To work 25 hours per week from mid June to late August. Minimum period of work 6 weeks. Minimum age 18; all applicants must speak reasonably good English. Overseas applicants welcome.
Work Placements (40). 4-8 weeks throughout the year – in hotel, restaurant, tourism, engineering, schools. Minimum age 17 years.

Applications from January to May to Carole Browne at the above address.

BLOOMSBURY AU PAIRS: 14 Tottenham Court Road, PO Box 625, London W1T 1JK (☎020-3122 0025; fax 020-7430 2325; e-mail bloomsburo@aol.com; www.bloomsburyaupairs.co.uk). This international au pair agency, established in 1971, with partner agents in most EU countries and Australia places Au Pairs in the UK, Ireland, Europe and Australia (Sydney area).
Au Pairs. Wages £60-£120 per week. Required to work 25 to 30 hours per week. Work includes an element of light domestic duties.. Minimum period of work is 10-12 months, with some opportunities for summer placements between June and September. Must be between 18 and 27 years old, have a good command of English and supply verifiable references proving previous training or experience in childcare. Only EU passport holders can be considered, as well as Australian, Canadian and New Zealand nationals. No charge is made to the Au Pairs, but all applicants must pay their own fare to the country of destination.
Apply by contacting Marcella Keswick at the above address.

BUNTERS AU PAIR AND NANNY AGENCY: The Old Malt House, 6 Church Street, Pattishall, Towcester, Northamptonshire NN12 8NB (☎01327-831144; fax 01327-831155; e-mail office@aupairsnannies.com; www.aupairsnannies.com).
Au Pairs. Minimum £55 for 25 hours and 2 evenings work over 5 days per week. Board and lodging included. Applicants should have some childcare experience such as babysitting. Must be aged between 18 and 27. Staff required from May to September,

minimum period of work 8 weeks. Overseas applicants with some knowledge of English and valid working visas welcome.

Apply before May to Mrs Caroline Jones at the above address.

CINDERELLA AU PAIR AGENCY: 291 Kirkdale, Sydenham, London SE26 4QE (☎020-8659 1689; fax 020-8265 2330; e-mail aupairs@cinderella.co.uk; www. cinderellaaupairs.co.uk).
Au Pairs And Au Pairs Plus placed in London and throughout UK. Wages/pocket money of £55 per week for standard au pair in the UK plus a contribution from family towards language school fees. Minimum stay: 3 month summer placements; otherwise 6-12 months. Must have record of childcare jobs and references. Male au pairs occasionally placed.

Applications to Trisha Waghorn, Au Pair Co-ordinator.

CZECH MATE AU PAIR AGENCY: 19 Warwick Road, Altrincham, Cheshire WA15 9NS (☎0161-928 0023).
Au pairs (50). Wages £60 plus living expenses. To work 25 hours per week. Some childcare experience preferred; must be aged 18 and 27 years. Placements can be anywhere from 2 months to 2 years in length. No fees are charged to the applicant. The company offers a follow-up service to help au pairs to settle.

Apply by contacting Eva Todd at the above address.

EDGWARE AND SOLIHULL AU PAIR & NANNY AGENCY: PO Box 147, Radlett WD7 8WX (☎01923-289737; fax 01923-289739; e-mail info@the-aupair-shop.com; www.the-aupair-shop.com). Edgware and Solihull agencies have been established separately since 1963 and have now amalgamated.
Places **Au Pair** girls and boys throughout Great Britain and Ireland. Au Pairs live with the host family as a family member and have their own bedroom and full B & L, plus an amount of pocket money each week (from £55). Pocket money is paid weekly in arrears. Period of work 6 months to 2 years. Applicants must have permission to work in the UK.

For *further details* consult the above website or write to Amanda Pampel at the above address.

EURO PAIR AGENCY: 28 Derwent Avenue, Pinner, Middlesex HA5 4QJ (☎020-8421 2100; fax 020-8428 6416; e-mail info@europair.net; www.euro-pair.co.uk). The agency supplies French speaking au pairs to British families in Great Britain and English speaking au pairs to French families in France. It takes great care in the selection of posts available and has a back-up service if things do not work out.
Au Pairs (100+). Live-in positions. Wages of £60 for 5 hours work a day, five days a week. Minimum period of work of 6 months; it is possible to find summer positions but no guarantee is given. Positions are available all year. Applicants should be 18 and over, childcare experience and driving licence helpful.

Applications should be made at any time to Mrs C. Burt at the above address. Telephone interview required.

EURO PAIRS: 87 Greenfield Crescent, Patcham, Brighton BN1 8HL (☎01273-563887; fax 01273-888678; e-mail info@euro-pairs.com; www.euro-pairs.com).
Au Pairs (25). Wages £55-£70. To work 25 hours per week. Three month minimum placement, two year maximum placement. Applicants should be between 19-27. Adequate evidence of childcare experience will be required where necessary. Applicants are not charged any fee. The company will give advice on travel and local

language classes.
Apply via the website above. Applicants must have regular access to e-mail.

GENEVIEVE BROWNE AU PAIRS: Banner Lodge, Cherhill, Calne, Wiltshire SN11 8XR (☎01249-812551; fax 01249-821533; e-mail enquiries@belaf.com; www.belaf.com).
Au Pairs. Wages from £50 for 25 hours work per week with board and accommodation. Usual au pair duties including housework and childcare. Minimum period of work of 4 weeks. Positions are available all year. Minimum age 18.
Applications should be made at any time to Carole Browne at the above address.

GLOGOVICH AU PAIR AGENCY: Gransden Cottage, Tydcombe Road, Warlingham, Surrey CR6 9LU (☎01883-624842; fax 01883-624662; e-mail info@au-pair-agency.com; www.au-pair-agency.com).
Au Pairs placed with families living near London. Wages minimum of £55-£60 per week; to work 25 hours per week. Females preferred, aged 20-27.
Au Pair Plus placed all over the UK. Wages minimum of £70-£90 per week; to work 30+ hours a week. Females preferred, aged 22-27, with good English and a clean driving licence.
Mother's Help placed throughout the UK. Wages minimum of £90 per week; to work 35+ hours a week. Females preferred, aged 22-27, with good English, a clean driving licence and excellent childcare experience. Minimum stay of 12 months. The company charges no fees to their applicants and offers a variety of support to the Au Pair throughout her stay.
To *apply*, contact Laura on the above e-mail address.

JOLAINE AU PAIR & DOMESTIC AGENCY: 18 Escot Way, Barnet, Hertfordshire EN5 3AN (☎020-8449 1334; fax 020-8449 9183; e-mail aupair@jolaine.prestel. co.uk; www.jolaineagency.com). Jolaine Agency has been successfully placing applicants in the UK and abroad since 1975 and operates a follow-up system to ensure that all applicants are happy with their stay.
Arranges **Au Pair/Plus and Mother's Help** positions in the UK throughout the year. Payment is from £160 per week for a Mother's Help and £55/£75 for an Au Pair/plus. Minimum stay is 6 months, maximum is 2 years. Also arranges paying guest family stays in the London suburbs throughout the year, from £100 per week. Accommodation available for individuals or groups of any size. Discounts given to groups and extended stays. Visits, excursions, activities and classes arranged on request.
For further information and application forms write at any time enclosing s.a.e. or IRC to the above address or email your details.

LARAH AU PAIRS: 1 Paxton Gardens, Woodham, Woking, Surrey GU21 5TR (☎01932-341704; fax 01932-341764; e-mail larahaupairs@ntlworld.co.uk; www. larahaupairs.co.uk). Agency cater mainly for families in the south of England, approximately 40 minutes from central London.
Summer Au Pairs wanted from June to September. Minimum stay 2 months. Approximately £60 pocket money for 25 hours per week. Approximately 5 hour day, 5 day week, but must be flexible. Must have childcare experience. Age limit 18-27 with at least basic English. The longer the stay, the easier it is to find a family. Must have references.
Applications to the above address.

LUCY LOCKETTS & VANESSA BANCROFT AGENCY: 400 Beacon Road, Wibsey, Bradford, West Yorkshire BD6 3DJ (tel/fax 01274-402822; e-mail lucylocketts@blueyonder.co.uk; www.lucylocketts.com). In business since 1984. **Au Pairs** for work around the UK. Pocket money £55+ per week. Childcare experience essential. Drivers and non-smokers preferred.

Summer placements available, also longer stays (minimum 6 months). Interviews given where possible; placement takes about 2 weeks to organise after all paperwork has been received and checked.

Apply by May for summer placements to Lucy Holland, Owner, at the above address.

M KELLY AU PAIR AGENCY: 17 Ingram Way, Greenford, Middlesex UB6 8QG (☎020-8575 3336; fax 020-8575 3336; e-mail info@mkellyaupair.co.uk; www. mkellyaupair.co.uk).

Au Pairs. Wages £55 per week minimum; to work at least 25 hours per week. Must be between 18 and 27 years of age. Applicants can be placed in all countries operating the Au Pair Programme. Minimum stay is 6 weeks, maximum 2 years. There are no fees charged to applicants.

To *apply*, contact Marian Kelly at the above address.

PARK AVENUE AU PAIR AGENCY: 36 Oakington Avenue, Wembley Park, Middlesex HA9 8HZ (☎020-8904 0340; fax 020-8904 2783; e-mail ruth@ aupairlondon.co.uk; www.aupairlondon.co.uk).

Au Pairs. Wages £60 per week; to work 25 hours per week. Placements are a minimum of two months. Must be between 17 and 27 years of age. Applicants are charged no fees.

Apply to Mrs Ruth Rosenthal at the above address.

QUICK AU PAIR & NANNY AGENCY: Cedar House, 41 Thorpe Road, Norwich NR1 1ES (☎0845-345 5945; fax 01603-219191; e-mail info@quickaupair.co.uk; www.quickaupair.co.uk). Agency covering the whole of the UK and Republic of Ireland. A very caring, fast and efficient Au Pair placement service.

Summer Au Pairs (30). Pocket Money from £55-£70 per week, free board and accommodation. To work 25 hours a week doing light housework and childcare duties with the possibility of overtime in the school holidays. Minimum period of work of 2 months. Positions are available from mid-June to mid-September. Applicants should be 17 and over, have childcare experience and an ability to help with light housework. Foreign applicants welcome.

Applications should be made from March onwards via post or e-mail to Bryan Levy at the above address. An application form is required, along with 2 character references, 2 childcare references, a 'Dear Family' letter, 2 (smiling) photos, a police check and a letter from the family doctor.

RICHMOND & TWICKENHAM AU PAIRS: The Old Rectory, Savey Lane, Yoxall, Staffordshire DE13 8PD (☎01543-473828; fax 01543-473838;e-mail info@ aupairsnationwide.co.uk; www.aupairsnationwide.co.uk). An established agency running since 1992, run by Vicki, who has been a Nanny/Au Pair. The agency places mainly French, Spanish and Danish girls, although they now place girls from Poland, Lithuania, Latvia, Bulgaria and Romania.

Au Pairs (500 Per Year). £55 per week plus accommodation. To work at least 25 hours per week all year round; minimum period of work 2 months in the summer. Must have childcare experience, and be happy and confident with a good command of the English language.

Duties involve childcare, ironing, washing up and 2 nights babysitting a week. Applicants must be aged between 18-27. Overseas applicants welcome; interview is not necessary. Most au pairs are placed in south-west London.

Applicants are requested to fill in *application* forms available on the company website, as above.

ROWAN NANNIES: The Rowans, Hollybush Close, Potten End, Berkhamsted, Hertfordshire (☎01442-876846; fax 01442-870865; e-mail info@rowanagency. com). Agency that places nannies and Au Pairs with host families in Hertfordshire, Bedfordshire and Buckinghamshire. Established since 1991.
Nannies and Au Pairs. Minimum stay for these placements is 6 months. Foreign applicants with permission to work in the UK welcome.

Applications should be made to Lesley Samson, Owner. Personal interview not required, but application processing will take 2-3 weeks.

SUPERSTUDY UK: 1-3 Manor Parade, Sheepcote Road, Harrow HA1 2JN (☎020-8861 5322; fax 020-8861 5169; e-mail superstudy@btinternet.com; www.superstudy. com). An English language school based in Harrow, North West London with over 23 years of experience. Open all year for work and study programmes and general English courses.
Work And Study Students. Students spend 15 hours per week as an au pair for their host family and 15 hours per week studying at the language school. They pay only for the language course and receive free board and lodgings in return for the au pair work. Work involves general housework and perhaps entertaining children. Students are required all year round, especially in July and August, for a minimum period of 8 weeks. EU and EEA nationals aged 19-29 with a reasonable standard of English should apply.

Applications at any time to the above address.

UK NANNIES AND AU PAIRS: 19 The Severals, Newmarket CB8 7YW (☎01638-560812; e-mail jobs@theuknannyagency.com; www.theuknannyagency.co.uk or www.theukaupairagency.co.uk).
Au Pairs and Nannies. Wages vary from £100-£400 per week; overtime is paid. To work between 25 and 60 hours a week. Placements can last from one month to two years. Must be over 18. Applicants are not charged any fees. Support for the au pair/ nanny is offered by the company.

Apply by e-mailing the above address.

UNIVERSAL AUNTS LTD: PO Box 304, London SW4 0NN (☎020-7738 8937; e-mail aunts@universalaunts.co.uk; www.universalaunts.co.uk). Established in 1921.
House Keepers, Nannies, Mother's Helps required, in both residential and non-residential positions. Must be available to sign on with the agency for minimum of 2 months. Please note the agency does not place au pairs.

Applications at any time to Universal Aunts Ltd.

USEFUL PUBLICATIONS

THE HOBSONS DIRECTORY: Hobsons PLC, Challenger House, 42 Adler Street, London E1 1EE (☎020-7958 5000; www.hobsons.com).
A careers guide for students that lists major employers; intended mainly for those choosing a career, but also a useful resource for those looking for vacation traineeships and internships. Normally distributed free to students, otherwise may be available for reference in careers departments or obtained from the above address.

ISCO PUBLICATIONS: 12A Princess Way, Camberley, Surrey GU15 3SP (☎01276-21188; fax 01276-691833; e-mail sylvie.pool@isco.org.uk; www.isco.org.uk).
ISCO publishes the book *Opportunities in the 'Gap' Year* which is aimed at school leavers taking a year off before going into higher education. It gives details of paid and voluntary work, inside and outside the UK, as well as study opportunities. It also includes sections on the armed forces, expeditions and outdoor work. The booklet is available from ISCO for £7.95 plus £1 for postage within the UK. Can also be ordered online at www.careerscope.info.

JOB MAGAZINE: Jobs Subs, University of London Careers Service, 49-51 Gordon Square, London WC1H 0PN (☎020-7554 4530; e-mail job.ads@careers.lon.ac.uk; www.careers.lon.ac.uk).
A weekly graduate careers magazine for London featuring part-time and vacation work as well as full-time graduate positions. A subscription costs £16 for twelve weeks (£25 in Europe and £31 other international destinations), including complimentary issues of *Prospects Today*; to subscribe send cheques payable to the University of London to the above address.

LIFETIME CAREERS PUBLISHING: 7 Ascot Court, White Horse Business Park, Trowbridge, Wiltshire BA14 0XA (☎01225-716000; www.lcw.uk.com).
Publishes *A Year Off ... A Year On?* in association with the University and Colleges Admissions Service (UCAS). This is a guide to employment, voluntary work and working holidays for gap year students and anyone considering taking a break during their education or career. It provides information, addresses, and ideas plus a variety of accounts of personal experiences. The book is priced £10.99 (ISBN 1902876326).

PROSPECTS PUBLICATIONS: Prospects House, Booth Street East, Manchester M13 9EP (☎0161- 277 5274; e-mail m.threlfall@prospects.ac.uk; www.prospects.ac.uk).
Graduate Prospects, the newly rebranded commercial subsidary of the Higher Education Careers Service Unit (HECSU), publish a number of guides, principally for the recent graduate. However, their *Prospects Directory* (priced £19.99) and *Prospects Work Experience* (priced £4.99) are a wealth of information for those seeking information on Summer Internships. Both books can be ordered from the website, which gives a full list of their publications, or found in careers departments.

RECRUITMENT UK: Part of the New Zealand News UK group, Quadrant House, 250 Kennington Road, London SE11 5RD (☎0845-270 7909; fax 0845-270 7904; e-mail sales@recruitment uk.net; www.recruitmentuk.net).
A free quarterly magazine aimed primarily at Australians and New Zealanders but relevant to anyone looking for work in the UK. Distributed in Australia and New Zealand. Website has active jobs board with new jobs added daily.

TNT MAGAZINE: 14-15 Childs Place, Earls Court, London SW5 9RX (☎020-7373 3377; e-mail enquiries@tntmag.co.uk; www.tntmagazine.com/uk). A twice-weekly magazine available free in London from dispensers around tube stations, packed with job news and advertisements. Aimed principally at working travellers from Australia, New Zealand and South Africa but could be useful to any job-seeker. It comes out in a Monday edition called *TNT Magazine* and a smaller Wednesday edition called *TNT Midweek*. The website also contains useful information on the job market.

VACATION WORK PUBLICATIONS: 9 Park End Street, Oxford OX1 1HH (☎01865-241978; fax 01865-790885; e-mail info@vacationwork.co.uk; www. vacationwork.co.uk). Publishes or distributes the following titles in the UK.
Working in Tourism – The UK, Europe & Beyond (£11.95). A comprehensive guide to short- and long-term work in the tourist industry.
Work Your Way Around The World (£12.95). Contains invaluable information on ways to find temporary work worldwide, both in advance and when abroad.
Teaching English Abroad (£14.95). Covers both short- and long-term opportunities for teaching English in Britain and abroad for both qualified and untrained teachers.
Working with the Environment (£11.95). A guide to the enormous range of possibilities for short- and long-term work with the environment, both in Britain and around the world.
The International Directory of Voluntary Work (£12.95). A comprehensive guide to worldwide residential and non-residential voluntary work.

VIRGIN BOOKS: Thames Wharf Studios, Rainville Road, London W6 9HA (☎020-7386 3300; fax 020-7386 3360; www.virginbooks.com).
Publishes *The Virgin Guide to Volunteering* (ISBN 0753508575). The book is priced £12.99 and can be bought off the website.

Vacation Work Publications

**Vacation Work Publications, 9 Park End Street, Oxford OX1 1HH
Tel 01865-241978 Fax 01865-790885**

Visit us online for more information on our unrivalled range of titles for work, travel and gap years, readers' feedback and regular updates:

www.vacationwork.co.uk

Books are available in the USA from the Globe Pequot Press, Guilford, Connecticut

www.globepequot.com

ANY COMMENTS?

We have made every effort to make this book as useful and accurate as possible for you. We would appreciate any comments that you may have concerning the employers listed.

Name:

Address:

Name of employer:

Entry on page:

Comments:

Have you come across any other employers who might merit inclusion in the book? (A free copy of a Vacation Work title of your choice will be sent to anyone who sends in the name and address of an employer subsequently included in the Directory.)

Please send this sheet to:
Guy Hobbs or David Woodworth, Vacation Work,
9 Park End Street, Oxford OX1 1HJ, U.K.